Beginning Oracle Database 12c Administration

From Novice to Professional

Second Edition

Ignatius Fernandez

■ ■ ■

⟨IOUG⟩
Independent oracle users group

Apress®

ISBN-13 (pbk): 978-1-4842-0194-7

ISBN-13 (electronic): 978-1-4842-0193-0

Managing Director: Welmoed Spahr
Lead Editor: Jonathan Gennick
Development Editor: Douglas Pundick
Technical Reviewer: Arup Nanda
Editorial Board: Steve Anglin, Mark Beckner, Gary Cornell, Louise Corrigan, Jim DeWolf,
    Jonathan Gennick, Robert Hutchinson, Michelle Lowman, James Markham, Susan McDermott,
    Matthew Moodie, Jeffrey Pepper, Douglas Pundick, Ben Renow-Clarke, Gwenan Spearing,
    Matt Wade, Steve Weiss
Coordinating Editor: Jill Balzano
Copy Editor: Tiffany Taylor
Compositor: SPi Global
Indexer: SPi Global
Artist: SPi Global
Cover Designer: Anna Ishchenko

Distributed to the book trade worldwide by Springer Science+Business Media New York, 233 Spring Street, 6th Floor, New York, NY 10013. Phone 1-800-SPRINGER, fax (201) 348-4505, e-mail orders-ny@springer-sbm.com, or visit www.springeronline.com. Apress Media, LLC is a California LLC and the sole member (owner) is Springer Science+Business Media Finance Inc (SSBM Finance Inc). SSBM Finance Inc is a Delaware corporation.

For information on translations, please e-mail rights@apress.com, or visit www.apress.com.

Apress and friends of ED books may be purchased in bulk for academic, corporate, or promotional use. eBook versions and licenses are also available for most titles. For more information, reference our Special Bulk Sales–eBook Licensing web page at www.apress.com/bulk-sales.

Any source code or other supplementary material referenced by the author in this text is available to readers at www.apress.com. For detailed information about how to locate your book's source code, go to www.apress.com/source-code/.

For Michelle, Cristina, and Elba.
"Oh Fame!—if I e'er took delight in thy praises,
'Twas less for the sake of thy high-sounding phrases,
Than to see the bright eyes of the dear one discover
She thought that I was not unworthy to love her."

—Byron

independent oracle users group

About IOUG Press

*IOUG Press is a joint effort by the **Independent Oracle Users Group (the IOUG)** and **Apress*** *to deliver some of the highest-quality content possible on Oracle Database and related topics. The IOUG is the world's leading, independent organization for professional users of Oracle products. Apress is a leading, independent technical publisher known for developing high-quality, no-fluff content for serious technology professionals. The IOUG and Apress have joined forces in IOUG Press to provide the best content and publishing opportunities to working professionals who use Oracle products.*

Our shared goals include:

- Developing content with excellence
- Helping working professionals to succeed
- Providing authoring and reviewing opportunities
- Networking and raising the profiles of authors and readers

To learn more about Apress, visit our website at **www.apress.com**. Follow the link for IOUG Press to see the great content that is now available on a wide range of topics that matter to those in Oracle's technology sphere.

Visit **www.ioug.org** to learn more about the Independent Oracle Users Group and its mission. Consider joining if you haven't already. Review the many benefits at www.ioug.org/join. Become a member. Get involved with peers. Boost your career.

www.ioug.org/join

Apress®

Contents at a Glance

About the Author xix

About the Technical Reviewer xxi

Acknowledgments xxiii

Foreword to the First Edition xxv

Introduction xxvii

■Part I: Database Concepts 1

■Chapter 1: Relational Database Management Systems 3

■Chapter 2: SQL and PL/SQL by Example 25

■Chapter 3: Oracle Architecture 47

■Part II: Database Implementation 59

■Chapter 4: Planning 61

■Chapter 5: Software Installation 73

■Chapter 6: Database Creation 91

■Chapter 7: Physical Database Design 117

■Chapter 8: User Management and Data Loading 135

■Part III: Database Support 159

■Chapter 9: Taking Control 161

■Chapter 10: Monitoring 175

■Chapter 11: Fixing Problems 191

■**Chapter 12: Backups** **217**

■**Chapter 13: Recovery** **235**

■**Chapter 14: Database Maintenance**.. **253**

■**Chapter 15: The Big Picture and the Ten Deliverables**.............................. **271**

■**Part IV: Database Tuning** **291**

■**Chapter 16: Database Tuning**.. **293**

■**Chapter 17: SQL Tuning** **313**

■**Index**.. **341**

Contents

About the Author xix

About the Technical Reviewer xxi

Acknowledgments xxiii

Foreword to the First Edition xxv

Introduction xxvii

■Part I: Database Concepts 1

■Chapter 1: Relational Database Management Systems.......................... 3

  A First Look at Oracle Database 12c 4

  What Is a Database?... 8

  What Is a Relational Database?.. 9

    The Secret Sauce 12

    Examples of Relational Operations...13

    Efficiency of Relational Operators 19

    Query Optimization 19

  What Is a Database Management System?.. 20

    Transaction Management...20

    The Atomicity Property of Transactions 21

    The Consistency Property of Transactions..21

    The Isolation Property of Transactions...21

    The Durability Property of Transactions...21

    Data Integrity 21

    Data Security...22

What Makes a Relational Database Management System Relational? 22

Summary 23

Further Reading 24

■ Chapter 2: SQL and PL/SQL by Example 25

Railroad Diagrams 27

Types of SQL 30

Data Definition Language 30

Database Manipulation Language 31

Embedded SQL 34

SQL*Plus and SQL Developer 35

Criticisms of SQL 36

Duplicates 37

Redundancy 37

Nullable Data Items 40

Introduction to PL/SQL 40

Summary 45

Exercises 45

Further Reading 46

■ Chapter 3: Oracle Architecture 47

Database vs. Instance 49

Database 49

Software 49

Configuration Files 49

Data Files 49

Temporary Files 50

Redo Log Files 50

Archived Redo Log Files 50

Control File 51

Event Logs 51

Database Backups 51

Instance..51

    System Global Area...51

    Buffer Cache...52

    Shared Pool..52

    Log Buffer..52

    Server Processes..52

    Background Processes..52

One-to-Many Configuration...53

Many-to-One Architecture...54

Life Cycle of a Database Session...55

Summary...56

Exercises..57

Further Reading...58

■**Part II: Database Implementation**... **59**

■**Chapter 4: Planning**.. **61**

Licensing..61

    Practical Example...61

    Free to Download, Free to Learn, Unlimited Evaluation..63

    Database Editions...63

Architectural Choices..64

    Dedicated Server..64

    Shared Server..65

    Real Application Clusters..65

    Standby Database...65

    Maximum Availability Architecture (MAA)...66

Sizing...66

    Disk Sizing...66

    Other Disk Considerations..67

    Memory Sizing...68

CPU Sizing 69

Network Sizing 69

Modern Options 69

Engineered Systems 69

Cloud Computing 70

Summary 71

Further Reading 72

■Chapter 5: Software Installation 73

Oracle Technology Network 74

The Forgotten Manuals 74

Prerequisites and Preinstallation Requirements 74

Client Installations 75

Instant Client 75

SQL Developer 78

Server Installations 80

Oracle Database Examples 89

Summary 90

■Chapter 6: Database Creation 91

Creating and Configuring a Listener 92

Creating and Configuring a Database 97

Common Options 110

Initialization Parameters 111

Data Files 111

Control Files 112

Redo Log Groups 112

Basic Database Administration Tasks 112

Stopping the Database 112

Stopping the Listener 113

Starting the Listener 113

Starting the Database 114

Enterprise Manager Database Express 114

Summary 116

■Chapter 7: Physical Database Design 117

Indexes 117

Unique vs. Non-Unique Indexes 118

Concatenated Indexes 118

Function-Based Indexes 119

Structure of an Index 119

What Indexes to Create? 120

Index-Organized Tables 121

Advanced Topics 121

Partitioning 121

Advantages of Partitioning 122

List Partitioning 122

Range Partitioning 123

Interval Partitioning 123

Hash Partitioning 124

Reference Partitioning 124

Composite Partitioning 125

Local and Global Indexes 126

Partitioned Views 126

Denormalization and Materialized Views 130

Clusters 131

Summary 132

■Chapter 8: User Management and Data Loading 135

Schemas 135

User Management 141

Creating Users 141

Giving Permissions to Users 144

Revoking Permissions Granted to Users..148

Modifying User Attributes 148

Removing Users..148

Data Loading 149

The Export and Import Utilities 149

The Data Pump Utilities 153

SQL*Loader...156

Summary 158

■Part III: Database Support 159

■Chapter 9: Taking Control 161

Enterprise Manager.. 162

SQL Developer... 163

Remote Diagnostic Agent 166

Dictionary Tables and Views... 168

Third-Party Tools 171

Summary.. 172

Exercises... 173

■Chapter 10: Monitoring 175

Monitoring Database Availability.. 176

Monitoring Changes 178

Monitoring Security... 179

Monitoring Backups 180

Monitoring Growth... 180

Monitoring Workload 182

Monitoring Performance 185

Monitoring Capacity 187

Third-Party Tools...189

Summary...189

Exercises..190

Further Reading..190

■Chapter 11: Fixing Problems 191

Systematic Five-Step Problem-Solving Method...193

The Book We All Want and Best Practices for Problem Management 194

Real-Life Example: Unresponsive Listener..196

Define the Problem..196

Investigate and Analyze the Problem 197

Solve and Implement the Problem 198

One Week Later 199

Opportunities for Improvement...199

Incident Management vs. Problem Management..200

Internet Resources 200

Working with Oracle Support 203

Remote Diagnostic Agent (RDA) 204

ORAchk Oracle Configuration Audit Tool 205

Automatic Diagnostic Repository (ADR)..207

Error Codes..207

Four Errors 209

ORA-01555: Snapshot Too Old...209

ORA-00060: Deadlock Detected 210

ORA-00600: Internal Error Code 211

ORA-07445: Exception Encountered...214

Summary..215

Exercises..216

■Chapter 12: Backups 217

Why Do You Need Backups? 217

Types of Backup 219

Tape Backups vs. Disk Backups 219

Full Backups vs. Partial Backups 219

Level 0 Backups vs. Level 1 Backups 220

Physical Backups vs. Logical Backups 220

Consistent Backups vs. Inconsistent Backups 220

Hot vs. Cold Backups 220

Oracle-Managed Backups vs. User-Managed Backups 220

Practical Demonstration: Physical Backups 221

Practical Demonstration: Logical Backups 226

Common RMAN Commands 228

Horror Stories 232

Summary 233

Exercises 233

■Chapter 13: Recovery 235

Horror Stories 235

Types of Recovery 236

Restore vs. Recover 236

Full Recovery vs. Partial Recovery 236

Complete Recovery vs. Incomplete Recovery 237

Traditional vs. Flashback 237

Physical Recovery vs. Logical Recovery 237

Flashback Technology 238

Flashback Query 238

Flashback Versions 239

Flashback Transaction 240

Flashback Table 240

Flashback Drop 241

Flashback Data Archive 242

Flashback Database 243

LogMiner 243

Data Recovery Advisor 244

Documentation and Testing 249

Summary 249

Exercises 250

■Chapter 14: Database Maintenance 253

The Maintenance Plan 253

Backups 254

Generic Best Practices for Database Backups 254

Best Practices for Oracle Database Backups 255

Statistics 256

Archiving and Purging 256

Rebuilding 257

Log File Maintenance 258

Auditing 260

User Management 262

Capacity Management 263

Time Series 263

Patching 267

Summary 268

Exercises 269

■Chapter 15: The Big Picture and the Ten Deliverables 271

An Instructive Job Interview 272

How I Became a DBA 273

ITIL 275

The Big Picture 275

IT Service Management Processes 276

Start with the End in Mind: The Ten Deliverables 280

The Book You Really Need and the Art of the SOP 281

Benefits of SOPs 282

Structure of an SOP 284

Suggested SOPs 287

Summary 288

Exercises 289

Further Reading 289

■Part IV: Database Tuning 291

■Chapter 16: Database Tuning 293

Using a Systematic Five-Step Tuning Method 293

Analyzing DB Time 296

Understanding the Oracle Wait Interface 300

V$SYSSTAT and V$SESSTAT 300

V$SESSION_EVENT and V$SYSTEM_EVENT 301

Mining the Statspack Repository 301

Using the Statspack Report 309

Summary 309

Exercises 310

Further Reading 312

■Chapter 17: SQL Tuning 313

Defining Efficiency 313

Identifying Inefficient SQL Statements 313

Understanding the Causes of Inefficient SQL 316

Ways to Improve SQL 317

Indexes 317

Hints 318

Statistics 319

Tuning by Example 321

    Creating and Populating the Tables 323

    Establishing a Baseline 324

    Examining the Query Plan 329

    Indexes and Statistics 331

    Using SQL Access Advisor 332

    Optimizer Hints 334

    Extreme Tuning 335

    But Wait, There's More! 337

Summary 338

Exercises 339

Index 341

About the Author

Iggy Fernandez has been working in the IT industry for almost three decades including almost two decades of experience as an Oracle Database administrator supporting databases big and small, for companies big and small, including a stint as the manager of the Oracle Database administration team of a large service provider. His favorite part of Oracle Database administration is database tuning and SQL tuning because they can often be puzzles that require a creative solutions. He edits the NoCOUG Journal (https://nocoug.wordpress.com/nocoug-journal-archive/), organizes the NoCOUG SQL Challenges, speaks at Oracle user group conferences, and blogs at https://iggyfernandez.wordpress.com/ and http://www.toadworld.com/members/iggy_5f00_fernandez/blogs/default.aspx. He is @OraTweets on Twitter.

About the Technical Reviewer

Arup Nanda has been an Oracle database administrator (DBA) since 1993, dealing with everything from modeling to security, and has a lot of gray hairs to prove it. He has coauthored five books, written 500+ published articles, presented 300+ sessions, delivered training sessions in 22 countries, and actively blogs at arup.blogspot.com. He is an Oracle ACE Director, a member of Oak Table Network, an editor for SELECT Journal (the IOUG publication), and a member of the Board for Exadata SIG. Oracle awarded him the DBA of the Year in 2003 and Architect of the Year in 2012. He lives in Danbury, CT, with his wife Anu and son, Anish.

Acknowledgments

I would like to thank to Bill Schwimmer—my manager at MCI Systemhouse—for giving me the chance to become an Oracle Database administrator many years ago, the long-suffering editors at Apress, Jonathan Gennick, Jill Balzano, and Douglas Pundick who tore their hair and bit their fingernails as they waited for me to finish writing, technical reviewers Bob Bryla (11g edition) and Arup Nanda (the present edition) for their thorough and insightful reviews, and the production team at Apress who created the finished product.

I would also like to thank all the colleagues and friends who helped me with the 11g edition, including Allen Tran, David Wolff, Gary Sadler, Malathy Thiruloganathan, Manoj Joshi, Raghav Vinjamuri, Rajesh Talreja, Rich Headrick, Scott Alexander, and Terry Sutton.

And all the members of the Oracle community who helped me with the present edition, including Biju Thomas, Chris Stephens, Fuad Arshad, Herlindo Velazquez, Jeremiah Peschka, Max Scalf, Niall Litchfield, Paul Houghton, Riyaj Shamsudeen, Timur Akhmadeev, and Toon Koppelaars.

And especially Jimmy Brock.

Foreword to the First Edition

There are so many computer books in the world. A few of them are lousy, most of them are pretty good, and several are excellent.

Fortunately for the Gross National Products of nations, we all buy many of these books.

Unfortunately, most of these books are never read, just skipped through and left to gather dust on the shelves with all the other good books (and course materials) that we never revisited.

So many wise words, wise thoughts, funny and instructive stories, and so many years of experience collected in these books. And so many people willing to commit (!) the same mistakes over and over again because they never read the books, but instead perform the famous skip/skim procedure.

Many authors ask for the skip/skim treatment of their books because, unlike Iggy, they either quote extensively from manuals or try to advise the reader about the chapters he or she can skip or skim.

The few people who actually read a handful of good Oracle database books from cover to cover, including trying out stuff on their test system as they read—they will have a much easier and more entertaining work life with Oracle's database.

Iggy is a workhorse. He wrote this book while holding down a day job at Database Specialists, editing the journal of the Northern California Oracle Users Group (NoCOUG), and making presentations at the RMOUG, IOUG, and Hotsos conferences. He's also a thinking man, who decided (I think) to write the book he wished he'd had when he started with databases.

So when I looked through the sections and chapters (all of them very useful, by the way), I saw a pattern:

Section I contains information you can easily find in manuals on http://tahiti.oracle.com or a good textbook on database theory. The information in Section II could also be extracted from the manuals if you knew what you were looking for in the first place—and had the many hours required at your disposal.

Sections III and IV, however, could only be written by someone who has acquired experience, has made mistakes (and learned from them), and has thought about his job and his role in the database world—and discussed it with others.

This is a very good book, Iggy. I want a signed copy of it.

—Mogens Nørgaard
CEO of Miracle A/S and co-founder of the OakTable network

Introduction

At the outset, I would like to say that this is not a perfect book. There are deadlines in the book publishing business and books have to go to print whether or not they are perfect. And, there is no living in writing technical books so authors like me have day jobs which means that we cannot devote as much time to perfecting our writing as we would like.

This book is really for *beginners* in database administration. If you are not a beginner in database administration, I recommend that you get *Pro Oracle Database 12c Administration* by my fellow Apress author Darl Kuhn instead. *Also*, did you know that Oracle Corp. provides excellent free reference materials at http://docs.oracle.com? For beginners in database administration, I particularly recommend *Oracle Database 2 Day DBA* in the "2 Day" series of publications. In fact, I suggest that you take a moment to check out *2 Day DBA* right now; it may be all that you want or need.

In general, I have found most Oracle Database professionals do not take enough advantage of the free Oracle Corp. publications. A plausible defense is that reference manuals are harder to read than books from Apress and other fine publishers. But, in addition to reference manuals, Oracle Corp. also provides many publications that are written in an extremely readable style. Throughout this book, I will be frequently referring you to the free Oracle Corp. publications for more information because I want you to get into the habit of referring to the best source of detailed and reliable information. Besides, I view myself as an interpreter and a teacher, not a regurgitator of free material.

The ancient Chinese classic text Tao Te Ching, Lao Tzu ("Old Master") says: "*The tree which fills the arms grew from the tiniest sprout; the tower of nine stories rose from a (small) heap of earth; the journey of a thousand [miles] commenced with a single step.*" I wrote this book to help you take the first steps of your Oracle Database journey. It's the book I wish I'd had when I first started using Oracle Database so many years ago. It's the book that I would have liked to have given to the many IT colleagues and friends who, over the years, have asked me to teach them the basics of Oracle Database.

I started my own journey almost two decades ago when my then manager, Bill Schwimmer, gave me the chance to become an Oracle Database administrator back in the days of Oracle 7. Books on Oracle Database were fewer then, and I relied on printed copies of the manuals, which I had to share with the rest of the team; this was in the days before Google, when Netscape Navigator had just appeared on the scene.

Today the Oracle Database manuals can be downloaded for free from the Oracle website. But their size has grown tremendously over the years. The Oracle Database 7.3 SQL reference manual had about 750 pages; the 12c version has almost 2000 pages. You definitely don't want to be carrying a printed copy of that in your backpack!

The book that you have in your hands is not an exhaustive reference manual by any stretch of the term; it is a more manageable introduction to key Oracle Database administration topics, including planning, installation, monitoring, troubleshooting, maintenance, backups, and performance tuning—to name just a few. You'll be getting the benefit of my experience not just the party line found in the manuals. For example, for reasons explained inside, I give equal time to both Statspack as well as Automatic Workload Repository (AWR).

In this book, you'll find information that you won't find in other books on Oracle Database. Here you'll find not just technical information but guidance on the work practices that are as vital to your success as technical skills. The most important chapter in the book is The Big Picture and the Ten Deliverables. If you take the lessons in that chapter to heart, you can quickly become a much better Oracle database administrator than you ever thought possible.

Who This Book Is For

I was a C programmer before I became a database administrator. For lack of a text like this, it took me quite a while to adjust to my new role. If you are an IT professional who has been thrust into an Oracle Database administration role without the benefit of formal training, or just want to understand how Oracle Database works, then I wrote this book for you.

How This Book Is Structured

The chapters of this book are logically organized into four parts that closely track the way your database administration career will naturally evolve. Part I is a necessary backgrounder in relational database theory and Oracle Database concepts, Part II will teach you how to implement an Oracle Database correctly, Part III will expose you to the daily routine of a database administrator, and Part IV will introduce you to the fine art of performance tuning. Each chapter has a section of exercises that are designed to help you apply the lessons of the chapter. Each chapter also includes a list of reference works that contain more information on the topic of the chapter.

Part I: Database Concepts

You may be in a hurry to learn how to create a database but I hope you will take the time to first understand the underlying theory. You won't regret it.

Chapter 1: Relational Database Management Systems

Leonardo da Vinci said: "*Those who are in love with practice without knowledge are like the sailor who gets into a ship without rudder or compass and who never can be certain [where] he is going. Practice must always be founded on sound theory.*" How can you competently administer a relational database management system like Oracle if you don't really know what makes a "relational" database relational or what a database management system manages for you? This chapter will help you find your bearings and prepare you for what is to come in the rest of the book. However, you probably won't be satisfied until you've seen an Oracle database management system. You will therefore connect to the fully-functional database in a "virtual machine" provided by Oracle Corporation.

Chapter 2: Structured Query Language

All database user activity is conducted in Structured Query Language (SQL), and therefore database administrators need to be intimately familiar with it. The greatest potential for performance improvement usually lies within the software application, not within the database where the application stores its data or within the physical infrastructure where the database is housed. An equally important reason why database administrators need to be intimately familiar with SQL is that all database administration activities such as database maintenance and user management are also conducted in SQL. A third reason is that SQL has deficiencies that must be guarded against. These deficiencies include redundancy, problems introduced by nullable data items, and the absence of prohibitions on duplicate data records.

Chapter 3: Oracle Architecture

Just as an automobile engine has a lot of interconnected parts that must all work well together, and just as an automobile mechanic must understand the individual parts and how they relate to the whole, the Oracle database engine has a lot of interconnected parts, and the database administrator must understand the individual parts and how they relate to the whole. This chapter provides a short overview of the Oracle engine.

Part II: Database Implementation

After spending some time on database theory, you'll be eager to create your first database. I hope that you take the opportunity to install Oracle on your own XP or Vista laptop—the best way to learn is by doing.

Chapter 4: Planning

Your goal as Oracle administrator is not simply to create a database but to be on time, on budget, and to meet the availability and performance targets of the business. As with any goal, careful planning is the key to success. You have little control over a number of factors that affect the success of your database; for example, application design and testing. This chapter discusses three important issues that are definitely within your circle of influence and that you cannot afford to ignore: licensing, architecture, and sizing.

Chapter 5: Software Installation

In this chapter, I'll go over a few prerequisites such as obtaining the software, installation guides, and reference manuals. I'll also discuss the installation of software that precedes the creation of a database. I'll show you how I installed the Oracle software on my laptop running Windows XP Professional.

Chapter 6: Database Creation

Database creation is easier that you would think; it's the tasks that come before and after that take a lot of time. In this chapter, I'll first discuss the "Next-Next-Next; click Finish" method of creating a database. I'll then briefly discuss some tasks that you should consider performing after you create a database; specifically, installing the RDA and Statspack tools and disabling database features that have not been licensed. Finally, I'll introduce the manual method of database creation and some basic administrative tasks.

Chapter 7: Physical Database Design

Performance considerations can come to the forefront at any time during the life of the database; new queries can be introduced at any time. Database administrators must therefore understand the mechanisms that can be used to improve performance, and this chapter discusses three broad categories. Indexes can be used to quickly find the data. Partitions and clusters can be used to organize the data. Finally, materialized views and denormalized tables can be used to perform expensive operations like Joins ahead of time.

Chapter 8: User Management and Data Loading

Your job does not end when you create a database; you still have to get the data into it and ensure that those who have a need to use it can do so. This chapter discusses how to control users and how to get large amounts of data in and out of databases. User management and data loading are two common chores performed by database administrators.

Part III: Database Support

The easy part is over. You have created a database and loaded it with data. Now you have to turn your attention to the care and feeding of it.

Chapter 9: Taking Control

If you are going to be responsible for a database, you need to know what it contains and how it is being used. Which are the biggest tables? How are the data files, control files, and log files laid out? How many people have database accounts? How many people use the database at a time? Your first action when you acquire responsibility for a database should be to thoroughly explore it.

In this chapter, you'll learn about form-based tools such as Enterprise Manager, SQL Developer, and Remote Diagnostic Agent which make it easy to explore the database and simplify the task of database administration.

Chapter 10: Monitoring

When I was growing up, I was sometimes awoken at night by the sound of a walking stick tapping on the ground—it was the night watchman patrolling the neighborhood. He would have had a better chance of surprising any burglars if he'd crept up on them quietly, but I never questioned why he advertised his presence so loudly. Armed only with a walking stick, he would have to rely on strong lungs to wake up the neighborhood if he saw any burglars, so perhaps it was best to advertise his presence and hope that burglars would flee when they heard him coming. Nevertheless, the sound of his stick was comforting—it was good to know that someone trustworthy was watching the neighborhood while we slept.

The database administrator is responsible for watching the database. If something goes wrong with the database that could have been prevented, there is nobody else to blame. As you'll learn in this chapter, database availability, changes, security, growth, backups, workload, performance, and capacity are some of the areas that should be monitored.

Chapter 11: Fixing Problems

In this chapter, you will watch a real-life problem as it progresses from detection to resolution. You will learn a five-step systematic approach to problem-fixing and the difference between incident management and problem management. I will cover the variety of Internet resources that are available to you, introduce an Oracle knowledge base called MetaLink, and explain how to get technical support from Oracle Corporation. Finally, I will discuss some common database problems.

Chapter 12: Backups

American national hero Benjamin Franklin often wrote anonymous letters to the Pennsylvania Gazette, a prominent newspaper that he himself owned and edited. In one such letter he coined the famous phrase "*an ounce of prevention is worth a pound of cure*" and, in addition to making several suggestions for the prevention of fires, he suggested that Philadelphia imitate his native Boston in establishing fire stations and employing firefighters; not only should all efforts be made to prevent fires but the city should be adequately prepared to handle the next inevitable fire.

Backups are to a database what fire stations and fire fighters are to a city; we may protect the database against damage the best we can, but we must be prepared if the database ever gets damaged, through user or operator error or hardware failure, and needs to be repaired. In this chapter you'll learn about the different kinds of backups and the tools used to create them.

Chapter 13: Recovery

In the previous chapter, you learned how to make backup copies of the database; you will now turn your attention to repairing the database if it gets damaged.

Chapter 14: Maintenance

In The Little Prince by Antoine de Saint-Exupéry, the protagonist meets a little prince whose home was on an asteroid. In one of their discussions, the little prince talked about the importance of proper maintenance, saying "*Sometimes, there is no harm in putting off a piece of work until another day. But when it is a matter of baobabs, that always means a catastrophe. I knew a planet that was inhabited by a lazy man. He neglected three little bushes ...*" You can quite imagine what might happen to an asteroid if three little bushes are allowed to grow into immense baobab trees.

In this chapter, we go over the maintenance that is needed to keep your database in peak operating condition.

Chapter 15: The Big Picture and the Ten Deliverables

This is the most important chapter in this book—I discuss the big IT picture and offer very specific guidance in the form of the database administration role's ten deliverables. Few, if any, other books address this topic. If you take the lessons in this one chapter to heart, you can quickly become a better Oracle Database administrator than you thought possible.

Competency in Oracle technology is only half of the challenge of being a database administrator. If you had very little knowledge of Oracle technology but knew exactly what needed to be done, you could always find out how to do it—there is Google and there are online manuals a-plenty. Too many Oracle database administrators don't know what to do and what they have when they are through is "*just a mess without a clue.*"

Part IV: Database Tuning

There's no such thing as a completely self-tuning car and there's no such thing as a completely self-tuning database. Performance tuning can often be a puzzle that requires a creative solution.

Chapter 16: Database Tuning

Database tuning can be a complex exercise but it can be facilitated by a systematic approach. This chapter describes a systematic five-step approach to performance tuning. It also presents the most important tools provided by Oracle to help with performance tuning; Statspack is emphasized because newer tools such as AWR and ADDM require costly licenses and are not available at most sites. In particular, you will learn a powerful method of mining the Statspack repository for data on performance trends. A highlight of this chapter is the very detailed performance tuning exercise at the end; it will reinforce the lessons of the chapter.

Chapter 17: SQL Tuning

Perhaps the most complex problem in database administration is SQL tuning, and it is not a coincidence that I left it for the very end. The paucity of books devoted to SQL tuning is evidence of the difficulty of the topic. The only way to interact with Oracle, to retrieve data, to change data, to administer the database, is via SQL. Oracle itself uses SQL to perform all the work that it does behind the scenes. SQL performance is therefore the key to database performance; all database performance problems are really SQL performance problems even if they express themselves as contention for resources.

In this chapter, I will present some of the causes of inefficient SQL and some of the common techniques of making SQL more efficient. Most of the time will be spent working through a case study; I will show you a fairly typical SQL statement and improve it in stages until it hits the theoretical maximum level of performance that is possible to achieve.

Source Code and Updates

As you work through the examples in this book, you may decide that you prefer to type in all the code by hand. You may want to do this because it is a good way to get familiar with the coding techniques that are being used.

Whether you want to type the code in or not, all the source code for this book is available in the Source Code section of the Apress web site (http://www.apress.com). If you like to type in the code, you can use the source code files to check the results you should be getting—they should be your first stop if you think you might have typed in an error. If you don't like typing, then downloading the source code from the Apress web site is a must! Either way, the code files will help you with updates and debugging.

Errata

Apress makes every effort to make sure that there are no errors in the text or the code. However, to err is human, and as such we recognize the need to keep you informed of any mistakes as they're discovered and corrected. Errata sheets are available for all our books at http://www.apress.com. If you find an error that hasn't already been reported, please let us know.

The Apress web site acts as a focus for other information and support, including the code from all Apress books, sample chapters, previews of forthcoming titles, and articles on related topics.

Contacting the Author

Join the Google group Beginning Oracle Database 12c Administration at https://groups.google.com/ forum/#!forum/beginning-oracle-database-12c-administration. There you will find additional materials and can discuss the material in this book. If you have private comments, you may send them to iggy_fernandez@hotmail.com.

## PART I

Database Concepts

CHAPTER 1

■ ■ ■

Relational Database Management Systems

Those who are in love with practice without knowledge are like the sailor who gets into a ship without rudder or compass and who never can be certain [where] he is going. Practice must always be founded on sound theory.

—*The Discourse on Painting* by Leonardo da Vinci

Thank you *very* much for buying this book (or for getting a legal copy). Database administrators have access to valuable and confidential data belonging to their organizations and therefore must possess high ethical standards. (Consider this your first lesson in Oracle Database administration.) Besides, royalties paid to textbook authors typically constitute no more than minimum wage for the long hours they spend writing, so the least you can do to respect their effort is to buy their books or get legal copies.

This book is really for *beginners* in database administration. If you aren't a beginner in database administration, I recommend that you get *Pro Oracle Database 12c Administration* by my fellow Apress author Darl Kuhn instead (2013). Also, did you know that Oracle provides excellent free reference materials at http://docs.oracle.com? For beginners in database administration, I particularly recommend *Oracle Database 2 Day DBA* in the "2 Day" series of publications. In fact, I suggest that you take a moment to check out *2 Day DBA* right now; it may be all that you want or need.

In general, I have found that most Oracle Database professionals don't take enough advantage of the free Oracle publications. A plausible defense is that reference manuals are harder to read than books from Apress and other fine publishers. But, in addition to reference manuals, Oracle also provides many publications that are written in an extremely readable style. Consider this your second lesson in Oracle Database administration! Throughout this book, I frequently refer you to the free Oracle publications for more information because I want you to get into the habit of referring to the best source of detailed and reliable information. Besides, I view myself as an interpreter and a teacher, not a regurgitator of free material.

With those little lessons and cautions out of the way, let's get our feet wet with Oracle Database 12c, shall we?

JOIN THE GOOGLE GROUP FOR THIS BOOK

Join the Google group Beginning Oracle Database 12c Administration at https://groups.google.com/forum/#!forum/beginning-oracle-database-12c-administration. There you can find errata and additional materials and can discuss the material in this book.

A First Look at Oracle Database 12c

I want to spend some time talking the theory of relational database management systems. What Leonardo da Vinci said is so important that I'll quote it again: "Those who are in love with practice without knowledge are like the sailor who gets into a ship without rudder or compass and who never can be certain [where] he is going. Practice must always be founded on sound theory." How can you competently administer a relational database management system like Oracle if you don't really know what makes a "relational" database relational or what a database "management" system manages for you?

However, if you're like most of my students, you won't be satisfied until you've seen an Oracle database management system. I'll grant that seeing a real system will make it easier for you to understand a few things. But it would take quite a while to coach you through the process of creating an Oracle database management system. Fortunately, there is a solution. Oracle provides a convenient *virtual machine* (VM) containing a complete and ready-to-use installation of Oracle Database 12c on Linux. All you need to do is to download and install the Oracle VirtualBox virtualization software and then import a ready-to-use VM. The instructions for doing so are at www.oracle.com/technetwork/community/developer-vm. Pick the Database App Development VM option, and follow the download and installation instructions. (I hope you don't want me to regurgitate the instructions here.) The instructions are short and couldn't be simpler, because you don't need to install and configure Oracle Database; rather, you import a prebuilt VM into Oracle VirtualBox. The only difficulty you may experience is that the prebuilt VM is almost 5GB in size, so you need a reliable and fast Internet connection.

If you follow the instructions and fire up the VM, you see the screen in Figure 1-1. It looks like a Windows or Mac screen, doesn't it? This is the Gnome Desktop, which makes it possible to use Linux without getting completely lost in a world of cryptic Linux commands.

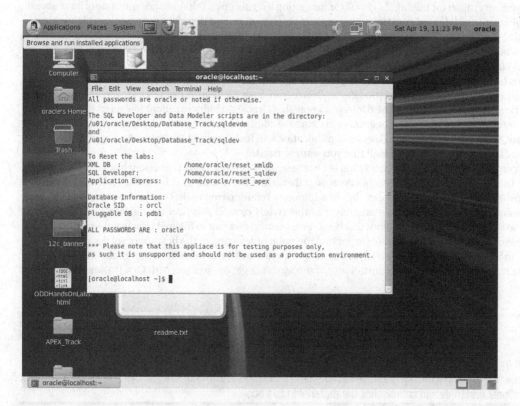

Figure 1-1. Starting screen of the Database App)VM

Next, minimize the terminal window that's taking up so much real estate, and click the SQL Developer icon in the top row of icons. SQL Developer is a GUI tool provided by Oracle for database administration. Because this is the first time, it will take a few minutes to start; that's normal. Figure 1-2 shows what you see at startup.

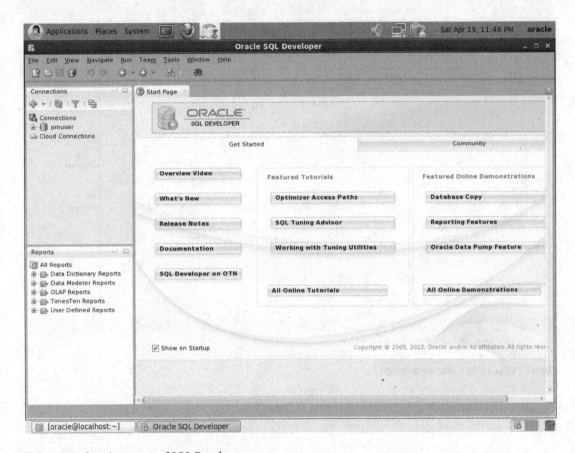

Figure 1-2. *Starting screen of SQL Developer*

As shown in Figure 1-3, click Connections, and create a new connection. Give the connection the name "hr" (Human Resources) or any other name you like. Use the following settings:

- Username "hr"
- Password "oracle"
- Connection Type "Basic"
- Role "Default"
- Hostname "localhost"
- Service Name "PDB1"

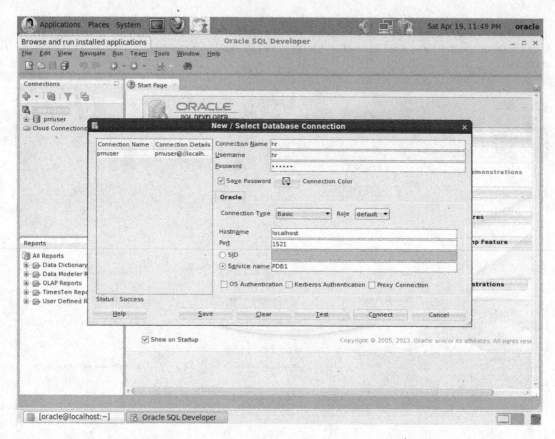

Figure 1-3. *Create a new connection*

Then click Connect. You see the screen shown in Figure 1-4.

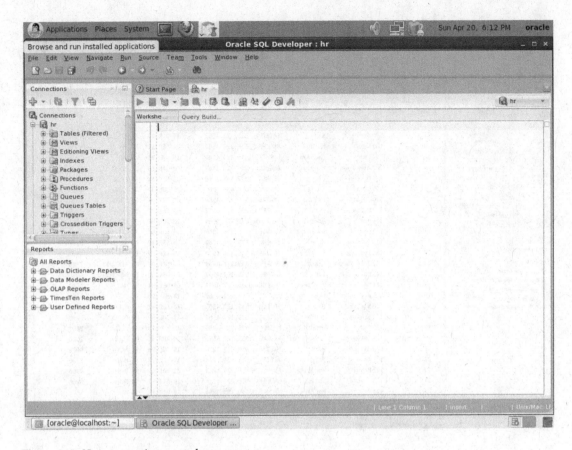

Figure 1-4. *New connection created*

Expand the Tables item in the navigation pane on the left. Six tables are shown; click the EMPLOYEES table. The data in the EMPLOYEES table is listed in a full-screen editor, as shown in Figure 1-5. If you like, you can make changes to the data and then either save your changes (commit) or discard them (roll back) using the Commit Changes and Rollback Changes buttons or the F11 and F12 keys.

7

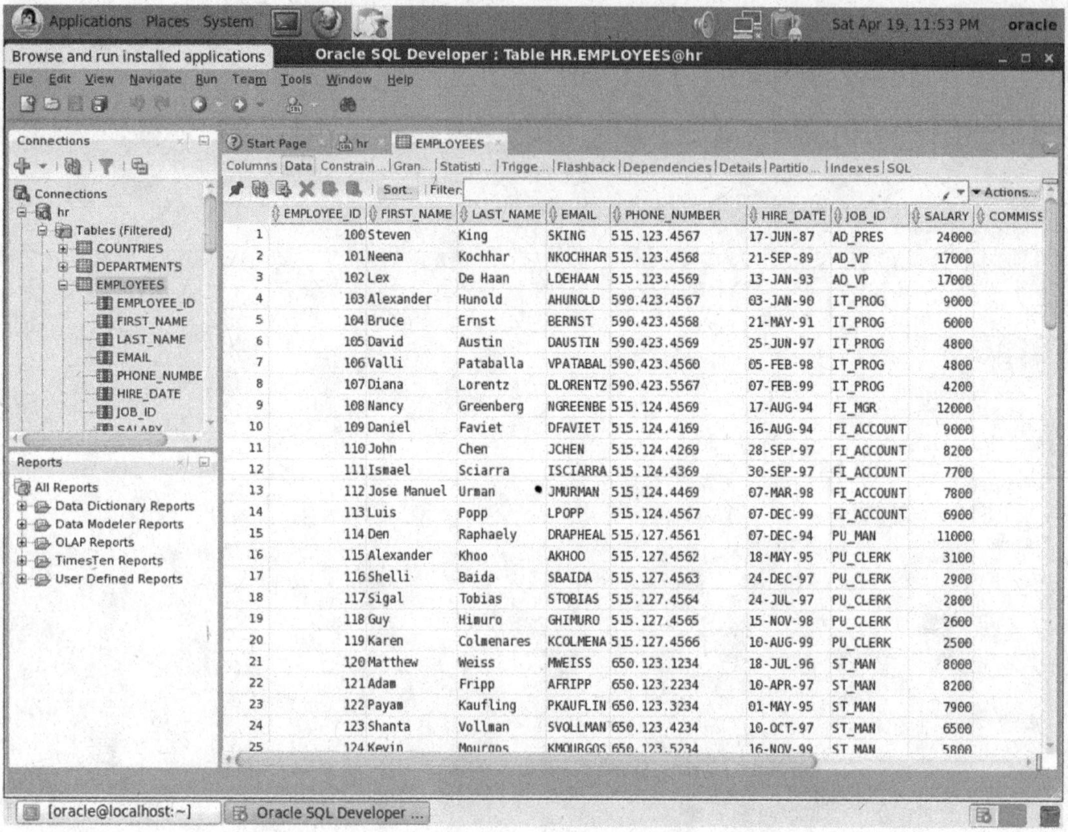

Figure 1-5. *Full-screen editor*

When I was a junior programmer, early in my career, my friends and I were assigned to work on a big software development project for which we would have to use unfamiliar technologies, although we were promised that training would be provided before the project started. All we knew in advance was that the operating system was something called VAX/VMS; we didn't know which programming language or database would be used. The very first thing the instructor said was (paraphrasing), "First you have to insert your definitions into the CDD," and then he walked to the chalkboard and wrote the commands that we needed for the purpose. Needless to say, we were quite flustered, because we had no idea what those "definitions" might be or what a "CDD" was and how it fit into the big picture.

I'm sure you're eager to learn how to create an Oracle database. Anybody can issue a command such as CREATE DATABASE or push a button in a GUI tool such as the Database Creation Assistant. But the mere knowledge of a few commands (or even a lot of commands) doesn't make anyone an Oracle Database administrator in my opinion.

What Is a Database?

Chris Date was the keynote speaker at one of the educational conferences organized by the Northern California Oracle Users Group (NoCOUG), of whose journal I am the editor. The local television news station sent out a crew to cover the event because Chris Date is a well-known database theoretician and one of the associates of Dr. Edgar Codd, an IBM researcher and the inventor of relational database theory. The news reporter cornered me and asked if I was willing to answer a few questions for the camera. I was flattered, but when the reporter pointed the camera at me and asked, "Why are databases important to society?" all I could think of to say was (paraphrasing), "Well, they're important because they're, like, really important, you know." All those years of database administration under my belt, and I still flunked the final exam!

I'd therefore like to spend a few minutes at the outset considering what the word *database* signifies. An understanding of the implications of the word and the responsibilities that go along with them will serve you well as a good database administrator.

I'll begin by saying that databases can contain data that is confidential and must be protected from prying eyes. Only authorized users should be able to access the data, their privileges must be suitably restricted, and their actions must be logged. Even if the data in the databases is for public consumption, you still may need to restrict who can update the data, who can delete from it, and who can add to it. Competent security management is therefore part of your job.

Databases can be critical to an organization's ability to function properly. Organizations such as banks and e-commerce web sites require their databases to be available around the clock. Competent *availability management* is thus an important part of your job. In the event of a disaster such as a flood or fire, the databases may have to be relocated to an alternative location using backups. Competent *continuitymanagement* is therefore another important element of your job. You also need competent *changemanagement* to protect a database from unauthorized or badly tested changes, *incident management* to detect problems and restore service quickly, *problem management* to provide permanent fixes for known issues, *configuration management* to document infrastructure components and their dependencies, and *release management* to bring discipline to the never-ending task of applying patches and upgrades to software and hardware.

I'll also observe that databases can be very big. The first database I worked with, for the semiconductor manufacturing giant Intel, was less than 100MB in size and had only a few dozen data tables. Today, databases used by enterprise application suites like PeopleSoft, Siebel, and Oracle Applications are tens or hundreds of gigabytes in size and might have 10,000 tables or more. One reason databases are now so large is that advancements in magnetic disk storage technology have made it feasible to efficiently store and retrieve large quantities of nontextual data such as pictures and sound. Databases can grow rapidly, and you need to plan for growth. In addition, database applications may consume huge amounts of computing resources. Capacity management is thus another important element of your job, and you need a capacity plan that accommodates both continuous data growth and increasing needs for computing resources.

When you stop thinking in terms of command-line syntax such as create database and GUI tools such as the Database Creation Assistant (dbca) and start thinking in terms such as security management, availability management, continuity management, change management, incident management, problem management, configuration management, release management, and capacity management, the business of database administration begins to make coherent sense and you become a more effective database administrator. These terms are part of the standard jargon of the IT Infrastructure Library (ITIL), a suite of best practices used by IT organizations throughout the world.

What Is a Relational Database?

Relational database theory was laid out by Codd in 1970 in a paper titled "A Relational Model for Data for Large Shared Data Banks." His theory was meant as an alternative to the "programmer as navigator" paradigm that was prevalent in his day.

In pre-relational databases, records were chained together by pointers, as illustrated in Figure 1-6. Each chain has an owner and zero or more members. For example, all the employee records in a department could be chained to the corresponding department record in the departments table. In such a scheme, each employee record points to the next and previous records in the chain as well as to the department record. To list all the employees in a department, you would first navigate to the unique department record (typically using the direct-access technique known as *hashing*) and then follow the chain of employee records.

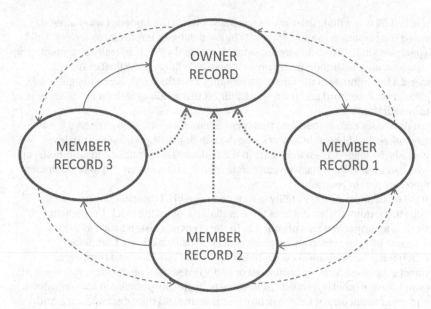

Figure 1-6. Chains of records

Records can participate in multiple chains; for example, all the employee records with the same job can be chained to the corresponding job record in the jobs table. To list all the employees performing a particular job, you can navigate to the job record and then follow the chain of employee records.

This scheme was invented by Charles Bachman, who received the ACM Turing Award in 1973 for his achievement. In his Turing Award lecture, titled "The Programmer as Navigator," Bachman enumerated seven ways in which you can navigate through such a database:

1. Records can be retrieved sequentially.

2. A specific record can be retrieved using its physical address if it's available.

3. A specific record can be retrieved using a unique key. Either a unique index or hash addressing makes this possible.

4. Multiple records can be retrieved using a non-unique key. A non-unique index is necessary.

5. Starting from an owner record, all the records in a chain can be retrieved.

6. Starting from any member record in a chain, the prior or next record in the chain can be retrieved.

7. Starting at any member record in a chain, the owner of the chain can be retrieved.

Bachman noted, "Each of these access methods is interesting in itself, and all are very useful. However, it is the synergistic usage of the entire collection which gives the programmer great and expanded powers to come and go within a large database while accessing only those records of interest in responding to inquiries and updating the database in anticipation of future inquiries."

In this scheme, you obviously need to know the access paths defined in the database. How else could you list all the employees in a record or all the employees holding a particular job without retrieving every single employee record?

STRANGE BUT TRUE

An example of a pre-relational database technology is so-called *network database* technology, one of the best examples of which was DEC/DBMS, created by Digital Equipment Corporation for the VAX/VMS and OpenVMS platforms—it still survives today as Oracle/DBMS. Yes, it's strange but it's true—Oracle, the maker of the world's dominant relational database technology, also sells a pre-relational database technology. According to Oracle, Oracle/DBMS is a very powerful, reliable, and sophisticated database technology that has continued relevance and that Oracle is committed to supporting.

In 1979, Codd made the startling statement that programmers *need not* and *should not* have to be concerned about the access paths defined in the database. The opening words of the first paper on the relational model were, "Future users of large data banks must be protected from having to know how the data is organized in the machine (the internal representation)" ("A Relational Model of Data for Large Shared Data Banks").

Productivity and ease of use were the stated goals of the relational model. In "Normalized Data Base Structure: A Brief Tutorial" (1971), Codd said,

> *What is less understandable is the trend toward more and more complexity in the data structures with which application programmers and terminal users directly interact. Surely, in the choice of logical data structures that a system is to support, there is one consideration of absolutely paramount importance—and that is the convenience of the majority of users. ... To make formatted data bases readily accessible to users (especially casual users) who have little or no training in programming we must provide the simplest possible data structures and almost natural language. ... What could be a simpler, more universally needed, and more universally understood data structure than a table?*

As IBM researcher Donald Chamberlin recalled later (*The 1995 SQL Reunion: People, Projects, and Politics*),

> *[Codd] gave a seminar and a lot of us went to listen to him. This was as I say a revelation for me because Codd had a bunch of queries that were fairly complicated queries and since I'd been studying CODASYL, I could imagine how those queries would have been represented in CODASYL by programs that were five pages long that would navigate through this labyrinth of pointers and stuff. Codd would sort of write them down as one-liners. These would be queries like, "Find the employees who earn more than their managers." He just whacked them out and you could sort of read them, and they weren't complicated at all, and I said, "Wow." This was kind of a conversion experience for me, that I understood what the relational thing was about after that."*

Donald Chamberlin and fellow IBM researcher Raymond Boyce went on to create the first relational query language based on Codd's proposals and described it in a short paper titled "SEQUEL: A Structured English Query Language" (1974). The acronym SEQUEL was later shortened to SQL because—as recounted by Chamberlin in *The 1995 SQL Reunion: People, Projects, and Politics*—SEQUEL was a trademarked name; this means the correct pronunciation of *SQL* is "sequel," not "es-que-el."

Codd emphasized the productivity benefits of the relational model in his acceptance speech for the 1981 Turing Award:

> *It is well known that the growth in demands from end users for new applications is outstripping the capability of data processing departments to implement the corresponding application programs. There are two complementary approaches to attacking this problem (and both approaches are needed): one is to put end users into direct touch with the information stored in computers; the other is to increase the productivity of data processing professionals in the development of application programs. It is less well known that a single technology, relational database management, provides a practical foundation to both approaches.*

In fact, the ubiquitous data-access language SQL was intended for the use of non-programmers. As explained by the creators of SQL in their 1974 paper, there is "a large class of users who, while they are not computer specialists, would be willing to learn to interact with a computer in a reasonably high-level, non-procedural query language. Examples of such users are *accountants, engineers, architects, and urban planners.* [emphasis added] It's for this class of users that SEQUEL is intended."

The Secret Sauce

Codd's secret was *relational algebra*, a collection of operations that could be used to combine tables. Just as you can combine numbers using the operations of addition, subtraction, multiplication, and division, you can combine tables using operations like *selection, projection, union, difference*, and *join* (more precisely, *Cartesian join*), listed in Table 1-1.

Table 1-1. *Five Relational Operators*

Operator	Definition
Selection	Form another table by extracting a subset of the rows of a table of interest using some criteria. This can be expressed in SQL as follows (the * character is a wildcard that matches all columns in the table that is being operated on)":
	``` select * from <table> where <criteria> ```
Projection	Form another table by extracting a subset of the columns of a table of interest. Any duplicate rows that are formed as a result of the projection operation are eliminated:
	``` select <column list> from <table> ```
Union	Form another table by selecting all rows from two tables of interest. If the first table has 10 rows and the second table has 20 rows, then the resulting table will have at most 30 rows, because duplicates are eliminated from the result:
	``` select * from <first table> union select * from <second table> ```

(continued)

Table 1-1. (*continued*)

Operator	Definition
Difference	Form another table by extracting from one table of interest only those rows that don't occur in a second table:
	``` select * from <first table> minus select * from <second table> ```
Join	Form another table by concatenating records from two tables of interest. For example, if the first table has 10 rows and the second table has 20 rows, then the resulting table has 200 rows. And if the first table has 10 columns and the second table has 20 columns, then the resulting table has 30 columns:
	``` select * from <first table>, <second column> ```

Why did Codd name this *relational* algebra? Codd based his theory on rigorous mathematical principles and used the esoteric mathematical term *relation* to denote what is loosely referred to as a table. I'm now ready to define what I mean by a relational database:

> *A relational database is a database in which: The data is perceived by the user as tables (and nothing but tables) and the operators available to the user for (for example) retrieval are operators that derive "new" tables from "old" ones.*[1]

Examples of Relational Operations

Let's use the five operations defined in Table 1-1 to answer this question: "Which employees have worked in all accounting positions—that is, those for which the job_id starts with the characters AC?" The current job of each employee is stored in the job_id column of the employees table. Any previous jobs are held in the job_history table. The list of job titles is held in the jobs table.

---

[1]Chris Date, *An Introduction to Database Systems*, 8th ed. (Addison-Wesley, 2003).

Here is the description of the employees table:

```
Name                                     Null?     Type
---------------------------------------- --------- ----------------------------
EMPLOYEE_ID                              NOT NULL  NUMBER(6)
FIRST_NAME                                         VARCHAR2(20)
LAST_NAME                               NOT NULL  VARCHAR2(25)
EMAIL                                   NOT NULL  VARCHAR2(25)
PHONE_NUMBER                                       VARCHAR2(20)
HIRE_DATE                               NOT NULL  DATE
JOB_ID                                  NOT NULL  VARCHAR2(10)
SALARY                                             NUMBER(8,2)
COMMISSION_PCT                                     NUMBER(2,2)
MANAGER_ID                                         NUMBER(6)
DEPARTMENT_ID                                      NUMBER(4)
```

Here is the description of the job_history table:

```
Name                                     Null?     Type
---------------------------------------- --------- ----------------------------
EMPLOYEE_ID                              NOT NULL  NUMBER(6)
START_DATE                               NOT NULL  DATE
END_DATE                                 NOT NULL  DATE
JOB_ID                                   NOT NULL  VARCHAR2(10)
DEPARTMENT_ID                                      NUMBER(4)
```

Here is the description of the jobs table:

```
Name                                     Null?     Type
---------------------------------------- --------- ----------------------------
JOB_ID                                   NOT NULL  VARCHAR2(10)
JOB_TITLE                                NOT NULL  VARCHAR2(35)
MIN_SALARY                                         NUMBER(6)
MAX_SALARY                                         NUMBER(6)
```

Given these three tables, you can execute the following steps to answer the business question that has been posed:

1.   This step uses only the employee_id column from the employees table. To do this, you need the projection operation. Following are the SQL command and its results. The employees table contains 107 rows, so this command also produces 107 rows. Only the first five rows are shown here:

     ```
     select employee_id
     from employees

             100
             101
             102
             103
             104
     ```

Note that certain formatting aspects of SQL statements, such as lowercase, uppercase, white space, and line feeds, are immaterial except in the case of string literals—that is, strings of characters enclosed within quote marks.

2. This step uses only the job_id column from the jobs table. To obtain this, you need the projection operation again. Following are the SQL command and its results. The jobs table contains 19 rows, so this command also produces 19 rows. Only the first five rows are shown here:

```
select job_id
from jobs
AC_ACCOUNT
AC_MGR
AD_ASST
AD_PRES
AD_VP
```

3. Remember that the result of any relational operation is always another table. You need a subset of rows from the table created by the projection operation used in step 2. To obtain this, you need the selection operation, as shown in the following SQL command and its results. * is a wildcard that matches all the columns of a table. % is a wildcard that matches any combination of characters. Note that the "table" that is operated on is actually the SQL command from step 2. The result contains only two rows:

```
select *
from (select job_id from jobs)
where job_id like 'AC%'
AC_ACCOUNT
AC_MGR
```

You can streamline this SQL command as follows. This version expresses both the projection from step 2 and the selection from step 3 using a unified syntax. Read it carefully, and make sure you understand it:

```
select job_id from jobs
where job_id like 'AC%'
```

4. You need the job title of every employee; that is, you need the job_id column from the employees table. The employees table has 107 rows, so the resulting table also has 107 rows; five of them are shown here:

```
select employee_id, job_id
from employees

        100 AD_PRES
        101 AD_VP
        102 AD_VP
        103 IT_PROG
        104 IT_PROG
```

5. Next, you need the `employee_id` and `job_id` columns from the `job_history` table. The `jobs` table contains 19 rows, so this command also produces 19 rows. Only the first five rows are shown here:

```
select employee_id, job_id
from job_history

        101 AC_ACCOUNT
        200 AC_ACCOUNT
        101 AC_MGR
        200 AD_ASST
        102 IT_PROG
```

6. Remember that the current job of each employee is stored in the `job_id` column of the `employees` table. Any previous jobs are held in the `job_history` table. The complete job history of any employee is therefore the union of the tables created in step 4 and step 5:

```
select employee_id, job_id
from employees
union
select employee_id, job_id
from job_history
```

7. You need to join the tables created in step 1 and step 3. The resulting table contains *all* possible pairings of the 107 emp_id values in the employees table with the two `job_id` values of interest. There are 214 such pairings, a few of which are shown next:

```
select *
from
  (select employee_id from employees),
  (select job_id from jobs where job_id like 'AC%')

        100 AC_ACCOUNT
        101 AC_ACCOUNT
        102 AC_ACCOUNT
        103 AC_ACCOUNT
        104 AC_ACCOUNT
```

You can streamline this SQL command as follows. This version expresses the projections from step 1 and step 2, the selection from step 3, as well as the join in the current step using a unified syntax. Read it carefully, and make sure you understand it. This pattern of combining multiple projection, join, and selection operations is the most important SQL pattern, so you should make sure you understand it. Note that you prefix the table names to the column names. Such prefixes are required whenever there are ambiguities. In this case, there is a `job_id` column in the employees table in addition to the `jobs` table:

```
select employees.employee_id, jobs.job_id
from employees, jobs
where jobs.job_id like 'AC%'
```

8.   From the table created in step 7, you need to subtract the rows in the table created in step 6! To do this, you need the difference operation, the appropriate SQL keyword being minus. The resulting table contains those pairings of employee_id and job_id that are *not* found in the job_history table. Here is the SQL command you need. The resulting table contains exactly 211 rows, a few of which are shown:

```
select employees.employee_id, jobs.job_id
from employees, jobs
where jobs.job_id like 'AC%'
minus
select employee_id, job_id
from job_history
```

```
100 AC_ACCOUNT
100 AC_MGR
102 AC_ACCOUNT
102 AC_MGR
103 AC_ACCOUNT
```

9.   Thus far, you've obtained pairings of employee_id and job_id that are *not* found in the employee's job history—that is, the table constructed in step 6. Any employee who participates in such a pairing is *not* an employee of interest; that is, any employee who participates in such a pairing isn't an employee who has worked in all positions for which the job_id starts with the characters AC. The first column of this table therefore contains the employees in which you're *not* interested. You need another projection operation:

```
select employee_id from
(
  select employees.employee_id, jobs.job_id
  from employees, jobs
  where jobs.job_id like 'AC%'
  minus
  select employee_id, job_id
  from job_history
)
```

```
100
100
102
102
103
```

10.   You've identified the employees who don't satisfy your criteria. All you have to do is to eliminate them from the table created in step 1! Exactly one employee satisfies your criteria:

```
select employee_id
from employees
minus
select employee_id from
```

```
(
  select employees.employee_id, jobs.job_id
  from employees, jobs
  where jobs.job_id like 'AC%'
  minus
  (
    select employee_id, job_id
    from job_history
    union
    select employee_id, job_id
    from job_history
  )
)
```

101

You had to string together 10 operations to produce the final answer: 5 projection operations, 1 selection operation, 1 union operation, and 2 difference operations.

You can express the final answer in a self-documenting way using *table expressions*, as shown in Listing 1-1. In practice, you wouldn't go to such great lengths to restrict yourself to a single relational operation in each step, because, as you saw in step 7, multiple projection, selection, and join operations can be expressed using a unified syntax. As I said earlier, this approach of combining multiple projection, join, and selection operations is the most important SQL pattern, so make sure you understand it.

Listing 1-1. Final Answer Using Table Expressions

```
WITH
  -- Step 1
  all_employees AS
  ( SELECT employee_id FROM employees
  ),
  -- Step 2
  all_jobs AS
  ( SELECT job_id FROM jobs
  ),
  -- Step 3
  selected_jobs AS
  ( SELECT * FROM all_jobs WHERE job_id LIKE 'AC%'
  ),
  -- Step 4
  selected_pairings AS
  ( SELECT * FROM all_employees, selected_jobs
  ),
  -- Step 5
  current_job_titles AS
  ( SELECT employee_id, job_id FROM employees
  ),
  -- Step 6
  previous_job_titles AS
  ( SELECT employee_id, job_id FROM job_history
  ),
```

```
-- Step 7
complete_job_history AS
( SELECT * FROM current_job_titles
UNION
SELECT * FROM previous_job_titles
),
-- Step 8
nonexistent_pairings AS
( SELECT * FROM selected_pairings
MINUS
SELECT * FROM complete_job_history
),
-- Step 9
undesired_employees AS
( SELECT employee_id FROM nonexistent_pairings
)
-- Step 10
SELECT * FROM all_employees
MINUS
SELECT * FROM undesired_employees
```

I resume the discussion of SQL in the next chapter. For now, note how formatting improves readability—the formatted version with vertical "rivers" and capitalized "reserved words" shown in Listing 1-1 was produced using the formatting options in SQL Developer.

Efficiency of Relational Operators

You may have noticed that the previous section made no mention of efficiency. The definitions of the table operations don't explain how the results can be efficiently obtained. This is intentional and is one of the greatest strengths of relational database technology—it's left to the database management system to provide efficient implementations of the table operations. In particular, the selection operation depends heavily on indexing schemes, and Oracle Database provides a host of such schemes, including B-tree indexes, index-organized tables, partitioned tables, partitioned indexes, function indexes, reverse-key indexes, bitmap indexes, table clusters, and hash clusters. I discuss indexing possibilities as part of physical database design in Chapter 7.

Query Optimization

Perhaps the most important aspect of relational algebra expressions is that, except in very simple cases, they can be rearranged in different ways to gain a performance advantage without changing their meaning or causing the results to change. The following two expressions are equivalent, except perhaps in the order in which data columns occur in the result—a minor presentation detail, not one that changes the meaning of the result:

```
Table_1 JOIN Table_2
Table_2 JOIN Table_1
```

The number of ways in which a relational algebra expression can be rearranged increases dramatically as the expression grows longer. Even the relatively simple expression (Table_1 JOIN Table_2) JOIN Table_3 can be arranged in the following 12 equivalent ways that produce results differing only in the order in which columns are presented—a cosmetic detail that can be easily remedied before the results are shown to the user:

```
(Table_1 JOIN Table_2) JOIN Table_3
(Table_1 JOIN Table_3) JOIN Table_2
(Table_2 JOIN Table_1) JOIN Table_3
(Table_2 JOIN Table_3) JOIN Table_1
(Table_3 JOIN Table_1) JOIN Table_2
(Table_3 JOIN Table_2) JOIN Table_1

Table_1 JOIN (Table_2 JOIN Table_3)
Table_1 JOIN (Table_3 JOIN Table_2)
Table_2 JOIN (Table_1 JOIN Table_3)
Table_2 JOIN (Table_3 JOIN Table_1)
Table_3 JOIN (Table_1 JOIN Table_2)
Table_3 JOIN (Table_2 JOIN Table_1)
```

It isn't obvious at this stage what performance advantage, if any, is gained by rearranging relational algebra expressions. Nor is it obvious what criteria should be used while rearranging expressions. Suffice it to say that a relational algebra expression is intended to be a nonprocedural specification of an intended result, and the query optimizer may take any actions intended to improve the efficiency of query processing as long as the result isn't changed. Relational query optimization is the subject of much theoretical research, and the Oracle query optimizer continues to be improved in every release of Oracle Database. I return to the subject of SQL query tuning in Chapter 17.

What Is a Database Management System?

Database management systems such as Oracle are the interface between users and databases. Database management systems differ in the range of features they provide, but all of them offer certain core features such as transaction management, data integrity, and security. And, of course, they offer the ability to create databases and to define their structure, as well as to store, retrieve, update, and delete the data in the databases.

Transaction Management

A *transaction* is a unit of work that may involve several small steps, all of which are necessary in order not to compromise the integrity of the database. For example, a logical operation such as inserting a row into a table may involve several physical operations such as index updates, trigger operations, and recursive operations. A transaction may also involve multiple logical operations. For example, transferring money from one bank account to another may require that two separate rows be updated. A DBMS needs to ensure that transactions are atomic, consistent, isolated, and durable.

The Atomicity Property of Transactions

It's always possible for a transaction to fail at any intermediate step. For example, users may lose their connection to the database, or the database may run out of space and may not be able to accommodate new data that a user is trying to store. If a failure occurs, the database management system performs automatic rollback of the work that has been performed so far. Transactions are therefore atomic or indivisible from a logical perspective. The end of a transaction is indicated by an explicit instruction such as COMMIT.

The Consistency Property of Transactions

Transactions also have the consistency property. That is, they don't compromise the integrity of the database. However, it's easy to see that a database may be temporarily inconsistent during the operation of the transaction. In the previous example, the database is in an inconsistent state when money has been subtracted from the balance in the first account but has not yet been added to the balance in the second account.

The Isolation Property of Transactions

Transactions also have the isolation property; that is, concurrently occurring transactions must not interact in ways that produce incorrect results. A database management system must be capable of ensuring that the results produced by concurrently executing transactions are *serializable*: the outcome must be the same as if the transactions were executed in serial fashion instead of concurrently.

For example, suppose that one transaction is withdrawing money from a bank customer's checking account, and another transaction is simultaneously withdrawing money from the same customer's savings account. Let's assume that negative balances are permitted as long as the sum of the balances in the two accounts isn't negative. Suppose that the operation of the two transactions proceeds in such a way that each transaction determines the balances in both accounts before either of them has had an opportunity to update either balance. Unless the database management system does something to prevent it, this can potentially result in a negative sum. This kind of problem is called *write skew*.

A detailed discussion of isolation and serializability properly belongs in an advanced course on application development, not in a beginner text on database administration. If you're interested, you can find more information in the Oracle 12c Advanced Application Developer's Guide, available at https://docs.oracle.com/cd/E11882_01/appdev.112/e41502/toc.htm.

The Durability Property of Transactions

Transactions also have the durability property. This means once all the steps in a transaction have been successfully completed and the user notified, the results must be considered permanent even if there is a subsequent computer failure, such as a damaged disk. I return to this topic in the chapters on database backups and recovery; for now, note that the end of a transaction is indicated by an explicit command such as COMMIT.

Data Integrity

Data loses its value if it can't be trusted to be correct. A database management system provides the ability to define and enforce what are called *integrity constraints*. These are rules you define, with which data in the database must comply. For example, you can require that employees not be hired without being given a salary or an hourly pay rate.

The database management system rejects any attempt to violate the integrity constraints when inserting, updating, or deleting data records and typically displays an appropriate error code and message. In fact, the very first Oracle error code, ORA-00001, relates to attempts to violate an integrity constraint. It's possible to enforce arbitrary constraints using trigger operations; these can include checks that are as complex as necessary, but the more common types of constraints are check constraints, uniqueness constraints, and referential constraints. These work as follows:

- *Check constraints*: Check constraints are usually simple checks on the value of a data item. For example, a price quote must not be less than $0.00.

- *Uniqueness constraints*: A uniqueness constraint requires that some part of a record be unique. For example, two employees may not have the same employee number. A unique part of a record is called a *candidate key*, and one of the candidate keys is designated as the primary key. Intuitively, you expect every record to have at least one candidate key; otherwise, you would have no way of specifying which records you needed. Note that the candidate key can consist of a single item from the data record, a combination of items, or even all the items.

- *Referential constraints*: Consider an employee database in which all payments to employees are recorded in a table called SALARY. The employee number in a salary record must obviously correspond to the employee number in some employee record; this is an example of a referential constraint.

Data Security

A database management system gives the owners of the data a lot of control over their data—they can delegate limited rights to others if they choose to. It also gives the database administrator the ability to restrict and monitor the actions of users. For example, the database administrator can disable the password of an employee who leaves the company, to prevent them from gaining access to the database. Relational database management systems use techniques such as *views* (virtual tables defined in terms of other tables) and query modification to give individual users access to just those portions of data they're authorized to use.

Oracle also offers extensive query-modification capabilities under the heading Virtual Private Database (VPD). Additional query restrictions can be silently and transparently appended to the query by *policy functions* associated with the tables in the query. For example, the policy functions may generate additional query restrictions that allow employees to retrieve information only about themselves and their direct reports between the hours of 9 a.m. and 5 p.m. on weekdays only.

I return to the subject of data security in Chapter 8.

What Makes a Relational Database Management System Relational?

Having already discussed the meaning of both *relational database* and *database management system*, it may appear that the subject is settled. But the natural implications of the relational model are so numerous and profound that critics contend that, even today, a "truly relational" database management system doesn't exist. For example, Dr. Edgar Codd wanted the database management system to treat views in the same manner as base tables whenever possible, but the problem of view updateability is unsolved to the present day. Codd listed more than 300 separate requirements that a database management system must meet in order to fulfill his vision properly, and I have time for just one of them: physical data independence. Here is the relevant quote from Codd's book:

> *RP-1 Physical Data Independence: The DBMS permits a suitably authorized user to make changes in storage representation, in access method, or in both—for example, for performance reasons. Application programs and terminal activities remain logically unimpaired whenever any such changes are made.*[2]

What Codd meant was that you and I shouldn't have to worry about implementation details such as the storage structures used to store data.

Summary

I hope that you now have an appreciation for the theoretical foundations of Oracle Database 12*c*. You can find more information about the subjects I touched on in the books mentioned in the bibliography at the end of the chapter. Here is a short summary of the concepts discussed in this chapter:

- A *database* is an information repository that must be competently administered using the principles laid out in the IT Infrastructure Library (ITIL), including security management, availability management, continuity management, change management, incident management, problem management, configuration management, release management, and capacity management.

- *Relation* is a precise mathematical term for what is loosely called a *data table*. Relational database technology swept aside earlier technologies because of the power and expressiveness of relational algebra and because it made performance the responsibility of the database management system instead of the application developer.

- A database management system provides efficient algorithms for the processing of table operations as well as indexing schemes for data storage. The query optimizer rearranges relational algebra expressions in the interests of efficiency but without changing the meaning or the results that are produced.

- A *database management system* is defined as a software layer that provides services such as transaction management, data security, and data integrity.

- A *transaction* is a logical unit of work characterized by atomicity, consistency, isolation, and durability.

- Relational database theory has many consequences, including logical data independence, which implies that changes to the way in which data is stored or indexed shouldn't affect the logical behavior of application programs.

---

[2]E. F. Codd, *The Relational Model for Database Management: Version 2* (Addison Wesley, 1990).

Further Reading

- Bachman, Charles. "The Programmer as Navigator." ACM Turing Award Lecture, 1973. http://amturing.acm.org/award_winners/bachman_9385610.cfm. To properly understand Codd's theory, you must understand what preceded it.

- Codd, E. F. "Relational Database: A Practical Foundation for Productivity." ACM Turing Award Lecture, 1981. http://amturing.acm.org/award_winners/codd_1000892.cfm. It's a shame that almost no database professionals have read the papers and articles written by the inventor of relational database theory. In my opinion, the 1981 ACM Turing Award Lecture should be required reading for every database professional.

- Silberschatz, Abraham, Henry Korth, and S. Sudarshan. *Database System Concepts*. 6th ed. McGraw-Hill, 2010. If you're going buy just one book on database theory, this is the one I recommend. This college textbook, now in its sixth edition, offers not only copious amounts of theory but also some coverage of commercial products such as Oracle Database.

CHAPTER 2

■ ■ ■

SQL and PL/SQL by Example

*A number of our established "powerful" programming language features, even beloved
ones, could very well turn out to belong rather to "the problem set" than to "the solution set."*

—Dutch computer scientist Edsger Dijkstra, advocate of structured
programming and winner of the 1972 Turing Award, in
"Correctness Concerns and, Among Other Things, Why They Are Resented"

All database activity is conducted in SQL, and therefore database administrators need to be intimately
familiar with it. Figure 2-1 illustrates that the greatest potential for performance improvement usually lies
within the software application, not within the database where the application stores its data or within the
physical infrastructure where the database is housed.[1]

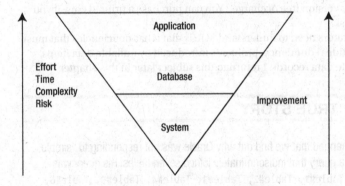

Figure 2-1. *The performance improvement pyramid*

---

[1]Based on a discussion in *Oracle Rdb Guide to Database Performance and Tuning*.

A common example of performance problems caused by applications is that the applications aren't designed to take advantage of indexing schemes. As an example of a performance problem that you might encounter in SQL, consider the query in Listing 2-1, which retrieves the names of employees with first_name "Steven" and last_name "King". An index exists on the first_name and last_name columns of the employees table, but the query can't use the index because it uses the upper function in the restriction. Because Oracle Database can't use the index, it has to retrieve and examine every single record in the employees table.[2]

Listing 2-1. An Inefficient SQL Query

```
SELECT first_name, last_name
  FROM employees
 WHERE upper(first_name) = 'STEVEN'
   AND upper(last_name) = 'KING';
```

Another source of performance problems is the temptation to use the Oracle Database engine as a calculator to perform arithmetic calculations and string manipulations. This is a highly inefficient use of SQL and is better done using math and string libraries instead. However, it is usually fine to issue a simple query against dual such as in Listing 2-2 that executes just one time.

Listing 2-2. Finding the Day of the Week

```
select to_char(sysdate, 'DAY') from dual;
```

An equally important reason why database administrators need to understand SQL is that all database administration activities such as database maintenance and user management are also conducted in SQL. It should come as no surprise, therefore, that the *Oracle Database 12c SQL Language Reference* is almost 2,000 pages—compare this with the 20 or so pages in this chapter. Fortunately, you can go online and search the SQL manual or download the electronic version free of charge.[3] You can purchase a printed copy if you like having a mountain of paper on your desk.

A third reason why database administrators need to understand SQL is that it has deficiencies that must be guarded against. These deficiencies include redundancy, problems introduced by nullable data items, and the absence of prohibitions on duplicate data records. I return to this subject later in this chapter.

TRUE STORY

One day, an angry software developer demanded that we find out why Oracle was not responding to "simple queries." We found that he had submitted a query that indiscriminately joined seven tables. His query was of the form SELECT COUNT(*) ... FROM Table#1, Table#2, Table#3, Table#4, Table#5, Table#6, Table#7.[4] The number of rows produced by such a query equals the product of the number of rows in each table; if each specified table contained 1,000 rows, the query would produce 100 trillion rows.

When we asked the software developer why he hadn't specified any joining criteria, he said that he first wanted to determine whether Oracle could handle a "simple" query before submitting a "complex" query!

It happened to me—it could happen to you!

---

[2] It's possible to create a *function-based index* for the upper(first_name) and upper(last_name) columns.
[3] The URL is http://docs.oracle.com.
[4] Such a query is called a *Cartesian product*.

Railroad Diagrams

SQL statements have many optional clauses, so the Oracle reference manuals use *railroad diagrams* as a visual aid. Figure 2-2 is an example of a railroad diagram for a hypothetical ROW command.

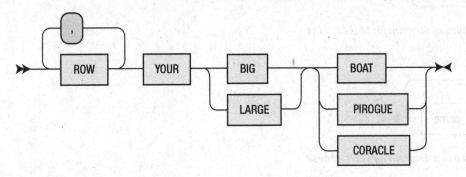

Figure 2-2. *A railroad diagram for a hypothetical ROW command*

Start at the left of the diagram, and take any path the diagram allows you to take. Along the way, you encounter mandatory words and clauses as well as optional words and clauses and even subdiagrams. The diagram indicates that the ROW command can take the forms indicated in Listing 2-3.

Listing 2-3. Examples of ROW Commands

```
ROW YOUR BOAT
ROW, ROW YOUR BOAT
ROW, ROW, ROW YOUR CORACLE
ROW, ROW, ROW, ROW YOUR PIROGUE
ROW, ROW, ROW, ROW, ROW YOUR LARGE CORACLE
```

Let's look at some railroad diagrams for a simplified version of the SELECT statement. The SELECT statement starts with the keyword SELECT and is used to retrieve data from a relational database. What you see here is a very small subset of the complete syntax, but it's powerful enough for many purposes.

The diagrams in Figures 2-3 through 2-8 show that the keyword SELECT is followed a number of clauses: the mandatory SELECT_list and FROM_clause and the optional WHERE_clause, GROUP_BY_clause, and ORDER_BY_clause. Separate railroad diagrams are also shown for each of the clauses.

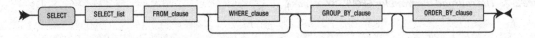

Figure 2-3. *A simplified railroad diagram for the SELECT statement*

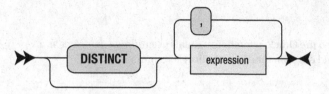

Figure 2-4. *The railroad diagram for SELECT_list*

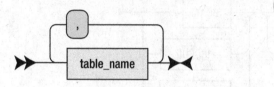

Figure 2-5. *The railroad diagram for FROM_clause*

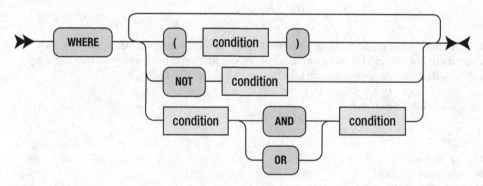

Figure 2-6. *The railroad diagram for WHERE_clause*

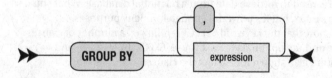

Figure 2-7. *The railroad diagram for GROUP_BY_clause*

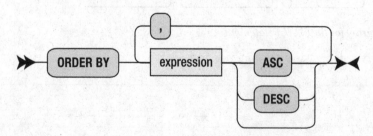

Figure 2-8. *The railroad diagram for ORDER_BY_clause*

As an example, let's generate a report of the total salary in each department, sorted by descending order of average salary. Let's assemble the necessary clauses.

The SELECT_list clause is a comma-separated list of column names or expressions in which you're interested. Here's what you need. The upper function produces the uppercase version of a character string, and the avg function produces the average of values in a group:

```
SELECT upper(department_name),
  AVG(salary)
```

The WHERE_clause portion of the statement is a list of tables that must be joined. You need the departments table and the employees table. You give each table a short alias that will come in handy in other clauses:

```
FROM departments d,
  employees e
```

The optional GROUP_BY_clause portion of the statement tells Oracle Database that you apply aggregate functions such as avg to groups of records. In this case, you need to group by upper(department_name):
```
GROUP BY upper(department_name)
```
Finally, the ORDER_BY_clause portion of the statement specifies how you want the report sorted. In this case, you need to sort by descending values of AVG(salary):

```
ORDER BY AVG(salary) DESC;
```

Let's put this all together:

```
SELECT upper(department_name),
  AVG(salary)
FROM departments d,
  employees e
WHERE e.department_id = d.department_id
GROUP BY upper(department_name)
ORDER BY AVG(salary) DESC;
```

And here is the result:

UPPER(DEPARTMENT_NAME)	AVG(SALARY)
EXECUTIVE	19333.3333
ACCOUNTING	10150 .
PUBLIC RELATIONS	10000
MARKETING	9500
SALES	8955.88235
FINANCE	8600
HUMAN RESOURCES	6500
IT	5760
ADMINISTRATION	4400
PURCHASING	4150
SHIPPING	3475.55556

Notice the formatting of the results. Formatting instructions aren't part of the SQL query; the formatting is left to the application program—SQL*Plus in this case—that sent the SQL query to the Oracle Database engine for processing.

Now take a minute and check out the complete syntax of the SELECT statement in the SQL reference manual. Notice the subquery diagram in particular and how it references *itself*; just before the ORDER BY clause, you can optionally specify a UNION, INTERSECT, or MINUS clause followed by another subquery. Also observe that the subquery diagram is referenced by other diagrams. For example:

- If you check the Subquery Factoring Clause diagram, you see that it too refers to the subquery diagram.

- If you check the Table Reference subdiagram, you see that a table reference can include a subquery. This kind of subquery is called an *inline view*.

- Subqueries that produce a single value can be used any place where a single value is indicated. This kind of subquery is called a *scalar subquery*. For example, scalar subqueries can be used in a SELECT list and in a WHERE clause.

Types of SQL

Only a small fraction of the SQL reference manual is devoted to the sort of SQL statements you've encountered so far. SQL statements are commonly classified into Database Manipulation Language (DML) statements to modify data and Database Definition Language (DDL) statements to create and modify the different types of objects that compose an Oracle database. The SQL reference manual also describes commands that can create and modify databases and perform database administration activities such as stopping and starting databases.

Data Definition Language

A large portion of the SQL reference manual is devoted to DDL: commands that are used to create, alter, and drop different types of database objects such as tables and indexes. Listing 2-4 shows the DDL commands that can be used to create the employees table in the HR schema. These commands specify a data type such as *variable character* (VARCHAR2) or numeric for each data item, the length of each data item, and, in the case of numeric data items, the precision. For example, VARCHAR2(32) indicates no more than 32 data characters, and NUMBER(8, 2) indicates a decimal number with no more than 8 digits, 2 of which are to the right of the decimal point. Some of the columns are specified to be NOT NULL, and you also have check, unique-key, and primary-key constraints.

Using SQL Developer, you can review the DDL-creation commands of other tables in the HR schema. Simply go to the SQL tab for each table.

Listing 2-4. DDL Commands to Create the employees Table

```
CREATE TABLE employees
  (
    employee_id    NUMBER(6,0),
    first_name     VARCHAR2(20),
    last_name      VARCHAR2(25) CONSTRAINT emp_last_name_nn NOT NULL enable,
    email          VARCHAR2(25) CONSTRAINT emp_email_nn NOT NULL enable,
    phone_number   VARCHAR2(20),
    hire_date      DATE CONSTRAINT emp_hire_date_nn NOT NULL enable,
    job_id         VARCHAR2(10) CONSTRAINT emp_job_nn NOT NULL enable,
```

```
    salary          NUMBER(8,2),
    commission_pct  NUMBER(2,2),
    manager_id      NUMBER(6,0),
    department_id   NUMBER(4,0),
    CONSTRAINT emp_salary_min CHECK (salary > 0) enable,
    CONSTRAINT emp_email_uk UNIQUE (email) enable,
    CONSTRAINT emp_emp_id_pk PRIMARY KEY (employee_id) enable,
    CONSTRAINT emp_dept_fk FOREIGN KEY (department_id)
      REFERENCES departments (department_id) enable,
    CONSTRAINT emp_job_fk FOREIGN KEY (job_id)
      REFERENCES jobs (job_id) enable,
    CONSTRAINT emp_manager_fk FOREIGN KEY (manager_id)
      REFERENCES employees (employee_id) enable
)
```

Database Manipulation Language

You've already seen several examples of the SELECT statement. Next, let's consider the INSERT, UPDATE, DELETE, and MERGE statements.

The INSERT Statement

The INSERT statement is the way in which data enters the relational database. In Listing 2-5, a new record is being added to the employees table. However, if you were to try this command using SQL Developer, it would fail because the employee_id column is the primary-key column and the value 100 is already in use. Also, values in the email column are required to be unique, and the value "SKING" is already in use. Try this statement using SQL Developer, and observe the error message. Then change the value to one that will succeed.

Listing 2-5. A DML statement to record a new employee

```
INSERT
INTO employees
  (
    employee_id,
    first_name,
    last_name,
    email,
    phone_number,
    hire_date,
    job_id,
    salary,
    commission_pct,
    manager_id,
    department_id
  )
VALUES
  (
    100,
    'Steven',
    'King',
```

```
  'SKING',
  '515.123.4567',
  TO_DATE('17-JUN-1987', 'dd-MON-yyyy'),
  'AD_PRES',
  24000,
  NULL,
  NULL,
  90
);
```

The UPDATE Statement

The UPDATE statement enables you to specify a subset of data rows and instructions for modifying them. In Listing 2-6, the e-mail address of an employee is being changed. However, if you were to try this command using SQL Developer, it would fail because the values in the email column are required to be unique and the value "NKOCHAR" is already in use. Try this statement using SQL Developer, and observe the error message. Then change the value "NKOCHAR" to one that will succeed.

Listing 2-6. DML Command to Modify the Values of Data Items

```
UPDATE employees SET email='NKOCHHAR' WHERE employee_id=100;
```

The DELETE Statement

The DELETE statement lets you specify a subset of data rows to delete. In Listing 2-7, an employee record is being deleted. However, if you were to try this statement using SQL Developer, it would fail, because the employee_id column is referenced by a foreign-key constraint specifying that the value in the manager_id column must be a valid employee_id (or be left unspecified). The employee_id column is also referenced by a foreign-key constraint on the job_history table, which specifies that the values in the employee_id column should all be valid. Try this statement using SQL Developer, and observe the error message. This statement won't succeed as long as there any rows for which the manager_id column has the value 101.

Listing 2-7. DML Command to Delete a Data Record from the employees Table

```
DELETE FROM employees WHERE employee_id = 101;
```

The MERGE Statement

MERGE is a powerful statement that combines the capabilities of the INSERT statement, the UPDATE statement, and the DELETE statement. Consider the following example. Suppose you have employee updates in a table called employee_updates. If a record contains an employee_id that already exists in the table, then the corresponding record in the employees table has to be updated. If a record contains an employee_id that doesn't exist in the table, then the values must be inserted into the employees table. Finally, if the terminated column has value 1, then the corresponding record has to be deleted from the database. You can merge the contents of the employee_updates table into the employees table by using the MERGE statement—inserting, updating, or deleting records as necessary—as shown in Listing 2-8.

Listing 2-8. DML Command to Merge the Contents of One Table into Another Table

```
MERGE INTO employees e USING employee_updates u ON (
  e.employee_id = u.employee_id)
WHEN matched THEN
  UPDATE
  SET last_name      = u.last_name,
    email            = u.email,
    phone_number     = u.phone_number,
    hire_date        = u.hire_date,
    job_id           = u.job_id,
    salary           = u.salary,
    commission_pct   = u.commission_pct,
    manager_id       = u.manager_id,
    department_id    = u.department_id
  DELETE WHERE terminated = 1
WHEN NOT matched THEN
  INSERT
    (
      employee_id,
      first_name,
      last_name,
      email,
      phone_number,
      hire_date,
      job_id,
      salary,
      commission_pct,
      manager_id,
      department_id
    )
  VALUES
    (
      u.employee_id,
      u.first_name,
      u.last_name,
      u.email,
      u.phone_number,
      u.hire_date,
      u.job_id,
      u.salary,
      u.commission_pct,
      u.manager_id,
      u.department_id
    );
```

Embedded SQL

Application programs written by application software developers can communicate with an Oracle database only by using SQL. These application programs must therefore be linked with Oracle-supplied routines that give them the capability to communicate with an Oracle database.

Listing 2-9 shows an example of SQL statements embedded in a Java program. Each embedded SQL statement is prefixed with the phrase #sql (refer to the text in boldface in the example). The example lists the names of all parts supplied by a specified supplier and the price quote in each case; the account name and password required to connect to the database must be provided by the user at runtime.

Listing 2-9. SQL Commands Embedded in a Java Program

```java
import sqlj.runtime.*;
import sqlj.runtime.ref.*;
import java.sql.*;

public class PrintQuote
{
  public static void main(String[] args)
  {
    Connection connection = null;

    #sql iterator quote_iterator (
      String partname,
      double quote);

    quote_iterator quote = null;

    try
    {

      // Connect to the database
      // The account name and password are provided to the program by the user

      DriverManager.registerDriver(
        new oracle.jdbc.driver.OracleDriver());
      connection = DriverManager.getConnection(
        "jdbc:oracle:thin:@localhost:1521:ORCL",
        args[0],
        args[1]);
      DefaultContext.setDefaultContext(
        new DefaultContext(connection));

      // Retrieve the data for one supplier
      // The supplier's name is provided to the program by the user

      String suppliername = args[2];

      #sql quote = {
        SELECT
          upper(department_name) AS department_name,
          AVG(salary) AS average_salary
```

```
    FROM
      departments d,
      employees e
    WHERE e.department_id = d.department_id
    GROUP BY upper(department_name)
    ORDER BY AVG(salary) DESC
    };

    // Print one row of data on each line

    while (quote.next()) {
      System.out.printf(
        "%-40s%10.2f\n",
        quote.department_name(),
        quote.average_salary());
    }

    connection.close();

  }
  catch (SQLException exception) {
    exception.printStackTrace();
  }
 }
}
}
```

SQL*Plus and SQL Developer

Oracle Database provides a command-line tool called *SQL*Plus* that enables you to interact with the database without having to embed SQL in an application program; this is the tool that database administrators most frequently use in their work besides *SQL Developer*. The advantage of a command-line tool such as SQL*Plus is that it can be used to automate tasks—that is, a series of SQL statements can be placed in a file and automatically executed at prescribed times.

The SQL*Plus utility can also be used as a simple report-writing tool to produce neatly formatted reports. The commands in Listing 2-10 cause the entire employees table to be listed. The average salary is also printed for each department. Listing 2-11 shows the output produced by the commands in Listing 2-10.

Listing 2-10. A SQL*Plus Program to Produce a Neatly Formatted Report

```
-- Print page titles and a closing line
SET pagesize 66
SET linesize 74
TTITLE center "SALARY LISTING" RIGHT "Page:" sql.pno skip 2
REPFOOTER skip 1 center "END OF REPORT"

-- Print suitable titles for each column of information
COLUMN deartment_name format a30 heading "Department Name"
COLUMN employee_name format a30 heading "Employee Name"
COLUMN salary format 99999990.00 heading "Salary"
```

```
-- Print the department name only once and skip a line when the supplier name changes
BREAK ON department_name skip 1

-- Print the number of parts supplied by each supplier
COMPUTE AVG OF salary ON department_name

-- Print all information in the quote table
SELECT upper(department_name) AS department_name,
  upper(last_name || ', ' ||first_name) AS employee_name,
  salary
FROM departments d,
  employees e
WHERE e.department_id = d.department_id
ORDER BY department_name,
  employee_name;
```

Listing 2-11. A Neatly Formatted Report with Page Headings, Column Headings, and Summary Lines

```
SALARY LISTING      Page: 1

DEPARTMENT_NAME                 Employee Name                           Salary
----------------------------    ----------------------------    ------------
ACCOUNTING                      GIETZ, WILLIAM                        8300.00
                                HIGGINS, SHELLEY                     12000.00
****************************                                    ------------
Avg                                                                 10150.00

ADMINISTRATION                  WHALEN, JENNIFER                      4400.00
****************************                                    ------------
Avg                                                                  4400.00

EXECUTIVE                       DE HAAN, LEX                         17000.00
                                KING, STEVEN                        24000.00
                                KOCHHAR, NEENA                      17000.00
****************************                                    ------------
Avg                                                                 19333.33
```

Criticisms of SQL

The IBM team that developed SQL made certain decisions that violated relational principles—chief among them that duplicate rows were allowed. The inventor of relational database technology, Dr. Edgar Codd, was not part of IBM's development team, and, despite his urging, these deficiencies were not corrected in subsequent revisions of the language. In the opinion of some commentators, the gap then continued to widen. Nevertheless, no one has been successful in providing an alternative to SQL, and you must learn to live with its deficiencies. Chris Date makes the point forcefully in *An Introduction to Database Systems*:

> *SQL is now so far from being a true embodiment of relational principles—it suffers from so many sins of both omission and commission—that I would frankly prefer not to discuss it at all! However, SQL is obviously important from a commercial point of view; thus, every database professional needs to have some familiarity with it...*

Michael Stonebraker makes the point that SQL is the intergalactic language. Everybody in the galaxy speaks SQL, so, like it or not, we have to be masters of it.

Duplicates

The SQL standard allows tables to contain duplicate data records and doesn't require that duplicates be eliminated from the results of a projection or union operation, thus violating the principles laid down by Codd. Date has published an example in which 12 formulations of a certain SQL query returned 9 different results because duplicate data rows existed in the tables in question. Not only does this become a programming nightmare, but Date points out that this is one reason why the query optimizer can't always rewrite queries into alternative forms that are more efficient—the optimizer can't be sure the result will be unaffected by the rewrite.

Redundancy

Redundancy isn't a violation of relational principles but creates a serious performance problem that database administrators must understand. There are usually many ways to rephrase the same SQL query. For various reasons (such as the one described in the previous section), the query optimizer might not find the optimal query execution plan in all cases even though all the plans retrieve the same data and, therefore, the query plan that is optimal in one case is equally optimal in all other cases.

Listing 2-12 shows lots of different ways to express the query *Departments that have at least one employee*. Only the first version conforms to the simplified railroad diagram in Figure 2-3 and is obviously an abbreviated way of specifying the application of three separate relational algebra operators: join, restriction, and projection.

Listing 2-12. Departments That Have at Least One Employee

```
SELECT DISTINCT d.department_name
FROM departments d,
  employees e
WHERE e.department_id = d.department_id
AND e.job_id          = 'SH_CLERK';

SELECT DISTINCT d.department_name
FROM departments d NATURAL
JOIN employees e
WHERE e.job_id = 'SH_CLERK';

SELECT DISTINCT d.department_name
FROM departments d
JOIN employees e USING (department_id)
WHERE e.job_id = 'SH_CLERK';

SELECT DISTINCT d.department_name
FROM departments d
JOIN employees e
ON (e.department_id = d.department_id)
WHERE e.job_id       = 'SH_CLERK';
```

```
SELECT department_name
FROM departments
WHERE department_id IN
  ( SELECT department_id FROM employees WHERE job_id = 'SH_CLERK'
  );


SELECT department_name
FROM departments d
WHERE department_id = ANY
  ( SELECT department_id FROM employees e WHERE job_id = 'SH_CLERK'
  );


SELECT department_name
FROM departments d
WHERE 'SH_CLERK' IN
  ( SELECT job_id FROM employees e WHERE e.department_id = d.department_id
  );


SELECT department_name FROM departments
MINUS
SELECT department_name
FROM departments d
WHERE 'SH_CLERK' NOT IN
  ( SELECT job_id FROM employees e WHERE e.department_id = d.department_id
  );


SELECT d.department_name
FROM departments d
WHERE 'SH_CLERK' = ANY
  ( SELECT job_id FROM employees WHERE department_id = d.department_id
  );


SELECT d.department_name
FROM departments d
WHERE EXISTS
  (SELECT *
  FROM employees
  WHERE department_id = d.department_id
  AND job_id          = 'SH_CLERK'
  );


SELECT department_name FROM departments
MINUS
SELECT department_name
FROM departments d
WHERE NOT EXISTS
  (SELECT *
  FROM employees
  WHERE department_id = d.department_id
  AND job_id          = 'SH_CLERK'
  );
```

```
SELECT department_name
FROM departments d
WHERE (SELECT COUNT(*)
  FROM employees
  WHERE department_id = d.department_id
  AND job_id         = 'SH_CLERK' ) > 0;

SELECT DISTINCT d.department_name
FROM departments d
LEFT JOIN employees e
ON (e.department_id = d.department_id)
WHERE e.job_id        = 'SH_CLERK';

SELECT DISTINCT d.department_name
FROM departments d,
  lateral
  (SELECT 1
  FROM employees e
  WHERE e.department_id = d.department_id
  AND e.job_id          = 'SH_CLERK'
  );
```

In Chapter 1, you saw the SQL answer to the problem *Which employees have worked in all accounting positions; that is, those for which the* job_id *starts with the characters AC*? Listing 2-13 shows two alternative formulations: the first formulation uses correlated subqueries, and the second formulation uses aggregate functions.

Listing 2-13. Alternative Solutions to the Problem Which employees have worked in all accounting positions; that is, those for which the job_id starts with the characters AC?

```
SELECT employee_id
FROM employees e
WHERE NOT EXISTS
  (SELECT *
  FROM jobs j
  WHERE job_id LIKE 'AC%'
  AND NOT ( e.job_id = j.job_id
  OR EXISTS
    (SELECT *
    FROM job_history
    WHERE employee_id = e.employee_id
    AND job_id         = j.job_id
    ) )
  );
```

```
SELECT employee_id
FROM
  ( SELECT employee_id, job_id FROM job_history WHERE job_id LIKE 'AC%'
  UNION
  SELECT employee_id, job_id FROM employees WHERE job_id LIKE 'AC%'
  )
GROUP BY employee_id
HAVING COUNT(DISTINCT job_id) =
  (SELECT COUNT(*) FROM jobs WHERE job_id LIKE 'AC%'
  );
```

Nullable Data Items

Sometimes the value of a data item isn't known. If you permit a record to be stored even if the values of some data items aren't known, those data items are said to be *nullable*. Missing information leads to "fuzzy" logic in which there is a third alternative—unknown—to truth and falsehood of a statement such as department_id=90. Nullable data items are commonly used by database designers, but three-valued logic isn't intuitive. In the employees table, manager_id is a nullable column. Intuitively, the following queries should return the value 107—the number of rows in the employees table—but instead they return the value 106 because one record doesn't contain a value for department_id:

```
SELECT COUNT(*) FROM employees WHERE manager_id = 100 OR manager_id != 100;
SELECT COUNT(*) FROM employees WHERE manager_id = manager_id;
SELECT COUNT(*) FROM employees WHERE manager_id != -1;
```

To obtain the expected answer, you need to add the clause OR manager_id IS NULL to the preceding SQL queries; you can find more information about the problems created by nullable data items in any good book on SQL.

Introduction to PL/SQL

Oracle Database gives you the ability to store programs in the database using a language called *Procedural Language/SQL* (*PL/SQL*). PL/SQL offers the entire suite of structured programming mechanisms, such as condition checking, loops, and subroutines, as shown in Figure 2-9. Just like programs written in other languages, PL/SQL programs use SQL to interact with the database.

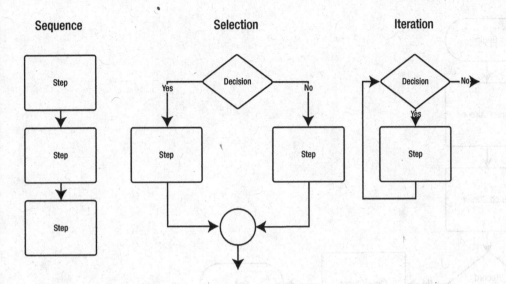

Figure 2-9. Programming patterns provided by all programming languages

A common use of PL/SQL is to write *triggers*. Triggers are tied to actions such as the action of inserting a record into a table. For example, the HR schema contains a trigger that inserts a history record into the job_history table whenever the job_id in the employees table is updated. This preserves the history of changes to an employee's position.

Figure 2-10 diagrams the logic of a PL/SQL program to merge the contents of the employee_updates table with the employees table. This is *not* the way you should do things, because the merge command is available, but the approach in the figure nicely illustrates the capabilities of PL/SQL. The program corresponding to Figure 2-10 is shown in Listing 2-14. It uses a *cursor*, which is a mechanism that allows you to iterate through the rows of data returned by a SQL query.

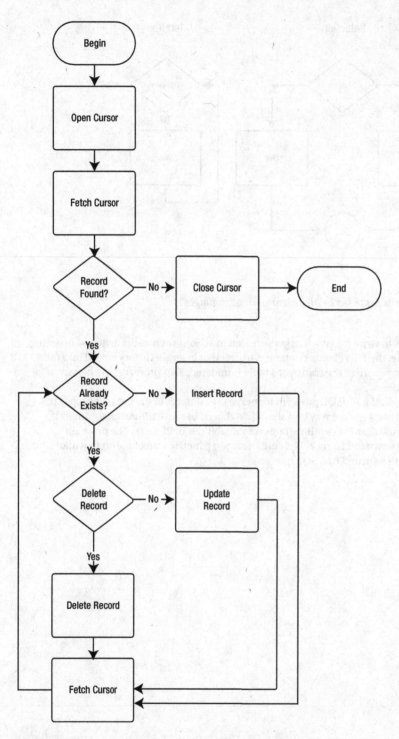

Figure 2-10. *Flow chart for the* employee_updates *procedure*

Listing 2-14. PL/SQL Program to Merge the Contents of the employee_updates table with the employees table

```
CREATE OR REPLACE
PROCEDURE employee_updates_proc
IS
  CURSOR l_cursor
  IS
    SELECT terminated,
      employee_id,
      first_name,
      last_name,
      email,
      phone_number,
      hire_date,
      job_id,
      salary,
      commission_pct,
      manager_id,
      department_id
    FROM employee_updates;
  l_record l_cursor%rowtype;
  l_count pls_integer;
BEGIN
  OPEN l_cursor;
  FETCH l_cursor INTO l_record;
  WHILE NOT l_cursor%notfound
  LOOP
    l_count := 0;
    SELECT COUNT(*)
    INTO l_count
    FROM employees
    WHERE employee_id        = l_record.employee_id;
    IF l_count               = 1 THEN
      IF l_record.terminated = 1 THEN
        DELETE FROM employees WHERE employee_id =
          l_record.employee_id;
      ELSE
        UPDATE employees
        SET last_name        = l_record.last_name,
          email              = l_record.email,
          phone_number       = l_record.phone_number,
          hire_date          = l_record.hire_date,
          job_id             = l_record.job_id,
          salary             = l_record.salary,
          commission_pct     = l_record.commission_pct,
          manager_id         = l_record.manager_id,
          department_id      = l_record.department_id;
      END IF;
```

```
    ELSE
      INSERT
      INTO employees
        (
          employee_id,
          first_name,
          last_name,
          email,
          phone_number,
          hire_date,
          job_id,
          salary,
          commission_pct,
          manager_id,
          department_id
        )
      VALUES
        (
          l_record.employee_id,
          l_record.first_name,
          l_record.last_name,
          l_record.email,
          l_record.phone_number,
          l_record.hire_date,
          l_record.job_id,
          l_record.salary,
          l_record.commission_pct,
          l_record.manager_id,
          l_record.department_id
        );
    END IF;
    FETCH l_cursor INTO l_record;
  END LOOP;
  CLOSE l_cursor;
END;
```

Storing programs in the database has many advantages. Special PL/SQL programs called *triggers* can be executed whenever a user performs a specified action. This gives you the ability to enforce business rules, control access to data, and keep records of who accessed the data and how it changed. Storing sequences of commands in the database greatly reduces the amount of communication between client and server and improves efficiency. Also, PL/SQL functions can be used in SQL statements; this increases the power and flexibility of SQL.

Summary

Database administrators need to understand SQL in all its forms. Many Oracle experts have devoted their entire careers to the study of SQL, and I have hardly been able to scratch the surface in this chapter. I highly recommend the books listed at the end of this chapter; and, of course, you can always download the official Oracle reference works from the Oracle web site. Here is a short summary of the concepts discussed in this chapter:

- All database activity, including database administration activities, is transacted in SQL.

- Oracle reference works use railroad diagrams to teach the SQL language. Railroad diagrams can include subdiagrams and can even refer to themselves in recursive fashion. For instance, a table reference can be an entire subquery—this kind of subquery is called an *inline view*. The SELECT list can include scalar subqueries—that is, subqueries that return exactly one data item from exactly one data row.

- SQL is divided into Data Manipulation Language (DML) and Data Definition Language (DDL). DML includes the SELECT, INSERT, UPDATE, MERGE, and DELETE statements. DDL includes the CREATE, ALTER, and DROP statements for the different classes of objects in an Oracle database. The SQL reference manual also describes commands that can be used to perform database administration activities such as stopping and starting databases.

- SQL needs to be embedded into software application programs so they can communicate with the database.

- SQL has been criticized because it doesn't prohibit duplicates; the absence of a prohibition against duplicates causes queries that are seemingly equivalent to produce differing results and inhibits the query optimization process.

- Using nullable data items can lead to results that contradict common sense.

- SQL queries can usually be formulated in several ways. The Oracle Database optimizer may not always choose the same query execution plan in all cases, even though the query plan that is most efficient in one case is obviously the most efficient for all other cases.

- Programs written in PL/SQL can be stored in an Oracle database. Using these programs has many advantages, including efficiency, control, and flexibility. PL/SQL offers a full complement of structured programming mechanisms such as condition checking, loops, and subroutines.

Exercises

- Download *Oracle Database 12c SQL Reference* from http://docs.oracle.com. Review the railroad diagram for the SELECT statement and all the subdiagrams.

- Using SQL Developer, try the INSERT, UPDATE, and DELETE statements in Listing 2-5, Listing 2-6, and Listing 2-7. Construct a solution in each case.

- Use SQL Developer to perform the following tasks:

    a. Create an employee_updates table by cloning the employees table.

    b. Add a terminated column to the employee_updates table.

    c. Insert records into the employee_updates table.

    d. Merge the data in the employee_updates table into the employees table using the MERGE command.

Further Reading

- De Haan, Lex, and Tim Gorman. *Beginning Oracle SQL: For Oracle Database 12*c. Apress, 2009. The work of the late Lex De Haan, a well-known Oracle expert and teacher has been revised for Oracle Database 12c by Tim Gorman, an Oracle ACE Director and a member of the OakTable network.

- Feuerstein, Steven. *Oracle Magazine*. www.oracle.com/technetwork/issue-archive/index-087690.html. A 12-part series on PL/SQL starting in the March/April 2011 issue and ending in the March/April 2013 issue. Part 2, "Controlling the Flow of Execution," and Part 12, "Working with Cursors," are especially relevant to the PL/SQL example in this chapter.

- Feuerstein, Steven, and Bill Pribyl. *Oracle PL/SQL Programming*. O'Reilly, 2014. Steven Feuerstein is the world's top expert in PL/SQL and has a highly readable style. If you're planning to invest in a PL/SQL book, I recommend this one.

- Gennick, Jonathan. *Oracle SQL*Plus: The Definitive Guide*. O'Reilly, 2009. Oracle reference works are good at documenting every detail of a product but not as good at describing how to use the product to maximum advantage. This book will help you do that.

- McJones, Paul. "The 1995 SQL Reunion: People, Projects, and Politics." www.hpl.hp.com/techreports/Compaq-DEC/SRC-TN-1997-018.pdf.

CHAPTER 3

■ ■ ■

Oracle Architecture

Try to imagine, how Confucius, Buddha, Jesus, Mohammed or Homer would have reacted when they had been offered a [computer].

—Edsger Dijkstra, advocate of structured programming and winner of the 1972 Turing Award, in "Correctness Concerns and, Among Other Things, Why They Are Resented"

Just as an automobile engine has a lot of interconnected parts that must all work well together, and just as an automobile mechanic must understand the individual parts and how they relate to the whole, the Oracle Database engine has a lot of interconnected parts, and the database administrator must understand the individual parts and how they relate to the whole. This chapter summarizes the Oracle engine. It is impossible to document the workings of a complex piece of machinery in a short chapter—for a full treatment, refer to *Oracle Database 12c Concepts*, which, like all the reference manuals, is searchable and downloadable for free at the Oracle web site.

As an introduction, Figure 3-1 shows an interesting diagram of the inner workings of the Oracle Database engine. This diagram was produced by a software tool called Spotlight from Quest Software. The name of the database—pdb1—is seen in the upper-right corner of the diagram.

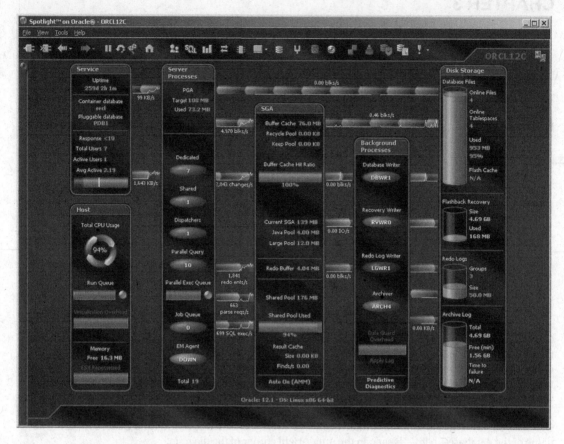

Figure 3-1. *The Spotlight tool's diagrammatic representation of the Oracle engine*

In Figure 3-1, the various components of the Oracle Database architecture are grouped as follows:

- The *Service* panel represents the users who are using the database.

- The *Host* panel represents the host computer of the database.

- The *Server Processes* panel represents the computer processes on the host computer performing all the work requested by the users.

- The *SGA* panel represents an area of computer memory used as a work area by the database. SGA stands for System Global Area.

- The *Background Processes* panel represents a core set of computer processes that are independent of the user sessions and that perform specialized tasks such as storing information about transactions in the redo log files.

- The *Disk Storage* panel represents the files in which data is stored and supporting files such as redo log files and archived redo log files.

The other terms used in the diagram are explained in the following sections.

Database vs. Instance

In Oracle terminology, the word *database* is used to collectively indicate the data files and supporting files on the storage disks attached to the host computer, and the word *instance* is used to describe the computer processes resident in computer memory and memory areas shared by these processes. The relationship between Oracle instances and databases is *one-to-one* (one instance per database), *many-to-one* (multiple instances per database), or *one-to-many* (Oracle Database 12c only). The many-to-one configuration is called Real Application Clusters (RAC)—the database lives on shared disks, and instances on multiple computers attach to the database. The one-to-many configuration is called the *Oracle Multitenant option* and—as the name implies—is an extra-cost optional feature of Oracle Database 12c.

Database

The most concrete aspect of a database is the files on the storage disks connected to the database host. This section briefly discusses each category of file. Placement, sizing, and other configuration details are discussed in Chapters 5 and 6.

Software

The location of the database software is called the *Oracle home*, and the path to that location is usually stored in the environment variable ORACLE_HOME. There are two species of database software: server software and client software. *Server software* is necessary to create and manage the database and is required only on the database host. *Client software* is necessary to utilize the database and is required on every user's computer—the most common example is the SQL*Plus command-line tool.

Configuration Files

The most important database configuration file is the one containing the settings used during database startup. It comes in two versions: a text version called a *pfile* and a binary version called an *spfile*. (You see an example in Chapter 6.) The pfile and spfile specify such details as the amount of computer memory that Oracle may use during operation. The pfile is traditionally referred to as the init.ora file.

Another important server-side configuration file is the listener.ora file. It controls the operation of the listener—an important process that comes into play when users start a database session. You see an example of this in Chapter 6. The tnsnames.ora file is a client-side configuration file that contains location information for databases. You see an example later in this chapter.

Data Files

The biggest component of a database is usually the files where data is stored. You could create a database with just one data file if you wanted to prove a point, but most databases have dozens of data files.

Data files are logically grouped into tablespaces and are usually given descriptive names such as DATA, INDEX, UNDO, and TEMP that indicate their intended purpose. Use a tablespace only for the purpose indicated by its name—for example, the SYSTEM tablespace should be used to store only the data dictionary (tables containing information about the rest of the database). Except for the SYSTEM and SYSAUX tablespaces, which are always created and whose names are mandated by Oracle, the number and names of the other tablespaces are left to you.

Each Oracle table and index is assigned to a single tablespace, and their growth is therefore limited by the availability of space in that assigned tablespace. They share the space with all the other tables or indexes also assigned to the tablespace. Data files can grow automatically as required; but, for reasons associated with manageability, you should limit how big they can grow. You can also create large data files of fixed size, and you can create additional data files during the life of the database.

The names chosen for data files typically include the name of the tablespace and the extension dbf or ora —for example, SYSTEM01.dbf might be the name given to the first data file in the SYSTEM tablespace. But this is only a convention, not a requirement, and you may invent your own convention or choose not to have one.

The space within data files is organized into data blocks (sometimes called *pages*) of equal size: 2, 4, 8, 16, 32, or 64 kilobytes (KB). 8KB is a commonly used block size. Each block contains data from just one table. The size of data records should be considered when deciding what size block to use. Oracle allows data records to span data blocks, but it is more efficient to retrieve one data block instead of multiple blocks from different locations on the storage disks. All the data files in one tablespace use blocks of the same size, and the block size should be a factor in the decision to assign a table or an index to a particular tablespace. When a table needs more space, it grabs a contiguous range of data blocks called an *extent*; it is conventional to use uniformly sized extents for all tables in the same tablespace.

Temporary Files

Each dedicated Oracle server process (a process that is dedicated to a single database connection) uses a private work area called a *Program Global Area* in computer memory to hold intermediate results: for example, data that must be sorted. The temporary files are used for intermediate storage when sufficient memory is unavailable.

Redo Log Files

Redo log files help Oracle ensure that the effects of a user's transaction are durable even if there is a computer failure. Before any data in the data files is changed, the log-writer (LGWR) process stores a copy of the old data (undo information) and the new data (redo information) in the redo log file. In the event of a computer failure, the redo log files enable Oracle to undo the effects of incomplete transactions (uncommitted transactions) and redo committed transactions.

The sizes of the redo log files are decided by the database administrator. It is conventional but not required for all redo log files to be the same size. An Oracle database needs at least two redo log files. Oracle uses the redo log files in round-robin fashion; when one redo log file is filled, Oracle begins filling the next one, and so on.

Because the redo log files defend the database against computer failure, they must be well protected. It is typical to mirror each redo log file; a mirrored set of redo log files is referred to as a *redo log group*. It is also typical to put each member of a redo file group on a different storage disk. All the members of a redo file group have the same size; the log writer process stores the same information in all members of a redo file group. Oracle can therefore continue to operate as long as at least one member of each redo file group is undamaged.

Archived Redo Log Files

When a redo file fills up, an Oracle component called the *archiver* makes one or more copies in locations specified by the database administrator. Multiple copies improve the chances that at least one will survive if the storage disks are damaged.

These copies make it possible to reconstruct data files if they are ever damaged. If a data file is damaged, the database administrator can first restore the most recent backup copy of the data file, and the information contained in the archived redo files can be systematically processed to reproduce the effects of all the transactions that modified the data file since the backup copy was created.

It is possible to make copies of redo files directly on computer tapes, but it is more common to make copies on dedicated disks and to periodically sweep them to the tapes.

Control File

Oracle uses the control file while starting the database. This file contains information about the rest of the database, such as the names and locations of the data files. It also contains information—such as the names and locations of the archived redo log files—needed for recovery of damaged data files. It is continuously updated during the operation of the database.

Because of the criticality of the control file, it is conventional to have multiple copies—that is, mirrors. Oracle keeps all copies in perfect synchronization.

Event Logs

Oracle records important events in various log files. Events such as startup and shutdown, important Data Definition Language (DDL) operations such as ALTER TABLESPACE ADD DATAFILE, and space shortages are some of the events recorded in the alert log. A record is written to the listener log every time a user establishes a connection to the database. A detailed trace file is produced every time certain severe errors occur; examples include the ORA-600 error, which usually indicates that an Oracle bug has been encountered. You see examples of event logs in Chapters 10 and 11.

Database Backups

You must protect the database from storage failures by creating backup copies of the data files. If not enough disk space is available, backup copies of the data files can be stored on magnetic tapes. If enough disk space is available, backup copies can be stored on the disks, although they should not be stored on the disks where data files are stored. The location of the backup copies is traditionally referred to as the *flashback recovery area*. The backups stored on disk are usually copied to tapes for added safety.

We return to the topic of database backups in Chapters 12 and 13.

Instance

The Oracle *instance* is the engine that processes requests for data from the database—it is composed of foreground processes, background processes, and a large shared memory area called the System Global Area (SGA).

System Global Area

The SGA is typically a very large memory area shared by all Oracle processes. It is divided into distinct areas such as the buffer cache, the shared pool, and the log buffer, whose sizes are specified in the database configuration file (pfile or spfile). The Oracle processes coordinate their access to these areas by using inter-process communication (IPC) mechanisms called *latches*.

Buffer Cache

Typically, the buffer cache is the largest portion of the SGA. For reasons of efficiency, copies of data blocks (block buffers) are cached in computer memory whenever possible. When a foreground process needs a data block, it first checks the buffer cache, hoping to find the block there. If a block is not found in the cache, query processing has to be delayed until the foreground process retrieves the block from the storage disks.

When the buffer cache fills up, the least recently used blocks are removed to make space for new requests. You can try various strategies to improve the efficiency of the cache. A special keep pool can be created in the buffer cache to store data blocks from frequently used data tables—for example, lookup tables. A recycle pool can be created to hold data blocks that are not likely to be reused. Other techniques include partitioning and clusters—more information is provided in Chapter 7.

Shared Pool

The shared pool is another large component of the SGA and has many uses. The best-known use is caching query-execution plans for potential reuse by the user who first submitted the query or by any another user who submits the identical query—this is done in an area called the *shared SQL area*. Another well-known use is caching information from the data dictionary; this is done in an area within the shared pool called the *dictionary cache*.

Log Buffer

The log buffer is a queue of undo entries and redo entries. The log writer copies undo and redo entries to the redo log file. Typically, the size of this area is only a few megabytes.

Server Processes

A dedicated server process is typically started whenever a user connects to the database—it performs all the work requested by the user. An alternative model called *multithreaded server (MTS)*, in which all user connections are serviced by a small set of dispatchers and shared servers, is also available but is not very suitable for general-purpose use and is not widely used.

These processes perform activities such as checking whether the user has permission to access the data, generating a query-execution plan for the SQL query submitted by the user, and retrieving data blocks into the buffer cache and modifying them. Before changing the contents of block buffers, it gains exclusive control to them by using a latch. Before modifying a data block, the foreground process first makes a copy of the block in an undo segment in the UNDO tablespace; it also creates the undo and redo entries that the log writer will store in the redo log files.

Dedicated server processes are terminated when the corresponding database sessions are terminated.

Background Processes

Unlike dedicated foreground processes, background processes live from database startup until database shutdown. The following are some of the better-known categories of background processes:

- The *database writer (DBWn)* processes are responsible for transferring all modified data blocks in the data caches to the data files. Multiple database writer processes can be created to share the load.

- The *log writer (LGWR)* process transfers all undo and redo entries in the log buffer to the redo log files.

- The *archiver (ARCHn)* processes are responsible for making copies of the redo log files when they fill up. These archived redo log files will be required if a data file is damaged and needs repair. Multiple archiver processes can be created to share the load.

- When a data block in the data cache is modified, it is not immediately transferred to the data files. In the interest of efficiency, it is better to copy changes in batches—this is the function of the database writer processes. However, at frequent intervals, the contents of the data caches are synchronized with the data files. Any modified data blocks remaining in memory are flushed to disk, and the file headers are updated with a special indicator called the *system change number (SCN)*. This activity is called a *checkpoint*; coordination of this activity is performed by a dedicated process called the *checkpoint process (CKPT)*.

- The *process monitor (PMON)* watches the progress of database connections. If a connection terminates abnormally, the process monitor initiates rollback activity on behalf of any transaction in progress.

- The *system monitor (SMON)* is responsible for any cleanup activities necessary if the database is restarted after an abnormal shutdown resulting from system failure. It uses the contents of the redo logs to perform cleanup activity. It also performs certain space-management activities during normal database operation.

One-to-Many Configuration

The one-to-many configuration has always been the standard configuration used by other database products including IBM DB2, Microsoft SQL, MySQL, and PostgreSQL; but Oracle Database 12*c* is the first version of Oracle Database to support this configuration. The official name for this feature is the Oracle Multitenant option, and—as the name implies—it is an extra-cost optional feature of Oracle Database 12*c*; that is, both the traditional one-to-one-configuration and the new one-to-many configurations are supported in Oracle Database 12*c*. In the one-to-many configuration, multiple databases share an Oracle home directory, SGA, background processes such as PMON and SMON, an UNDO tablespace, online redo logs, and (optionally) a TEMP tablespace. Each such database is referred to as a *pluggable database (PDB)* to indicate that it "plugs" into a *container database (CDB)* and can be plugged or unplugged when necessary. For example, a PDB can be unplugged from one CDB and plugged into another CDB with more hardware resources or a CDB to which software patches and upgrades have been applied. In other words, PDBs are easily transportable.

The one-to-many architecture is compatible with the one-to-one architecture. Oracle Distinguished Product Manager Bryn Llewellyn calls this the *PDB/non-CDB compatibility guarantee*. Any database application designed on the one-to-one architecture will continue to work without change in the one-to-many architecture. Llewellyn asserts that all questions about backward compatibility can immediately be answered in the affirmative by virtue of this guarantee. For example:

- Can two PDBs in same CDB each have a user called scott? Yes.

- Can you create a database link between two PDBs to allow applications connected to one PDB to access data in another PDB? Yes.

- Can you set up data replication between two PDBs or between a PDB and a non-CDB? Yes.

- Can a PDB be rolled back to a prior point in time without affecting other PDBs that share the same CDB? Yes.

The answer to the last question is particularly important because one of the defining characteristics of a database is that it is a logical unit of recovery.

Oracle Multitenant can only be licensed in conjunction with Enterprise Edition (Chapter 4 discusses the various editions of Oracle Database). However, a limited license is available for free. You can freely use Oracle Multitenant with any edition of Oracle Database and without paying any extra charges as long as you restrict yourself to a single PDB. You can reduce the downtime associated with database upgrades by creating an upgraded CDB and then painlessly unplugging a PDB from its current CDB and plugging it into the upgraded CDB. However, because of the PDB/non-CDB compatibility guarantee, this book does not need to spend much time on Oracle Multitenant, even though it is the signature feature of Oracle Database 12c.

Many-to-One Architecture

When you need to scale a database to support more users and transactions, there are two solutions: scale up or scale out. *Scale up* means additional hardware resources are added to the computer server housing the database. *Scale out* means the database is spread over multiple computer servers. Oracle Real Application Clusters (RAC) is Oracle's scale-out architecture. In this architecture, multiple Oracle instances, each housed in a separate computer server, all connect to a single set of database files on a network-attached storage (NAS) or storage area network (SAN) storage server. This approach is called the *shared disk approach* to contrast it with the *shared nothing* or *federated* approach used by other database products such as IBM DB2. In the shared nothing approach, each instance manages a part of the database such that, if one instance stops, that part of the database becomes inaccessible until the failed instance is restarted. In the shared disk approach, the failure of one instance impacts the availability of the database. Another distinguishing feature of the Oracle scheme is *cache fusion,* in which each instance can request data held in the data caches of other instances.

The many-to-one architecture is much harder to configure and administer than the one-to-many architecture. In a nod to the increased complexity of RAC, Oracle Corporation sells an engineered system— that is, a combined hardware and software package—called the Oracle Database Appliance (ODA) . The ODA is a two-node RAC cluster with sufficient power for all but the largest organizations. Here are some of the advantages of the ODA:

- *Push-button configuration:* An ODA can be unboxed, installed, hooked up, and configured in just half a day, compared to the several weeks it typically takes to provision a RAC environment.

- *Push-button patching:* Oracle Corporation provides push-button patches for the entire technology stack—that is, operating system as well as database.

- *Pay-as-you-go licensing:* Oracle licensing is based on CPU cores (discussed in Chapter 4). However, not all the cores in the ODA need to be licensed at the same time. You can license only the CPU cores you need at the outset and license additional cores as time passes and your computing needs increase.

Oracle RAC is outside the scope of this introductory text, so it is not mentioned again.

Life Cycle of a Database Session

Now let's consider the life cycle of a database session, from initiation to termination. For simplicity, I am restricting the example to a traditional client-server connection and assuming the use of dedicated servers instead of shared servers. Here are the phases that each database session goes through:

1. The program residing on the user's computer tries to connect to a database. One of the methods it can use to locate the database is to refer to the tnsnames.ora file in the ORACLE_HOME/network/admin directory on the user's computer. There, it finds the name of the database host computer and the number of the network port where connections are being accepted. Here is an example of an entry for a database service called pdb1 on a host with IP address 192.168.56.101:

    ```
    pdb1 =
      (description =
        (address = (protocol = tcp)(host = 192.168.56.101)(PORT = 1521))
        (connect_data =
          (server = dedicated)
          (service:name = pdb1)
        )
      )
    ```

2. The user's program sends a message to the port number specified in the tnsnames.ora file. The Oracle listener process receives the message and creates a dedicated server process to process the user's requests.

3. The user's program provides the user's credentials (name and password) to the dedicated server process. The dedicated server checks the data dictionary and verifies that the user's credentials are valid and that the user has permission to access the database.

4. The user's program sends an SQL statement to the dedicated server for processing.

5. The dedicated server prepares the SQL statement for execution. First it verifies that the SQL statement is syntactically correct. Next it verifies that the tables mentioned in the SQL statement exist and that the user has permission to access those tables. Then it creates a query-execution plan for the SQL statement. The query-execution plan is saved in the plan cache in the shared SQL area so it can be reused later by the same user or another user.

6. The dedicated server checks whether the required blocks of data are in the buffer cache. If the needed blocks are not in the buffer cache, the dedicated server retrieves them from the data files.

7. If the SQL statement involves no modifications to the data, the required data rows are transmitted to the user. If the SQL statement involves modification to the data, the dedicated server first copies the relevant data blocks to a rollback segment. It also creates undo and redo entries in the log buffer. The log writer copies undo and redo entries to the redo log files.

8. If the SQL statement involved modification to the data, the user's program sends a COMMIT command to the dedicated server process. The dedicated server process puts the COMMIT instruction in the log buffer and waits for confirmation from the log writer that it has recorded the transaction's redo entries and the COMMIT instruction in the redo log files—this guarantees the durability of the modifications.

9. The database writer processes copy-modified data blocks from the data cache to the data files. The checkpoint process wakes up periodically and initiates a systematic synchronization procedure on all data files that includes updating the system-change number in the heading of each data file.

10. When the current redo log file fills up, the log writer closes the file and opens the next one. An archiver process subsequently makes a copy of the closed file in case a data file ever gets damaged and needs to be repaired.

11. The user's program disconnects from the database. This terminates the dedicated server process.

Summary

The information in this chapter summarizes the contents of *Oracle Database 12c Concepts*. Here is a summary of the concepts the chapter touched on:

- In Oracle terminology, the word *database* is used to collectively indicate the data files and supporting files on the storage disks attached to the host computer. The word *instance* is used to indicate the computer processes resident in computer memory and memory areas shared by these processes.

- The relationship between Oracle instances and databases is one-to-one, one-to-many (the Multitenant option of Oracle Database 12c), or many-to-one (Real Application Clusters).

- The location of the database software is called the Oracle home and is usually stored in the environment variable ORACLE_HOME.

- Well-known configuration files include init.ora, listener.ora, and tnsnames.ora.

- Data files are logically grouped into tablespaces. Each Oracle table or index is assigned to one tablespace and shares the space with the other tables assigned to the same tablespace. Data files can grow automatically if the database administrator wishes. The space within data files is organized into equally sized blocks; all data files belonging to a tablespace use the same block size. When a data table needs more space, it grabs a contiguous range of data blocks called an extent; it is conventional to use the same extent size for all tables in a tablespace.

- Temporary files are used if a large work area does not fit in computer memory.

- Redo log files guarantee atomicity and durability of a transaction. Redo logs are of fixed size and are mirrored for safety. Oracle fills the redo logs in round-robin fashion. The redo logs should be archived when they fill up—this makes it possible to repair data files if they get damaged.

- The control file is used by Oracle while starting the database; it contains the names and locations of the data files, among other things.

- Oracle records important events and errors in the alert log. A detailed trace file is created when a severe error occurs.

- The System Global Area (SGA) is composed of the buffer cache, the shared pool, and the log buffer. The best-known use of the shared pool is to cache query-execution plans. It is also used to store information from the data dictionary.

- A dedicated server is started whenever a user connects to the database; it is terminated when the user disconnects from the database. In the multithreaded server (MTS) mode of operation, all user connections are serviced by a few dispatchers and shared servers. Multithreaded server is a form of connection pooling for conserving memory and CPU resources but is rarely used today, having been overtaken by middle-tier connection pooling.

- Background processes are not tied to user connections and live from database startup until database shutdown. The best-known background processes are the database writer (DBWn), the log writer (LGWR), the archiver processes (ARCn), the checkpoint process (CKPT), the process monitor (PMON), and the system monitor (SMON).

- The Oracle Multitenant option is an extra-cost, optional feature of Oracle Database 12*c* only available in conjunction with the higher-cost Enterprise Edition. In this configuration, multiple databases share an Oracle home directory, SGA, background processes such as PMON and SMON, an UNDO tablespace, online redo logs, and optionally a TEMP tablespace. You can freely use Oracle Multitenant with any edition of Oracle Database and without paying any extra charges if you restrict yourself to a single pluggable database (PDB) in the container database (CDB). The PDB/non-CDB compatibility guarantee means any database application designed on the one-to-one architecture will continue to work without change in the one-to-many architecture.

- Oracle Real Application Clusters (RAC) is Oracle's scale-out architecture. In this architecture, multiple Oracle instances, each housed in a separate computer server, all connect to a single set of database files on a network-attached storage (NAS) or storage area network (SAN) storage server. In a nod to the increased complexity of RAC, Oracle Corporation sells an engineered system—that is, a combined hardware and software package—called the Oracle Database Appliance (ODA). The ODA is a two-node RAC cluster with sufficient power for all but the largest organizations. Its advantages are push-button installations, push-button upgrades, and pay-as-you-go licensing.

Exercises

- In your virtual machine, connect to the service orcl using the SYSTEM account. The password is oracle. Issue the SQL command select * from cdb_pdbs. Interpret the result.

- Search Figure 3-1 for terms that have not been explained in this chapter. Find their definitions in the Oracle Database 12*c* Master Glossary available at http://docs.oracle.com.

Further Reading

- Llewellyn, Bryn. "Oracle Multitenant." Oracle white paper, June 2013. A wonderfully eloquent white paper by am Oracle Distinguished Product Manager.

- Oracle Database 12*c* Concepts Chapter 11 (Physical Storage Structures), Chapter 14 (Memory Architecture), Chapter 15 (Process Architecture), and Chapter 17 (Introduction to the Multitenant Architecture). http://docs.oracle.com.

■ ■ ■

Database Implementation

CHAPTER 4

■ ■ ■

Planning

1. Start with the end in mind.

—*The 7 Habits of Highly Effective People*, by Stephen Covey

Your goal as Oracle administrator is not simply to create a database but to be on time, be on budget, and meet the availability and performance targets of the business. As with any goal, careful planning is the key to success. You have little control over a number of factors that affect the success of your database: for example, application design and testing. This chapter discusses three important issues that are definitely within your circle of influence and that you cannot afford to ignore: licensing, architecture, and sizing.

Licensing

Oracle provides a choice of licenses, ranging from free licenses to licenses for basic functionality or more advanced functionality, and a wide range of individually priced extra-cost options. You do not need licensing keys to unlock Oracle software; anyone may freely download software from the Oracle web site and begin using it. This is an unusual practice that separates Oracle from other software vendors and has probably contributed to Oracle's success in the marketplace. It is, therefore, very easy to make the mistake of using software for which you do not have the required licenses. Make sure the licensing question is answered as early in the software development project as possible.

Practical Example

Suppose you are considering using a high-end configuration of four Sun UltraSPARC T2 servers—each with four four-core CPUs—for an e-commerce web site. For extra horsepower and reliability, the production database will be handled by two servers clustered together using Oracle Real Application Clusters (RAC) technology. For protection against a catastrophe such as fire or flood, the third server will be located in a separate data center and will handle a standby database, which will be kept synchronized with the production database using Oracle's Data Guard technology; you can also use the standby database for reporting purposes and backups if the Active Data Guard option is purchased. The fourth server is needed to house multiple development and testing databases.

Table 4-1 shows the license and support fees I calculated for a high-end configuration using the pricing document on the Oracle web site when I wrote this chapter; the prices are subject to change, so you should always download the latest version of the pricing document. I've included typical options that you might consider licensing, such as table partitioning, Diagnostics Pack, and Tuning Pack. Note that because each CPU has multiple cores, you have to multiply the number of cores by a factor of 0.75 to compute the number of equivalent CPUs that must be licensed. You can find more information on the treatment of multicore CPUs in the pricing document listed at the end of this chapter; AMD and Intel CPUs are treated differently than Sun CPUs.

Table 4-1. *Oracle Licensing Cost for a High-End Configuration*

Description	License Cost per Equivalent CPU	Number of Licensed Servers	Total Number of CPUs	Total Number of Cores	Total Number of Equivalent CPUs	Cost
Enterprise Edition	$47,500	4	16	64	48	$2,280,000
Real Application Clusters	$23,000	2	8	32	24	$552,000
Partitioning Option	$11,500	4	16	64	48	$552,000
Active Data Guard	$11,500	3	12	48	36	$552,000
Diagnostic Pack	$7,500	2	8	32	24	$180,000
Tuning Pack	$5,000	2	8	32	24	$120,000
Total Purchase Price						$4,236,000
Annual Support Fees						$931,920

Table 4-2 shows the prices I calculated for a low-end configuration consisting of four Windows servers, each with two Intel Xeon four-core CPUs.

Table 4-2. *Oracle Licensing Cost for a Low-End Configuration*

Description	License Cost per Equivalent CPU	Number of Licensed Servers	Total Number of CPUs	Total Number of Cores	Total Number of Equivalent CPUs	Cost
Standard Edition (SE)	$17,500	4	8	32	16	$280,000
Real Application Clusters	Included with SE					
Partitioning Option	Unavailable with SE					
Active Data Guard	Unavailable with SE					
Diagnostic Pack	Unavailable with SE					
Tuning Pack	Unavailable with SE					
Total Purchase Price						$280,000
Annual Support Fees						$61,600

The calculations may lead you to select a different hardware configuration or to license only the options that you really need. However, licensing costs, support fees, and feature sets are not the only considerations when making technology choices; development costs, personnel costs, hardware compatibility, and performance benchmarks are some of the other considerations.

Free to Download, Free to Learn, Unlimited Evaluation

You can freely download Oracle database software from the Oracle web site and use it for self-education, evaluate its suitability for a project, or develop a prototype of an application. The following language is found at www.oracle.com/technology/software/index.html:

> *All software downloads are free, and each comes with a Development License that allows you to use full versions of the products at no charge while developing and prototyping your applications (or for strictly self-educational purposes).*

No license keys are required to unlock Oracle database software, there is no limit to the length of the evaluation period, there are no restrictions on the use of the product, and you don't need to provide information about yourself or your company if you don't want to do so. Oracle does not appear to be worried about the potential for illegal use of its software and stands alone in the software industry in allowing its product to be downloaded and used in this way; some of its commercial success can undoubtedly be traced to its liberal download and usage policies.

Database Editions

Just as Microsoft does with Windows Vista, Oracle packages its software into different versions. Those who need only basic database functionality can buy a less expensive edition than a large international corporation that needs high-end features. Here are some of the editions that you can choose from:

- *Oracle Express Edition*: Provides a significant subset of Oracle Database functionality—comparable to that of Standard Edition, described next—as a free starter edition. There are significant restrictions on its use (for example, the database size is restricted to 4GB) but Express Edition can be used without charge even in commercial settings (for example, a starter database bundled with a software product) and formal classroom settings. A significant attraction is its ease of deployment; it is provided as a self-extracting executable for Windows or an RPM package for Linux.

- *Standard Edition*: Includes a significant subset of Oracle Database functionality. There are no restrictions on the size of the database, but there is a restriction on the size of the server; Standard Edition can only be installed on servers with a maximum capacity of four CPUs. It is not suitable for the largest databases, because performance and management options such as partitioning are not included; they can only be licensed along with Enterprise Edition, described next. Management packs such as Configuration Management and Change Management are also not available with Standard Edition. However, in an effort to promote the use of RAC technology (a high-availability feature), Oracle permits its use with Standard Edition if there are no more than four CPUs in the cluster.

- *Enterprise Edition*: Includes performance and management features required by the largest and most demanding databases, such as parallel query, query-results caching, parallel backup and recovery, and so on. Enterprise Edition costs much more than Standard Edition: $47,500 per single-core CPU, at time of writing. However, a number of features are not included even with Enterprise Edition and cost even more, the most significant being RAC, partitioning (a management and performance feature needed when dealing with the largest data tables), and Advanced Security (for encryption of data as well as network traffic). Other important features that also require additional license fees are the management packs, such as Configuration Management Pack, Change Management Pack, Provisioning Pack (for release management), Diagnostic Pack, and Tuning Pack.

Oracle licenses can be purchased on the Web at http://store.oracle.com. However, it is conventional to contact an Oracle sales representative so that discounts can be negotiated on large purchases. If your organization already uses Oracle, you have an assigned sales representative. If your organization is using Oracle for the first time, you can get in touch with a sales representative by calling the toll-free number listed on the Oracle web site.

■ **Note**   Further licensing topics that this book must omit for lack of space include the named user metric, Personal Edition, Standard Edition One, and term licenses. I also do not have space to list the features that are bundled in the various editions and the restrictions on each edition. The documents containing all this information are listed at the end of this chapter.

As already indicated, Oracle software can be freely downloaded from the Oracle web site. Media packs (CD sets) can also be ordered from the online store for a nominal price. Reference manuals can be downloaded in PDF format from the Oracle web site at no charge, regardless of whether you buy licenses for Oracle software. Of particular interest to you at this stage are the installation guides for various operating system platforms. Printed copies of the reference manuals can be purchased if necessary, but they are quite expensive.

Architectural Choices

Oracle provides a variety of architectural choices to suit every need. The choice of architecture is determined by factors such as performance, availability, and scalability. For example, if you require very high availability, you could consider Oracle's Data Guard architecture. If you need to start small and scale to very high volumes, you could consider Oracle's RAC architecture. The following sections explore the most common architectural choices for Oracle databases.

Dedicated Server

This is the simplest Oracle configuration as well as the most common. It requires that each connection to the database be handled by a dedicated Oracle process; if 100 users were connected to the database, then 100 Oracle processes are required to handle them. You use dedicated server architecture when creating a database on your laptop in Chapter 6.

Shared Server

The dedicated server architecture does not work well for large numbers of connections because the Oracle Database processes contend for the limited amount of RAM. Large numbers of database connections are typically observed in Online Transaction Processing (OLTP) situations, but most of the connections are typically idle most of the time.

For example, suppose that all the employees of a company use the same computer program on their individual workstations to do their daily work. They remain connected to the database throughout the day, but each of them usually makes a very reasonable number of requests for information. The total time required to process each user's requests is generally a very small fraction of the time the user is connected.

In such a situation, shared Oracle Database processes can be used to conserve RAM. The program running on the user's workstation communicates with an Oracle Database dispatcher process instead of a dedicated Oracle Database process. The dispatcher process places the request on a request queue. Any available shared process handles the request and places the results on a response queue. The dispatcher then communicates the results to the user. Any information that has to be preserved until the next request—that is, any state information—is preserved in the SGA.

Real Application Clusters

A computer can efficiently handle only a certain number of requests at a time; this number is greatly dependent on the number of CPUs and the amount of RAM. As the number of requests increases beyond a certain threshold, processes begin competing for scarce resources, and all of them suffer. The easiest solution is to increase the number of CPUs and the amount of RAM, but large and powerful computers are also very expensive.

RAC is a technology that combines the resources of more than one computer. Two or more Oracle Database instances share access to the same set of disks and coordinate with each other over a fast network. Additional instances can be added to the cluster as the workload increases. This allows you to start with cheap commodity hardware and scale out as the workload increases instead of scaling up to a more powerful (and more expensive) computer.

RAC also has implications for database availability. For example, any single instance can be shut down for hardware maintenance or OS patching without affecting the availability of the database. In some cases, it is even possible to apply Oracle patches in rolling upgrade fashion.

Standby Database

A standby database can improve application availability. In this scenario, redo information from the main database is shipped and applied to another database, called the *standby* (which started life as a clone of the main database). In the event of a primary-database outage, applications can use the standby database. Applications can also be switched to the standby database when hardware maintenance or operating system maintenance needs to be performed on the primary database; even the outages associated with Oracle patch sets and upgrades can be avoided. Note that maintenance of the standby database can be automated and simplified using an Oracle product called Data Guard, which is part of Enterprise Edition.

To save money, it is typical for the standby database to have less hardware resources (CPU and memory) than the primary database; it is also typical to use a non-RAC standby database for an RAC primary database. Another interesting option is to use an active-active configuration of two or more computers. A typical active-active configuration has two databases, each on a separate server; the standby database of the first database is placed on the second server, and the standby database of the second database is placed on the first server. Each server thus hosts a primary database as well as a standby database. If one server suffers an outage, the standby database on the other node can be activated; this is a very cost-effective way of using hardware resources.

Maximum Availability Architecture (MAA)

Maximum Availability Architecture (MAA) can be used when both availability and performance are important and budgets are generous. The typical standby configuration uses less hardware resources for the standby database because the probability of a switchover is low; that is, there will be some amount of degradation in performance if the applications are pointed to the standby database. The MAA configuration combines RAC technology with standby technology and uses identically configured primary and secondary sites. The primary and standby databases both have the same number of RAC nodes.

MAA can be extended to the application tier, too; the details are in the white paper listed at the end of this chapter. Of course, identically configured primary and secondary sites (both database and application tiers) can be extremely expensive.

Sizing

The hardware resources your database needs depend on a number of factors such as the characteristics of the application (for example, OLTP vs. OLAP), the expected amount of activity, and the performance targets (such as the response time of business-critical transactions). However, it is rare to get good information on the expected amount of activity; ask how many simultaneously active sessions can be expected on average, and you may get a blank stare in return. Even if you have good information, sizing can still be tricky. Here are some strategies you can use:

- Ask vendors for help. Both hardware and software vendors have a great deal of experience in hardware sizing. You might even consider including the question of hardware sizing in the request for proposal (RFP) process.

- Use the results obtained from volume testing during the development phase.

- Use information about similar systems in the enterprise; for example, an enterprise may own several brands, each of which has a similar e-commerce database.

- Early in the exercise, set the expectation that the hardware sizing is only a best guess and additional hardware may have to be procured once the initial results are in.

- Be very generous in your estimates, if you are not on a tight budget. You can also use this strategy if the application is critical to the enterprise; in such cases it is preferable to be oversized than undersized.

- Ensure that there is room for expandability; for example, ensure that the system can accommodate more CPUs and memory if the estimates are found to be inadequate.

Disk Sizing

It is easy to underestimate the amount of space you need for the database. Another common mistake is not to leave sufficient room for growth. The following sections describe the different types of files that you have to worry about in forecasting disk-space needs for a database.

Data Files

Data files store your tables and indexes, and therefore you need to have some idea of how much data will be stored in tables in the foreseeable future. To estimate the amount of space required for a table, you have to estimate the average size of each row of data and the number of rows in the table. A reasonable rule of thumb is to allow as much room for indexes as you allow for tables. There is a fair amount of overhead space and white space in tables and indexes, and it would not be unreasonable to estimate that only 50% of the allocated space is usable. To summarize: estimate the amount of space required for tables, then double the number to allow for indexes, and then double the number again to allow for overhead space and white space.

You also need to allow room for the SYSTEM and SYSAUX tablespaces used by Oracle. Oracle uses the SYSTEM tablespace to store the data dictionary and the SYSAUX tablespace for other kinds of management information: for example, Active Workload Repository (AWR).

If you do not have a license for the Diagnostics Pack (which is required in order to use AWR), you can and should use a free Oracle-provided alternative called Statspack to collect performance data. In this case, you should reserve a sufficient amount of space for Statspack data.

You must also allow a sufficient amount of undo and temporary space. *Undo* refers to a copy of a data block that is made before the block is changed; it is used to restore the block in case the transaction does not commit its work. Temporary space is used for sorting operations during SQL queries. Don't forget to leave a margin of error, especially if your estimates are not very reliable.

Control Files and Online Redo Logs

The space required for control files and online redo log files is usually modest; 2GB should suffice for most databases. In a highly demanding OLTP environment, you should pay careful attention to the placement of these files because they can quickly become a performance bottleneck.

Archived Redo Logs

Redo logs contain the information necessary to redo the database; they hold a record of all changes to the database. When redo logs fill up, they have to be copied to the archive destination before they can be reused. The amount of space required for the storage of archived redo logs depends on the amount of activity in the database; it also depends on retention preferences. An amount of space equal to the size of the database is not unreasonable for a busy OLTP database.

Backups and Exports

Allocating an area twice the size of the database for backups is not an unreasonable thing to do, unless you plan to put backups directly onto tape.

Software Executables and Related Files

You must allocate some space for the Oracle software and for various categories of error logs such as the alert log, listener log, and trace files. A reasonable rule of thumb for most databases is 4GB of space.

Other Disk Considerations

There's more to worry about when it comes to files than just the amount of space they take. Usable space, file placement, and disk speed are some of the issues to consider.

Usable Space

When specifying the amount of space required for data, be clear that you are talking about usable space. For data protection, most disks use some form of redundant array of inexpensive disks (RAID) layout, which reduces the amount of usable space. RAID 10 (mirroring plus striping) reduces the amount of usable space by 50%. RAID 5 has the most usable space but reduces write performance; the details are outside the scope of this book. RAID 10 is the best choice for databases.

File Placement

Some attention must be paid to the placement of different categories of files; for example, data files should not be placed on the same file system where software, archived redo log files, or backups are stored. Optimal Flexible Architecture (OFA) is a set of recommendations provided by Oracle for the placement of different categories of files. OFA is automatically used by Database Configuration Assistant (DBCA) when creating databases.

Disk Speed

Pay attention to your disk ratings, because disk I/O can be a big performance bottleneck. If it takes 10 milliseconds to retrieve 1 data block (typically 8KB in size), then an SQL query may not be able to read more than 100 data rows per second, because the required rows will probably be spread out over many data blocks.

Memory Sizing

Memory sizing is heavily dependent on the characteristics of your application. The amount of space you need to meet performance targets is very difficult to estimate unless you have good information, such as the results of volume testing. The cost of memory is a consideration, but memory becomes cheaper every year, and it is no longer unusual to find databases using many gigabytes of memory. Here are the main considerations when planning memory requirements:

- *Buffer cache*: You need to allow enough space for Oracle to cache data blocks in memory, because disk I/O can slow your application tremendously. Note that you must a use a 64-bit operating system and the 64-bit version of Oracle to create very large buffer caches, because the 32-bit versions cannot handle large amounts of memory.

- *Shared pool*: The shared pool contains the library cache and the dictionary cache. Query-execution plans are stored in the library cache, and information about database objects is stored in the dictionary cache. It is rare to find a database that needs more than 1GB of memory for the shared pool.

- *Stack space*: You need to provide stack space for each Oracle connection. A commonly used rule of thumb is 512KB for each connection: for example, 50MB for 100 connections.

CPU Sizing

The number of CPUs you need depends not only on the speed of the CPUs—the faster the CPUs, the fewer you need—but also on the application load. A good rule of thumb is as many CPUs as the average number of simultaneously active sessions during the critical period of the day; the database for a big e-commerce application may require 16 CPUs to meet performance targets.

Note that if you use more than four CPUs, you will need to purchase Oracle Enterprise Edition, which is far costlier than Oracle Standard Edition.

Network Sizing

Finally, you must give some consideration to network requirements. A database that services hundreds of connections may require multiple network cards to meet performance targets. Fast connections are required to the storage area network (SAN) and between the nodes in an RAC cluster.

Modern Options

Recent years have seen several innovations that reduce the complexity and cost of provisioning Oracle Database: engineered systems and various flavors of cloud computing.

Engineered Systems

Instead of designing and implementing your own hardware and software configuration, you can simply buy a complete hardware and software package—a.k.a. an *engineered system*—directly from Oracle Corporation. Two examples are Oracle Database Appliance (ODA) and Exadata.

Oracle Database Appliance

Deploying RAC is a complex endeavor. ODA is a two-node plug-and-play RAC cluster running Enterprise Edition; it reduces typical deployment times from weeks to less than a day. ODA eliminates or automates the following classes of complex and error-prone work involved in a typical RAC deployment:

- Hardware sizing and design
- Special networking requirements for RAC
- SAN or NAS storage sizing and provisioning (ODA uses locally attached storage)
- Operating system installation and configuration (the operating system comes preinstalled)
- Security requirements (ODA uses best practices for operating system and database security)
- Oracle Database installation (the installation is automated)
- System testing and validation
- Project management for these activities

ODA offers more advantages than simplified provisioning. Oracle licenses can be purchased using the "pay-as-you-grow" model; that is, you can license only the number of CPU cores you need and disable the rest. Also, software patching is automated for all tiers (BIOS, firmware, operating system, and database).

If you are planning to use RAC and Enterprise Edition, you should check whether ODA has enough capacity for you .in terms of CPU cores, storage, and IOPS. If so, there is simply no reason for you not to use ODA. Each new generation of ODA has more capacity than the previous generation; at the time of writing, each of the two nodes in ODA has two 12-core Intel Xeon processors and 256GB of memory, and the configuration includes 9TB of usable storage (doubly mirrored) and four 200GB solid-state disks for the online redo logs.

Exadata

Exadata is the big brother of ODA and should be considered if your organization has outgrown the capacity of ODA. It comes in four progressively more powerful configurations: *eighth-rack* (two RAC nodes), *quarter-rack* (two RAC nodes), *half-rack* (four RAC nodes), and *full-rack* (eight RAC nodes). Like ODA, each new generation of Exadata has more capacity at the previous generation. At the time of writing, *each* Exadata node has two 12-core Intel Xeon processors (in an eighth-rack configuration, only half the number of cores are enabled on each server) and up to 512GB of memory. A full-rack configuration also uses 14 storage servers *each* with 12 CPU cores, 12 × 1.2 TB 10,000 RPM disks (or 12 × 4 TB 7,200 RPM disks), and 3.2TB of flash cache.

Expansion capabilities are available if you have even higher storage needs. This makes Exadata suitable for today's most demanding workloads and database consolidation on a massive scale.

Cloud Computing

Cloud computing is "the delivery of computing as a service instead of a product" (Wikipedia). Gone are the days when the only option was to purchase dedicated hardware and software when your computing needs changed or increased. In a large sense, cloud computing represents a return to the earliest days of the computing era when mainframe computers and time sharing were the norm. Cloud computing not only is more economical than owning hardware and software outright but also offers the key advantage of *elasticity*; that it, you can acquire more computing resources as your needs grow.

Platform as a Service (PaaS)

In the PaaS model, you have the ability to create tables, indexes, views, and other kinds of database objects in a dedicated database schema. This schema is a tenant in a multi-tenanted Oracle database containing many tenants. Of course, each tenant is completely isolated from the others. Key aspects of database administration such as backups and monitoring are automatically handled for you. The schema is accessed using web interfaces. Oracle Corporation offers PaaS with a choice of 5GB, 20GB, or 50GB of database storage.

Infrastructure as a Service (IaaS)

In the IaaS model, customers receive access not just to a database schema but to an entire server. This server is accessible over the Internet and is typically a virtual machine carved out of a very powerful server. In mere minutes, you can have complete access to a fully configured and operational Linux or Windows server containing a fully configured and operational Oracle Database instance. As your needs grow, you can add CPU cores, memory, or disk storage. You can either bring your own Oracle Database licenses (BYOL) or pay a per-minute charge for each minute the servers are running. At the time of writing, Microsoft Azure was charging $1.60 per hour for access to a four-core server with 7GB of RAM. Storage and network bandwidth are charged for separately. Such a pay-per-use model with no long-term contractual commitments is an irresistible attraction to businesses that wish to avoid heavy capital expenditures (CAPEX). In some service plans, key aspects of database administration such as backups and monitoring are automatically handled for you (IT as a service).

At the time of writing, the two major providers of Oracle Database servers are Amazon EC2 and Microsoft Azure, with Oracle making its first steps into the field. If your company is an Oracle shop, you will definitely want to check Oracle's offering.

Summary

Here is a short summary of the concepts touched on in this chapter:

- Oracle offers a variety of licensing options. Standard Edition is attractively priced but can only be used on servers with a maximum capacity of four CPUs. Enterprise Edition is expensive but offers high-end features such as parallelism. Certain other features that are only available with Enterprise Edition require additional fees; the list includes features such as partitioning, and management packs such as Diagnostics Pack and Tuning Pack.

- Oracle software can be used free of charge for prototyping and self-education.

- The dedicated server configuration is the most common configuration; each user session is handled by a dedicated process.

- The shared server configuration conserves resources; a small set of shared processes and dispatchers handles all sessions.

- Real Application Clusters (RAC) involve multiple Oracle instances connecting to the same database. This allows you to use cheap commodity hardware and scale out as the workload increases instead of scaling up to a more powerful (and more expensive) computer. RAC databases can improve application availability; for example, hardware maintenance can be performed on one node of the RAC database without affecting the availability of the application.

- A standby database can improve application availability. In this scenario, redo information from the main database is shipped and applied to another database.

- Maximum Available Architecture (MAA) requires identically configured primary and standby sites; for example, if the primary database uses RAC, then the standby database also uses RAC. The redundancy is extended to the application tier. MAA maximizes availability but can be very expensive.

- Sizing is a difficult task involving a lot of best guesses. Strategies to use include asking vendors for help, using results obtained from volume testing, studying similar systems in the enterprise, setting expectations correctly, estimating generously, oversizing when possible, and ensuring that there is room for expansion.

- Disk sizing must take the following categories of files into account: data files, control files, online redo logs, archived redo logs, backups, exports, software, error logs, and trace files. The use of RAID layouts is standard practice but reduces the amount of usable space. Raid 10 is the best choice for databases. Certain categories of files must be separated from each other.

- The main categories of memory usage to consider are the buffer cache, the shared pool, and stack space for user sessions.

- Instead of designing and implementing your own hardware and software configuration, you can buy a complete hardware and software package—an engineered system—directly from Oracle Corporation. Oracle Database Appliance is a two-node plug-and-play RAC cluster running Enterprise Edition. Exadata is suitable for today's most demanding workloads and database consolidation on a massive scale.

- Cloud computing is "the delivery of computing as a service instead of a product." In the PaaS model, you can create tables, indexes, views, and other kinds of database objects in a dedicated database schema. In the IaaS model, customers receive access not just to a database schema but to a virtual machine carved out of a very powerful server.

Further Reading

- *Oracle Database Licensing Information 12c Release 1*. Describes the various bundles, extra-cost options, and licensing restrictions. http://docs.oracle.com/database/121/index.htm.

- *Software Investment Guide*. Provides a management overview of licensing options. www.oracle.com/us/corporate/pricing/index.html.

- *US Oracle Technology Commercial Price List*. Lists the prices of the various bundles and the extra cost options; it is updated whenever prices change. www.oracle.com/us/corporate/pricing/price-lists/index.html.

Software Installation

The third little pig met a man with a load of bricks, and said, "Please, man, give me those bricks to build a house with;" so the man gave him the bricks, and he built his house with them. So the wolf came, as he did to the other little pigs, and said,—

"Little pig, little pig, let me come in."

"No, no, by the hair of my chiny chin chin."

"Then I'll huff, and I'll puff, and I'll blow your house in."

Well, he huffed, and he puffed, and he huffed, and he puffed, and he puffed, and he huffed; but he could not get the house down.

—*The Nursery Rhymes of England* by James Orchard Halliwell (1886)

You're almost ready to create a database. Chapter 4 covered the planning process. This chapter first goes over a few prerequisites such as obtaining the software, installation guides, and reference manuals. I also discuss the installation of software that precedes the creation of a database. I then demonstrate the process of installing the Oracle software in your VM. I hope you take the opportunity to perform the software installation exercise yourself—the best way to learn is by doing. Besides, software installation is one of the most common tasks of a database administrator.

Once you've learned how to install the Oracle software, you'll be ready to create a database. You create your first database in Chapter 6. To get maximum value out of this book, please repeat all the demonstrations yourself in your VM.

■ **Note**   To make it possible to repeat the software installation procedure multiple times, make sure you have taken a snapshot of the VM before installing the Oracle software into it. You can then restore the snapshot at will to repeat the procedure if you desire.

Oracle Technology Network

One of the reasons Oracle dominates the database market is that it makes its software and its software manuals available for download without any artificial restrictions such as license keys and limited trials. Oracle's motto is, "free to download, free to learn, unlimited evaluation." All you need is an Oracle Technology Network (OTN) account, available free of charge.

In addition to software and software manuals, OTN offers forums, articles, sample code, and tutorials. Go to www.oracle.com/technology/index.html and create an account for yourself; there's no reason not to do so.

The Forgotten Manuals

Beginning with Oracle Database 8, Oracle discontinued the practice of providing free printed copies of reference manuals to customers who purchased database licenses. In the early days of the Internet, when broadband access was not common, Oracle put the manuals on a CD. Today, you can search and read the manuals online; they are available in both HTML and PDF formats. For convenience, you can also download selected manuals—or the entire set of manuals—to your laptop computer for offline reading. You can purchase printed copies of the manuals at http://store.oracle.com, but they are huge. *Oracle Database 12c SQL Language Reference* alone is almost 1,500 pages, twice the size of the Oracle Database 7 version.

The manuals for Oracle Database 12*c* are available at docs.oracle.com; the manuals for older database versions are also available, all the way back to Oracle Database 7. For this chapter, you need the installation guides for the Linux operating system—separate guides are available for client installations and server installations.

■ **Note**   A very short version of the server installation guide, called a Quick Installation Guide, is also available in each case; it covers the most common scenarios.

Prerequisites and Preinstallation Requirements

You need to pay attention to the sections of the installation guides that discuss prerequisites and preinstallation requirements. If you have chosen a complex architecture such as Real Application Clusters (RAC), these prerequisites are themselves fairly complex, but RAC is outside the scope of this book.

Of course, a common prerequisite for all operating systems is adequate space for database files, archived redo logs, and backups. In a Linux environment, you need to install and run Oracle using a dedicated account, and there are also numerous other prerequisites. There was a time when you had to perform all the prerequisites manually; but when using Oracle Enterprise Linux (OEL), as is the case for your VM, they are bundled into an RPM package that is installed from the root account by the yum installer as follows:

```
yum install oracle-rdbms-server-12cR1-preinstall -y
```

Of course, you don't need to perform the prerequisites on the VM, because it already contains a full Oracle installation and therefore all the necessary prerequisites have been completed.

Client Installations

A *client installation* refers to the software that needs to be installed on every machine from which a connection to the database is initiated. This could be a user's laptop or an application server. This section shows you two types of client installations—Instant Client and SQL Developer—and demonstrates how to install them on a Windows desktop or laptop and connect to a database in your VM.

Instant Client

Prior to Oracle 10g, a typical client installation was a large collection of software including dozens of components. Installation was a time-consuming process that required the use of Oracle Universal Installer (OUI).

Beginning with Oracle Database 10g, Oracle provides the most essential software in a bundle called *Instant Client*. OUI is not needed for installation; you can simply copy a few files to a directory of your choice. The entire process takes only a few minutes:

1. Use your OTN account to download the necessary zipped files from Oracle Technology Network to your desktop or laptop. Several choices are offered. The most common choices are Basic and SQL*Plus. The Basic package contains the dynamic link libraries required by Oracle applications, and SQL*Plus is the traditional command-line tool favored by database administrators. Download both of them.

2. Unzip the two zip files into the same directory. Here's what I found in the directory after I did that:

```
$ dir
 Volume in drive C is System
 Volume Serial Number is 1C02-18A4

 Directory of C:\Users\iggy\Desktop\Iggy\Downloads\instantclient_12_1

08/03/2014  07:15 PM    <DIR>          .
08/03/2014  07:15 PM    <DIR>          ..
06/28/2013  04:04 AM            40,448 adrci.exe
06/28/2013  04:04 AM            19,672 adrci.sym
06/28/2013  04:04 AM               567 BASIC_README
06/28/2013  04:04 AM            84,992 genezi.exe
06/28/2013  04:04 AM            52,656 genezi.sym
01/13/2006  12:36 AM               342 glogin.sql
06/28/2013  04:02 AM           641,024 oci.dll
06/28/2013  04:02 AM           472,392 oci.sym
06/26/2013  04:38 AM           150,016 ocijdbc12.dll
06/26/2013  04:38 AM            29,912 ocijdbc12.sym
06/28/2013  03:39 AM           505,856 ociw32.dll
06/28/2013  03:39 AM            79,840 ociw32.sym
06/26/2013  04:38 AM         3,389,454 ojdbc6.jar
06/28/2013  03:33 AM            67,072 oramysql12.dll
06/28/2013  03:33 AM            32,472 oramysql12.sym
06/25/2013  12:30 PM         4,736,000 orannzsbb12.dll
06/25/2013  12:30 PM           859,960 orannzsbb12.sym
06/28/2013  03:13 AM         1,095,680 oraocci12.dll
```

```
06/28/2013  04:04 AM              842,704 oraocci12.sym
06/28/2013  03:26 AM            1,121,792 oraocci12d.dll
06/28/2013  04:04 AM              944,272 oraocci12d.sym
06/28/2013  04:03 AM          161,174,528 oraociei12.dll
06/28/2013  04:04 AM           10,604,136 oraociei12.sym
06/25/2013  08:25 AM              207,872 oraons.dll
06/28/2013  04:00 AM              310,272 orasql12.dll
06/28/2013  04:00 AM               53,712 orasql12.sym
06/25/2013  04:36 AM            1,559,040 Orasqlplusic12.dll
06/25/2013  04:36 AM              946,176 sqlplus.exe
06/28/2013  04:05 AM              150,856 sqlplus.sym
06/28/2013  04:05 AM                  571 SQLPLUS_README
08/03/2014  07:32 PM                  187 tnsnames.ora
06/28/2013  04:04 AM               40,448 uidrvci.exe
06/28/2013  04:04 AM               19,672 uidrvci.sym
08/03/2014  07:08 PM    <DIR>             vc10
08/03/2014  07:08 PM    <DIR>             vc11
06/28/2013  03:47 AM               71,231 xstreams.jar
              34 File(s)    190,305,824 bytes
               4 Dir(s)  28,239,732,736 bytes free
```

3. Use any text editor to create a file called tnsnames.ora containing an entry that describes an existing database. The following sample describes the database that you saw in Chapter 1; the Oracle listener is listening on port 1521. Save the file to the directory that you used in step 2:

```
$ type tnsnames.ora
orcl12c =
  (description =
    (address = (protocol = tcp)(host = 192.168.56.101)(PORT = 1521))
    (connect_data =
      (server = dedicated)
      (service:name = orcl)
    )
  )
```

4. Log in to your VM, and switch to the root account using the su - command; the password is oracle. Modify the /etc/sysconfig/iptables file to open port 1521 on the VM. You can either edit the file directly or use the sed command as shown in the following example. The extra line that you need is shown in boldface—it is similar to the line for port 22, the ssh port:

```
[oracle@localhost ~]$ su -
Password:

[root@localhost ~]# cat /etc/sysconfig/iptables
# Generated by iptables-save v1.4.7 on Sun Aug  3 22:31:09 2014
*filter
:INPUT ACCEPT [0:0]
:FORWARD ACCEPT [0:0]
:OUTPUT ACCEPT [0:0]
```

```
-A INPUT -m state --state RELATED,ESTABLISHED -j ACCEPT
-A INPUT -p icmp -j ACCEPT
-A INPUT -i lo -j ACCEPT
-A INPUT -p tcp -m state --state NEW -m tcp --dport 22 -j ACCEPT
-A INPUT -j REJECT --reject-with icmp-host-prohibited
-A FORWARD -j REJECT --reject-with icmp-host-prohibited
COMMIT
# Completed on Sun Aug  3 22:31:09 2014
```

```
[root@localhost ~]# sed -i '/dport 22/a-A INPUT -p tcp -m state --state
NEW -m tcp --dport 1521 -j ACCEPT' /etc/sysconfig/iptables
```

```
[root@localhost ~]# cat /etc/sysconfig/iptables
# Generated by iptables-save v1.4.7 on Sun Aug  3 22:31:09 2014
*filter
:INPUT ACCEPT [0:0]
:FORWARD ACCEPT [0:0]
:OUTPUT ACCEPT [0:0]
-A INPUT -m state --state RELATED,ESTABLISHED -j ACCEPT
-A INPUT -p icmp -j ACCEPT
-A INPUT -i lo -j ACCEPT
-A INPUT -p tcp -m state --state NEW -m tcp --dport 22 -j ACCEPT
-A INPUT -p tcp -m state --state NEW -m tcp --dport 1521 -j ACCEPT
-A INPUT -j REJECT --reject-with icmp-host-prohibited
-A FORWARD -j REJECT --reject-with icmp-host-prohibited
COMMIT
# Completed on Sun Aug  3 22:31:09 2014
```

```
[root@localhost ~]# /etc/init.d/iptables restart
iptables: Setting chains to policy ACCEPT: filter       [  OK  ]
iptables: Flushing firewall rules:                      [  OK  ]
iptables: Unloading modules:                            [  OK  ]
iptables: Applying firewall rules:                      [  OK  ]
```

5.   Switch back to your desktop or laptop, and define a variable called TNS_ADMIN to tell Oracle where you have placed the tnsnames.ora file—typically in the same location as the Instant Client software. You're ready to connect to the targeted database using the sqlplus program, as shown here:

```
$ cd "C:\Users\iggy\Desktop\Iggy\Downloads\instantclient_12_1"
```

```
$ set TNS_ADMIN="C:\Users\iggy\Desktop\Iggy\Downloads\instantclient_12_1"
```

```
$ type tnsnames.ora
```

```
orcl12c =
  (description =
    (address = (protocol = tcp)(host = 192.168.56.101)(PORT = 1521))
    (connect_data =
```

```
    (server = dedicated)
    (service:name = pdb1)
  )
)
```

$ sqlplus hr/oracle@orcl12c

```
SQL*Plus: Release 12.1.0.1.0 Production on Sun Aug 3 21:44:34 2014

Copyright (c) 1982, 2013, Oracle.  All rights reserved.

ERROR:
ORA-28002: the password will expire within 7 days


Last Successful login time: Sun Aug 03 2014 21:16:51 -07:00

Connected to:
Oracle Database 12c Enterprise Edition Release 12.1.0.1.0 - 64bit Production
With the Partitioning, OLAP, Advanced Analytics and Real Application Testing options

SQL> select count(*) from employees;

  COUNT(*)
----------
       107

SQL> exit
Disconnected from Oracle Database 12c Enterprise Edition Release 12.1.0.1.0 - 64bit
Production
With the Partitioning, OLAP, Advanced Analytics and Real Application Testing options
```

SQL Developer

Another form of client installation that you have already seen is SQL Developer—a Java-based GUI tool that is useful to application developers as well as database administrators. It is a client installation in its own right and does not depend on other client software such as Instant Client.

Installing SQL Developer is painless:

1.   Use your OTN account to download the necessary zipped files from Oracle Technology Network, and unzip the contents into a directory of your choice. Note that SQL Developer needs Java to operate, and the first invocation of the tool asks you for the location of Java. You have the option of downloading Java along with SQL Developer, but most people don't need to do so because they already have a Java installation.

2.   Click the sqldeveloper.exe program, and provide the details of the target database, as shown in Figure 5-1. Click Connect.

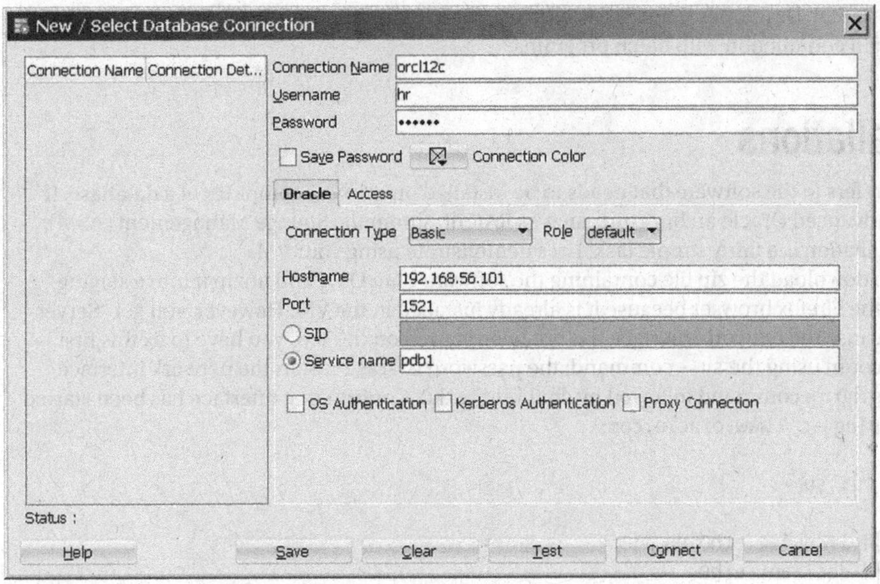

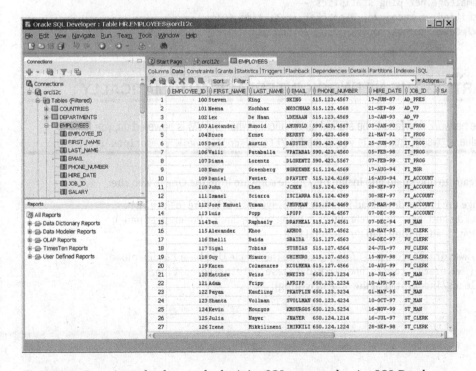

Figure 5-1. *Connecting to a database using SQL Developer*

3. As illustrated in Figure 5-2, you can browse the database by using the navigation panel at left on the SQL Developer screen or submit SQL commands from the SQL worksheet.

Figure 5-2. *Browsing a database and submitting SQL commands using SQL Developer*

A GUI tool such as SQL Developer is much easier to use than a command-line tool such as SQL*Plus, but it cannot be used in conjunction with batch programs.

Server Installations

A *server installation* refers to the software that needs to be installed on the host computer of a database. If you're not using an advanced Oracle architecture such as RAC or Automatic Storage Management (ASM), creating a server installation is a fairly simple task. Let's demonstrate using your VM.

First you have to download the zip file containing the software from OTN and unzip it into a staging directory. You'll use the Firefox browser because it is already installed in the VM. However, you get "Server not found" errors because the network interface has not been started on the VM; you have to fix this first. Switch to the root account using the su - command; the password is oracle. Start the network interface using the ifconfig eth0 up command followed by dhclient eth0. Confirm that interface has been started using the command ping -c 1 www.oracle.com:

```
[oracle@localhost ~]$ su -
Password:
[root@localhost ~]# ifconfig eth0 up
[root@localhost ~]# dhclient eth0
[root@localhost ~]# ping -c 1 www.oracle.com
PING e7075.x.akamaiedge.net (23.7.198.140) 56(84) bytes of data.
64 bytes from a23-7-198-140.deploy.static.akamaitechnologies.com
(23.7.198.140): icmp_seq=1 ttl=57 time=30.0 ms

--- e7075.x.akamaiedge.net ping statistics ---
1 packets transmitted, 1 received, 0% packet loss, time 104ms
rtt min/avg/max/mdev = 30.093/30.093/30.093/0.000 ms
```

STARTING THE NETWORK INTERFACE AUTOMATICALLY

If you want the network interface to be started automatically when the VM is powered on, you have to change the value of ONBOOT from no to yes in the file /etc/sysconfig/network-scripts/ifcfg-eth0.

You're now ready to download and install the Oracle software from the Oracle web site:

1. Change the Firefox download location to Always Ask Me Where to Save Files (click Edit and then click Preferences to bring up the Firefox Preferences panel; the Downloads setting is in the General tab).

2. Go to www.oracle.com, and find your way to the Oracle Database 12*c* download page (www.oracle.com/technetwork/database/enterprise-edition/downloads/index.html at the time of writing).

3. Click Accept License Agreement, and then download the two zip files containing the software for the Linux x86-64 operating system (File 1 and File 2). You are prompted for your OTN username and password; provide the same username and password that you used in Chapter 1 to download the VM. Save both files to the /tmp directory, because you want to conserve space in the other filesystems. The files are very large (2.3GB at the time of writing), so they may take a long time to download.

4. When you are done downloading the files, go to the /tmp directory and unzip them:

```
unzip linuxamd64_12c_database_1of2.zip
unzip linuxamd64_12c_database_2of2.zip
```

5. Unzipping the files creates a directory called database. Switch to that directory using the command cd /tmp/database, and then invoke the runInstaller script using the command ./runInstaller. Doing so starts Oracle Universal Installer (OUI), as shown in Figure 5-3.

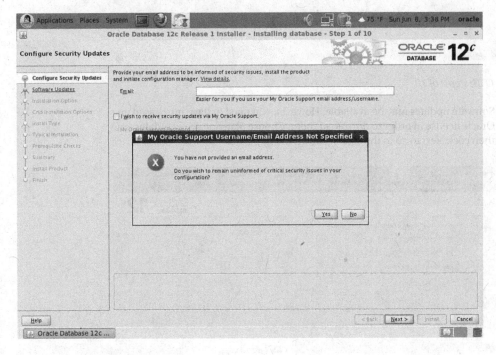

Figure 5-3. *OUI: step 1 of 10*

6. Leave the Email field blank, and uncheck I Wish to Receive Security Updates via My Oracle Support. Click Next.

7. A prompt appears with the message "You have not provided an email address. Do you wish to remain uninformed of critical security issues in your configuration?" Click Yes to go to the screen shown in Figure 5-4.

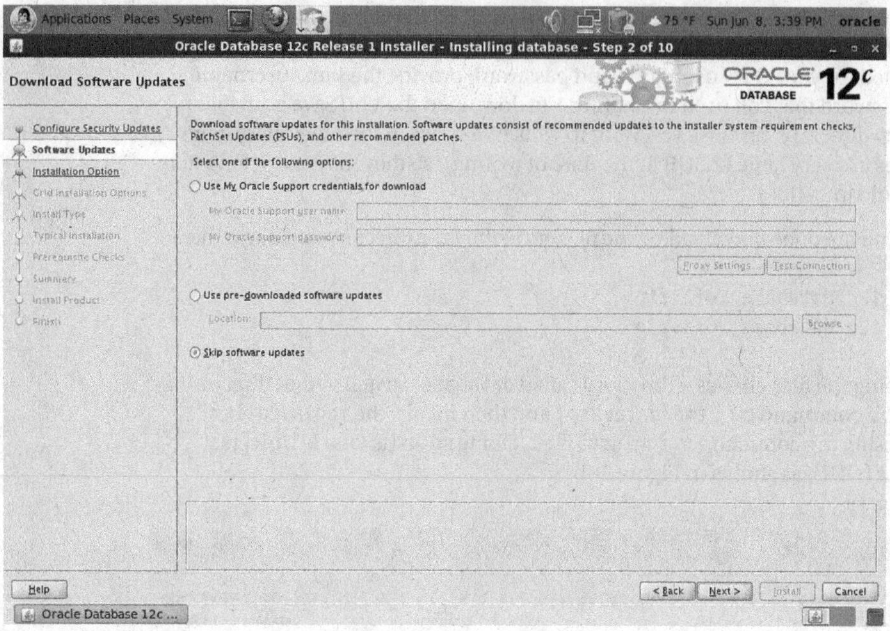

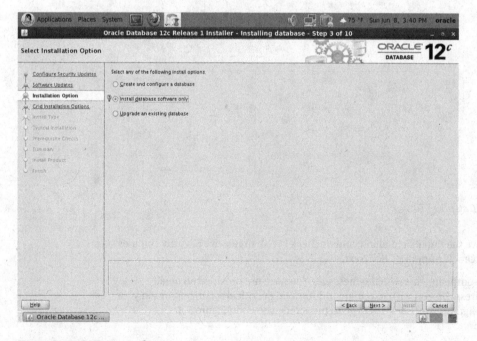

Figure 5-4. OUI: step 2 of 10

8. Software updates may be available. However, you need to have purchased an Oracle license in order to download them. Choose Skip Software Updates, and then click Next to go to the screen shown in Figure 5-5.

Figure 5-5. OUI: step 3 of 10

9. Choose Install Database Software Only, and click Next to go to the screen shown in Figure 5-6.

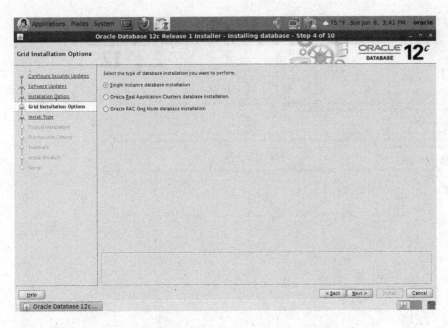

Figure 5-6. *OUI: step 4 of 10*

10. Choose Single Instance Database Installation, and click Next to go to the screen shown in Figure 5-7.

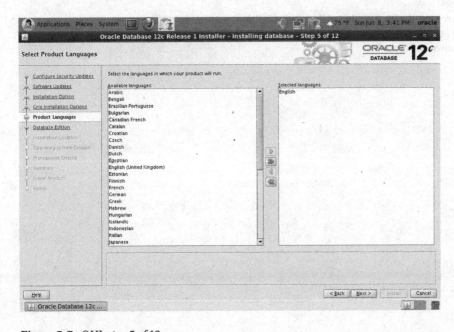

Figure 5-7. *OUI: step 5 of 12*

11. You are presented with a list of languages. Click Next to go to the screen shown in Figure 5-8.

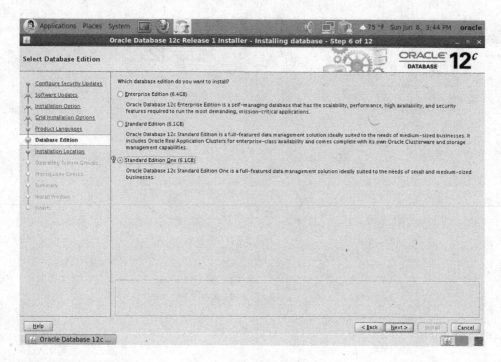

Figure 5-8. *OUI: step 6 of 12*

12. You are presented with a choice of Enterprise Edition, Standard Edition, or Standard Edition One. Choose Standard Edition, and click Next to go to the screen shown in Figure 5-9.

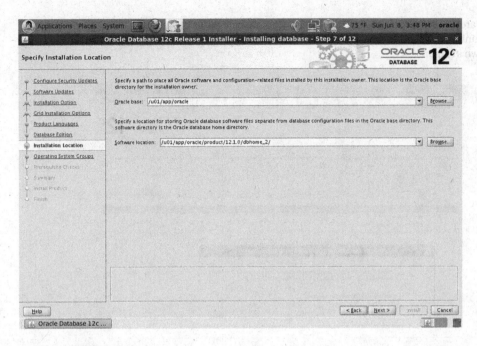

Figure 5-9. *OUI: step 7 of 12*

13. Change the last component of the Software Location path from dbhome_1 to dbhome_2. Click Next to go to the screen shown in Figure 5-10.

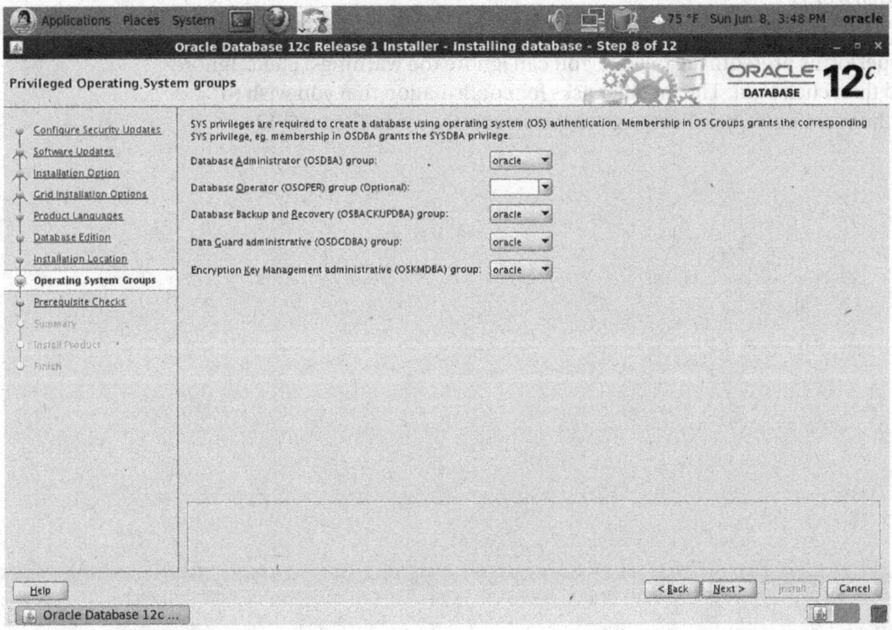

Figure 5-10. *OUI: step 8 of 12*

14. You are asked to designated OS groups for different categories of database administrators. In this case, the defaults will suffice. Click Next to go to the screen shown in Figure 5-11.

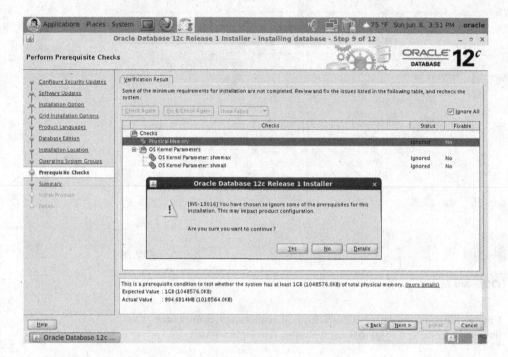

Figure 5-11. *OUI: step 9 of 12*

15. Oracle performs prerequisite checks. You can ignore the warnings: check Ignore All, and then click Next. The installer asks for confirmation that you wish to ignore the warnings. Click Next to go to the screen shown in Figure 5-12.

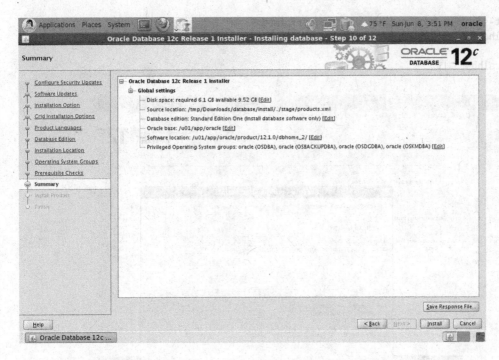

Figure 5-12. *OUI: step 10 of 12*

16. The installer displays a summary of your choices. Click Install, and the installer begins installing the software. A progress bar is displayed; note that the installation may take a long time.

17. When the installation is complete, OUI asks you to execute a script called root.sh, as shown in Figure 5-13. Open a terminal window, switch to the root account, and execute the script as follows:

```
[oracle@localhost ~]$ su -
Password:
[root@localhost ~]# /u01/app/oracle/product/12.1.0/dbhome_2/root.sh
Performing root user operation for Oracle 12c

The following environment variables are set as:
    ORACLE_OWNER= oracle
    ORACLE_HOME=  /u01/app/oracle/product/12.1.0/dbhome_2

Enter the full pathname of the local bin directory: [/usr/local/bin]:
The contents of "dbhome" have not changed. No need to overwrite.
The contents of "oraenv" have not changed. No need to overwrite.
The contents of "coraenv" have not changed. No need to overwrite.

Entries will be added to the /etc/oratab file as needed by
Database Configuration Assistant when a database is created
Finished running generic part of root script.
```

```
Now product-specific root actions will be performed.
[root@localhost ~]# exit
logout
[oracle@localhost ~]$
```

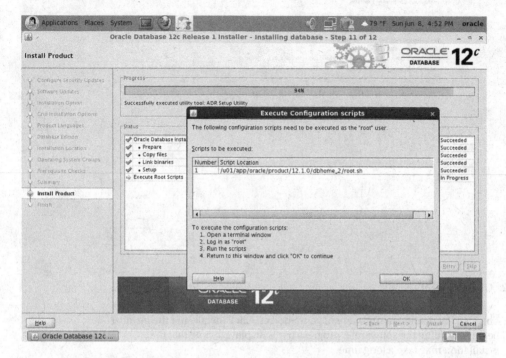

Figure 5-13. *OUI: step 11 of 12*

18. Go back to the installer window, and click OK to go to the screen shown in
Figure 5-14.

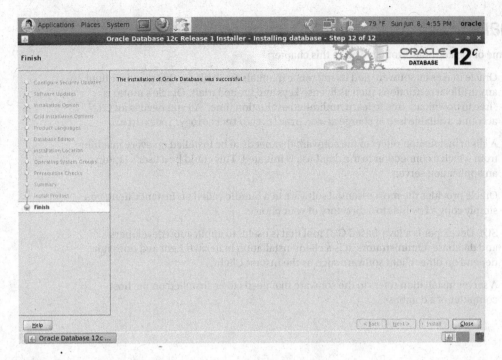

Figure 5-14. *OUI: step 12 of 12*

19. Oracle displays a success message. Click Close to terminate OUI.

Oracle Database Examples

Oracle provides examples and demos that you can install for learning purposes. The steps are as follows:

1. Download the zip file containing the examples from OTN, and unzip it into a staging directory.

2. Navigate to the staging directory, and click setup.exe to start OUI. The installer displays a welcome screen. Click Next.

3. Specify the Oracle Home into which the examples should be installed. Click Next.

4. OUI checks that all prerequisites are satisfied. Click Next.

5. OUI displays a summary screen. Click Install.

6. OUI begins installing the examples and demos. When the installation is complete, OUI displays a success message. Click Exit.

Summary

Here are some of the key points touched on in this chapter:

- Oracle makes its software and its reference manuals available for download without any artificial restrictions such as license keys and limited trials. Oracle's motto is "free to download, free to learn, unlimited evaluation time." All you need is an OTN account, available free of charge at www.oracle.com/technology/index.html.

- A client installation refers to the software that needs to be installed on every machine from which a connection to the database is initiated. This could be a user's laptop or an application server.

- Oracle provides the most essential software in a bundle called an Instant Client; you simply copy a few files to a directory of your choice.

- SQL Developer is a Java-based GUI tool that is useful to application developers and database administrators. It is a client installation in its own right and does not depend on other client software such as the Instant Client.

- A server installation refers to the software that needs to be installed on the host computer of a database.

■ ■ ■

Database Creation

Who verily knows and who can here declare it, whence it was born and whence comes this creation?

The Gods are later than this world's production. Who knows then whence it first came into being?

He, the first origin of this creation, whether he formed it all or did not form it,

Whose eye controls this world in highest heaven, he verily knows it, or perhaps he knows not.

—*The Hymns of the Rigveda* by Ralph T. H. Griffith (E. J. Lazarus and Co., Benares, 1897)

Oracle makes the process of creating a database as easy as pie—you can create a database from scratch in a few minutes to an hour. Mogens Norgaard, the ex-CEO of a Danish company called Miracle A/S, recorded one of his employees, Morten Egan, clad in a straitjacket and creating a database in about 30 minutes by typing on his keyboard with his *nose!*

The reason for this demonstration was that a service provider had quoted 50 hours of labor to create a database. When viewers of the video protested that Egan had only created a very simple database, Norgaard recorded a video of Egan creating a more complex database in less than an hour, once again clad in a straitjacket and typing on the keyboard with his *nose*. In the same video, a 14-year-old intern named Daniel Christensen demonstrated that he, too, was capable of creating an Oracle database; he did it in 26 minutes.

To find both videos, search the YouTube catalog for the phrase *Unconventional Oracle Installation*. Here are the opening remarks from the second video:

Norgaard: Mr. Egan, we've had some flak from our first "Nosejob" video. People say it's not a very serious way to show what [the service provider] was actually asked to do. Is that correct?

Egan: No, that is not correct. The thing that [the service provider] was asked to do was to install the database. The job of actually finding out how the database should be installed, what options should be in there, what parameters should be set, was done by me beforehand, and that took a month. So the paper that [the service provider] got to do the job was: install the database, change these two parameters, click Finish.

I had made an entire list of what to do; so it was basically a next-next-next installation type and I think the criticism is based on that. Well, the difficult thing is not to install the database, and that's correct; it's not difficult to install the database. The thing that takes time is the precursor thing where you think about how it should be set up and after you install the database where you say: OK, how do I design this thing for the application?

The only thing that [the service provider] was asked to do was the tiny part of installing the database because we did not have access to the machines, the only reason why [the service provider] was asked to do this. And I gave them a piece of paper with basically eight steps and listed the two parameters that need to be changed. And that was it.

In other words, the work of actually creating a database is trivial compared to the planning, approval, and hardware provisioning that precede it. In this chapter, you learn the "Next-Next-Next; click Finish" method of creating a database.

First you have to spend a minute creating a listener. A minute is all it takes!

■ **Tip**   To make it possible to repeat the database procedure multiple times, make sure you have taken a snapshot of the VM before creating a database. You can then restore the snapshot at will to repeat the procedure if you so desire.

The graphical user interfaces demonstrated in this chapter depend on the X Window System. If you are creating a database on a server other than your VM, ask the system administrator for instructions for running graphical user interfaces.

Creating and Configuring a Listener

The Net Configuration Assistant (NetCA) is used to create a listener. To use it to create and configure a listener, follow these steps:

1. The NetCA program (netca) is located in the $ORACLE_HOME/bin directory. In your VM, change the value of the ORACLE_HOME environment variable from /u01/app/oracle/product/12.1.0/dbhome_1/ to /u01/app/oracle/product/12.1.0/dbhome_2/, and start NetCA:

```
[oracle@localhost ~]$ echo $ORACLE_HOME
/u01/app/oracle/product/12.1.0/dbhome_1/
[oracle@localhost ~]$ export ORACLE_HOME=/u01/app/oracle/product/12.1.0/dbhome_2/
[oracle@localhost ~]$ $ORACLE_HOME/bin/netca
```

The opening screen shown in Figure 6-1 is displayed.

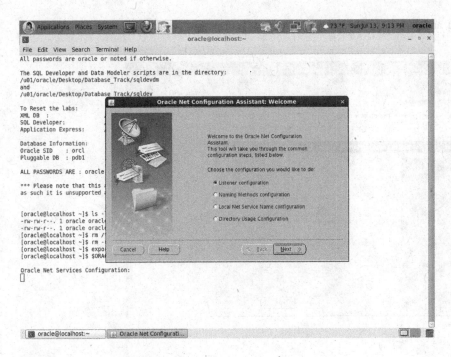

Figure 6-1. *NetCA opening screen*

2.   Select Listener Configuration, and click Next. The screen in Figure 6-2 is displayed.

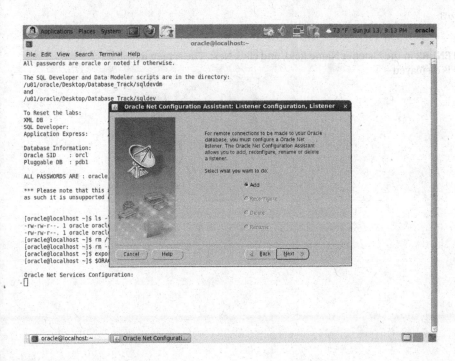

Figure 6-2. *NetCA step 2*

3. Select Add, and click Next. The screen in Figure 6-3 is displayed.

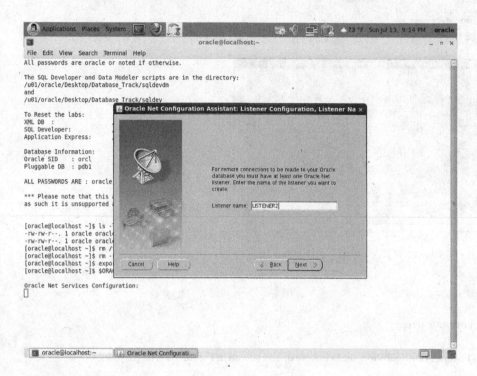

Figure 6-3. NetCA step 3

4. Type **LISTENER2** in the Listener Name field, and click Next. The screen in Figure 6-4 is displayed.

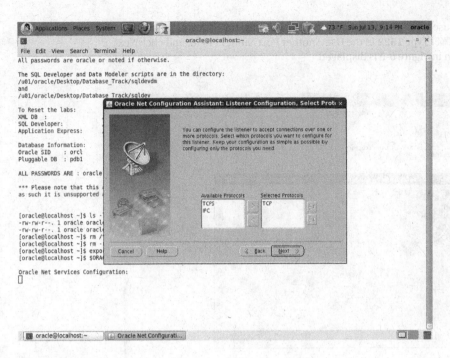

Figure 6-4. *NetCA step 4*

5. Retain the default selection of protocols, and click Next. The screen in Figure 6-5 is displayed.

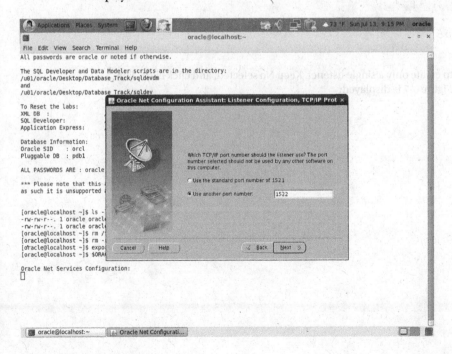

Figure 6-5. *NetCA step 5*

6. You can't use port 1521 because it is already used by the listener in the first ORACLE_HOME. Type **1522** in the Use Another Port Number field, and click Next. The screen in Figure 6-6 is displayed.

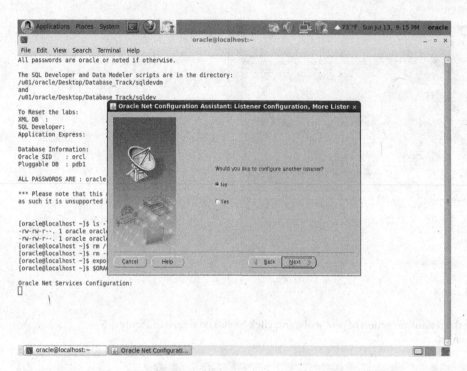

Figure 6-6. *NetCA step 6*

7. You wish to create only a single listener. Keep No selected, and click Next. The screen in Figure 6-7 is displayed.

Figure 6-7. *NetCA final screen*

8. Oracle displays a success message. Click Next. This takes you back to the starting
    screen (Figure 6-1), where you can click Cancel to exit NetCA.

That was easy, wasn't it?

Creating and Configuring a Database

The Database Configuration Assistant (DBCA) streamlines the process of creating and configuring a
database and ensures that no steps are forgotten. The use of *database templates* further speeds up and
standardizes the database-creation process. The process is described in the following sections.

The DBCA program dbca is located in the $ORACLE_HOME/bin directory. You have already changed the
value of the ORACLE_HOME environment variables to /u01/app/oracle/product/12.1.0/dbhome_2/, so go
ahead and start the DBCA:

```
[oracle@localhost ~]$ $ORACLE_HOME/bin/dbca
```

As the opening screen in Figure 6-8 indicates, DBCA can be used to create a database, reconfigure an
existing database, delete a database, or manage database templates. A *database template* is a copy of all
the settings that were used to create a previous database. I recommend that you save the settings of every
database you create; this makes it easy to create another database with the same settings. Another good idea
is to create an organizational standard and use it for all your databases. For convenience, Oracle provides
three database templates, but their configurations are not suitable for production databases—for example,
redo logs are not mirrored—so some customization of the Oracle provided templates is usually necessary.

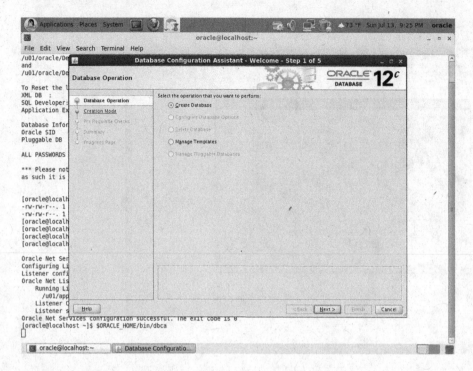

Figure 6-8. *DBCA opening screen*

To create a database with DBCA, continue with these steps:

1. Select Create Database on the DBCA Welcome screen, and click Next to go to the next step, shown in Figure 6-9.

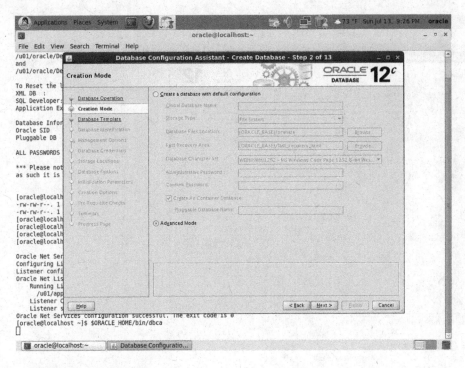

Figure 6-9. DBCA step 2

■ **Tip** Every DBCA screen sports a Help button that you can click to display information on how to use the screen.

---

2. The screen in Figure 6-9 gives you the option to short-circuit the process by specifying a few options and going directly to the Finish stage. I don't recommend choosing this option, because the defaults are unsatisfactory; for example, the online redo logs are not mirrored. Select Advanced Mode, and click Next to go to the next step, shown in Figure 6-10.

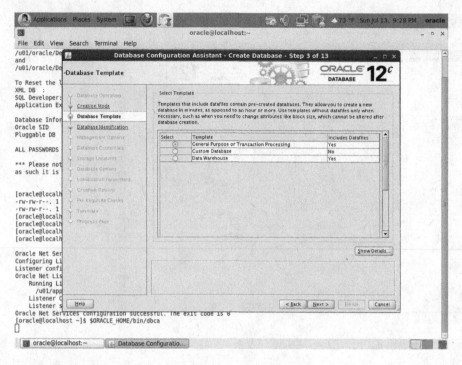

Figure 6-10. DBCA step 3

This screen lists the available templates containing initialization parameters and other choices you need to make when creating a database. Using templates is a good practice because standardization usually improves quality and maintainability.

Oracle provides three default templates: General Purpose or Transaction Processing, Custom Database, and Data Warehouse. It is always tempting to choose the general-purpose template, because it is first in the list and the name indicates that it will suit most purposes. However, note that this template—along with the data warehouse template—is pre-seeded; that is, it includes pre-created data files. Pre-seeded templates are less customizable but allow you to create databases very quickly. But as you'll see in Table 6-1 later in this chapter, the pre-created data files are loaded with optional software that you may not need. In the Exercises section, you are asked to create your own pre-seeded template with just the software you need and with certain desirable settings.

3. Choose the General Purpose or Transaction Processing template. Click the Show Details button, and examine the details of the template; in the screens that follow, you are given the opportunity to modify some of the settings listed in the template. Click Next to go to the next step, shown in Figure 6-11.

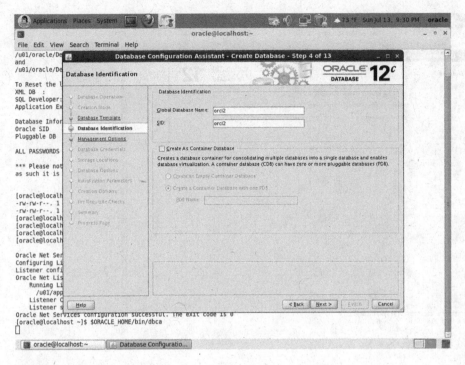

Figure 6-11. *DBCA step 4*

Here you choose a *database* name and an *instance* name (SID) . A database is a group of files on disk, whereas an instance is a group of operating system processes that provide access to a database. Specify **orcl2** as the database name as well as the instance name. You next have to decide whether to use the new container architecture, discussed in Chapter 3.

4. For the purpose of this exercise, stick with the traditional architecture. Leave the Create As Container Database option unchecked, and click Next to go to the next screen, shown in Figure 6-12.

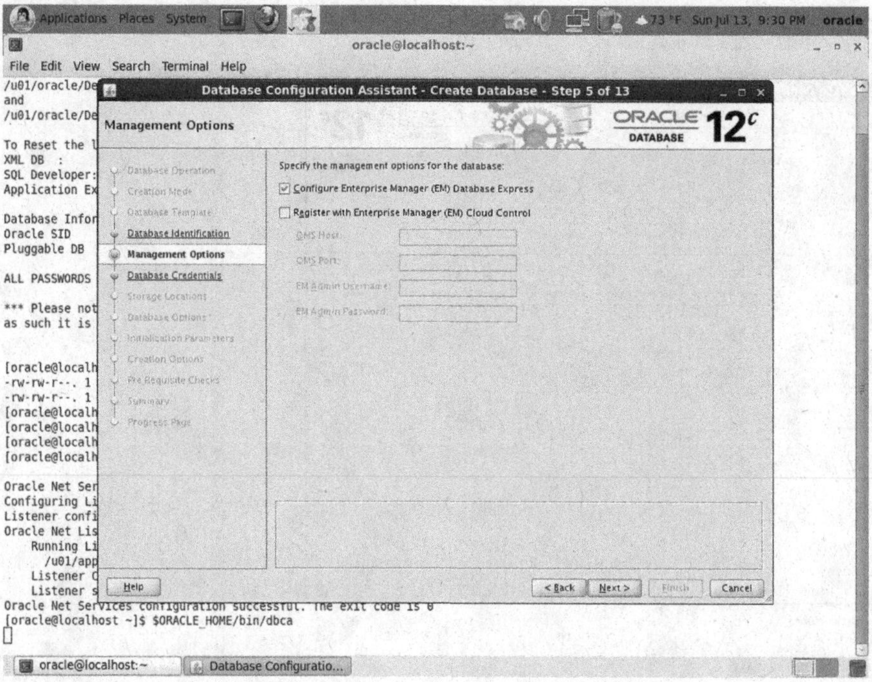

Figure 6-12. *DBCA step 5*

On this screen, you decide which flavors of Enterprise Manager you would like to use. You can configure a standalone component called Enterprise Manager Database Express (EM Express), and you can also optionally register the new database with an enterprise-wide monitoring framework called Enterprise Manager Cloud Control (EM Cloud Control). EM Express is a very lightweight browser-based tool suitable for common database administration tasks. EM Cloud Control is a sophisticated framework for lights-out database monitoring and backup (among other things).

5. Select Configure Enterprise Manager (EM) Database Express, and then click Next to go to the next screen, shown in Figure 6-13.

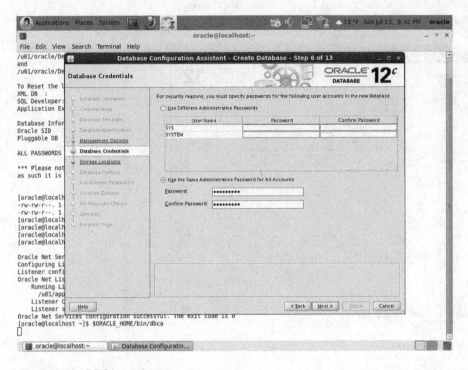

Figure 6-13. *DBCA step 6*

You need to choose passwords for the four most important administrative accounts in the database: SYS, SYSTEM, DBSNMP, and SYSMAN. The SYS account owns the core tables in the Oracle data dictionary, whereas the SYSTEM account owns administrative views and other components of Oracle's management infrastructure. The DBSNMP and SYSMAN views are used by Enterprise Manager. There are a number of other administrative accounts, but they are all locked out when the database is created and should be enabled on an as-needed basis only. You can elect to use the same password for all four accounts. Use a password that meets the complexity requirements of your organization's security policy but is fairly easy to remember.

6. Select Use the Same Administrative Password for All Accounts, and specify a password. Then click Next to go to the next step, shown in Figure 6-14.

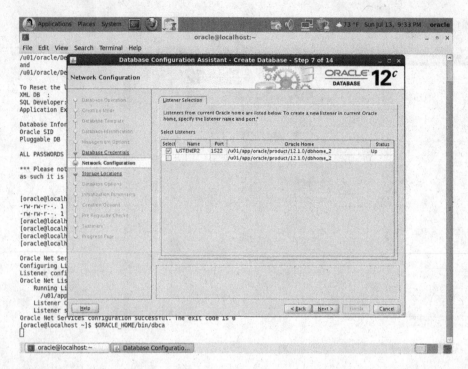

Figure 6-14. *DBCA step 7*

7. Select LISTENER2 to specify which listener the database should register with. Then click Next to go to the next screen, shown in Figure 6-15.

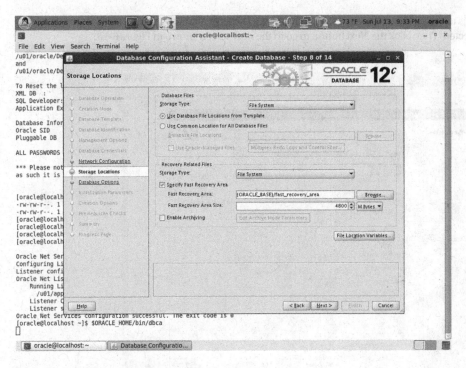

Figure 6-15. *DBCA step 8*

Next you make decisions about storage. You can use a traditional file system for file storage or use Automatic Storage Management (ASM), an advanced Oracle technology for disk management. A number of data files are automatically created by DBCA; you can let DBCA decide their names and locations, or you can specify a name and location for each data file. If you let Oracle choose, it constructs names and locations from the values of variables such as ORACLE_BASE, ORACLE_HOME, DB_NAME, and SID. Click the File Location Variables button to review these variables' values; ORACLE_HOME is the location of the Oracle software, ORACLE_BASE is the parent directory of ORACLE_HOME, DB_NAME is the name of the database, and SID is the name of the instance. If you wish, you may alter the names and locations of individual files later. One of the options you can choose on this screen is Oracle-Managed Files; this option gives Oracle control over the naming of data files and their properties.

You must also specify whether to use a common area called the *fast recovery area* to store backups created with Recovery Manager (RMAN) and archived redo logs; this is the recommended practice. To increase safety, you should specify a location that is on a different file system than the one containing the database. You must also specify the maximum amount of space that Oracle may use for the purpose; this value depends on the size of the database, the backup scheme, and the expected volume of archived redo logs. The default value is not adequate, even for a starter database.

8. Change the Fast Recovery Area Size value to 8192 MB (8 GB) for now; you can adjust it at a later date if it does not meet your needs.

On this screen, you also specify whether you would like redo logs to be archived; this too is the recommended practice. Remember that if you do not archive redo logs, you cannot make a backup copy of the database unless you first shut it down; and, if the database ever requires recovery, you cannot recover any changes made to the database after the latest backup.

9. For this exercise, select Specify Fast Recovery Area but leave Enable Archiving unselected. Then click the Next button to go to the next screen shown in Figure 6-16.

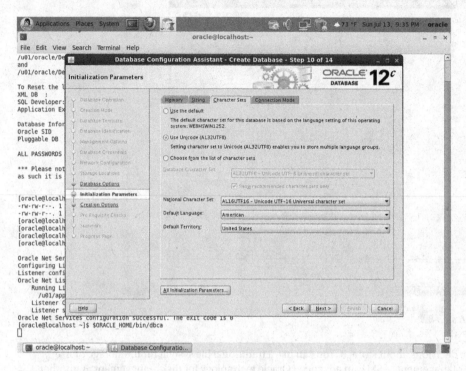

Figure 6-16. *DBCA step 10*

A lot of options are packed into this screen's four tabs. In the Memory tab, you specify how much computer memory you are willing to devote to the Oracle database. The simplest option is to choose a single number and leave it to Oracle to manage it appropriately; this is called *automatic memory management*. Alternatively, you can explicitly specify how much memory Oracle should use for each purpose—for example, the shared pool and the buffer cache.

In the Sizing tab, you specify the maximum number of simultaneous connections to the database that can be expected and the default block size of the database. In this example, the block size is set to 8192 bytes (8KB) and cannot be changed (because the template you are using includes pre-created data files containing blocks of this size).

In the Character Sets tab, you specify character sets that accommodate the languages spoken by your users. It is common to choose Unicode (also called AL32UTF8) in order to support the maximum number of languages.

In the Connection Mode tab, you choose between dedicated server mode and shared server mode; these are discussed in Chapter 4.

You can click the All Initialization Parameters button if you would like to modify initialization parameters that are not presented on this screen.

10. For this exercise, the only change you should make is to choose AL32UTF8 as the database character set in the Character Sets tab instead of the default value. Click Next to go to the next screen, shown in Figure 6-17.

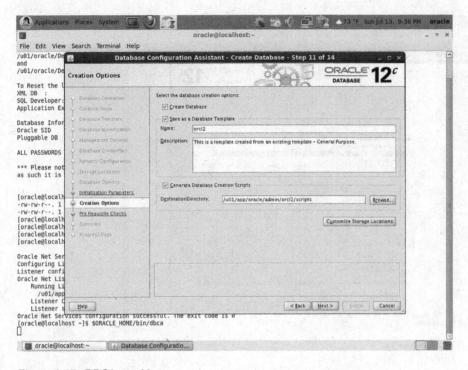

Figure 6-17. *DBCA step 11*

Here you can choose whether to save your work as a template and whether to generate database-creation scripts. *Always* save your work as a template, *even if you did not make any changes to the default template.* Saving your work as a template keeps a record of your work; it also allows you to create other databases using the same settings. In the interest of further documenting your work, you should also select the option that generates database-creation scripts—these are the scripts that DBCA runs behind the scenes to create the database.

11. Select Create Database, Save as a Database Template, and Generate Database
     Creation Scripts; then click Next to go to the next step, shown in Figure 6-18.

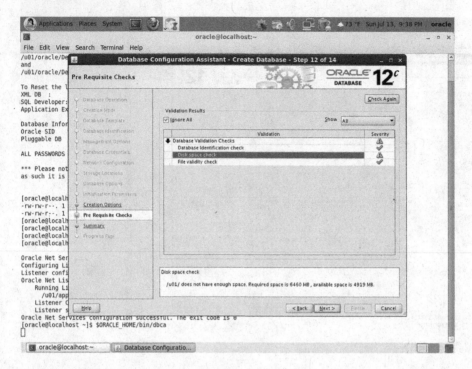

Figure 6-18. *DBCA step 12*

On this screen, Oracle displays the results of validity checks. One of the checks fails because the DBCA believes there is not enough disk space for the new database. You can ignore this failure because you do in fact have enough disk space.

12. Select Ignore All, and then click Next to go to the next step, shown in Figure 6-19.

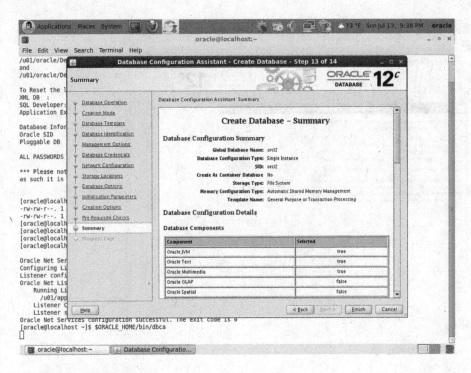

Figure 6-19. *DBCA step 13*

13. DBCA displays a confirmation screen that lists all the options you have selected. Click Finish to begin the process of database creation. This process is particularly speedy if you use a template that includes pre-created data files. Once the database is created, DBCA displays a success message similar to the one shown in Figure 6-20. Make a note of the EM Database Express URL.

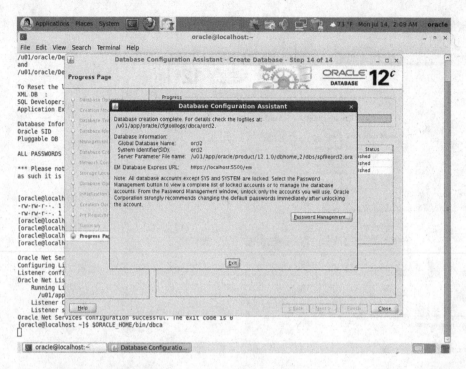

Figure 6-20. *DBCA final screen*

Common Options

Because you chose a template that included data files, Oracle did not allow you to pick and choose optional components for installation. Table 6-1 shows which options are installed. The option you really need is Sample Schemas, but it is not automatically installed. I leave this as an exercise for you.

Table 6-1. *Common Options*

Component	Selected
Oracle JVM	True
Oracle Text	True
Oracle Multimedia	True
Oracle OLAP	False
Oracle Spatial	False
Oracle Label Security	False
Sample Schemas	False
Oracle Application Express	True
Oracle Database Vault	False

Initialization Parameters

Oracle databases have hundreds of initialization parameters, most of which have default values. Table 6-2 lists the few parameters that were set by DBCA.

***Table 6-2.** Initialization Parameters*

Name	Value
audit_file_dest	{ORACLE_BASE}/admin/{DB_UNIQUE_NAME}/adump
audit_trail	db
compatible	12.1.0.0.0
control_files	("{ORACLE_BASE}/oradata/{DB_UNIQUE_NAME}/control01.ctl", "{ORACLE_BASE}/fast_recovery_area/{DB_UNIQUE_NAME}/control02.ctl")
db_block_size	8KB
db_name	
db_recovery_file_dest	{ORACLE_BASE}/fast_recovery_area
db_recovery_file_dest_size	MB
diagnostic_dest	{ORACLE_BASE}
dispatchers	(PROTOCOL=TCP) (SERVICE={SID}XDB)
memory_target	250MB
open_cursors	300
processes	300
remote_login_passwordfile	EXCLUSIVE
undo_tablespace	UNDOTBS1

Data Files

All the data files listed in Table 6-3 were included in the template; you could have changed their names and locations if you wished to do so.

***Table 6-3.** Data Files*

Name	Tablespace	Size (MB)
{ORACLE_BASE}/oradata/{DB_UNIQUE_NAME}/system01.dbf	SYSTEM	770
{ORACLE_BASE}/oradata/{DB_UNIQUE_NAME}/sysaux01.dbf	SYSAUX	650
{ORACLE_BASE}/oradata/{DB_UNIQUE_NAME}/undotbs01.dbf	UNDOTBS1	25
{ORACLE_BASE}/oradata/{DB_UNIQUE_NAME}/users01.dbf	USERS	5
{ORACLE_BASE}/oradata/{DB_UNIQUE_NAME}/temp01.dbf	TEMP	60

Control Files

Table 6-4 shows the control files created by DBCA. It is conventional to triply mirror the control file because it is critical. However, at least one mirror copy should be placed in a different location for extra safety—this is not automatically performed by DBCA.

Table 6-4. Control Files

Name
{ORACLE_BASE}/oradata/{DB_UNIQUE_NAME}/control01.ctl
{ORACLE_BASE}/fast_recovery_area/{DB_UNIQUE_NAME}/control02.ctl

Redo Log Groups

Table 6-5 shows the redo log groups created by DBCA. It is conventional to create at least three redo log groups; high-volume environments need even more. Mirroring the redo log files is recommended—DBCA does not do this automatically. Also, the sizes chosen by DBCA are fairly low.

Table 6-5. Redo Log Groups

Group	Size (KB)
1	51,200
2	51,200
3	51,200

Basic Database Administration Tasks

The most basic database administration tasks are stopping and starting the database and the listener. First you must define the environment variables ORACLE_SID and ORACLE_HOME correctly. You do so using the oraenv program, as follows:

```
[oracle@localhost ~]$ source oraenv
ORACLE_SID = [orcl] ? orcl2
The Oracle base has been set to /u01/app/oracle
```

Stopping the Database

You typically stop the database before stopping the listener. Let's stop the database first:

```
[oracle@localhost ~]$ sqlplus "/ as sysdba"

SQL*Plus: Release 12.1.0.1.0 Production on Mon Aug 4 02:59:55 2014

Copyright (c) 1982, 2013, Oracle.  All rights reserved.
```

```
Connected to:
Oracle Database 12c Release 12.1.0.1.0 - 64bit Production

SQL> shutdown immediate;
Database closed.
Database dismounted.
ORACLE instance shut down.
SQL> exit
Disconnected from Oracle Database 12c Release 12.1.0.1.0 - 64bit Production
```

Stopping the Listener

After stopping the database, you can stop the listener:

```
[oracle@localhost ~]$ lsnrctl stop listener2

LSNRCTL for Linux: Version 12.1.0.1.0 - Production on 04-AUG-2014 03:00:53

Copyright (c) 1991, 2013, Oracle.  All rights reserved.

Connecting to (DESCRIPTION=(ADDRESS=(PROTOCOL=TCP)(HOST=localhost)(PORT=1522)))
The command completed successfully
```

Starting the Listener

The listener is typically started before starting the database. Let's start the listener first:

```
[oracle@localhost ~]$ lsnrctl start listener2

LSNRCTL for Linux: Version 12.1.0.1.0 - Production on 04-AUG-2014 03:03:44

Copyright (c) 1991, 2013, Oracle.  All rights reserved.

Starting /u01/app/oracle/product/12.1.0/dbhome_2/bin/tnslsnr: please wait...

TNSLSNR for Linux: Version 12.1.0.1.0 - Production
System parameter file is /u01/app/oracle/product/12.1.0/dbhome_2/network/admin/listener.ora
Log messages written to /u01/app/oracle/diag/tnslsnr/localhost/listener2/alert/log.xml
Listening on: (DESCRIPTION=(ADDRESS=(PROTOCOL=tcp)(HOST=localhost)(PORT=1522)))
Listening on: (DESCRIPTION=(ADDRESS=(PROTOCOL=ipc)(KEY=EXTPROC1522)))

Connecting to (DESCRIPTION=(ADDRESS=(PROTOCOL=TCP)(HOST=localhost)(PORT=1522)))
STATUS of the LISTENER
------------------------
Alias                     listener2
Version                   TNSLSNR for Linux: Version 12.1.0.1.0 - Production
Start Date                04-AUG-2014 03:03:44
Uptime                    0 days 0 hr. 0 min. 0 sec
Trace Level               off
Security                  ON: Local OS Authentication
```

```
SNMP                        OFF
Listener Parameter File     /u01/app/oracle/product/12.1.0/dbhome_2/network/admin/listener.ora
Listener Log File           /u01/app/oracle/diag/tnslsnr/localhost/listener2/alert/log.xml
Listening Endpoints Summary...
  (DESCRIPTION=(ADDRESS=(PROTOCOL=tcp)(HOST=localhost)(PORT=1522)))
  (DESCRIPTION=(ADDRESS=(PROTOCOL=ipc)(KEY=EXTPROC1522)))
The listener supports no services
The command completed successfully
```

Starting the Database

After starting the listener, you can start the database:

```
[oracle@localhost ~]$ sqlplus "/ as sysdba"

SQL*Plus: Release 12.1.0.1.0 Production on Mon Aug 4 03:03:52 2014

Copyright (c) 1982, 2013, Oracle.  All rights reserved.

Connected to an idle instance.

SQL> startup
ORACLE instance started.

Total System Global Area  438423552 bytes
Fixed Size                  2289304 bytes
Variable Size             255852904 bytes
Database Buffers          176160768 bytes
Redo Buffers                4120576 bytes
Database mounted.
Database opened.
SQL> exit
Disconnected from Oracle Database 12c Release 12.1.0.1.0 - 64bit Production
```

Enterprise Manager Database Express

As mentioned earlier, Enterprise Manager Database Express is a lightweight browser-based tool suitable for common database administration tasks (other than stopping and starting the database or listener). You first need to open port 5500 on the VM. Switch to the root account using the su - command; the password is oracle. Modify the /etc/sysconfig/iptables file as shown next. You can either edit the file directly or use the sed command as shown. The extra line you need is shown in boldface; it is similar to the line for port 22, the ssh port:

```
[oracle@localhost ~]$ su -
Password:

[root@localhost ~]# cat /etc/sysconfig/iptables
# Generated by iptables-save v1.4.7 on Sun Aug  3 22:31:09 2014
*filter
:INPUT ACCEPT [0:0]
```

```
:FORWARD ACCEPT [0:0]
:OUTPUT ACCEPT [0:0]
-A INPUT -m state --state RELATED,ESTABLISHED -j ACCEPT
-A INPUT -p icmp -j ACCEPT
-A INPUT -i lo -j ACCEPT
-A INPUT -p tcp -m state --state NEW -m tcp --dport 22 -j ACCEPT
-A INPUT -p tcp -m state --state NEW -m tcp --dport 1521 -j ACCEPT
-A INPUT -j REJECT --reject-with icmp-host-prohibited
-A FORWARD -j REJECT --reject-with icmp-host-prohibited
COMMIT
# Completed on Sun Aug  3 22:31:09 2014


[root@localhost ~]# sed -i '/dport 22/a-A INPUT -p tcp -m state --state
NEW -m tcp --dport 5500 -j ACCEPT' /etc/sysconfig/iptables


[root@localhost ~]# cat /etc/sysconfig/iptables
# Generated by iptables-save v1.4.7 on Sun Aug  3 22:31:09 2014
*filter
:INPUT ACCEPT [0:0]
:FORWARD ACCEPT [0:0]
:OUTPUT ACCEPT [0:0]
-A INPUT -m state --state RELATED,ESTABLISHED -j ACCEPT
-A INPUT -p icmp -j ACCEPT
-A INPUT -i lo -j ACCEPT
-A INPUT -p tcp -m state --state NEW -m tcp --dport 22 -j ACCEPT
-A INPUT -p tcp -m state --state NEW -m tcp --dport 5500 -j ACCEPT
-A INPUT -p tcp -m state --state NEW -m tcp --dport 1521 -j ACCEPT
-A INPUT -j REJECT --reject-with icmp-host-prohibited
-A FORWARD -j REJECT --reject-with icmp-host-prohibited
COMMIT
# Completed on Sun Aug  3 22:31:09 2014


[root@localhost ~]# /etc/init.d/iptables restart
iptables: Setting chains to policy ACCEPT: filter         [  OK  ]
iptables: Flushing firewall rules:                        [  OK  ]
iptables: Unloading modules:                              [  OK  ]
iptables: Applying firewall rules:                        [  OK  ]
```

The URL was displayed by DBCA after it created the database. Replace localhost with the IP address of your VM. The screen shown in Figure 6-21 is displayed.

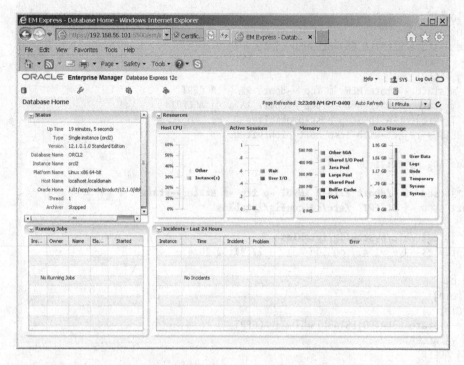

Figure 6-21. *Home screen of Enterprise Manager Database Express*

Summary

Here is a short summary of the concepts touched on in this chapter.

- You can use NetCA to configure a listener. You can use DBCA to create a database, reconfigure existing databases, delete a database, and manage database templates.

- A database template is a copy of all the settings used to create a previous database.

- Oracle provides three database templates: General Purpose or Transaction Processing, Custom Database, and Data Warehouse.

- Saving your work as a template allows you to review your work later; it also lets you create other databases using the same settings.

CHAPTER 7

■ ■ ■

Physical Database Design

In most people's vocabularies, design means veneer. It's interior decorating. It's the fabric of the curtains and the sofa. But to me, nothing could be further from the meaning of design. Design is the fundamental soul of a man-made creation that ends up expressing itself in successive outer layers of the product or service.

—Apple CEO Steve Jobs, interviewed in Fortune magazine; January 24, 2000

The two stages of database design are *logical* and *physical* design. Logical database design, also referred to as *data modeling*, is done first. It is the process of studying the workings of a business organization, constructing a set of tables to store the business data, and understanding the constraints on the data, the dependencies between the tables, and the business rules concerning the data. The logical database design process is conducted without reference to any specific database technology such as Oracle or Microsoft SQL Server. Tools such as SQL Developer Data Modeler and Toad Data Modeler can be used for the purpose. *Physical* database design follows logical database design. First, the logical model is mapped to the proprietary features of the chosen database technology. Security requirements, integrity requirements, and business rules are also implemented. Finally, you consider performance: the ability of the database engine to handle work requests efficiently. This typically involves the creation of *indexes* on the data, and Oracle Database provides a wealth of indexing mechanisms to choose from.

Performance considerations can come to the forefront at any time during the life of the database; new queries can be introduced whenever you like. Database administrators must therefore understand the mechanisms that can be used to improve performance.

Three broad categories of performance mechanisms are available for physical database design. *Indexes* can be used to quickly find data. *Partitions* and *clusters* can be used to organize data. Finally, *materialized views* and *denormalized tables* can be used to perform expensive operations like joins ahead of time.

Indexes

An Oracle index is analogous to the index of words at the back of this book. For example, if you wanted to quickly locate information about indexes in this book, you would refer to the index at the back of this book, which would direct you to this page. Similarly, an Oracle index allows Oracle to quickly locate a row of data that satisfies a query. Consider this query: SELECT * FROM employee WHERE last_name = 'FERNANDEZ'. If an index of last names was available, Oracle could quickly identify rows of data that satisfy the query. For each row of data in the table, this index would store the ROWID (address) of the row together with the value of LAST_NAME. In the absence of the index, Oracle would be forced to check every row of data in the table. Note that an index is tied to a single table; the following command creates an index of last names and gives it the name employee_i1:

```
CREATE INDEX employee_i1 ON employee(last_name)
```

Paradoxically, the use of an index does not always reduce the time taken to process a query. To understand why this might be so, suppose that you wanted to underline all lines in this book containing the word *the*. A great many lines would qualify, and it would be faster to read the entire book, underlining as you went, instead of flipping back and forth between the index and the pages of the book. Now, consider the query `SELECT * FROM employee WHERE hire_date > '1-Jan-1900'`. It is very probable that a large percentage of data rows in the employee table will satisfy the query. Suppose that an index of hire dates is available. It would be faster to retrieve all rows of data in the quickest possible manner—that is, to scan the full table—than to flip back and forth from the index to the table. The decision to use an index is left to the query optimizer, which uses statistical information such as histograms to make its decisions.

More than one data item in a table may need to be indexed. However, a proliferation of indexes can negatively impact efficiency. To understand why, consider that Oracle must update all the relevant indexes whenever the data in a table is modified; for example, when a new row of data is inserted, Oracle must create a new index record in every single one of the indexes associated with the table. When a row of data is deleted, Oracle must delete the corresponding index record from every index associated with the table. And, of course, indexes themselves require space in the database.

■ **Tip**   Use the `MONITORING USAGE` clause of the `CREATE INDEX` or `ALTER INDEX` command to track whether your indexes are being used by your queries.

Unique vs. Non-Unique Indexes

Sometimes, the collection of indexed values should not include duplicates. For example, no two employees should have the same employee ID number. You can use the `UNIQUE` clause of the `CREATE INDEX` command to enforce the uniqueness requirement, as in the following example:

```
CREATE UNIQUE INDEX employee_i1 ON employee(employee_ID)
```

Concatenated Indexes

Consider the following query, which retrieves all red cars registered in the state of California: `SELECT * FROM automobile WHERE state = 'CA' and color = 'RED'`. The query would probably benefit from an index of states or an index of colors, but an even more selective index would be an index of state and color *combinations*. The following command creates an index of state and color combinations and names it `automobile_i1`:

```
CREATE INDEX automobile_i1 ON automobile(state, color)
```

Oracle is capable of using the information in a concatenated index even if all relevant data items are not restricted in the SQL query. Instead of separate indexes, one of states and one of colors, let's suppose that a concatenated index has been created as in the previous paragraph. Also suppose that the query specifies only the state or the color but not both. Oracle can use the concatenated index even in such a case. For example, consider the query `SELECT * FROM automobile WHERE state = 'CA'`. In this case, it makes perfect sense to use the concatenated index described in the previous paragraph. Now consider the query `SELECT * FROM automobile WHERE color = 'RED'`. Because color is not the leading item in the concatenated index, it may appear at first sight that the concatenated index is not useful. However, Oracle can check the index 50 times, once for each state in the union, and thus identify rows satisfying both restrictions. It makes sense to do so because indexes are relatively compact objects, compared to tables. Also, database indexes are structured for easy lookup, just as the index of keywords at the back of this book is sorted in alphabetical order.

Function-Based Indexes

Indexes of the type considered so far are not as useful if the restrictions listed in the query include anything more complex than simple equality and inequality checks. For example, an index of salaries will not help if you are trying to identify employees for whom the *total* of salary and bonus is greater than a certain amount. Therefore, Oracle provides the ability to create indexes of the results of expressions. For example, the following command creates an index of the total of salary and bonus:

```
CREATE INDEX employee_i3 ON (salary + bonus)
```

Structure of an Index

Oracle indexes are structured for ease of use. To consider why structure is important, observe that the index of words at the back of this book would be far less useful if it were not sorted in alphabetical order. The typical Oracle index is a *balanced tree* or *b-tree*. The details are beyond the scope of this introductory text, but suffice it to say that the indexing information is stored in the "leaves" of a balanced tree as illustrated in Figure 7-1.

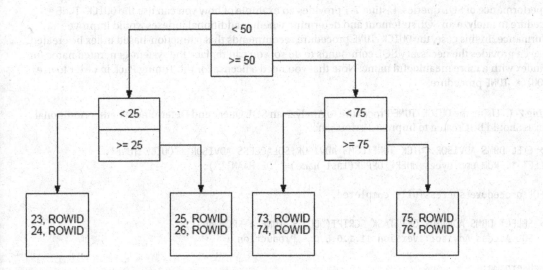

Figure 7-1. A balanced tree

What Indexes to Create?

Which indexes to create is a question that is not easily answered. The temptation is to create too many, but it is equally easy to forget to create any. Oracle will do the best it can with the available indexes, and powerful modern hardware can sometimes compensate for the lack of appropriate indexes. A commonly used rule is to create an index for every column that is restricted in a query. This may be too many, because the query optimizer bases the decision to use an index on the available statistical information about the table, and some indexes may never be used. Also, as I explained earlier, indexes must be modified whenever the data is modified; and, therefore, indexes can slow down the database. However, there are some situations where indexes are not optional:

- Unique indexes are required to efficiently enforce the requirement of uniqueness; for example, no two employees can share a Social Security number. This is particularly true of any column or combination of columns designated as a primary key.

- Indexes should always be created on foreign keys. A *foreign key* is a column or set of columns that is required to map to the primary key of another table. Full table scans and table-level locks can result if a foreign key is not indexed. In *Expert One-On-One Oracle*, Tom Kyte says: "I sometimes wish I had a dollar for every time I was able to solve the insolvable hanging issue by simply running the query to detect un-indexed foreign keys and suggesting that we index the one causing the problem—I would be very rich." Tom provides the script in the book—it can also be found at http://tkyte.blogspot.com/2009/10/httpasktomoraclecomtkyteunindex.html.

Oracle Database provides several "advisors" that can generate recommendations for improving the performance of SQL queries. Listing 7-1 provides an example of how you can use the QUICK_TUNE procedure to analyze an SQL statement and determine whether additional indexes would improve performance. In this case, the QUICK_TUNE procedure recommends that a function-based index be created and even provides the necessary SQL commands to do so; you can replace the system-generated name for the index with a more meaningful name. Note that you need a license for the Tuning Pack in order to use the QUICK_TUNE procedure.

Listing 7-1. Using the QUICK_TUNE Procedure to Analyze an SQL Query and Determine Whether Additional Indexes Should Be Created to Improve Performance

```
SQL> EXEC DBMS_ADVISOR.QUICK_TUNE(DBMS_ADVISOR.SQLACCESS_ADVISOR, 'QUICK_TUNE',
'SELECT * FROM employees WHERE UPPER(last_name)=''DE HAAN''');

PL/SQL procedure successfully completed.

SQL> SELECT DBMS_ADVISOR.GET_TASK_SCRIPT('QUICK_TUNE') FROM dual;
Rem   SQL Access Advisor: Version 11.1.0.6.0 - Production
Rem
Rem   Username:         HR
Rem   Task:             QUICK_TUNE
Rem   Execution date:
Rem

CREATE INDEX "HR"."EMPLOYEES_IDX$$_00440000"
    ON "HR"."EMPLOYEES"
    (UPPER("LAST_NAME"))
    COMPUTE STATISTICS;
```

Index-Organized Tables

Ordinary Oracle tables are often referred to as *heaps* because the data they contain is not sorted in any way; separate structures—indexes—are needed in order to identify the records of interest efficiently. The *index-organized table* (*IOT*) is a single structure that unites a table and an index for its primary key. No separate index for the primary key is necessary, because the table itself is structured exactly as if it were an index for the primary key; all the non-key data is stored on the leaf blocks together with the key data. Indexes for other columns can be created in precisely the same way as indexes on ordinary tables.

Index-organized tables have a number of advantages. The union of table and primary key index in a single structure results in increased efficiency of retrieval operations. Certain maintenance operations (such as the MOVE operation) can be performed on them without invalidating all the indexes. Finally, index-organized tables can offer dramatic performance improvements if the primary key is composed of multiple data items and the leading item partitions the data in a natural way: for example, the store name in a table that contains sales data. The performance improvement comes from the physical clustering of related data that naturally results, the increased likelihood of finding the required data in the buffer cache, and the consequent reduction in disk activity.

Advanced Topics

An advanced type of index known as the *bitmap index* uses a single bit (0 or 1) to represent each row. A *bitmap* is generated for each distinct value contained in the indexed column.

If the indexed column contains ever-increasing values, Oracle attempts to insert the index information into the same leaf block each time. This dramatically increases the frequency of splitting and balancing operations. The solution is to create a reverse key index.

Partitioning

Because Oracle tables are stored as heaps, with no discernible internal organization, new rows of data are simply appended to the end of the table or anywhere else in the table there happens to be room. The strategy of using indexes to find the required rows of data quickly works well up to a point. But it begins to reveal its limitations as the amount of data and the number of users approach the levels seen in modern data warehouses and in online stores such as Amazon.com.

To understand the problem with heaps, imagine a history book containing facts like the following: "The Declaration of Independence was adopted by the Second Continental Congress on July 4, 1776." Suppose that these facts are not naturally organized into separate chapters for, say, individual countries, but are randomly scattered throughout the book. You can still use the alphabetical index at the back of the book to discover facts about the United States relatively easily; but each time you retrieve a fact, you may have to visit a different page. This would obviously not be an efficient process.

A page of a book is analogous to a data block on a storage disk, and a chapter of related information in a book is analogous to an Oracle *partition*. Partitions divide data tables into separate storage pools; rows of data can be allocated to each storage pool using some criterion. Suppose you have a very large table of credit-card transactions, and they are randomly stored throughout the table without regard to date. To process the transactions completed in the last month, Oracle must retrieve more blocks of data from the storage disks than if transactions were stored with regard to date. The solution is to create a separate partition for each month. If a query spans partitions, Oracle need only visit the appropriate partitions; this is called *partition pruning*.

Oracle provides several methods of partitioning large tables, including list partitioning, range partitioning, and interval partitioning. The partitions can themselves be subpartitioned. Indexes can also be partitioned, and it makes a lot of sense to do so.

■ **Tip**   Partitioning is a separately licensed, extra-cost option and must be purchased together with Oracle
Enterprise Edition; it cannot be used with Oracle Standard Edition or with Oracle Express Edition.

Advantages of Partitioning

I have already alluded to the fact that partitioning may improve performance of SQL queries by reducing the
number of data blocks that have to be retrieved from the storage disks, but this is not the only advantage.
Here are some others:

- A join operation on two tables that are partitioned in the same manner can be parallelized.
  That is, Oracle can perform simultaneous join operations, each one joining a partition
  of one table to the related partition in the other table; the results are pooled. This
  technique is suitable when you are dealing with large data warehouses; it requires more
  computing power but can reduce the time required to process an SQL query.

- Partitions make it particularly easy to purge unneeded data. Dropping a partition
  can be a painless operation; deleting large numbers of records from an unpartitioned
  table is a resource-intensive operation.

- Making a backup copy of a large data warehouse is a time-consuming and
  resource-intensive operation. If the data in an old partition does not need to be
  modified and the partition is located in a dedicated tablespace, the tablespace
  can be put into read-only mode and one last backup copy of the tablespace can be
  created for archival purposes. From that point onward, the tablespace need not be
  included in backup copies.

- If an old partition cannot be removed from the database, an alternative is to move
  it to slower and cheaper storage. The faster and more expensive storage can be
  reserved for more current and frequently queried data.

- Maintenance operations can be performed on individual partitions without affecting
  the availability of the rest of the data in the rest of the table. For example, old
  partitions can be moved to cheaper storage without impacting the availability of the
  data in the rest of the table.

List Partitioning

In this form of partition, the refinancing criterion for each partition is a list of values. Consider a retail
chain that has stores in three states. You might store sales data in a table created in the manner illustrated
in Listing 7-2.

Listing 7-2. Example of List Partitioning

```
CREATE TABLE sales
(
    item# INTEGER,
    quantity INTEGER,
    store_name VARCHAR(30),
    state_code VARCHAR(2),
    sale_date DATE
)
```

```
PARTITION BY LIST (state_code)
(
    PARTITION california VALUES ('CA'),
    PARTITION oregon VALUES ('OR'),
    PARTITION washington VALUES ('WA')
);
```

Range Partitioning

In this form of partition, the refinancing criterion for each partition is a range of values. In the case described in the previous section, you might alternatively store sales data in a table created in the manner illustrated in Listing 7-3.

Listing 7-3. Example of Range Partitioning

```
CREATE TABLE sales
(
    item# INTEGER,
    quantity INTEGER,
    store_name VARCHAR(30),
    state_code VARCHAR(2),
    sale_date DATE
)
PARTITION BY RANGE (sale_date)
(
    PARTITION olddata VALUES LESS THAN (TO_DATE('01-JAN-2008','DD-MON-YYYY')),
    PARTITION jan2008 VALUES LESS THAN (TO_DATE('01-FEB-2008','DD-MON-YYYY')),
    PARTITION feb2008 VALUES LESS THAN (TO_DATE('01-MAR-2008','DD-MON-YYYY')),
    PARTITION mar2008 VALUES LESS THAN (TO_DATE('01-APR-2008','DD-MON-YYYY')),
    PARTITION apr2008 VALUES LESS THAN (TO_DATE('01-MAY-2008','DD-MON-YYYY')),
    PARTITION may2008 VALUES LESS THAN (TO_DATE('01-JUN-2008','DD-MON-YYYY')),
    PARTITION jun2008 VALUES LESS THAN (TO_DATE('01-JUL-2008','DD-MON-YYYY')),
    PARTITION jul2008 VALUES LESS THAN (TO_DATE('01-AUG-2008','DD-MON-YYYY')),
    PARTITION aug2008 VALUES LESS THAN (TO_DATE('01-SEP-2008','DD-MON-YYYY')),
    PARTITION sep2008 VALUES LESS THAN (TO_DATE('01-OCT-2008','DD-MON-YYYY')),
    PARTITION oct2008 VALUES LESS THAN (TO_DATE('01-NOV-2008','DD-MON-YYYY')),
    PARTITION nov2008 VALUES LESS THAN (TO_DATE('01-DEC-2008','DD-MON-YYYY')),
    PARTITION dec2008 VALUES LESS THAN (TO_DATE('01-JAN-2009','DD-MON-YYYY'))
); .
```

Interval Partitioning

One difficulty with partitioning by monotonically increasing data items such as dates is that new partitions have to be periodically added to the table; this can be accomplished using the ADD PARTITION clause of the ALTER TABLE command. Interval partitioning eliminates this difficulty by having Oracle automatically create new partitions as necessary. The example in the previous section can be rewritten as illustrated in Listing 7-4. Only one partition called olddata is initially created. New partitions are automatically created by Oracle as necessary when data is inserted into the table.

Listing 7-4. Example of Interval Partitioning

```
CREATE TABLE sales
(
    item# INTEGER,
    quantity INTEGER,
    store_name VARCHAR(30),
    state_code VARCHAR(2),
    sale_date DATE
)
PARTITION BY RANGE (sale_date)
INTERVAL(NUMTOYMINTERVAL(1, 'MONTH'))
(
    PARTITION olddata VALUES LESS THAN (TO_DATE('01-JAN-2008','DD-MON-YYYY'))
);
```

Hash Partitioning

Hash partitioning was useful before large RAID arrays became commonplace; it can be used to *stripe* data across multiple disks in order to prevent the reading and writing speed of a single disk from becoming a performance bottleneck in OLTP and other environments requiring very high levels of throughput. A *hashing function* (randomizing function) is applied to the data item used as the partitioning criterion in order to allocate new rows to partitions randomly. Listing 7-5 illustrates the use of this technique; the data is spread over four tablespaces, which are presumably located on separate disk drives.

Listing 7-5. Example of Hash Partitioning

```
CREATE TABLE sales
(
    item# INTEGER,
    quantity INTEGER,
    store_name VARCHAR(30),
    state_code VARCHAR(2),
    sale_date DATE
)
PARTITION BY HASH (sale_date)
PARTITIONS 4
STORE IN (data1, data2, data3, data4); .
```

Reference Partitioning

Sometimes it makes sense to partition two or more tables using the same data item as the partitioning criterion *even though the tables do not share the data item.* As an example, consider the Orders and LineItems tables in Listing 7-6. The two tables are linked by the purchase order number. It makes sense to partition the Orders table using the OrderDate data item. It would also make sense to partition the LineItems table using the same data item as the criterion *even though it is not part of the table.* This can be accomplished using *referential partitioning.* Any number of tables can thus be partitioned using a common partitioning criterion that *appears in only one of the tables.*

Listing 7-6. Example of Reference Partitioning

```
CREATE TABLE Orders
(
    PONo NUMBER(5),
    Custno NUMBER(3),
    OrderDate DATE,
    ShipDate DATE,
    ToStreet VARCHAR2(20),
    ToCity VARCHAR2(20),
    ToState CHAR(2),
    ToZip VARCHAR2(10),
    CONSTRAINT Orders_PK PRIMARY KEY (PONo),
    CONSTRAINT Orders_FK1 FOREIGN KEY (CustNo) REFERENCES Customers
)
PARTITION BY RANGE (OrderDate)
(
    PARTITION olddata VALUES LESS THAN (TO_DATE('01-JAN-2008','DD-MON-YYYY')),
    PARTITION jan2008 VALUES LESS THAN (TO_DATE('01-FEB-2008','DD-MON-YYYY')),
    PARTITION feb2008 VALUES LESS THAN (TO_DATE('01-MAR-2008','DD-MON-YYYY')),
    PARTITION mar2008 VALUES LESS THAN (TO_DATE('01-APR-2008','DD-MON-YYYY')),
    PARTITION apr2008 VALUES LESS THAN (TO_DATE('01-MAY-2008','DD-MON-YYYY')),
    PARTITION may2008 VALUES LESS THAN (TO_DATE('01-JUN-2008','DD-MON-YYYY')),
    PARTITION jun2008 VALUES LESS THAN (TO_DATE('01-JUL-2008','DD-MON-YYYY')),
    PARTITION jul2008 VALUES LESS THAN (TO_DATE('01-AUG-2008','DD-MON-YYYY')),
    PARTITION aug2008 VALUES LESS THAN (TO_DATE('01-SEP-2008','DD-MON-YYYY')),
    PARTITION sep2008 VALUES LESS THAN (TO_DATE('01-OCT-2008','DD-MON-YYYY')),
    PARTITION oct2008 VALUES LESS THAN (TO_DATE('01-NOV-2008','DD-MON-YYYY')),
    PARTITION nov2008 VALUES LESS THAN (TO_DATE('01-DEC-2008','DD-MON-YYYY')),
    PARTITION dec2008 VALUES LESS THAN (TO_DATE('01-JAN-2009','DD-MON-YYYY'))
);

CREATE TABLE LineItems
(
    LineNo NUMBER(2),
    PONo NUMBER(5) NOT NULL,
    StockNo NUMBER(4),
    Quantity NUMBER(2),
    Discount NUMBER(4,2),
    CONSTRAINT LineItems_PK PRIMARY KEY (LineNo, PONo),
    CONSTRAINT LineItems_FK1 FOREIGN KEY (PONo) REFERENCES Orders,
    CONSTRAINT LineItems_FK2 FOREIGN KEY (StockNo) REFERENCES StockItems
)
PARTITION BY REFERENCE (LineItems_FK1); .
```

Composite Partitioning

Oracle offers the ability to further divide a partition into subpartitions using different criteria; this can make sense if a table is very large. In Listing 7-7, you first create one partition for each month (using the interval partitioning method) and then create subpartitions for each state.

Listing 7-7. Example of List Partitioning

```
CREATE TABLE sales
(
    item# INTEGER,
    quantity INTEGER,
    store_name VARCHAR(30),
    state_code VARCHAR(2),
    sale_date DATE
)
PARTITION BY RANGE (sale_date)
INTERVAL(NUMTOYMINTERVAL(1, 'MONTH'))
SUBPARTITION BY list (state_code)
(
    PARTITION olddata VALUES LESS THAN (TO_DATE('01-JAN-2008','DD-MON-YYYY'))
    (
        SUBPARTITION california VALUES ('CA'),
        SUBPARTITION oregon VALUES ('OR'),
        SUBPARTITION washington VALUES ('WA')
    )
); .
```

Local and Global Indexes

Partitioning a table does not eliminate the need for any of its indexes. However, you must make a design choice for each index; indexes on partitioned tables can be either *local* or *global*. A local index is itself partitioned in exactly the same way as its table; you only need to specify the LOCAL clause when creating the index to automatically create the necessary partitions for the use of the index. Local indexes are most suitable when the query specifies the partitioning criterion. They also promote *partition independence*; that is, they preserve your ability to perform maintenance operations on a partition without impacting the availability of the rest of the data in the table. Global indexes are most suitable when the query does not specify the partitioning criterion. A global index may or may not be partitioned and can even have a different partition scheme than its table.

Partitioned Views

The partitioning capabilities you have just learned about were introduced in Oracle 8 and have their roots in much older capabilities called *partition views* or—more properly—*partitioned views*. Partition views are simply views formed by the UNION ALL of separate tables, each of which contains a range of data values. The following paragraph is found in the Oracle7 Tuning guide:

> *You can avoid downtime with very large or mission-critical tables by using partition views. You create a partition view by dividing a large table into multiple physical tables using partitioning criteria. Then create a UNION-ALL view of the partitions to make the partitioning transparent for queries. Queries that use a key range to select from a partition view retrieve only the partitions that fall within that range. In this way partition views offer significant improvements in availability, administration and table scan performance.*

Partitioned views do not offer all the features of the partitioning feature, but the prime reason to consider them is that—unlike regular partitions—they can be used with Standard Edition.

Consider the Sales fact table from the SH sample schema, one of the sample schemas provided by Oracle. The Sales table has five *dimensions*—product, customer, time, channel, and promotion—and two *measurements*—quantity sold and amount sold. It is partitioned into 28 partitions using the time dimension. The five dimensions are linked by foreign key constraints to the dimension tables, and there is a bitmap index on each of the dimensions. Here is the definition of the table:

```
CREATE TABLE SALES
(
  -- dimensions
  PROD_ID NUMBER NOT NULL,
  CUST_ID NUMBER NOT NULL,
  TIME_ID DATE NOT ENABLE,
  CHANNEL_ID NUMBER NOT NULL,
  PROMO_ID NUMBER NOT NULL,
  -- measurements
  QUANTITY_SOLD NUMBER(10,2) NOT NULL,
  AMOUNT_SOLD NUMBER(10,2) NOT NULL,
  -- constraints
  CONSTRAINT SALES_CHANNEL_FK FOREIGN KEY (CHANNEL_ID) REFERENCES SH.CHANNELS (CHANNEL_ID),
  CONSTRAINT SALES_TIME_FK FOREIGN KEY (TIME_ID) REFERENCES SH.TIMES (TIME_ID),
  CONSTRAINT SALES_PRODUCT_FK FOREIGN KEY (PROD_ID) REFERENCES SH.PRODUCTS (PROD_ID),
  CONSTRAINT SALES_CUSTOMER_FK FOREIGN KEY (CUST_ID) REFERENCES SH.CUSTOMERS (CUST_ID),
  CONSTRAINT SALES_PROMO_FK FOREIGN KEY (PROMO_ID) REFERENCES SH.PROMOTIONS (PROMO_ID)
)
-- partition by the time dimension
PARTITION BY RANGE (TIME_ID)
(
  -- annual partitions for 1995 and 1996
  PARTITION SALES_1995 VALUES LESS THAN '1996-01-01',
  PARTITION SALES_1996 VALUES LESS THAN '1997-01-01',
  -- semi-annual partitions for 1997
  PARTITION SALES_H1_1997 VALUES LESS THAN '1997-07-01',
  PARTITION SALES_H2_1997 VALUES LESS THAN '1998-01-01',
  -- quarterly partitions for 1998
  PARTITION SALES_Q1_1998 VALUES LESS THAN '1998-04-01',
  PARTITION SALES_Q2_1998 VALUES LESS THAN '1998-07-01',
  PARTITION SALES_Q3_1998 VALUES LESS THAN '1998-10-01',
  PARTITION SALES_Q4_1998 VALUES LESS THAN '1999-01-01',
  … intervening sections for 1999, 2000, 2001, and 2002 not shown
  -- quarterly partitions for 2003
  PARTITION SALES_Q1_2003 VALUES LESS THAN '2003-04-01',
  PARTITION SALES_Q2_2003 VALUES LESS THAN '2003-07-01',
  PARTITION SALES_Q3_2003 VALUES LESS THAN '2003-10-01',
  PARTITION SALES_Q4_2003 VALUES LESS THAN '2004-01-01'
);
```

And here are the definitions of the five indexes on each partition. The keyword LOCAL means the indexes are partitioned in the same manner as the table. In other words, each partition has a local index:

```
CREATE BITMAP INDEX SALES_CHANNEL_BIX ON SALES (CHANNEL_ID) LOCAL;
CREATE BITMAP INDEX SALES_CUST_BIX ON SALES (CUST_ID) LOCAL;
CREATE BITMAP INDEX SALES_PROD_BIX ON SALES (PROD_ID) LOCAL;
CREATE BITMAP INDEX SALES_PROMO_BIX ON SALES (PROMO_ID) LOCAL;
CREATE BITMAP INDEX SALES_TIME_BIX ON SALES (TIME_ID) LOCAL;
```

Let's work on recasting the Sales table into a partition view composed of 28 separate tables with the same names as the partitions of the original table, each with its own indexes. Although this may seem like an unnecessary proliferation of tables and indexes, remember that table and index partitions are also independent, have explicitly assigned storage, and can be independently maintained. Here are the table-creation statements for four quarters of data:

```
CREATE TABLE SALES_Q1_2003 AS
  SELECT * FROM sales PARTITION (SALES_Q1_2003) NOLOGGING;

CREATE TABLE SALES_Q2_2003 AS
  SELECT * FROM sales PARTITION (SALES_Q2_2003) NOLOGGING;

CREATE TABLE SALES_Q3_2003 AS
  SELECT * FROM sales PARTITION (SALES_Q3_2003) NOLOGGING;

CREATE TABLE SALES_Q4_2003 AS
  SELECT * FROM sales PARTITION (SALES_Q4_2003) NOLOGGING;
```

Next, let's create *check constraints* on the time dimension for each of the 28 tables. These check constraints are critical to the success of the partition view; you need some way to ensure that data is not inserted into the wrong table. Here are some examples:

```
-- the oldest table is only bounded on one side and may contain data from prior years
ALTER TABLE SALES_1995 ADD CONSTRAINT SALES_1995_C1 CHECK
 (time_id < '1996-01-01');

-- tables other than the SALES_1995 table are bounded on both sides
ALTER TABLE SALES_Q1_1998 ADD CONSTRAINT SALES_Q1_1998_C1 check
  (time_id >= '1998-01-01' AND time_id < '1998-04-01');

ALTER TABLE SALES_Q1_1998 ADD CONSTRAINT SALES_Q2_1998_C1 check
  (time_id >= '1998-04-01' AND time_id < '1998-07-01');

ALTER TABLE SALES_Q1_1998 ADD CONSTRAINT SALES_Q3_1998_C1 check
  (time_id >= '1998-07-01' AND time_id < '1998-10-01');

ALTER TABLE SALES_Q1_1998 ADD CONSTRAINT SALES_Q4_1998_C1 check
  (time_id >= '1998-10-01' AND time_id < '1999-01-01');
```

You need to create bitmap indexes on the individual tables that make up the partition views. Each of the 28 partitions has 5 bitmap indexes, for a total of 140 indexes:

```
CREATE BITMAP INDEX SALES_Q1_1998_SALES_CHAN_BIX ON SALES_Q1_1998(channel_id);
CREATE BITMAP INDEX SALES_Q1_1998_SALES_CUST_BIX ON SALES_Q1_1998(cust_id);
CREATE BITMAP INDEX SALES_Q1_1998_SALES_PROD_BIX ON SALES_Q1_1998(prod_id);
CREATE BITMAP INDEX SALES_Q1_1998_SALES_PROM_BIX ON SALES_Q1_1998(promo_id);
```

You also need to add foreign key constraints on the individual partitions. Each of the 28 partitions has 5 constraints, for a total of 140 constraints:

```
ALTER TABLE SALES_Q1_1998 ADD CONSTRAINT SALES_Q1_1998_CHAN_FK
  FOREIGN KEY (channel_id) REFERENCES channels;

ALTER TABLE SALES_Q1_1998 ADD CONSTRAINT SALES_Q1_1998_CUST_FK
  FOREIGN KEY (cust_id) REFERENCES customers;

ALTER TABLE SALES_Q1_1998 ADD CONSTRAINT
  SALES_Q1_1998_PROD_FK FOREIGN KEY (prod_id) REFERENCES products;

ALTER TABLE SALES_Q1_1998 ADD CONSTRAINT SALES_Q1_1998_PROM_FK
  FOREIGN KEY (promo_id) REFERENCES promotions;

ALTER TABLE SALES_Q1_1998 ADD CONSTRAINT SALES_Q1_1998_TIME_FK
  FOREIGN KEY (time_id) REFERENCES times;
```

You're now ready to create the partition view; let's call it sales2. Notice that the partition view is a UNION ALL of 28 SELECT * sections. Note that each section includes the restriction on the time dimension. This gives the optimizer the information it needs to perform partition pruning during query execution:

```
CREATE OR REPLACE VIEW sales2 AS
SELECT * FROM SALES_1995 WHERE time_id<'1996-01-01'
UNION ALL SELECT * FROM SALES_1996 WHERE time_id >= '1996-01-01' AND time_id<'1997-01-01'
UNION ALL SELECT * FROM SALES_H1_1997 WHERE time_id>='1997-01-01' AND time_id<'1997-07-01'
UNION ALL SELECT * FROM SALES_H2_1997 WHERE time_id>='1997-07-01' AND time_id<'1998-01-01'
UNION ALL SELECT * FROM SALES_Q1_1998 WHERE time_id>='1998-01-01' AND time_id<'1998-04-01'
UNION ALL SELECT * FROM SALES_Q2_1998 WHERE time_id>='1998-04-01' AND time_id<'1998-07-01'
UNION ALL SELECT * FROM SALES_Q3_1998 WHERE time_id>='1998-07-01' AND time_id<'1998-10-01'
UNION ALL SELECT * FROM SALES_Q4_1998 WHERE time_id>='1998-10-01' AND time_id<'1999-01-01'
... intervening lines not shown
UNION ALL SELECT * FROM SALES_Q1_2003 WHERE time_id>='2003-01-01' AND time_id<'2003-04-01'
UNION ALL SELECT * FROM SALES_Q2_2003 WHERE time_id>='2003-04-01' AND time_id<'2003-07-01'
UNION ALL SELECT * FROM SALES_Q3_2003 WHERE time_id>='2003-07-01' AND time_id<'2003-10-01'
UNION ALL SELECT * FROM SALES_Q4_2003 WHERE time_id>='2003-10-01' AND time_id<'2004-01-01';
```

Denormalization and Materialized Views

Denormalization is a technique that is used to improve the efficiency of join operations. Consider the Orders and LineItems tables from the order-management database described in *Oracle Database 11g Java Developer's Guide*. To avoid having to join these tables, you can replace them with a table that contains all the data items from both tables. This eliminates the need to join the two tables frequently, but it introduces its own set of problems. Data items such as ToStreet, ToCity, ToState, and ToZip must now be duplicated if there is more than one line in an order. And if any of these data items needs to be changed, multiple data rows must be updated. The duplication of data thus creates the possibility that mistakes will be made.

You can use materialized views to avoid the problems created by denormalization. Instead of replacing the Orders and LineItems tables with a denormalized table, you could prejoin the tables and store the results in a structure called a *materialized view,* as illustrated in Listing 7-8.

Listing 7-8. Example of a Materialized View

```
CREATE MATERIALIZED VIEW Orders_LineItems
REFRESH ON COMMIT
ENABLE QUERY REWRITE
AS SELECT
    -- data items from the Orders table
    Orders.PONo,
    Orders.Custno,
    Orders.OrderDate,
    Orders.ShipDate,
    Orders.ToStreet,
    Orders.ToCity,
    Orders.ToState,
    Orders.ToZip,
    -- data items from the LineItems table
    LineItems.LineNo,
    LineItems.StockNo,
    LineItems.Quantity,
    LineItems.Discount
FROM Orders, LineItems
WHERE LineItems.PONo = Orders.PONo;
```

The data items from the Orders tables are still duplicated, but the responsibility for accurate modifications to the materialized view rests with Oracle, which modifies the data in the materialized view whenever the data in the underlying tables is modified. For example, if the ToStreet data item of an order is modified, Oracle modifies all occurrences in the materialized view. Note that materialized views need to be indexed just like regular tables and can be partitioned if appropriate.

Materialized views can be directly referenced in SQL queries, but the same level of performance enhancement is obtained even if they are not directly referenced. Notice the ENABLE QUERY REWRITE clause in the command used to create the Orders_LineItems materialized view: the optimizer silently *rewrites* queries and incorporates materialized views if possible.

Clusters

In his book *Effective Oracle by Design* (Osborne Oracle Press, 2003), Tom Kyte quotes Steve Adams as saying, "If a schema has no IOTs or clusters, that is a good indication that no thought has been given to the matter of optimizing data access." Although most people wouldn't agree with Steve's conclusion, it is true that most databases use only the simplest of table and index organizations—heap and b-tree, respectively—and don't exploit the wealth of data-access mechanisms provided by Oracle.

Clusters improve the efficiency of the memory cache (and consequently of join operations) because data from related tables can be stored in the *same* data blocks. Oracle itself uses the cluster mechanism to access some of the most important tables in the data dictionary; the C_OBJ# cluster contains 17 tables including TAB$ (tables), COL$ (columns of tables), IND$ (indexes) and ICOL$ (columns of indexes). Oracle also uses the cluster mechanism in its spectacular TPC benchmarks; in one benchmark that was submitted in February 2007, an Oracle database achieved a throughput of more than 4 million transactions per minute.

Hash clusters provide quick access without the need for an index (if the value of the clustering key is specified in the SQL query). Listing 7-9 first *preallocates* space for a cluster called Orders_LineItems with 10,000 *hash buckets*, each of size 2KB. When inserting a new data row in the cluster, Oracle uses a *hash function* to convert the cluster key (PONo in this case) into the address of a random hash bucket where it will store the row. When the row is retrieved later, all Oracle has to do is use the same hash function to locate the row.

You use the cluster to store rows from the Orders table as well as the LineItems table, which means related rows from the LineItems table are stored in the same storage bucket al*ong with the corresponding row from the* Orders *table*. SQL queries that join the two tables and specify what value the PONo data item should have can now be expected to be very efficient.

Listing 7-9. Example of a Cluster

```
CREATE CLUSTER Orders_LineItems (PONo NUMBER(5))
HASHKEYS 10000 SIZE 2048;

CREATE TABLE Orders
(
    PONo NUMBER(5),
    Custno NUMBER(3),
    OrderDate DATE,
    ShipDate DATE,
    ToStreet VARCHAR2(20),
    ToCity VARCHAR2(20),
    ToState CHAR(2),
    ToZip VARCHAR2(10),
    CONSTRAINT Orders_PK PRIMARY KEY (PONo),
    CONSTRAINT Orders_FK1 FOREIGN KEY (CustNo) REFERENCES Customers
)
CLUSTER Orders_LineItems (PONo);
```

```
CREATE TABLE LineItems
(
    LineNo NUMBER(2),
    PONo NUMBER(5) NOT NULL,
    StockNo NUMBER(4),
    Quantity NUMBER(2),
    Discount NUMBER(4,2),
    CONSTRAINT LineItems_PK PRIMARY KEY (LineNo, PONo),
    CONSTRAINT LineItems_FK1 FOREIGN KEY (PONo) REFERENCES Orders,
    CONSTRAINT LineItems_FK2 FOREIGN KEY (StockNo) REFERENCES StockItems
)
CLUSTER Orders_LineItems (PONo);
```

Summary

Performance considerations can remain at the forefront throughout the life of a database. For example, new queries may be introduced at any time. Database administrators must therefore understand the mechanisms that can be used to improve performance. This chapter provided an overview of these mechanisms. Here is a short summary of the concepts touched on in this chapter:

- The first stage in database design is called logical database design or data modeling and is conducted without reference to any specific database technology such as Oracle or Microsoft SQL Server.

- Physical database design follows logical database design. First, the logical model is mapped to the proprietary data types, language elements, and mechanisms provided by the chosen database technology. Next, security requirements are implemented using the various mechanisms provided by the technology, such as views. Finally, you consider performance—the ability of the database engine to handle work requests efficiently.

- The three broad categories of performance mechanisms are indexes to quickly find data, partitions and clusters to organize data, and materialized views and denormalized tables to perform expensive operations like joins ahead of time.

- An Oracle index is analogous to the index of words at the back of this book and allows Oracle to quickly locate a row of data that satisfies the restrictions of a query. However, indexes don't help much if a large percentage of rows in the table satisfy the restrictions of the query.

- A proliferation of indexes can negatively affect efficiency because Oracle must update all the relevant indexes whenever the data in a table is modified.

- Oracle indexes are structured for ease of use. The typical Oracle index is a balanced tree or b-tree.

- SQL Access Advisor can analyze an SQL query and determine whether an additional index would improve performance.

- An index-organized table (IOT) is a single structure that unites a table and an index for its primary key.

- Partitions divide data tables into separate storage pools. Rows of data can be allocated to each storage pool using some criterion. The partitioning methods provided by Oracle include list partitioning, range partitioning, interval partitioning, reference partitioning, hash partitioning, and composite partitioning.

- Indexes on partitioned tables can be local or global. A local index is itself partitioned in the same way as its table. Local indexes are most suitable when the query specifies the partitioning criterion; they also promote partition independence. Global indexes are most suitable when the query does not specify the partitioning criterion. A global index may or may not be partitioned and can even have a different partition scheme than its table.

- Partitioned views offer some of the advantages of the partitioning feature—partition pruning in particular. They can be used even with Standard Edition.

- Denormalized tables and materialized views can be used to improve the efficiency of join operations. Oracle automatically modifies the data in a materialized view whenever the data in the underlying tables is modified. The optimizer silently rewrites queries and incorporates materialized vies if possible. Materialized views can also be used to aggregate information or to synchronize satellite databases.

- Hash clusters provide quick access without the need for an index (if the value of the clustering key is specified in the SQL query). They improve the efficiency of the memory cache (and consequently of join operations) because data from related tables can be stored in the same data blocks.

CHAPTER 8

■■■

User Management and Data Loading

The woods are lovely, dark and deep.

But I have promises to keep,

And miles to go before I sleep,

And miles to go before I sleep.

"Stopping by Woods on a Snowy Evening" *by Robert Frost*

Your job does not end when you create a database; you still have to get the data into it and ensure that those who need to use it can do so. This chapter discusses how to control users and how to get large amounts of data in and out of databases. User management and data loading are two common chores performed by database administrators.

Schemas

Every object in a database is explicitly owned by a single owner, and the owner of an object must explicitly authorize its use by somebody else. The collection of objects owned by a user is called a *schema*. To illustrate, Listing 8-1 shows a summary of the contents of the HR schema, one of the sample schemas that Oracle provides for educational purposes. Note that the terms *user*, *schema*, *schema owner*, and *account* are used interchangeably; for example, youcan speak of either the HR user or the HR schema.

Listing 8-1. Objects Commonly Found in Schemas

```
[oracle@localhost ~]$ sqlplus sys/oracle as sysdba

SQL*Plus: Release 12.1.0.1.0 Production on Sat Oct 4 13:46:01 2014

Copyright (c) 1982, 2013, Oracle.  All rights reserved.

Connected to:
Oracle Database 12c Enterprise Edition Release 12.1.0.1.0 - 64bit Production
With the Partitioning, OLAP, Advanced Analytics and Real Application Testing options
```

```
PDB1@ORCL> SELECT object_type, COUNT (*)
  2   FROM dba_objects
  3   WHERE owner = 'HR'
  4   GROUP BY object_type
  5   ORDER BY 2 DESC;

OBJECT_TYPE    COUNT(*)
---------------------- ----------
INDEX19
TABLE 7
SEQUENCE 3
PROCEDURE 2
TRIGGER 2
VIEW 1

6 rows selected.

PDB1@ORCL> exit
Disconnected from Oracle Database 12c Enterprise Edition Release 12.1.0.1.0 - 64bit
Production
With the Partitioning, OLAP, Advanced Analytics and Real Application Testing options
```

The object types shown in Listing 8-1 are very common. *Tables* are the containers for your data; *indexes* help you find the data; *sequences* are continuously incrementing counters that generate unique identification numbers for data records; *procedures* are blocks of application logic that are stored in the database; *triggers* are specialized blocks of application logic that are triggered by specific events, such as a data record being added to a table; and *views* are "virtual tables" that can combine data from multiple tables.

Notice that you found the information you needed in a view called DBA_OBJECTS. It is a *dictionary view* in the SYS schema. Because Oracle Database strives to follow the principles of the relational model, it is no surprise that Oracle Database manages objects owned by users using its own tables, indexes, sequences, procedures, triggers, and views; these are stored in the SYS schema. For example, Listing 8-2 shows the contents of the SYS schema; notice the wide variety of object types.

■ **Tip**   Because SQLDeveloper is a graphical user interface (GUI), it is the tool of choice to get information about objects in your database. However, you should also practice using and SQL*Plus and SQL to query the dictionary views, because there will be times when SQLDeveloper does not go far enough.

Listing 8-2. Objects Found in the SYS Schema

```
PDB1@ORCL> SELECT object_type, COUNT (*)
  2   FROM dba_objects
  3   WHERE owner = 'SYS'
  4   GROUP BY object_type
  5   ORDER BY 2 DESC;
```

```
OBJECT_TYPE COUNT(*)
---------------------- ----------
JAVA CLASS 27971
VIEW  5454
TYPE   1640
INDEX      1395
TABLE      1234
JAVA RESOURCE        921
PACKAGE   705
PACKAGE BODY        678
JAVA DATA      301
LOB    196
TABLE PARTITION          193
LIBRARY        161
SEQUENCE      157
TYPE BODY        147
PROCEDURE       140
FUNCTION99
INDEX PARTITION 92
TABLE SUBPARTITION32
CONSUMER GROUP18
JOB18
SYNONYM 17
QUEUE17
UNDEFINED15
JOB CLASS14
RULE SET13
TRIGGER 11
RESOURCE PLAN11
DIRECTORY10
CONTEXT 10
PROGRAM 10
EVALUATION CONTEXT10
CLUSTER 10
WINDOW 9
LOB PARTITION 8
OPERATOR 7
UNIFIED AUDIT POLICY 5
SCHEDULE 4
SCHEDULER GROUP  4
DESTINATION 2
JAVA SOURCE 2
RULE 1
EDITION  1

42 rows selected.
```

■ **Tip**   Definitions of Oracle terms and links to the relevant sections of the reference manuals can be found in the Master Glossary available at www.oracle.com/pls/db121/homepage. Try using the Master Glossary to find the meanings of the terms you see in Listing 8-2.

Some of the objects in a schema, such as tables and indexes, represent blocks of storage; the others are just definitions that are stored as rows in tables. For example, the view DBA_OBJECTS is simply a definition stored as rows in the VIEW$ table in the SYS schema. An object that represents blocks of storage is called a *segment*. Listing 8-3 shows that only 11 of the object types displayed in Listing 8-2 actually represent blocks of storage; the others are only definitions stored as rows in tables.

Listing 8-3. Segment Types Found in the SYS Schema

```
PDB1@ORCL> SELECT segment_type, COUNT(*)
  2  FROM dba_segments
  3  WHERE owner = 'SYS'
  4  GROUP BY segment_type
  5  ORDER BY 2 DESC;


SEGMENT_TYPE    COUNT(*)
------------------ ----------
INDEX   484
TABLE   388
LOBINDEX    89
LOBSEGMENT    89
NESTED TABLE    12
TABLE PARTITION    11
CLUSTER    10
INDEX PARTITION    7
LOB PARTITION    6
ROLLBACK    1

10 rows selected.
```

You can find more information about each type of object in the appropriate dictionary view. Listing 8-4 is a list of the columns found in the DBA_TABLES view; you can do the same for any table or view using the DESCRIBE command. Coincidentally, a complete list of dictionary views can be found in a view called DICTIONARY; the actual SQL definitions of the views can be found in another view called DBA_VIEWS. You'll explore additional data dictionary views in the exercises at the end of this chapter, and Chapter 9 discusses the topic further.

Listing 8-4. Information about Tables in the DBA_TABLES View

```
PDB1@ORCL> describe dba_tables
 Name    Null?    Type
------------------------------------------------- -------- ----------------------------
 OWNER    NOT NULL VARCHAR2(128)
 TABLE_NAME NOT NULL VARCHAR2(128)
 TABLESPACE_NAME    VARCHAR2(30)
 CLUSTER_NAME    VARCHAR2(128)
 IOT_NAME  VARCHAR2(128)
```

```
STATUS VARCHAR2(8)
PCT_FREENUMBER
PCT_USED NUMBER
INI_TRANSNUMBER
MAX_TRANS NUMBER
INITIAL_EXTENT NUMBER
NEXT_EXTENT NUMBER
MIN_EXTENTSNUMBER
MAX_EXTENTSNUMBER
PCT_INCREASE    NUMBER
FREELISTSNUMBER
FREELIST_GROUPSNUMBER
LOGGINGVARCHAR2(3)
BACKED_UPVARCHAR2(1)
NUM_ROWSNUMBER
BLOCKS NUMBER
EMPTY_BLOCKS    NUMBER
AVG_SPACENUMBER
CHAIN_CNTNUMBER
AVG_ROW_LEN NUMBER
AVG_SPACE_FREELIST_BLOCKSNUMBER
NUM_FREELIST_BLOCKS    NUMBER
DEGREE VARCHAR2(10)
INSTANCES  VARCHAR2(10)
CACHE    VARCHAR2(5)
TABLE_LOCK  VARCHAR2(8)
SAMPLE_SIZE NUMBER
LAST_ANALYZED    DATE
PARTITIONED VARCHAR2(3)
IOT_TYPE VARCHAR2(12)
TEMPORARY    VARCHAR2(1)
SECONDARY VARCHAR2(1)
NESTED    VARCHAR2(3)
BUFFER_POOL    VARCHAR2(7)
FLASH_CACHE VARCHAR2(7)
CELL_FLASH_CACHEVARCHAR2(7)
ROW_MOVEMENT    VARCHAR2(8)
GLOBAL_STATS    VARCHAR2(3)
USER_STATS VARCHAR2(3)
DURATIONVARCHAR2(15)
SKIP_CORRUPT    VARCHAR2(8)
MONITORING VARCHAR2(3)
CLUSTER_OWNER    VARCHAR2(128)
DEPENDENCIES    VARCHAR2(8)
COMPRESSION VARCHAR2(8)
COMPRESS_FOR    VARCHAR2(30)
DROPPEDVARCHAR2(3)
READ_ONLYVARCHAR2(3)
SEGMENT_CREATED VARCHAR2(3)
RESULT_CACHE    VARCHAR2(7)
CLUSTERING VARCHAR2(3)
```

```
ACTIVITY_TRACKING VARCHAR2(23)
DML_TIMESTAMP    VARCHAR2(25)
HAS_IDENTITY     VARCHAR2(3)
CONTAINER_DATA   VARCHAR2(3)
```

■ **Tip**   Explanations of the information contained in the dictionary views can be found in the *Oracle Database Reference* available at www.oracle.com/pls/db121/homepage. Try using it to figure out the meaning of each of the columns in DBA_TABLES.

Ordinary users don't have access to the dictionary views whose names begin with DBA_, because that would give them the ability to obtain information about other users. Instead, they have access to special sets of views whose names begin with USER_ and ALL_. The views whose names begin with USER_show only those objects the current user owns. As illustrated in Listing 8-5, Oracle displays an error message when user hr tries to query the DBA_OBJECTS view. When user hr queries the USER_OBJECTS view instead, Oracle displays the same information you saw in Listing 8-1. And, interestingly enough, when user hr queries the ALL_OBJECTS table, the user has access to tables in several other schemas.

Listing 8-5. Querying the DBA_, USER_, and ALL_ Dictionary Views

```
SQL> CONNECT hr
Enter password:
Connected.
SQL> SELECT    object_type,
  2            COUNT (*)
  3       FROM dba_objects
  4   GROUP BY object_type
  5   ORDER BY 2 DESC;
     FROM dba_objects
          *
ERROR at line 3:
ORA-00942: table or view does not exist

SQL> SELECT    object_type,
  2            COUNT (*)
  3       FROM user_objects
  4   GROUP BY object_type
  5   ORDER BY 2 DESC;

OBJECT_TYPE           COUNT(*)
------------------- ----------
INDEX                       19
TABLE                        7
SEQUENCE                     3
PROCEDURE                    2
TRIGGER                      2
VIEW                         1

6 rows selected.
```

```
SQL> SELECT    owner,
  2            object_type,
  3            COUNT (*)
  4    FROM all_objects
  5    WHERE object_type = 'TABLE'
  6  GROUP BY owner,
  7            object_type
  8  ORDER BY 3 DESC;

OWNER                           OBJECT_TYPE           COUNT(*)
------------------------------  --------------------  ----------
MDSYS                           TABLE                         47
SYS                             TABLE                         27
XDB                             TABLE                         18
WKSYS                           TABLE                         10
HR                              TABLE                          7
SYSTEM                          TABLE                          8
CTXSYS                          TABLE                          5
FLOWS_030000                    TABLE                          3
OLAPSYS                         TABLE                          2
EXFSYS                          TABLE                          1

10 rows selected.
```

User Management

As you might expect, nobody can store data in the database or retrieve data from it unless they are properly authorized to do so. The following sections explore the five commands required for user management: CREATE USER, ALTER USER, DROP USER, GRANT, and REVOKE. Only users with the appropriate privileges can execute these commands. For example, only a user with the Create User privilege can execute the CREATE USER command. Database administrators typically perform user-management tasks using the SYSTEM account.

Creating Users

The CREATE USER command is used to specify the alias by which the database knows a user. A typical convention is to use the first character of the user's first name and the first seven characters of the person's last name—for example, ifernand in the case of a user named Iggy Fernandez. Listing 8-6 shows a minimalist example of the CREATE USER command; the IDENTIFIED BY clause is used to specify the password that the user must specify to gain access to the database.

Listing 8-6. Minimalist Form of the CREATE USER Command

```
SQL> CONNECT system
Enter password:
Connected.
SQL>CREATE USER ifernand
  2 IDENTIFIED BY qazwsxedc;

User created.
```

The CREATE USER statement should typically specify a value for DEFAULT TABLESPACE—the tablespace where the user's tables and indexes are automatically placed if another tablespace is not explicitly specified—and TEMPORARY TABLESPACE—the tablespace used for sorting operations and other operations that require temporary space. If you do not specify values, DEFAULT TABLESPACE and TEMPORARY TABLESPACE are automatically set to the values listed in the DATABASE_PROPERTIES view. This example also neglects to assign a value to the user's *profile*; this is automatically set to the value DEFAULT. Listing 8-7 shows some information from the DBA_USERS view; note especially the attributes of user ifernand.

Listing 8-7 is interesting because it also shows you just how many schemas are automatically created when a database is created. The creation date provides a clue as to the origin of these schemas; the creation date of August 30, 2005 tells me that those schemas were part of the database template I used to create my database. The creation date of February 21, 2008 is when I installed the sample schemas in the database, soon after creating the database.

Listing 8-7. Schema Attributes Stored in DBA_USERS

```
SQL> CONNECT system
Enter password:
Connected.
SQL> COLUMN username format a20 heading "USER|NAME"
SQL> COLUMN created format a10 heading "CREATED"
SQL> COLUMN default_tablespace format a10 heading "DEFAULT|TABLESPACE"
SQL> COLUMN temporary_tablespace format a10 heading "TEMPORARY|TABLESPACE"
SQL> COLUMN profile format a20 heading "PROFILE"
SQL>
SQL> SELECT    username,
  2            created,
  3            default_tablespace,
  4            temporary_tablespace,
  5            PROFILE
  6       FROM dba_users
  7   ORDER BY created;
```

USER NAME	CREATED	DEFAULT TABLESPACE	TEMPORARY TABLESPACE	PROFILE
SYS	30-AUG-05	SYSTEM	TEMP	DEFAULT
SYSTEM	30-AUG-05	SYSTEM	TEMP	DEFAULT
OUTLN	30-AUG-05	SYSTEM	TEMP	DEFAULT
DIP	30-AUG-05	USERS	TEMP	DEFAULT
TSMSYS	30-AUG-05	USERS	TEMP	DEFAULT
DBSNMP	30-AUG-05	SYSAUX	TEMP	MONITORING_PROFILE
WMSYS	30-AUG-05	SYSAUX	TEMP	DEFAULT
EXFSYS	30-AUG-05	SYSAUX	TEMP	DEFAULT
DMSYS	30-AUG-05	SYSAUX	TEMP	DEFAULT
CTXSYS	30-AUG-05	SYSAUX	TEMP	DEFAULT
XDB	30-AUG-05	SYSAUX	TEMP	DEFAULT
ANONYMOUS	30-AUG-05	SYSAUX	TEMP	DEFAULT
ORDSYS	30-AUG-05	SYSAUX	TEMP	DEFAULT
SI_INFORMTN_SCHEMA	30-AUG-05	SYSAUX	TEMP	DEFAULT
ORDPLUGINS	30-AUG-05	SYSAUX	TEMP	DEFAULT
MDSYS	30-AUG-05	SYSAUX	TEMP	DEFAULT
OLAPSYS	30-AUG-05	SYSAUX	TEMP	DEFAULT

```
MDDATA          30-AUG-05   USERS     TEMP   DEFAULT
SYSMAN          30-AUG-05   SYSAUX    TEMP   DEFAULT
MGMT_VIEW       30-AUG-05   SYSTEM    TEMP   DEFAULT
SCOTT           30-AUG-05   USERS     TEMP   DEFAULT
HR              21-FEB-08   USERS     TEMP   DEFAULT
OE              21-FEB-08   USERS     TEMP   DEFAULT
SH              21-FEB-08   USERS     TEMP   DEFAULT
IX              21-FEB-08   USERS     TEMP   DEFAULT
PM              21-FEB-08   USERS     TEMP   DEFAULT
BI              21-FEB-08   USERS     TEMP   DEFAULT
IFERNAND        27-APR-08   USERS     TEMP   DEFAULT

28 rows selected.
```

The user's *profile* specifies a number of behaviors and quotas that apply to the user. For example, IDLE_TIME specifies the length of time after which an idle session is automatically disconnected in order to conserve system resources, and CPU_PER_SESSION specifies the maximum number of CPU cycles that any single session may utilize.You can find a detailed description of these behaviors and quotas in the CREATE PROFILE section of the *Oracle Database 12c SQL Language Reference*. You can customize the default profile using the ALTER PROFILE command, and you can create custom profiles using the CREATE PROFILE command. Listing 8-8 shows the definition of the DEFAULT profile.

Listing 8-8. Definition of the DEFAULT Profile

```
SQL> CONNECT system
Enter password:
Connected.
SQL> COLUMN resource:type format a15 heading "RESOURCE TYPE"
SQL> COLUMN resource:name format a30 heading "RESOURCE NAME"
SQL> COLUMN limit format a15 heading "LIMIT"
SQL> SELECT    resource:type,
  2            resource:name,
  3            LIMIT
  4      FROM dba_profiles
  5     WHERE PROFILE = 'DEFAULT'
  6   ORDER BY resource:type, resource:name;

RESOURCE TYPE    RESOURCE NAME                    LIMIT
---------------  ------------------------------   ---------------
KERNEL           COMPOSITE_LIMIT                  UNLIMITED
KERNEL           CONNECT_TIME                     UNLIMITED
KERNEL           CPU_PER_CALL                     UNLIMITED
KERNEL           CPU_PER_SESSION                  UNLIMITED
KERNEL           IDLE_TIME                        UNLIMITED
KERNEL           LOGICAL_READS_PER_CALL           UNLIMITED
KERNEL           LOGICAL_READS_PER_SESSION        UNLIMITED
KERNEL           PRIVATE_SGA                      UNLIMITED
KERNEL           SESSIONS_PER_USER                UNLIMITED
PASSWORD         FAILED_LOGIN_ATTEMPTS            10
PASSWORD         PASSWORD_GRACE_TIME              UNLIMITED
PASSWORD         PASSWORD_LIFE_TIME               UNLIMITED
```

PASSWORD	PASSWORD_LOCK_TIME	UNLIMITED
PASSWORD	PASSWORD_REUSE_MAX	UNLIMITED
PASSWORD	PASSWORD_REUSE_TIME	UNLIMITED
PASSWORD	PASSWORD_VERIFY_FUNCTION	NULL

```
16 rows selected.
```

Giving Permissions to Users

Oracle gives you tight control over what users are permitted to do; the GRANT command is the main tool for this purpose. User ifernand may be known to Oracle, but he won't be able to start an interactive session. Here's what happens when he tries to do so:

```
SQL> CONNECT ifernand
Enter password:
ERROR:
ORA-01045: user IFERNAND lacks CREATE SESSION privilege; logon denied
```

To give the database administrator more flexibility in managing users, the ability to start a session is not automatically available to database users, even if they own objects in the database. The ability to start a session can be granted when necessary, and revoking a user's ability to start a session does not remove any objects owned by the user. Let's give user ifernand the ability to start a session:

```
SQL> CONNECT system
Enter password:
Connected.
SQL>GRANT CREATE SESSION TO ifernand;

Grant succeeded.
```

User ifernand is now able to connect, but Oracle does not let him create any tables:

```
SQL> CONNECT ifernand
Enter password:
Connected.
SQL> CREATE TABLE TEST AS
  2  SELECT * FROM DUAL;
SELECT * FROM DUAL
              *
ERROR at line 2:
ORA-01031: insufficient privileges
```

You must explicitly give user ifernand permission to create tables; this is done with the GRANT command. Here's an example:

```
SQL> CONNECT system
Enter password:
Connected.
SQL>GRANT CREATE TABLE TO ifernand;

Grant succeeded.
```

User ifernand encounters another problem when he tries to create a table—he does not have a quota of space in any tablespace:

```
SQL> CONNECT ifernand
Enter password:
Connected.
SQL> CREATE TABLE TEST AS
  2  SELECT * FROM DUAL;
SELECT * FROM DUAL
             *
ERROR at line 2:
ORA-01950: no privileges on tablespace 'USERS'
```

You must explicitly give user ifernand a quota of space in at least one tablespace. You do so with the ALTER USER command:

```
SQL> CONNECT system
Enter password:
Connected.
SQL>ALTER USER ifernand QUOTA 128 m ON users;

User altered.
```

User ifernandcan now create a table in his default tablespace, USERS, but not in any other tablespace. Here's what happens when he tries to create a table in another tablespace:

```
SQL> CONNECT ifernand
Enter password:
Connected.
SQL> CREATE TABLE TEST (dummy VARCHAR2(1))
  2  STORAGE (INITIAL 128 m)
  3  TABLESPACE example;
CREATE TABLE TEST (dummy VARCHAR2(1))
*
ERROR at line 1:
ORA-01950: no privileges on tablespace 'EXAMPLE'
```

As shown next, user ifernandcan only successfully create tables in the USERS tablespace. If he does not explicitly specify a tablespace when creating a table (or index), it is automatically created in the USERS tablespace, because that is his default tablespace:

```
SQL> CONNECT ifernand
Enter password:
Connected.
SQL> CREATE TABLE TEST (dummy VARCHAR2(1))
  2  STORAGE (INITIAL 128 m);

Table created.
```

```
SQL> SELECT tablespace:name
  2    FROM user_segments
  3    WHERE segment_name = 'TEST';

TABLESPACE_NAME
------------------------------
USERS
```

Once user ifernand exhausts his quota of space, his tables cannot grow any more, and he cannot create new tables (or indexes):

```
SQL> CONNECT ifernand
Enter password:
Connected.
SQL> ALTER TABLE TEST ALLOCATE EXTENT (SIZE 64 k);
ALTER TABLE TEST ALLOCATE EXTENT (SIZE 64 k)
*
ERROR at line 1:
ORA-01536: space quota exceeded for tablespace 'USERS'

SQL> CREATE INDEX test_i1 ON TEST(dummy);
CREATE INDEX test_i1 ON TEST(dummy)
                            *
ERROR at line 1:
ORA-01536: space quota exceeded for tablespace 'USERS'

SQL> SELECT tablespace:name,
  2         BYTES / 1048576 AS mb
  3    FROM user_ts_quotas;

TABLESPACE_NAME                      MB
------------------------------ ----------
USERS                               128
```

Note that other users cannot retrieve or modify the contents of tables owned by user ifernand unless he explicitly gives them the necessary privileges. Listing 8-9 shows some examples of granting *table privileges* to users—the word PUBLIC denotes all users of the database.

Listing 8-9. Granting Table Privileges to Users

```
SQL> CONNECT ifernand
Enter password:
Connected.
SQL> GRANT SELECT ON TEST TO PUBLIC;

Grant succeeded.

SQL> GRANT INSERT ON TEST TO hr;

Grant succeeded.

SQL> GRANT UPDATE ON TEST TO clerical_role;

Grant succeeded.
```

TABLE, SYSTEM, AND ROLE PRIVILEGES

A recurring theme in this chapter's discussion is that Oracle gives you the ability to control tightly what users are permitted to do. *Object privileges* are privileges to perform operations on objects; examples include SELECT, INSERT, UPDATE, and DELETE privileges on tables. *System privileges* are privileges that do not apply to specific objects; examples are CREATE SESSION and CREATE TABLE. *Roles* are collections of privileges that are created for convenience; all the privileges in a collection can be assigned to a user with a single command. For example, if you want to give a user the ability to perform database administration functions, you can give them theDBA role—it includes such privileges as CREATE USER and DROP USER.

The permissions granted to each user of the database are tracked in the dba_sys_privs, dba_role_privs, and dba_tab_privs views.Here are their definitions:

```
SQL> CONNECT system
Enter password:
Connected.
SQL> DESCRIBE dba_sys_privs
 Name                                      Null?    Type
 ----------------------------------------- -------- ----------------------------

 GRANTEE                                   NOT NULL VARCHAR2(30)
 PRIVILEGE                                 NOT NULL VARCHAR2(40)
 ADMIN_OPTION                                       VARCHAR2(3)

SQL> DESCRIBE dba_role_privs
 Name                                      Null?    Type
 ----------------------------------------- -------- ----------------------------

 GRANTEE                                            VARCHAR2(30)
 GRANTED_ROLE                              NOT NULL VARCHAR2(30)
 ADMIN_OPTION                                       VARCHAR2(3)
 DEFAULT_ROLE                                       VARCHAR2(3)

SQL> DESCRIBE dba_tab_privs
 Name                                      Null?    Type
 ----------------------------------------- -------- ----------------------------

 GRANTEE                                   NOT NULL VARCHAR2(30)
 OWNER                                     NOT NULL VARCHAR2(30)
 TABLE_NAME                                NOT NULL VARCHAR2(30)
 GRANTOR                                   NOT NULL VARCHAR2(30)
 PRIVILEGE                                 NOT NULL VARCHAR2(40)
 GRANTABLE                                          VARCHAR2(3)
 HIERARCHY                                          VARCHAR2(3)
```

You explore these views in the exercises at the end of this chapter, where you are asked to audit the privileges of users.

Revoking Permissions Granted to Users

The REVOKE command can be used to revoke a privilege granted by a GRANT command. In Listing 8-10, user ifernand is revoking the privileges on the table test that he previously granted to various users. In the exercises at the end of this chapter, you are asked to review the permissions granted to PUBLIC and revoke those that pose a security risk.

Listing 8-10. Revoking Table Privileges from Users

```
SQL> CONNECT ifernand
Enter password:
Connected.
SQL> REVOKE SELECT ON test FROM PUBLIC;

Revoke succeeded.

SQL> REVOKE INSERT ON test FROM hr;

Revoke succeeded.

SQL> REVOKE INSERT ON test FROM clerical_role;

Revoke succeeded.
```

Modifying User Attributes

You can use the ALTER USER command to change any of the attributes specified by the CREATE USER command. One very common use of the command is to change a user's password.This particular use is not restricted to database administrators—users can use the ALTER USER command to change their own passwords, as shown in Listing 8-11. As you saw in the previous section, ALTER USER can also be used to give users a quota of space in a tablespace.

Listing 8-11. Changing Your Own Password

```
SQL> CONNECT ifernand
Enter password:
Connected.
SQL>ALTER USER ifernand IDENTIFIED BY t0ps3cr3t;

User altered.
```

Removing Users

The final command in the suite of user-management commands is DROP USER.It removes all trace of the user from the database. As shown in Listing 8-12, if the user has created any objects with the database, then either those objects must first be removed manually or the CASCADE option must be specified when using the DROP USER command. CASCADE automatically removes all objects owned by the user being removed from the database.

Listing 8-12. Dropping a User

```
SQL> CONNECT system
Enter password:
Connected.
SQL> DROP USER ifernand;
DROP USER ifernand
*
ERROR at line 1:
ORA-01922: CASCADE must be specified to drop 'IFERNAND'

SQL> SELECT object_type,
  2          object_name
  3    FROM dba_objects
  4   WHERE owner = 'IFERNAND';

OBJECT_TYPE          OBJECT_NAME
-------------------  -------------------------------
TABLE                TEST

SQL> DROP USER ifernand CASCADE;

User dropped.

SQL> SELECT object_type,
  2          object_name
  3    FROM dba_objects
  4   WHERE owner = 'IFERNAND';

no rows selected
```

Data Loading

Any user with the requisite privileges can insert data into tables, but database administrators are routinely called on to help with bulk loading of data.This typically happens when a new software application is deployed, but it can happen on a routine basis in *data marts* and *data warehouses*. The simplest way to load data is to use scripts containing INSERT commands—one INSERT command per row—but this approach is only useful for small amounts of data. The sections that follow discuss some of the tools and techniques provided by Oracle for data loading.

The Export and Import Utilities

The exp and imp utilities—used for exporting data out of and importing data into a database, respectively—were once the workhorses of the Oracle world. The *data pump* utilities, which were introduced in Oracle Database 10g, have more features but also have the drawback of using PL/SQL routines for reading and writing; as a result, they can only read and create server-side files. On the other hand, the exp and imp utilities read and create client-side files such as those located on a user's laptop. Also, the data pump utilities do not work with magnetic tapes and standby databases. As a result of limitations like these, the exp and imp utilities have not been fully supplanted by the new utilities. I discuss them here for completeness even though their use is now expressly discouraged by Oracle.[1]

The exp and imp utilities are rich in features; you can list them with the help=y clause. Listing 8-13 shows the features of the exp utility—the imp utility has very similar features.

Listing 8-13. Features of the exp Utility

```
C:\Documents and Settings\IGNATIUS>exp help=y

Export: Release 11.1.0.6.0 - Production on Sat Nov 15 18:15:45 2008

Copyright (c) 1982, 2007, Oracle.  All rights reserved.

You can let Export prompt you for parameters by entering the EXP
command followed by your username/password:

    Example: EXP SCOTT/TIGER

Or, you can control how Export runs by entering the EXP command followed
by various arguments. To specify parameters, you use keywords:

    Format:   EXP KEYWORD=value or KEYWORD=(value1,value2,...,valueN)
    Example: EXP SCOTT/TIGER GRANTS=Y TABLES=(EMP,DEPT,MGR)
             or TABLES=(T1:P1,T1:P2), if T1 is partitioned table

USERID must be the first parameter on the command line.

Keyword     Description (Default)       Keyword       Description (Default)
--------------------------------------------------------------------------
USERID      username/password          FULL          export entire file (N)
BUFFER      size of data buffer        OWNER         list of owner usernames
FILE        output files (EXPDAT.DMP)  TABLES        list of table names
COMPRESS    import into one extent (Y) RECORDLENGTH  length of IO record
GRANTS      export grants (Y)          INCTYPE       incremental export type
INDEXES     export indexes (Y)         RECORD        track incr. export (Y)
DIRECT      direct path (N)            TRIGGERS      export triggers (Y)
LOG         log file of screen output  STATISTICS    analyze objects (ESTIMATE)
ROWS        export data rows (Y)       PARFILE       parameter filename
CONSISTENT  cross-table consistency(N) CONSTRAINTS   export constraints (Y)
```

---

[1]The following language appears in *Oracle Database 11g Utilities*: "Original export is desupported for general use as of Oracle Database 11g. The only supported use of Original Export in 11g is backward migration of XMLType data to a database version 10g release 2 (10.2) or earlier. Therefore, Oracle recommends that you use the new Data Pump Export and Import utilities, except in the following situations which require Original Export and Import:
You want to import files that were created using the original Export utility (exp).).
You want to export files that will be imported using the original Import utility (imp).). An example of this would be if you wanted to export data from Oracle Database 10g and then import it into an earlier database release."

```
OBJECT_CONSISTENT       transaction set to read only during object export (N)
FEEDBACK                display progress every x rows (0)
FILESIZE                maximum size of each dump file
FLASHBACK_SCN           SCN used to set session snapshot back to
FLASHBACK_TIME          time used to get the SCN closest to the specified time
QUERY                   select clause used to export a subset of a table
RESUMABLE               suspend when a space related error is encountered(N)
RESUMABLE_NAME          text string used to identify resumable statement
RESUMABLE_TIMEOUT       wait time for RESUMABLE
TTS_FULL_CHECK          perform full or partial dependency check for TTS
TABLESPACES             list of tablespaces to export
TRANSPORT_TABLESPACE    export transportable tablespace metadata (N)
TEMPLATE                template name which invokes iAS mode export

Export terminated successfully without warnings.
```

Listing 8-14 shows an example of the use of the exp utility. You export the contents of the hr sample schema into a file called hr.dmp.Using the consistent=y clause ensures that all the contents of the file accurately represent a single point in time.

Listing 8-14. Using the exp Utility

```
C:\Documents and Settings\IGNATIUS>exp hr file=hr.dmp consistent=y
tables=(countries,departments,employees,jobs,job_history,locations,regions)

Export: Release 11.1.0.6.0 - Production on Sun May 4 09:24:28 2008

Copyright (c) 1982, 2007, Oracle.  All rights reserved.

Password:

Connected to: Oracle Database 11g Enterprise Edition Release 11.1.0.6.0 - Production
With the Partitioning, OLAP, Data Mining and Real Application Testing options
Export done in WE8MSWIN1252 character set and AL16UTF16 NCHAR character set

About to export specified tables via Conventional Path ...
. . exporting table                     COUNTRIES         25 rows exported
. . exporting table                   DEPARTMENTS         27 rows exported
. . exporting table                     EMPLOYEES        107 rows exported
. . exporting table                          JOBS         19 rows exported
. . exporting table                   JOB_HISTORY         10 rows exported
. . exporting table                     LOCATIONS         23 rows exported
. . exporting table                       REGIONS          4 rows exported
Export terminated successfully without warnings.
```

Next, let's import the data into another schema using the imp utility, as illustrated in Listing 8-15.You can take advantage of the fromuser and touser clauses.

Listing 8-15. *Using the imp Utility*

```
C:\Documents and Settings\IGNATIUS>imp ifernand file=hr.dmp fromuser=hr
touser=ifernand
tables=(countries,departments,employees,jobs,job_history,locations,regions)

Import: Release 11.1.0.6.0 - Production on Sun May 4 09:26:15 2008

Copyright (c) 1982, 2007, Oracle.  All rights reserved.

Password:

Connected to: Oracle Database 11g Enterprise Edition Release 11.1.0.6.0 - Production
With the Partitioning, OLAP, Data Mining and Real Application Testing options

Export file created by EXPORT:V11.01.00 via conventional path

Warning: the objects were exported by HR, not by you

import done in WE8MSWIN1252 character set and AL16UTF16 NCHAR character set
. importing HR's objects into IFERNAND
. . importing table                     "COUNTRIES"           25 rows imported
. . importing table                   "DEPARTMENTS"          27 rows imported
. . importing table                     "EMPLOYEES"         107 rows imported
. . importing table                          "JOBS"          19 rows imported
. . importing table                   "JOB_HISTORY"          10 rows imported
. . importing table                     "LOCATIONS"          23 rows imported
. . importing table                       "REGIONS"           4 rows imported
IMP-00041: Warning: object created with compilation warnings
 "CREATE TRIGGER "IFERNAND".secure_employees"
 "  BEFORE INSERT OR UPDATE OR DELETE ON employees"
 "BEGIN"
 "  secure_dml;"
 "END secure_employees;"
IMP-00041: Warning: object created with compilation warnings
 "CREATE TRIGGER "IFERNAND".update_job_history"
 "  AFTER UPDATE OF job_id, department_id ON employees"
 "  FOR EACH ROW"
 "BEGIN"
 "  add_job_history(:old.employee_id, :old.hire_date, sysdate,"
 "                  :old.job_id, :old.department_id);"
 "END;"
About to enable constraints…
Import terminated successfully with warnings.
```

Notice the warnings produced by the utility; it reports compilation errors for two triggers. This is because, in the absence of an explicit prohibition, the exp utility exported not only the data but also the definitions of indexes, constraints, triggers, and grants associated with the tables as well as the table and index statistics. The triggers on the employee table refer to stored procedures that do not exist in the destination schema.

The Data Pump Utilities

The expdp (Data Pump Export) and impdp (Data Pump Import) utilities were introduced in Oracle Database 10g with support for parallelism, compression, and encryption, among other things. They were intended to supplant the exp and imp utilities but could not do so completely, for the reasons already stated. The invocation syntax for expdp and impdp is fairly similar to that for the exp and imp utilities; you can use the help=y clause to list their features.

Listing 8-16 illustrates use the expdp and impdp utilities to export and import the same tables referenced in Listing 8-14 and Listing 8-15. Notice the reference to a special directory called data_pump_dir and how intervention by the database administrator becomes necessary to give users permission to use this directory.

Listing 8-16. Using the expdp and impdp Utilities

```
C:\Documents and Settings\IGNATIUS>expdp hr directory=data_pump_dir dumpfile=hr.dmp
flashback_time="to_timestamp(sysdate)"
tables=(countries,departments,employees,jobs,job_history,locations,regions)

Export: Release 11.1.0.6.0 - Production on Sunday, 04 May, 2008 10:27:47

Copyright (c) 2003, 2007, Oracle.  All rights reserved.
Password:

Connected to: Oracle Database 11g Enterprise Edition Release 11.1.0.6.0 - Production
With the Partitioning, OLAP, Data Mining and Real Application Testing options
ORA-39002: invalid operation
ORA-39070: Unable to open the log file.
ORA-39087: directory name DATA_PUMP_DIR is invalid

C:\Documents and Settings\IGNATIUS>sqlplus system

SQL*Plus: Release 11.1.0.6.0 - Production on Sun May 4 10:34:42 2008

Copyright (c) 1982, 2007, Oracle.  All rights reserved.

Enter password:

Connected to:
Oracle Database 11g Enterprise Edition Release 11.1.0.6.0 - Production
With the Partitioning, OLAP, Data Mining and Real Application Testing options

SQL>grant read, write on directory data_pump_dir to hr;

Grant succeeded.

SQL> exit
Disconnected from Oracle Database 11g Enterprise Edition Release 11.1.0.6.0 -
Production
With the Partitioning, OLAP, Data Mining and Real Application Testing options
```

```
C:\Documents and Settings\IGNATIUS>expdp hr directory=data_pump_dir dumpfile=hr.dmp
flashback_time="to_timestamp(sysdate)"
tables=(countries,departments,employees,jobs,job_history,locations,regions)

Export: Release 11.1.0.6.0 - Production on Sunday, 04 May, 2008 10:43:41

Copyright (c) 2003, 2007, Oracle.  All rights reserved.
Password:

Connected to: Oracle Database 11g Enterprise Edition Release 11.1.0.6.0 - Production
With the Partitioning, OLAP, Data Mining and Real Application Testing options
Starting "HR"."SYS_EXPORT_TABLE_01":  hr/******** directory=data_pump_dir
dumpfile=hr/********.dmp flashback_time=to_timestamp(sysdate)
tables=(countries,departments,employees,jobs,job_history,locations,regions)
Estimate in progress using BLOCKS method…
Processing object type TABLE_EXPORT/TABLE/TABLE_DATA
Total estimation using BLOCKS method: 448 KB
Processing object type TABLE_EXPORT/TABLE/TABLE
Processing object type TABLE_EXPORT/TABLE/GRANT/OWNER_GRANT/OBJECT_GRANT
Processing object type TABLE_EXPORT/TABLE/INDEX/INDEX
Processing object type TABLE_EXPORT/TABLE/CONSTRAINT/CONSTRAINT
Processing object type TABLE_EXPORT/TABLE/INDEX/STATISTICS/INDEX_STATISTICS
Processing object type TABLE_EXPORT/TABLE/COMMENT
Processing object type TABLE_EXPORT/TABLE/CONSTRAINT/REF_CONSTRAINT
Processing object type TABLE_EXPORT/TABLE/TRIGGER
Processing object type TABLE_EXPORT/TABLE/STATISTICS/TABLE_STATISTICS
. . exported "HR"."COUNTRIES"                    6.375 KB      25 rows
. . exported "HR"."DEPARTMENTS"                  7.015 KB      27 rows
. . exported "HR"."EMPLOYEES"                    16.80 KB     107 rows
. . exported "HR"."JOBS"                         6.984 KB      19 rows
. . exported "HR"."JOB_HISTORY"                  7.054 KB      10 rows
. . exported "HR"."LOCATIONS"                    8.273 KB      23 rows
. . exported "HR"."REGIONS"                      5.484 KB       4 rows
Master table "HR"."SYS_EXPORT_TABLE_01" successfully loaded/unloaded
********************************************************************************
Dump file set for HR.SYS_EXPORT_TABLE_01 is:
  C:\APP\IGNATIUS\ADMIN\TRAINING\DPDUMP\HR.DMP
Job "HR"."SYS_EXPORT_TABLE_01" successfully completed at 10:44:19

C:\Documents and Settings\IGNATIUS>impdp ifernand directory=data_pump_dir
dumpfile=hr.dmp remap_schema=hr:ifernand
tables=(countries,departments,employees,jobs,job_history,locations,regions)

Import: Release 11.1.0.6.0 - Production on Sunday, 04 May, 2008 10:49:44

Copyright (c) 2003, 2007, Oracle.  All rights reserved.
Password:

Connected to: Oracle Database 11g Enterprise Edition Release 11.1.0.6.0 - Production
With the Partitioning, OLAP, Data Mining and Real Application Testing options
ORA-39002: invalid operation
```

```
ORA-39070: Unable to open the log file.
ORA-39087: directory name DATA_PUMP_DIR is invalid

C:\Documents and Settings\IGNATIUS>sqlplus system

SQL*Plus: Release 11.1.0.6.0 - Production on Sun May 4 10:49:53 2008

Copyright (c) 1982, 2007, Oracle.  All rights reserved.

Enter password:

Connected to:
Oracle Database 11g Enterprise Edition Release 11.1.0.6.0 - Production
With the Partitioning, OLAP, Data Mining and Real Application Testing options

SQL>grant read, write on directory data_pump_dir to ifernand;

Grant succeeded.

SQL> exit
Disconnected from Oracle Database 11g Enterprise Edition Release 11.1.0.6.0 -
Production
With the Partitioning, OLAP, Data Mining and Real Application Testing options

C:\Documents and Settings\IGNATIUS>impdp ifernand directory=data_pump_dir
dumpfile=hr.dmp remap_schema=hr:ifernand
tables=(countries,departments,employees,jobs,job_history,locations,regions)

Import: Release 11.1.0.6.0 - Production on Sunday, 04 May, 2008 10:50:45

Copyright (c) 2003, 2007, Oracle.  All rights reserved.
Password:

Connected to: Oracle Database 11g Enterprise Edition Release 11.1.0.6.0 - Production
With the Partitioning, OLAP, Data Mining and Real Application Testing options
Master table ifernand."SYS_IMPORT_TABLE_01" successfully loaded/unloaded
Starting ifernand."SYS_IMPORT_TABLE_01":   ifernand/******** directory=data_pump_dir
dumpfile=hr.dmp remap_schema=hr:ifernand/********
tables=(countries,departments,employees,jobs,job_history,locations,regions)
Processing object type TABLE_EXPORT/TABLE/TABLE
Processing object type TABLE_EXPORT/TABLE/TABLE_DATA
. . imported ifernand."COUNTRIES"                      6.375 KB      25 rows
. . imported ifernand."DEPARTMENTS"                    7.015 KB      27 rows
. . imported ifernand."EMPLOYEES"                      16.80 KB     107 rows
. . imported ifernand."JOBS"                           6.984 KB      19 rows
. . imported ifernand."JOB_HISTORY"                    7.054 KB      10 rows
. . imported ifernand."LOCATIONS"                      8.273 KB      23 rows
. . imported ifernand."REGIONS"                        5.484 KB       4 rows
Processing object type TABLE_EXPORT/TABLE/GRANT/OWNER_GRANT/OBJECT_GRANT
Processing object type TABLE_EXPORT/TABLE/INDEX/INDEX
Processing object type TABLE_EXPORT/TABLE/CONSTRAINT/CONSTRAINT
Processing object type TABLE_EXPORT/TABLE/INDEX/STATISTICS/INDEX_STATISTICS
```

```
Processing object type TABLE_EXPORT/TABLE/COMMENT
Processing object type TABLE_EXPORT/TABLE/CONSTRAINT/REF_CONSTRAINT
Processing object type TABLE_EXPORT/TABLE/TRIGGER
ORA-39082: Object type TRIGGER:ifernand."SECURE_EMPLOYEES" created with compilation
warnings
ORA-39082: Object type TRIGGER:ifernand."SECURE_EMPLOYEES" created with compilation
warnings
ORA-39082: Object type TRIGGER:ifernand."UPDATE_JOB_HISTORY" created with
compilation warnings
ORA-39082: Object type TRIGGER:ifernand."UPDATE_JOB_HISTORY" created with
compilation warnings
Processing object type TABLE_EXPORT/TABLE/STATISTICS/TABLE_STATISTICS
Job ifernand."SYS_IMPORT_TABLE_01" completed with 4 error(s) at 10:50:55
```

SQL*Loader

The SQL*Loader utility (sqlldr) is used to import data from sources located in other Oracle databases. It is similar to the DB2 load utility and the SQL Server bcp utility. It imports data from one or more data files whose structure is described in a SQL*Loader *control file*.

SQL*Loader offers tremendous flexibility in dealing with data files. For example:

- Fixed-length data items and variable-length (delimited) data items are both supported.

- Header records can be skipped.

- Bad records can be discarded.

- Data items from multiple lines can be combined.

- Data items can be selectively imported.

- Data records can be selectively imported.

- Data items from the same row of data can be inserted into multiple tables.

Listing 8-17 shows the contents of a simple SQL*Loader control file that describes how to load three columns of information from a *comma-delimited file* into a table. The INFILE * clause indicates that there is no separate data file or *infile*; that is, the data is part of the control file itself.

Listing 8-17. A Simple SQL*Loader Control File

```
LOAD DATA
INFILE *
INTO TABLE DEPT
FIELDS TERMINATED BY ',' OPTIONALLY ENCLOSED BY '"'
(DEPTNO, DNAME, LOC)
BEGINDATA
12,RESEARCH,"SARATOGA"
10,"ACCOUNTING",CLEVELAND
11,"ART",SALEM
13,FINANCE,"BOSTON"
21,"SALES",PHILA.
22,"SALES",ROCHESTER
42,"INT'L","SAN FRAN"
```

This control file belongs to the first in a series of 11 case studies included with the Oracle software. The control files (ulcase*.ctl) and data files (ulcase*.dat) can be found in the ORACLE_HOME\rdbms\ demo directory. SQL scripts for creating the necessary tables are also provided (ulcase*.sql). Complete instructions for testing the examples can be found in the comments section of each control file; they are also discussed in Chapter 6 of *Oracle Database 12c Utilities*, available at www.oracle.com/pls/db121/homepage. Listing 8-18 shows the results of performing the first case study.

Listing 8-18. A Sample SQL*Loader Session

```
C:\app\IGNATIUS\product\11.1.0\db_1\RDBMS\demo>sqlldr USERID=scott
CONTROL=ulcase1.ctl LOG=ulcase1.log
Password:

SQL*Loader: Release 11.1.0.6.0 - Production on Mon Nov 17 07:20:58 2008

Copyright (c) 1982, 2007, Oracle.  All rights reserved.

Commit point reached - logical record count 7

C:\app\IGNATIUS\product\11.1.0\db_1\RDBMS\demo>type ulcase1.log

SQL*Loader: Release 11.1.0.6.0 - Production on Mon Nov 17 07:20:58 2008

Copyright (c) 1982, 2007, Oracle.  All rights reserved.

Control File:    ulcase1.ctl
Data File:       ulcase1.ctl
  Bad File:      ulcase1.bad
  Discard File:  none specified

 (Allow all discards)

Number to load: ALL
Number to skip: 0
Errors allowed: 50
Bind array:     64 rows, maximum of 256000 bytes
Continuation:   none specified
Path used:      Conventional

Table DEPT, loaded from every logical record.
Insert option in effect for this table: INSERT

  Column Name         Position  Len  Term Encl Datatype
----------------------- ---------- ----- ---- ---- ---------------------
DEPTNO                    FIRST     *    ;   O(") CHARACTER
DNAME                     NEXT      *    ,   O(") CHARACTER
LOC                       NEXT      *    ,   O(") CHARACTER

Table DEPT:
  7 Rows successfully loaded.
  0 Rows not loaded due to data errors.
  0 Rows not loaded because all WHEN clauses were failed.
  0 Rows not loaded because all fields were null.
```

157

```
Space allocated for bind array:                      49536 bytes(64 rows)
Read    buffer bytes: 1048576

Total logical records skipped:          0
Total logical records read:             7
Total logical records rejected:         0
Total logical records discarded:        0

Run began on Mon Nov 17 07:20:58 2008
Run ended on Mon Nov 17 07:21:00 2008

Elapsed time was:       00:00:01.84
CPU time was:           00:00:00.02
```

■ **Tip**   Oracle does not provide a "SQL*Unloader" utility to complement the SQL*Loader utility—this is possibly the longest-standing gap in the Oracle Database product suite.

Summary

Here are some of the key points touched on in this chapter:

- Every object in a database is explicitly owned by a single owner, and the owner of an object must explicitly authorize its use by anybody else. The collection of objects owned by a user is called a *schema*. Oracle manages the contents of a database using its own tables, indexes, sequences, procedures, triggers, and views; these are stored in the SYS schema.

- The fivecommands required for user management are CREATE USER, ALTER USER, DROP USER, GRANT, and REVOKE.

- Object privileges are privileges to perform operations on objects; examples include SELECT, INSERT, UPDATE, and DELETE privileges on tables. System privileges are privileges that do not apply to specific objects; examples are CREATE SESSION and CREATE TABLE. Roles are collections of privileges that are created for convenience; all the privileges in a collection can be assigned to a user with a single command.

- The exp and imp utilities used to be the workhorses of the Oracle world; they are used to transfer data from one Oracle database to another. They are not as sophisticated as the data pump utilities introduced in Oracle Database 10g, but their advantage is that they can work with client-side files, named pipes, magnetic tapes, and standby databases (when opened in read-only mode).

- The expdp (Data Pump Export) and impdp (Data Pump Import) utilities were introduced in Oracle Database 10g with support for parallelism, compression, and encryption, among other things.

- The SQL*Loader utility is used to import data from sources in other Oracle databases; it is similar to the DB2 load utility and the SQL Server bcp utility. A complementary "SQL*Unloader" utility is not available.

Database Support

CHAPTER 9

■■■

Taking Control

Then felt I like some watcher of the skies
When a new planet swims into his ken;
Or like stout Cortez, when with eagle eyes
He stared at the Pacific—and all his men
Look'd at each other with a wild surmise—
Silent, upon a peak in Darien.

"On First Looking into Chapman's Homer" by John Keats

If you are going to be responsible for a database, you need to know what it contains and how it is being used. Which are the biggest tables? How are the data files, control files, and log files laid out? How many people have database accounts? How many people use the database at a time? Your first action when you acquire responsibility for a database should be to thoroughly explore it. Form-based tools such as Enterprise Manager, SQL Developer, and Remote Diagnostic Agent make it easy to explore the database.

Form-based tools also simplify the task of database administration. A long time ago in my career, I remember a manager looking on as I fixed a database problem. It took quite a while for me to get everything right, because the only tool I had was the SQL*Plus command-line tool and I was constructing SQL commands on the fly to fix the problem. A workman is as good as his tools. The manager was not very impressed.

As illustrated in Listing 9-1, I suggest that you create an account with DBA privileges for your personal use so that you are not tempted to use the SYS or SYSTEM account while browsing or performing chores. There are certainly times when you will have to use one of these accounts, but you should be able to do most of your daily work with your own account. This helps prevent unnecessary objects from being created in the SYS and SYSTEM schemas.

Listing 9-1. Creating an Account with DBA Privileges

```
SQL> CONNECT system
Enter password:
Connected.
SQL> CREATE USER ifernand
  2   IDENTIFIED BY change_immediately
  3   PASSWORD EXPIRE;

User created.

SQL> GRANT DBA TO ifernand;
```

```
Grant succeeded.

SQL> CONNECT ifernand
Enter password:
ERROR:
ORA-28001: the password has expired

Changing password for ifernand
New password:
Retype new password:
Password changed
Connected.
```

Enterprise Manager

Enterprise Manager comes in two flavors: Database Express and Grid Control. Both of them are web-based tools. Database Express is used to manage a single database, whereas Grid Control is used to manage multiple databases. Database Express is automatically installed when you create a database. I use the terms *Enterprise Manager* and *Database Express* interchangeably in this rest of this chapter.

As discussed in Chapter 6, Database Express can be installed by the Database Configuration Assistant if you so choose—this is the recommended method.

As you saw in Figure 6-20, the URL that you need to connect to Database Express is displayed after Database Configuration Assistant has finished creating the database. The URL shown in Figure 6-20 is https://localhost:5500/em.; this can be used to connect from within the VM if you first install the Adobe Flash plugin. Replace localhost with the IP address of your VM to connect from outside the VM if you have opened the Database Express port; Chapter 6 explains how to do so. The starting screen of Database Express was shown in Figure 6-21.

As illustrated in Figure 9-1, you can accomplish a subset of DBA tasks—such as password resets—by using EM Express instead of command-line tools such as SQL*Plus.

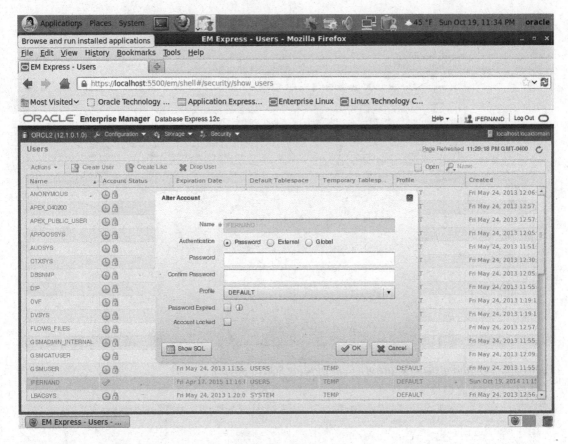

Figure 9-1. *Performing password resets by using Enterprise Manager*

■ **Tip** Before clicking the Apply or OK button on any task screen, click the Show SQL button to review the SQL statements that Oracle will use to perform the task. This is a great way to learn new SQL commands.

SQL Developer

Chapter 5 discussed the installation of SQL Developer. Until a few years ago, Oracle was very weak in the area of tools for software developers, but this changed with the release of SQL Developer. This Java-based tool for the Windows platform can be downloaded from the Oracle Technology Network (http://otn.oracle.com). The direct link is www.oracle.com/technology/software/products/sql/index.html.

SQL Developer is primarily a tool for software developers, but DBAs will find it extremely useful. Figure 9-2 and Figure 9-3 show common uses—examining the structure of a table and checking the execution plan for a query. Notice how easy it is to browse through collections of different types of objects by using the object tree in the left pane and the tabs in the right pane. The SQL tab in particular is very interesting; it displays SQL commands for creating the object. You can use these SQL commands as a template for creating a similar object.

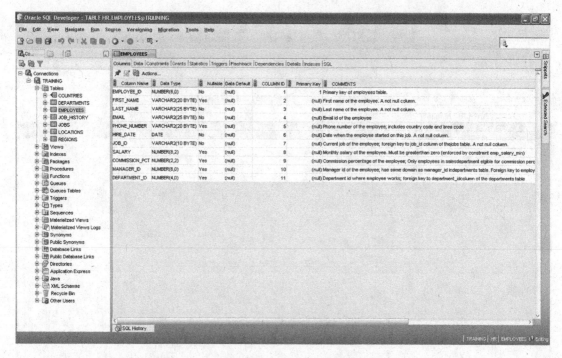

Figure 9-2. *Examining the structure of a table by using SQL Developer*

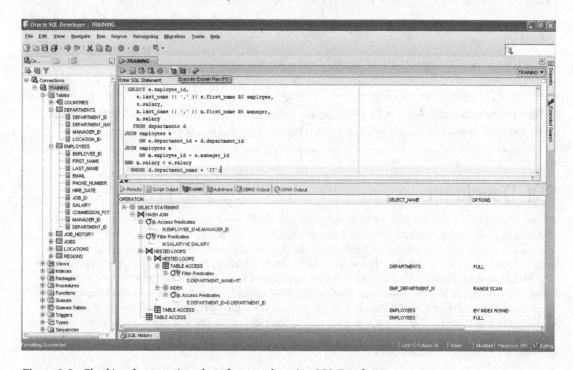

Figure 9-3. *Checking the execution plan of a query by using SQL Developer*

SQL Developer can also be used to perform typical database administration tasks such as identifying and terminating blocking sessions.[1] In Figure 9-4, you can see that session 128 has been blocked by session 125 for 2,500 seconds. In Figure 9-5, you can see that session 125 is idle. It is waiting for a "SQL*Net message from client," and you can decide to terminate the session.

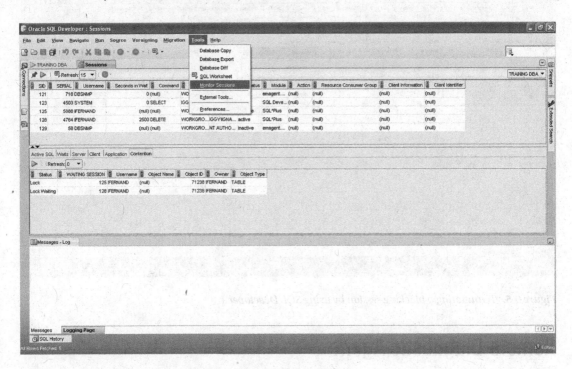

Figure 9-4. *Identifying a blocking session by using SQL Developer*

[1]You cannot use Enterprise Manager to identify and terminate blocking sessions unless you have a license for the Diagnostics Pack.

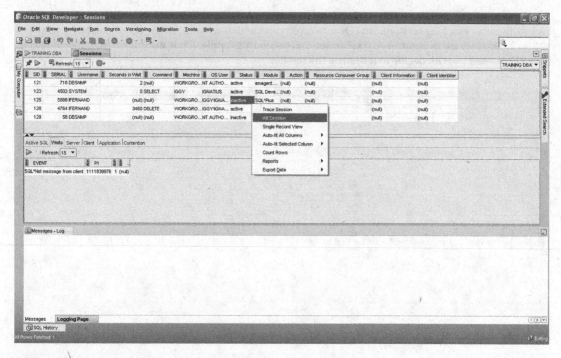

Figure 9-5. *Terminating a blocking session by using SQL Developer*

Remote Diagnostic Agent

Remote Diagnostic Agent (RDA) is provided by Oracle Support to collect all the information about a database and its host system that might aid in the diagnosis of a problem. Oracle Support typically asks that you use this tool and send the collected data to Oracle whenever you request help in solving a problem. Although it was created to aid in the diagnosis of a problem, it is of great help in exploring and documenting database configurations.

RDA organizes the information it gathers into an HTML framework for easy viewing; the starting URL is RDA__start.htm. This is a wonderful way to document all aspects of a system. Figure 9-6 shows an example of system information collected by RDA, and Figure 9-7 shows an example of database information.

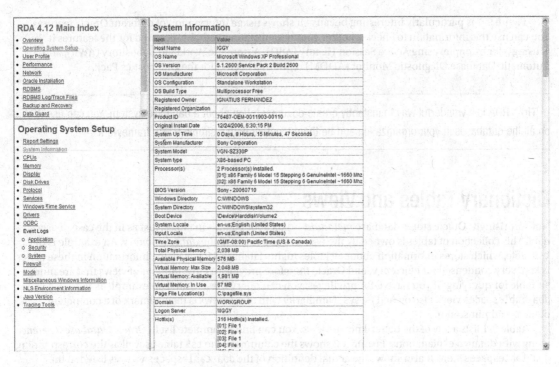

Figure 9-6. *System information collected by Remote Diagnostic Agent*

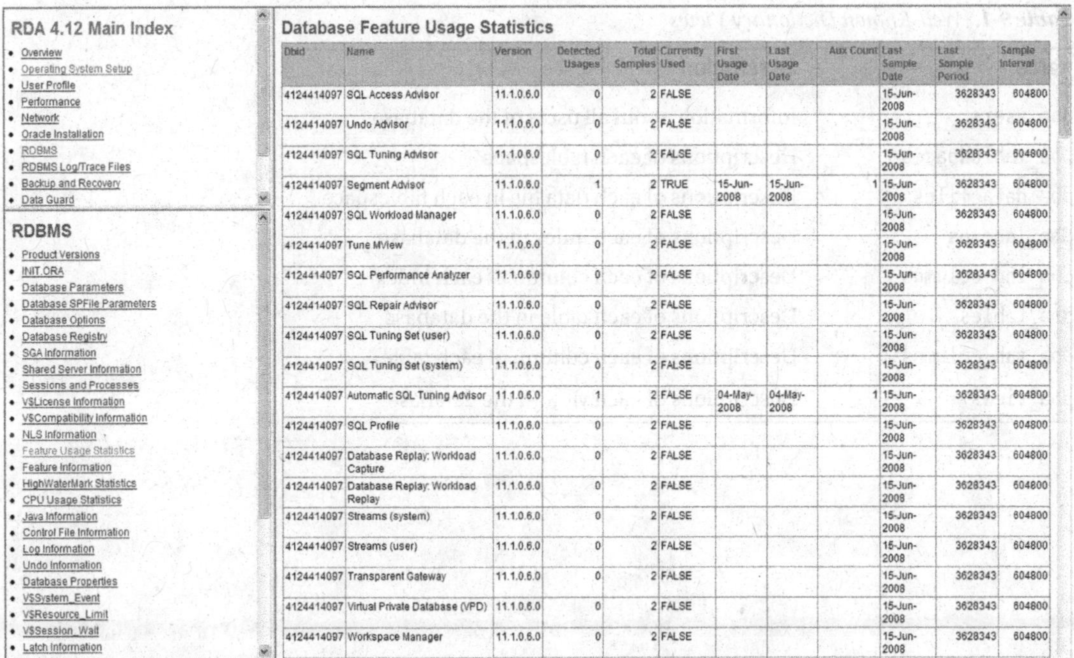

Figure 9-7. *Database information collected by Remote Diagnostic Agent*

Figure 9-7 is particularly interesting because it shows usage information of different Oracle features. You can use this information to check whether your organization is suitably licensed for the features it is using—for example, using Active Session History (ASH), Automatic Workload Repository (AWR), and Automatic Database Diagnostic Monitor (ADDM) requires a license for the Diagnostics Pack.

■ **Tip**   RDA is a wonderful way to instantly create documentation about a database system. You can use RDA on all the databases in your organization and tie them together with a simple HTML framework.

Dictionary Tables and Views

Not surprisingly, Oracle stores database *metadata*—data about data—in tables, just as in the case of user data. This collection of tables is owned by the user sys and is called the *data dictionary*. An example is the ts$ table, which stores information about all tables in the database. However, the information in these tables is kept very condensed for efficiency, and Oracle therefore provides a large number of views that are more suitable for querying. If you have DBA privileges, you can query these views; an example is the dba_tablespaces view, also owned by sys. Familiarity with these views is the hallmark of a competent database administrator.

Table 9-1 lists a few of the better-known views. You can find a complete list in *Oracle Database Reference* along with detailed explanations. Listing 9-2 shows the columns of the ts$ table as well as the corresponding dba_tablespaces view. It also shows the actual definition of the dba_tablespaces view as listed in the dba_views view.

Table 9-1. *Well-Known Dictionary Views*

Name	Description
dba_users	Information about all users of the database
dba_tablespaces	Descriptions of each tablespace
dba_data_files	Descriptions of each data file in each tablespace
dba_indexes	Descriptions of each index in the database
dba_ind_columns	Descriptions of each column of each index
dba_tables	Descriptions of each table in the database
dba_tab_columns	Descriptions of each column of each table
dba_views	Descriptions of each view in the database

Listing 9-2. A Sample Data Dictionary Table and View

```
SQL> DESCRIBE sys.ts$
 Name                                      Null?    Type
 ---------------------------------------- -------- -----------------------------
 TS#                                       NOT NULL NUMBER
 NAME                                      NOT NULL VARCHAR2(30)
 OWNER#                                    NOT NULL NUMBER
 ONLINE$                                   NOT NULL NUMBER
 CONTENTS$                                 NOT NULL NUMBER
 UNDOFILE#                                          NUMBER
 UNDOBLOCK#                                         NUMBER
 BLOCKSIZE                                 NOT NULL NUMBER
 INC#                                      NOT NULL NUMBER
 SCNWRP                                             NUMBER
 SCNBAS                                             NUMBER
 DFLMINEXT                                 NOT NULL NUMBER
 DFLMAXEXT                                 NOT NULL NUMBER
 DFLINIT                                   NOT NULL NUMBER
 DFLINCR                                   NOT NULL NUMBER
 DFLMINLEN                                 NOT NULL NUMBER
 DFLEXTPCT                                 NOT NULL NUMBER
 DFLOGGING                                 NOT NULL NUMBER
 AFFSTRENGTH                               NOT NULL NUMBER
 BITMAPPED                                 NOT NULL NUMBER
 PLUGGED                                   NOT NULL NUMBER
 DIRECTALLOWED                             NOT NULL NUMBER
 FLAGS                                     NOT NULL NUMBER
 PITRSCNWRP                                         NUMBER
 PITRSCNBAS                                         NUMBER
 OWNERINSTANCE                                      VARCHAR2(30)
 BACKUPOWNER                                        VARCHAR2(30)
 GROUPNAME                                          VARCHAR2(30)
 SPARE1                                             NUMBER
 SPARE2                                             NUMBER
 SPARE3                                             VARCHAR2(1000)
 SPARE4                                             DATE

SQL> DESCRIBE sys.dba_tablespaces
 Name                                      Null?    Type
 ---------------------------------------- -------- -----------------------------
 TABLESPACE_NAME                           NOT NULL VARCHAR2(30)
 BLOCK_SIZE                                NOT NULL NUMBER
 INITIAL_EXTENT                                     NUMBER
 NEXT_EXTENT                                        NUMBER
 MIN_EXTENTS                               NOT NULL NUMBER
 MAX_EXTENTS                                        NUMBER
 MAX_SIZE                                           NUMBER
 PCT_INCREASE                                       NUMBER
 MIN_EXTLEN                                         NUMBER
 STATUS                                             VARCHAR2(9)
 CONTENTS                                           VARCHAR2(9)
 LOGGING                                            VARCHAR2(9)
```

```
  FORCE_LOGGING                                    VARCHAR2(3)
  EXTENT_MANAGEMENT                                VARCHAR2(10)
  ALLOCATION_TYPE                                  VARCHAR2(9)
  PLUGGED_IN                                       VARCHAR2(3)
  SEGMENT_SPACE_MANAGEMENT                         VARCHAR2(6)
  DEF_TAB_COMPRESSION                              VARCHAR2(8)
  RETENTION                                        VARCHAR2(11)
  BIGFILE                                          VARCHAR2(3)
  PREDICATE_EVALUATION                             VARCHAR2(7)
  ENCRYPTED                                        VARCHAR2(3)
  COMPRESS_FOR                                     VARCHAR2(18)

SQL> SET LONG 10000
SQL> SELECT text
  2      FROM SYS.dba_views
  3    WHERE owner = 'SYS'
  4      AND view_name = 'DBA_TABLESPACES';

TEXT
--------------------------------------------------------------------------------
select ts.name, ts.blocksize, ts.blocksize * ts.dflinit,
        decode(bitand(ts.flags, 3), 1, to_number(NULL),
               ts.blocksize * ts.dflincr),
        ts.dflminext,
        decode(ts.contents$, 1, to_number(NULL), ts.dflmaxext),
        decode(bitand(ts.flags, 4096), 4096, ts.affstrength, NULL),
        decode(bitand(ts.flags, 3), 1, to_number(NULL), ts.dflextpct),
        ts.blocksize * ts.dflminlen,
        decode(ts.online$, 1, 'ONLINE', 2, 'OFFLINE',
               4, 'READ ONLY', 'UNDEFINED'),
        decode(ts.contents$, 0, (decode(bitand(ts.flags, 16), 16, 'UNDO',
               'PERMANENT')), 1, 'TEMPORARY'),
        decode(bitand(ts.dflogging, 1), 0, 'NOLOGGING', 1, 'LOGGING'),
        decode(bitand(ts.dflogging, 2), 0, 'NO', 2, 'YES'),
        decode(ts.bitmapped, 0, 'DICTIONARY', 'LOCAL'),
        decode(bitand(ts.flags, 3), 0, 'USER', 1, 'SYSTEM', 2, 'UNIFORM',
               'UNDEFINED'),
        decode(ts.plugged, 0, 'NO', 'YES'),
        decode(bitand(ts.flags,32), 32,'AUTO', 'MANUAL'),
        decode(bitand(ts.flags,64), 64,'ENABLED', 'DISABLED'),
        decode(bitand(ts.flags,16), 16, (decode(bitand(ts.flags, 512), 512,
               'GUARANTEE', 'NOGUARANTEE')), 'NOT APPLY'),
        decode(bitand(ts.flags,256), 256, 'YES', 'NO'),
        decode(tsattr.storattr, 1, 'STORAGE', 'HOST'),
        decode(bitand(ts.flags,16384), 16384, 'YES', 'NO'),
        decode(bitand(ts.flags,64), 0, null,
               decode(bitand(ts.flags,65536), 65536,'FOR ALL OPERATIONS',
               'DIRECT LOAD ONLY'))
from sys.ts$ ts, sys.x$kcfistsa tsattr
where ts.online$ != 3
and bitand(flags,2048) != 2048
and ts.ts# = tsattr.tsid
```

These views are typically queried by monitoring tools. For example, the query shown in Listing 9-3 displays the names of tablespaces that are more than 90 percent full.

Listing 9-3. Querying the Data Dictionary

```
COLUMN free_percentage format 990.00

WITH total_space AS
    (SELECT   tablespace:name,
              SUM (CASE
                      WHEN autoextensible = 'YES'
                          THEN maxbytes
                      ELSE BYTES
                  END) AS total_space
        FROM dba_data_files
     GROUP BY tablespace:name),
    used_space AS
    (SELECT   tablespace:name,
              SUM (BYTES) AS used_space
        FROM dba_segments
     GROUP BY tablespace:name)
SELECT tablespace:name,
       100 - (fs.used_space / ts.total_space) * 100 AS free_percentage
  FROM total_space ts NATURAL JOIN used_space fs
 WHERE 100 - (fs.used_space / ts.total_space) * 100 < 10;
```

■ **Tip**   You can find a complete list of data dictionary views in a data dictionary view called DICTIONARY.

Third-Party Tools

Several third-party tools are widely used; examples are Toad and DBArtisan. I particularly like DBArtisan because it allows access to multiple database technologies—Oracle, SQL Server, DB2, and MySQL—from a single console. Figure 9-8 shows the use of Toad to examine the structure of a table. Note the similarity to the corresponding screen of SQL Developer that you saw in Figure 9-2.

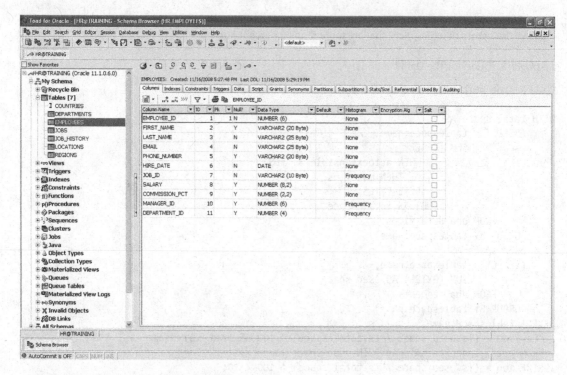

Figure 9-8. *Examining the structure of a table by using Toad*

Summary

Here are some of the key points touched on in this chapter:

- Enterprise Manager comes in two flavors: Database Express and Cloud Control. Both are web-based tools. Database Express is used to manage a single database, whereas Grid Control is used to manage multiple databases. You can accomplish most DBA tasks—from mundane tasks such as password resets and creating indexes, to complex tasks such as backup and recovery—by using Enterprise Manager instead of command-line tools such as SQL*Plus.

- SQL Developer is primarily a tool for software developers, but database administrators will find it very useful. Common uses are examining the structure of a table and checking the execution plan for a query. It can also be used to perform some typical database administration tasks such as identifying and terminating blocking sessions.

- Remote Diagnostic Agent (RDA) is a tool provided by Oracle Support to collect information about a database and its host system. RDA organizes the information it gathers into an HTML framework for easy viewing; it is a wonderful way to document all aspects of a database system.

- Oracle stores database metadata—data about data—in tables, just as in the case of user data. This collection of tables is called the data dictionary. The information in the data dictionary tables is very cryptic and condensed for maximum efficiency during database operation. The data dictionary views are provided to make the information more comprehensible to the database administrator.

Exercises

- Use any of the tools described in this chapter to answer the following questions about your database:

  - Which is the largest table in the database, and who owns it?

  - How many redo log groups have been created? Are the logs mirrored?

  - Which tables do not have indexes?

  - How many control files are being used? Where are they located?

  - What was the largest number of simultaneous sessions (high-water mark)?

  - Do the data files have fixed sizes, or do they expand automatically to accommodate more data?

- Use Oracle Enterprise Manager to perform the following tasks:

  - Reset the password of the hr user.

  - Add a data file to the USERS tablespace.

Monitoring

> *BEHOLD, the fool saith, "Put not all thine eggs in the one basket"—which is but a manner of saying, "Scatter your money and your attention;" but the wise man saith, "Put all your eggs in the one basket and—WATCH THAT BASKET."— Pudd'nhead Wilson's Calendar.*

> —*The Tragedy of Pudd'nhead Wilson* by Mark Twain

When I was growing up, I was sometimes woken at night by the sound of a walking stick tapping on the ground—it was the night watchman patrolling the neighborhood. He would have had a better chance of surprising any burglars if he'd crept up on them quietly, but I never questioned why he advertised his presence so loudly. Armed only with a walking stick, he would have had to rely on strong lungs to wake up the neighborhood if he saw any burglars, so perhaps it was best to advertise his presence and hope that burglars would flee when they heard him coming. Nevertheless, the sound of his stick was comforting—it was good to know that someone trustworthy was watching the neighborhood while we slept.

The database administrator is responsible for watching the database. If something goes wrong with the database that could have been prevented, there is nobody else to blame. Database availability, changes, security, growth, backups, workload, performance, and capacity are some of the areas that should be monitored. Luckily, Oracle offers many tools for database monitoring. Enterprise Manager puts the information at your fingertips and can send out e-mail messages when things go wrong. Oracle also maintains all sorts of totals and counts that keep track of database workload, performance, and capacity. All that remains is to create regular snapshots of these numbers—this is automatically done by tools such as Statspack and Automatic Workload Repository (AWR). This time-series data can be manipulated with SQL queries and turned into graphs. You saw how to enable Statspack snapshots in Chapter 6. Statspack is a free tool, whereas AWR requires you to be licensed for Enterprise Edition as well as Diagnostics Pack. For that reason, I give equal time to Statspack and AWR in this book.

■ **Tip**   The SQL scripts in this chapter use blank lines for extra readability. When executing them in SQL*Plus, use the command `set sqlblanklines on` to prevent them from erroring out.

Monitoring Database Availability

The DBA must continuously monitor the availability of the database and take the necessary action to restore service. The best source of information is the alert log, which contains error messages as well as alert messages. A sample excerpt covering database startup is shown in Listing 10-1.

Listing 10-1. An Extract from the Alert Log

```
Starting up:
Oracle Database 12c Enterprise Edition Release 12.1.0.1.0 - 64bit Production
With the Partitioning, OLAP, Advanced Analytics and Real Application Testing options.
ORACLE_HOME = /u01/app/oracle/product/12.1.0/dbhome_1
System name:    Linux
Node name:      localhost.localdomain
Release:        3.8.13-16.2.1.el6uek.x86_64
Version:        #1 SMP Thu Nov 7 17:01:44 PST 2013
Machine:        x86_64
Using parameter settings in server-side spfile /u01/app/oracle/product/12.1.0/dbhome_1/dbs/
spfileorcl.ora
System parameters with non-default values:
  processes                = 300
  memory_target            = 396M
  control_files            = "/u01/app/oracle/oradata/ORCL/controlfile/o1_mf_9fxn1csd_.ctl"
  control_files            = "/u01/app/oracle/fast_recovery_area/ORCL/controlfile/o1_
mf_9fxn1d0k_.ctl"
  db_block_size            = 8192
  compatible               = "12.1.0.0.0"
  db_create_file_dest      = "/u01/app/oracle/oradata"
  db_recovery_file_dest    = "/u01/app/oracle/fast_recovery_area"
  db_recovery_file_dest_size= 4800M
  undo_tablespace          = "UNDOTBS1"
  remote_login_passwordfile= "EXCLUSIVE"
  db_domain                = ""
  dispatchers              = "(PROTOCOL=TCP) (SERVICE=orclXDB)"
  audit_file_dest          = "/u01/app/oracle/admin/orcl/adump"
  audit_trail              = "DB"
  db_name                  = "orcl"
  open_cursors             = 300
  diagnostic_dest          = "/u01/app/oracle"
  enable_pluggable_database= TRUE
NOTE: remote asm mode is local (mode 0x1; from cluster type)
Starting background process PMON
Starting background process PSP0
Sat Jul 05 22:59:50 2014
PMON started with pid=2, OS id=2103
Starting background process VKTM
Sat Jul 05 22:59:50 2014
PSP0 started with pid=3, OS id=2105
Sat Jul 05 22:59:51 2014
VKTM started with pid=4, OS id=2107 at elevated priority
Starting background process GEN0
```

```
Sat Jul 05 22:59:51 2014
VKTM running at (1)millisec precision with DBRM quantum (100)ms
Starting background process MMAN
Sat Jul 05 22:59:51 2014
GENO started with pid=5, OS id=2111
Sat Jul 05 22:59:51 2014
MMAN started with pid=6, OS id=2113
Starting background process DIAG
Starting background process DBRM
Sat Jul 05 22:59:52 2014
DIAG started with pid=8, OS id=2117
Starting background process DIAO
Sat Jul 05 22:59:52 2014
DBRM started with pid=9, OS id=2119
Starting background process DBWO
Sat Jul 05 22:59:52 2014
DIAO started with pid=10, OS id=2121
Starting background process LGWR
Sat Jul 05 22:59:52 2014
DBWO started with pid=11, OS id=2123
Starting background process CKPT
Sat Jul 05 22:59:52 2014
LGWR started with pid=12, OS id=2125
Starting background process SMON
Sat Jul 05 22:59:53 2014
CKPT started with pid=13, OS id=2127
Starting background process RECO
Sat Jul 05 22:59:53 2014
SMON started with pid=14, OS id=2129
Starting background process LREG
Sat Jul 05 22:59:53 2014
RECO started with pid=15, OS id=2131
Starting background process MMON
Sat Jul 05 22:59:53 2014
LREG started with pid=16, OS id=2133
Starting background process MMNL
Sat Jul 05 22:59:53 2014
MMON started with pid=17, OS id=2135
Sat Jul 05 22:59:54 2014
starting up 1 dispatcher(s) for network address '(ADDRESS=(PARTIAL=YES)(PROTOCOL=TCP))'...
Sat Jul 05 22:59:54 2014
MMNL started with pid=18, OS id=2137
starting up 1 shared server(s) ...
ORACLE_BASE from environment = /u01/app/oracle
Sat Jul 05 22:59:56 2014
ALTER DATABASE   MOUNT
Sat Jul 05 22:59:56 2014
Using default pga_aggregate_limit of 2048 MB
Sat Jul 05 23:00:01 2014
Successful mount of redo thread 1, with mount id 1379942639
Sat Jul 05 23:00:01 2014
```

```
Database mounted in Exclusive Mode
Lost write protection disabled
Ping without log force is disabled.
Completed: ALTER DATABASE   MOUNT
Sat Jul 05 23:00:02 2014
ALTER DATABASE OPEN
```

■ **Tip**   List the contents of the V$DIAG_INFO view and look for the row containing the words Diag Trace—this gives you the location of the alert log. The name of the alert log is alert_*SID*.log, where *SID* is the name of your database instance such as orcl.

Fortunately, there is no need to stay glued to a computer the whole day, reviewing the alert log. You can use Oracle Enterprise Manager to monitor the database and send e-mail messages—or even open problem tickets—whenever problems are detected. Step-by-step instructions for configuring the monitoring capability can be found in the *Oracle Database 12c 2 Day DBA* manual provided on Oracle's website.

It is even possible to customize and extend the alerting capabilities of Enterprise Manager. For example, an alert could be generated if a batch job continued running past a defined maintenance window. Corrective action can be taken automatically if needed; for example, a job that continues running outside a defined maintenance window can be killed automatically, or an incident record can be created in an incident-management system.

■ **Tip**   The alert log contains informational messages in addition to error messages. Even if the database is being monitored by Enterprise Manager, the DBA should periodically review the alert log.

Monitoring Changes

The DBA can monitor changes to database objects using the Oracle auditing facilities. The command AUDIT ALL enables auditing for a wide variety of actions that modify the database and objects in it. Examples of such actions are ALTER SYSTEM, ALTER TABLESPACE, ALTER TABLE, and ALTER INDEX. The list of audited actions is contained in DBA_STMT_AUDIT_OPTS. Auditing of modifications to tables must be separately enabled, using the command AUDIT ALTER TABLE. If the database initialization parameter AUDIT_TRAIL is set to db_extended or xml:extended, Oracle also records the SQL statement associated with the action. As illustrated in Listing 10-2, you can find the information in the DBA_AUDIT_OBJECT view.

Listing 10-2. Monitoring the History of Modifications to Tables and Other Objects

```
SQL> SELECT   TIMESTAMP,
  2              action_name,
  3              sql_text
  4       FROM dba_audit_object
  5      WHERE owner = 'IFERNANDEZ'
  6   ORDER BY TIMESTAMP;
```

```
TIMESTAMP            ACTION_NAME      SQL_TEXT
----------------- ---------------  --------------------------------------------------
08/11/02 10:54:49 CREATE TABLE     CREATE TABLE mydual AS SELECT * FROM dual
08/11/02 10:54:57 ALTER TABLE      ALTER TABLE mydual ADD (dummy2 INTEGER)
08/11/02 10:55:28 DROP TABLE       DROP TABLE mydual
```

I have more to say on the subject of auditing in Chapter 14, in particular about the location and sizing of the audit trail.

Monitoring Security

The DBA can use the Oracle auditing facilities to monitor database usage. The AUDIT CREATE SESSION command causes all connections and disconnections to be recorded. Of particular interest for security purposes are the USERHOST, TERMINAL, and OS_USERNAME values in the DBA_AUDIT_SESSION view. These tell you where a connection originated; unusual values may indicate unauthorized intrusions. Listing 10-3 shows an example.

Listing 10-3. Monitoring the History of Connections and Disconnections

```
PDB1@ORCL> SELECT           userhost,
   2            os_username,
   3            username,
   4            COUNT (*)
   5      FROM dba_audit_session
   6   GROUP BY userhost,
   7            os_username,
   8            username
   9   ORDER BY userhost,
  10            os_username,
  11            username;

USERHOST                          OS_USERNAM USERNAME               COUNT(*)
------------------------------- ---------- --------------------- ----------
localhost.localdomain             oracle     APEX_LISTENER                 3
localhost.localdomain             oracle     APEX_PUBLIC_USER              6
localhost.localdomain             oracle     PMUSER                        1
localhost.localdomain             oracle     SOE                           5

PDB1@ORCL>
PDB1@ORCL> SELECT TIMESTAMP AS logon_time,
   2            logoff_time
   3      FROM dba_audit_session
   4   WHERE username = 'SOE'
   5   ORDER BY 1;

LOGON_TIM LOGOFF_TI
--------- ---------
18-APR-15 18-APR-15
18-APR-15 18-APR-15
18-APR-15 18-APR-15
18-APR-15 18-APR-15
18-APR-15 18-APR-15
```

You should also check the database's security settings. Here are two important questions to ask:

- Is there a password policy that forces users to change their passwords at regular intervals? Is password complexity enforced? Is an account automatically locked if there are too many failed login attempts? (The answers can be found in the DBA_PROFILES view.)

- Which users have DBA privileges? (The answer can be found in the DBA_ROLE_PRIVS view.)

Monitoring Backups

Oracle provides a utility called Recovery Manager (RMAN) for database backups and recovery. One of the advantages of RMAN is that it maintains detailed history information. You can use RMAN commands such as list backup to review the history of backups. You can issue commands such as report need backup and report unrecoverable to determine whether fresh backups are needed. You can also obtain a report of backups on the View Backup Report page of Enterprise Manager.

The use of RMAN for backups and recovery is discussed in Chapters 12 and 13, respectively.

Monitoring Growth

As illustrated in Listing 10-4, you can use the information in the DBA_DATA_FILES view to monitor the size of your database; the query shows the size in megabytes of each tablespace in the database.

Listing 10-4. Using the DBA_DATA_FILES View to Monitor the Size of the Database

```
SELECT    tablespace:name,
          SUM (BYTES) / 1048576 AS mb
   FROM dba_data_files
GROUP BY tablespace:name
ORDER BY tablespace:name;
```

You can incorporate the query in Listing 10-4 into a batch report with the SQL*Plus command-line tool, or you can execute it interactively with SQL Developer. Alternatively, as illustrated in Figure 10-1, Enterprise Manager offers a visual representation of space usage.

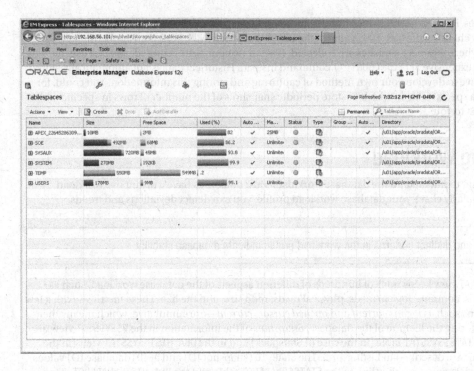

Figure 10-1. Database size report in Enterprise Manager

Table sizes can be monitored using the DBA_SEGMENTS view. The query in Listing 10-5 displays table sizes in megabytes; it uses the RANK function to limit the list to the ten biggest tables.

Listing 10-5. Using DBA_SEGMENTS to Determine the Ten Biggest Tables

```
WITH ranked_information AS

    (SELECT owner,
            segment_name,
            BYTES / 1048576 AS mb,
            RANK () OVER (ORDER BY BYTES DESC) AS RANK
      FROM dba_segments
     WHERE segment_type = 'TABLE')

SELECT  RANK,
        owner,
        segment_name,
        mb
   FROM ranked_information
  WHERE RANK <= 10

ORDER BY RANK;
```

In some cases, it is also useful to monitor the number of rows in specific tables; this is efficiently accomplished by checking the NUM_ROWS value in the DBA_TABLES view. NUM_ROWS is an approximate value that is updated when optimizer statistics are collected. If accurate counts are required, you can use the computationally expensive SELECT COUNT(*) command instead. Historical data is not automatically stored by Oracle; you have to develop your own method of capturing and storing this information. You could, for example, create a special table in which to store periodic snapshots of the number of rows in specific tables that are of interest to you.

Monitoring Workload

It is very important to understand the database workload. Most databases have a distinctive workload profile. If you regularly check your database workload profile, you can detect deviations and trends.

■ **Tip**   Regular and distinct patterns in the workload profile indicate database stability.

The V$SYSSTAT view keeps track of hundreds of different aspects of the database workload, such as logons, executions, commits, logical reads, physical reads, redo size, and the like. These metrics—with a few notable exceptions such as *logons current* and *opened cursors current*—are cumulative, which means their values increase during the lifetime of the database. *Snapshots* of the information in the V$SYSSTAT view are available in the STATS$SYSSTAT table (in the case of Statspack) and in the DBA_HIST_SYSSTAT view (in the case of AWR); they are described in Listing 10-6. The SNAP_ID (snapshot ID) and DBID (database ID) values are used to identify snapshots—they link to the STATS$SNAPSHOT table and the DBA_HIST_SNAPSHOT view, which contain details such as the time when the snapshot was created.

Listing 10-6. Tables and Views for Monitoring the Database Workload

```
SQL> DESCRIBE v$sysstat;
 Name                                      Null?    Type
 ----------------------------------------- -------- --------------------
 STATISTIC#                                         NUMBER
 NAME                                               VARCHAR2(64)
 CLASS                                              NUMBER
 VALUE                                              NUMBER
 STAT_ID                                            NUMBER

SQL> DESCRIBE stats$sysstat;
 Name                                      Null?    Type
 ----------------------------------------- -------- ----------------------------
 SNAP_ID                                   NOT NULL NUMBER
 DBID                                      NOT NULL NUMBER
 INSTANCE_NUMBER                           NOT NULL NUMBER
 STATISTIC#                                NOT NULL NUMBER
 NAME                                      NOT NULL VARCHAR2(64)
 VALUE                                              NUMBER
```

```
SQL> DESCRIBE dba_hist_sysstat
 Name                                        Null?     Type
 ------------------------------------------- --------- ----------------------------
 SNAP_ID                                     NOT NULL  NUMBER
 DBID                                        NOT NULL  NUMBER
 INSTANCE_NUMBER                             NOT NULL  NUMBER
 STAT_ID                                     NOT NULL  NUMBER
 STAT_NAME                                   NOT NULL  VARCHAR2(64)
 VALUE                                                 NUMBER
```

The Excel graph shown in Figure 10-2 was generated using the data produced by the SQL query shown in Listing 10-7. The graph shows a distinct pattern, indicating database stability. The PIVOT operator is used to produce new columns, and the LAG analytic function is used to operate on data in different rows. The use of subquery factoring breaks the query into logical pieces and makes it readable.

Listing 10-7. SQL Query to List Logical Reads per Second and Physical Reads per Second for a One-Week Period

```
WITH

    -- Pivot the data in the STATS$SYSSTAT table
    -- Create separate columns for physical reads and logical reads

    pivoted_data AS

    (SELECT *
       FROM (SELECT snap_id,
                    NAME,
                    VALUE
               FROM stats$sysstat)
            PIVOT (SUM(value)
              FOR name IN ('physical reads' AS physical_reads,
                           'session logical reads' AS logical_reads))),

    deltas AS

    -- Use the LAG analytic function to determine the amount of increase

    (SELECT snap_id,

            snap_time,

            snap_time
            - LAG (snap_time)
                OVER (PARTITION BY startup_time
                      ORDER BY snap_id)
              AS duration,
```

```
        physical_reads
          - LAG (physical_reads)
              OVER (PARTITION BY startup_time
                      ORDER BY snap_id)
            AS physical_reads,

        logical_reads
          - LAG (logical_reads)
              OVER (PARTITION BY startup_time
                      ORDER BY snap_id)
            AS logical_reads

    FROM pivoted_data NATURAL JOIN stats$snapshot)

SELECT   snap_id,
         to_char(snap_time, 'yyyy/mm/dd hh24:mi') as snap_time,
         physical_reads / duration / (24 * 60 * 60) as physical_reads_per_second,
         logical_reads / duration / (24 * 60 * 60) AS logical_reads_per_second
    FROM deltas

ORDER BY snap_id;
```

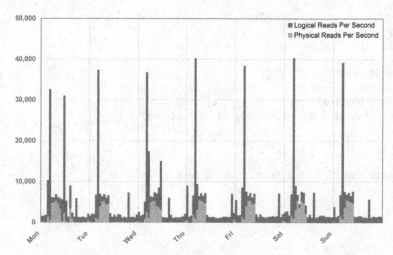

Figure 10-2. *Excel graph of logical reads and physical reads produced using the time-series data in the STATS$SYSSTAT table*

Monitoring Performance

Be sure to monitor the performance of important queries. The V$SQLAREA view records execution statistics such as executions, CPU time, elapsed time, logical reads, and physical reads for each SQL statement cached in the *library cache*—it is therefore a source of workload information as well as performance information. Snapshots of the information in the V$SQLAREA view are available in the STATS$SQL_SUMMARY table (in the case of Statspack) and in the DBA_HIST_SQLSTAT view (in the case of AWR). The SQL statement in Listing 10-8 retrieves the average execution times of each of two SQL queries of choice in successive time periods; the query can easily be modified to include additional queries that are critical to application performance. Notice the use of the LAST_VALUE analytic function to interpolate missing values.

Listing 10-8. SQL Query to List the Average Elapsed Times for Two SQL Queries of Choice

```
WITH pivoted_data AS

    -- Pivot the data in STATS$SQL_SUMMARY using two values of the SQL ID column.
    -- q1 and q2 refer to the two values of interest in the SQL ID column.
    -- Create new columns representing the total elapsed time and the number of
    -- executions of each of the two queries.
    -- The newly created columns are named as follows:
    --    q1_elapsed_time
    --    q1_executions
    --    q2_elapsed_time
    --    q2_executions

    (SELECT *
        FROM (SELECT snap_id,
                     sql_id,
                     elapsed_time,
                     executions
                FROM stats$sql_summary)
            PIVOT (SUM(elapsed_time) AS elapsed_time,
                   SUM(executions) AS executions
              FOR sql_id IN ('&&1' AS q1,
                             '&&2' AS q2))),

    interpolated_data AS

    -- Interpolate any missing values using the LAST_VALUE analytic function.
    -- Use the last non-null value after the database was started.
    -- The STATS$SNAPSHOT view tells us when the database was started.

    (SELECT snap_id,

            snap_time,

            startup_time,
```

```
          LAST_VALUE (q1_elapsed_time IGNORE NULLS)
            OVER (PARTITION BY startup_time
                  ORDER BY snap_id
                  ROWS BETWEEN UNBOUNDED PRECEDING AND CURRENT ROW)
              AS q1_elapsed_time_i,

          LAST_VALUE (q1_executions IGNORE NULLS)
            OVER (PARTITION BY startup_time
                  ORDER BY snap_id
                  ROWS BETWEEN UNBOUNDED PRECEDING AND CURRENT ROW)
              AS q1_executions_i,

          LAST_VALUE (q2_elapsed_time IGNORE NULLS)
            OVER (PARTITION BY startup_time
                  ORDER BY snap_id
                  ROWS BETWEEN UNBOUNDED PRECEDING AND CURRENT ROW)
              AS q2_elapsed_time_i,

          LAST_VALUE (q2_executions IGNORE NULLS)
            OVER (PARTITION BY startup_time
                  ORDER BY snap_id
                  ROWS BETWEEN UNBOUNDED PRECEDING AND CURRENT ROW)
              AS q2_executions_i

     FROM pivoted_data NATURAL JOIN stats$snapshot),

  deltas AS

  -- Use the LAG analytic function to determine the amount of increase.

  (SELECT snap_id,

          snap_time,

          q1_elapsed_time_i
            - LAG (q1_elapsed_time_i)
                OVER (PARTITION BY startup_time
                      ORDER BY snap_id)
              AS q1_elapsed_time_d,

          q1_executions_i
            - LAG (q1_executions_i)
                OVER (PARTITION BY startup_time
                      ORDER BY snap_id)
              AS q1_executions_d,

          q2_elapsed_time_i
            - LAG (q2_elapsed_time_i)
                OVER (PARTITION BY startup_time
                      ORDER BY snap_id)
              AS q2_elapsed_time_d,
```

```
            q2_executions_i
              - LAG (q2_executions_i)
                  OVER (PARTITION BY startup_time
                        ORDER BY snap_id)
              AS q2_executions_d

      FROM interpolated_data)

-- Print the number of executions and average execution time for each time period.
-- Convert microseconds to seconds when printing the average execution time.
-- Don't print any negative values.

SELECT   snap_id,

         TO_CHAR (snap_time, 'yyyy/mm/dd hh24:mi') AS snap_time,

         CASE
           WHEN q1_elapsed_time_d > 0 AND q1_executions_d > 0
             THEN q1_executions_d
         END AS q1_executions_d,

         CASE
           WHEN q1_elapsed_time_d > 0 AND q1_executions_d > 0
             THEN q1_elapsed_time_d / q1_executions_d / 1000000
         END AS q1_elapsed_time_a,

         CASE
           WHEN q2_elapsed_time_d > 0 AND q2_executions_d > 0
             THEN q2_executions_d
         END AS q2_executions_d,

         CASE
           WHEN q2_elapsed_time_d > 0 AND q2_executions_d > 0
             THEN q2_elapsed_time_d / q2_executions_d / 1000000
         END AS q2_elapsed_time_a

    FROM deltas

ORDER BY snap_id;
```

Monitoring Capacity

The V$OSSTAT view offers cumulative values for operating system metrics such as CPU usage. Snapshots of the information in the V$OSSTAT view are available in the STATS$OSSTAT table (in the case of Statspack) and in the DBA_HIST_OSSTAT view (in the case of AWR); they are described in Listing 10-9. The SQL statement in Listing 10-10 computes the CPU utilization percentage for each time period.

Listing 10-9. Tables and Views for Monitoring Database Capacity

```
SQL> DESCRIBE v$osstat;
Name                                        Null?     Type
------------------------------------------- --------- ---------------------------
STAT_NAME                                             VARCHAR2(64)
VALUE                                                 NUMBER
OSSTAT_ID                                             NUMBER
COMMENTS                                              VARCHAR2(64)
CUMULATIVE                                            VARCHAR2(3)


SQL> DESCRIBE stats$osstat
Name                                        Null?     Type
------------------------------------------- --------- ---------------------------
SNAP_ID                                     NOT NULL  NUMBER
DBID                                        NOT NULL  NUMBER
INSTANCE_NUMBER                             NOT NULL  NUMBER
OSSTAT_ID                                   NOT NULL  NUMBER
VALUE                                                 NUMBER


SQL> DESCRIBE dba_hist_osstat
Name                                        Null?     Type
------------------------------------------- --------- ---------------------------
SNAP_ID                                     NOT NULL  NUMBER
DBID                                        NOT NULL  NUMBER
INSTANCE_NUMBER                             NOT NULL  NUMBER
STAT_ID                                     NOT NULL  NUMBER
STAT_NAME                                   NOT NULL  VARCHAR2(64)
VALUE                                                 NUMBER
```

Listing 10-10. SQL Query to Compute the CPU Utilization Percentage

```
WITH

    pivoted_data AS

    -- Pivot the data in the STATS$OSSTAT table
    -- Create separate columns for total idle time and total busy time

    (SELECT *
       FROM (SELECT snap_id,
                    osstat_id,
                    VALUE
               FROM stats$osstat)
            PIVOT (SUM(value)
              FOR osstat_id IN (1 AS idle_time,
                                2 AS busy_time))),

    deltas AS

    -- Use the LAG analytic function to determine the amount of increase

    (SELECT snap_id,
```

```
          snap_time,

          idle_time
            - LAG (idle_time)
                OVER (PARTITION BY startup_time
                      ORDER BY snap_id)
            AS idle_time,

          busy_time
            - LAG (busy_time)
                OVER (PARTITION BY startup_time
                      ORDER BY snap_id)
            AS busy_time

        FROM pivoted_data NATURAL JOIN stats$snapshot)

SELECT    snap_id,
          to_char(snap_time, 'yyyy/mm/dd hh24:mi') as snap_time,
          busy_time / (idle_time + busy_time) AS cpu_utilization_p
    FROM deltas

ORDER BY snap_id;
```

■ **Tip**   If you have licensed the System Monitoring Plug-In for Hosts, Enterprise Manager can track disk and CPU utilization and alert you when thresholds are breached.

Third-Party Tools

Many organizations use third-party tools for enterprise-wide monitoring. Examples include Patrol from BMC, Tivoli from IBM, and OpenView from HP. Open source tools such as Nagios are also a popular choice. An enterprise-wide tool that is agnostic to database and server technologies will have more breadth than Oracle Enterprise Manager but not as much depth. However, Enterprise Manager is constrained by the number of extra-cost options that must be separately licensed—they include Provisioning Pack, Database Change Management Pack, Database Tuning Pack, Database Configuration Pack, Database Diagnostics Pack, System Monitoring Plug-in for Hosts, and so on.

If you join a team of DBAs, you should ask your colleagues for information about the monitoring tools being used in your organization.

Summary

Here is a short summary of the concepts touched on in this chapter:

- Database availability, changes, security, growth, backups, workload, performance, and capacity are some of the areas that should be monitored by the DBA.

- The alert log contains error messages and informational messages. The location of the alert log is listed in the V$DIAG_INFO view. The name of the alert log is alert_*SID*.log, where *SID* is the name of your database instance.

- Enterprise Manager monitors the database and sends e-mail messages when problems are detected.

- The command `AUDIT ALL` enables auditing for a wide variety of actions that modify the database and objects in it, such as `ALTER SYSTEM`, `ALTER TABLESPACE`, `ALTER TABLE`, and `ALTER INDEX`.

- The `AUDIT CREATE SESSION` command causes all connections and disconnections to be recorded.

- Recovery Manager (RMAN) maintains detailed history information about backups. RMAN commands such as `list backup`, `report need backup`, and `report unrecoverable` can be used to review backups. Enterprise Manager can also be used to review backups.

- Database size can be monitored using `DBA_DATA_FILES`; table size can be monitored using `DBA_SEGMENTS`.

- Oracle maintains a large number of totals and counts that keep track of database workload, performance, and capacity. Statspack and AWR create regular snapshots of these numbers—this time-series data can be manipulated with SQL queries and turned into graphs. The `V$SQLAREA` view records execution statistics such as executions, CPU time, elapsed time, logical reads, and physical reads for each SQL statement cached in the library cache. The `V$OSSTAT` view offers cumulative values of operating system metrics such as CPU usage.

Exercises

- Review the discussion of user management in Chapter 8. Also review the definitions of the `DBA_ROLE_PRIVS` and `DBA_PROFILES` views in *Oracle Database 12c Reference* in the Oracle documentation set. Answer the following questions about the database pdb1 in your VM: Which database users have DBA authority? Is there a password policy that forces database users to change their passwords at regular intervals? Is password complexity enforced? Is an account automatically locked if there are too many failed login attempts?

- Develop a system that tracks database growth and table growth. Create history tables to capture the information contained in the `DBA_DATA_FILES` and `DBA_SEGMENTS` views. Write SQL queries that report daily, weekly, and monthly growth.

- Modify the Statspack queries in this chapter for use with the corresponding AWR views: `DBA_HIST_SNAPSHOT`, `DBA_HIST_SYSSTAT`, `DBA_HIST_SQLSTAT`, and `DBA_HIST_OSSTAT`. The definitions of the AWR views can be found in the *Oracle Database 12c Reference* manual.

Further Reading

- *Oracle Database 12c 2 Day DBA* Chapter 3 (Introduction to Oracle Enterprise Manager Database Express. `http://docs.oracle.com`.

- Oracle by Example (OBE) tutorial "Getting Started with Oracle Enterprise Manager Express."

CHAPTER 11

■ ■ ■

Fixing Problems

Rise and shine, sleepy Joe

There are places to go

There are windows to clean on the way

You've got nothing to lose

But a shine on your shoes

Do the best things you can every day

> "Sleepy Joe," composed by John Carter and Russell Alquist and
> recorded by Herman's Hermits

To state the obvious, fixing problems is the part of the DBA's job that takes precedence over everything else. In his best-selling book *The 7 Habits of Highly Effective People*, Stephen Covey explains that our activities can be divided among four quadrants depending on their urgency and importance. Figure 11-1 illustrates these quadrants.

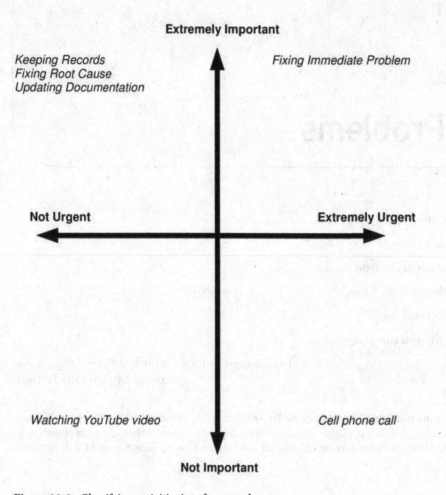

Extremely Important

Keeping Records
Fixing Root Cause
Updating Documentation

Fixing Immediate Problem

Not Urgent

Extremely Urgent

Watching YouTube video

Cell phone call

Not Important

Figure 11-1. Classifying activities into four quadrants

Restoring service when the database crashes is an example of an activity that is both important *and* urgent. Determining the root cause of the database crash is important but not as urgent. The loud ringing of your cell phone demands your immediate attention but is rarely more important than the task at hand. And, of course, watching the latest sensational video on YouTube is unimportant and not urgent.

We tend to spend most of our time in the quadrant of activities that are important and urgent. However, the ideal place to spend time is the quadrant of activities that are important but *not* urgent: for example, keeping records, identifying the root causes of incidents and eliminating them, updating documentation, automating common tasks, and so forth.

In this chapter, you watch a real-life problem as it progresses from detection to resolution. You learn a five-step systematic approach to problem-fixing and the difference between *incident management* and *problem management*. I cover the variety of Internet resources that are available to you, introduce an Oracle knowledge base called My Oracle Support, and explain how to get paid support from Oracle Corporation. Finally, I discuss a few common problems.

Systematic Five-Step Problem-Solving Method

In his book *The Art and Science of Oracle Performance Tuning*, Christopher Lawson describes a systematic five-step method for solving a performance-tuning problem. The method applies to any problem, not just to a performance problem. Oracle Database versions and software tools may change, but the five steps always remain the same. A problem may be simple and require only a few minutes of your time, or it may be tremendously complex and require weeks, but the five steps never change:

1. *Define* the problem. This requires patient listening, skillful questioning, and even careful observation. "Is the database having a problem?" is a question, not a problem statement. "The users are complaining" is a poorly defined problem statement. "I cannot connect to the database" is very precise. Ask the user for the history of the problem. Ask what previous efforts have been made to solve the problem. Ask what changed recently in the environment—for example, software or hardware upgrades. Ask whether all users are affected or only some. Ask whether the problem occurs at specific times of the day or week. Ask whether all parts of the application are equally affected or just parts. *Avoid confusing the problem with the solution—for example, "The problem is that we need to reboot the server."* A good way to end this phase is with a reproducible test case or with one or more Oracle error codes.

2. *Investigate* the problem, and collect as much pertinent evidence as possible. A good place to start is the Oracle alert log.

3. *Analyze* the data collected in step 2, and isolate the cause of the performance problem. This is often the most challenging part of the performance-tuning exercise. If the root cause is not found, you can go back to step 2 to continue your investigation of the problem or to step 1 to refine the definition of the problem.

4. *Solve* the problem by creating a solution that addresses the cause of the problem. Solutions are not always obvious, and, therefore, this part of the exercise may require a great deal of ingenuity and creativity.

5. *Implement* the solution in a safe and controlled manner. Conduct an appropriate level of testing in a suitable testing environment. Obtain necessary approvals, and follow the organization's change-management procedures. *Before* and *after* measurements should be obtained in the case of performance problems. If the *after* measurements indicate that the problem is not fixed, you can return to step 2 and continue your investigation of the problem.

The flowchart in Figure 11-2 illustrates the problem-solving work flow.

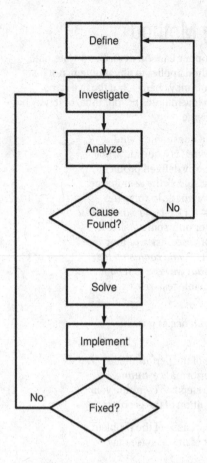

Figure 11-2. *Systematic five-step problem-solving method*

The Book We All Want and Best Practices for Problem Management

The book we all want is a book that has a clear description of every Oracle problem and step-by-step instructions for fixing them. That book will never be written. There are just too many problems that can occur. Problems can have multiple solutions. The solution may depend on *your particular circumstances*. In many cases, it is not even clear what the problem really is. The best you can do is to use best practices for problem management. Here are my suggestions:

- *Fix problems proactively.* Monitoring your database and preventing problems is better than fixing problems—for example, add space to a database before it fills up completely and jobs begin to fail.

- *Find the root cause of problems.* After the problem has been fixed, look for the underlying root cause—for example, find out why the database is growing and how much space will be needed over the medium term.

- *Use good tools.* Workers are only as good as their tools. The more tools you have, the better you are equipped to solve a problem. Commonly used tools include Oracle-supplied tools such as Enterprise Manager and SQL Developer and third-party tools such as Toad from Quest Software and DBArtisan from Embarcadero Technologies.

- *Use standard operating procedures (SOPs).* The two obvious advantages of SOPs are consistency and efficiency, but there are many others. Chapter 15 returns to the subject of SOPs.

- *Document the database environment.* Remote Diagnostic Agent (RDA), introduced in Chapter 9, is a simple tool that you can use to document your environment. An RDA collection collects all the information about the database and operating system into one compact package that is very useful in solving problems.

- *Ask for help.* Several online forums can help you solve a problem. If you have an Oracle support contract, you can escalate a problem to an Oracle engineer. We return to this subject later in this chapter.

- *Keep work records.* The most important thing to do is to keep work records. When a problem reoccurs, it helps to have access to the details of prior occurrences. Every environment is prone to certain problems—for example, Oracle Database 10.1.0.3 is affected by a bug that causes the nightly statistics-gathering job GATHER_STATS_JOB to fail—the characteristic error code is ORA-00904.

■ **Note**   An IT organization without work records is like a dentist's office without dental records. Work records are one of the ten deliverables of the database administration role listed in Chapter 15.

Figure 11-3, courtesy of Database Specialists, proves the value of work records in solving chronic problems: Three DBAs—Iggy Fernandez, Terry Sutton, and Roger Schrag—encountered an ORA-00904 error in the alert log, and a quick search of the work records told them each time that it was a known problem that had occurred many times in the same database.

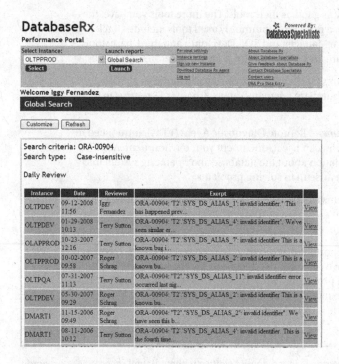

Figure 11-3. Searching work records

Real-Life Example: Unresponsive Listener

This section presents the transcripts—with some editing to preserve confidentiality—of several instant-messaging conversations between a DBA and another member of the IT staff. The problem puzzles the DBA the first time but is fixed very quickly the second time it occurs.

Define the Problem

A member of the IT staff tells the DBA that the database "seems to be locked up." This phase ends when the DBA is able to reproduce the problem—he cannot connect to the database from the reporting server. The DBA now has a clear definition of the problem:

```
User: help. our oracle database server seems to be locked up
User: if I do sql
User: it says cannot connect. I cannot connect from reporting server
DBA: ok let me try that
DBA: ok i cannot connect either
```

Investigate and Analyze the Problem

The DBA now begins looking for information that may shed light on the problem. The first thing he does is check the alert log. He finds that the database is healthy, and he is able to connect to it without going through the listener—that is, using a local session on the database server. This phase ends when he discovers that there are two listeners. This is apparently the cause of the problem, because the timestamp of the last good entry in the alert log coincides with the time when the second listener was started:

```
DBA: no errors in alert log
DBA: cpu and load average good check
DBA: without the @ i can connect
DBA: this tells me that the database is OK
DBA: connections to port 1521 are failing
User: listener ?
DBA: trying telnet localhost 1521 to find out if there is connectivity to the port
DBA: hmmmm there is
DBA: $ telnet localhost 1521
Trying 127.0.0.1...
Connected to localhost.localdomain (127.0.0.1).
Escape character is '^]'.
DBA: that is the behaviour i expect
DBA: can you try it from the reporting server
DBA: telnet should produce the same output
DBA: i.e. it should connect
User: ok. one sec
DBA: i.e. it should "connect" but not quite
DBA: i.e. it should detect somebody listening
DBA: but obviously there is no telnet daemon there
DBA: and it will hang
User: it hangs
DBA: same output as above
DBA: ok ...
DBA: the last connection recorded in tail /local/service/oracle/product/10.2.0/db/network/
log/listener.log
on the db server was at 14:17
DBA: it is now 15:05
DBA: 09-JUN-2007 14:17:47 *
(CONNECT_DATA=(SID=devdb)(CID=(PROGRAM=)(HOST=__jdbc__)(USER) *
(ADDRESS=(PROTOCOL=tcp)(HOST=127.0.0.1)(PORT=5009)) * establish * proddb * 0 09-JUN-
2007 14:17:47 * (CONNECT_DATA=(SID=devdb)(CID=(PROGRAM=)(HOST=__jdbc__)(USER) *
(ADDRESS=(PROTOCOL=tcp)(HOST=127.0.0.1)(PORT=5010)) * establish * proddb * 0
DBA: definitely a problem with the listener
DBA: but ....
DBA: my guess is that somehow the database server cannot talk to the world
DBA: the way it works is that ...
DBA: all traffic flows through the 1521 port
DBA: both inbound and outbound
DBA: for all sessions
DBA: there is one unix process servicing each client process
DBA: but everybody talks over the 1521 port
DBA: looks like the report server can reach the 1521 port
```

```
DBA: but perhaps the db cannot talk back
DBA: aah i have it
DBA: $ ps -ef |grep lsnr
oracle 19832 1 0 Mar31 ? 00:05:40
/local/service/oracle/product/10.2.0/db/bin/tnslsnr LISTENER -inherit
oracle 19987 19832 0 14:17 ? 00:00:00
/local/service/oracle/product/10.2.0/db/bin/tnslsnr LISTENER -inherit
DBA: look carefully
DBA: two listeners
DBA: one at 14:17
DBA: the second process is the child of the first
```

Solve and Implement the Problem

Having determined that the second listener is the problem, the DBA first tries to shut down the listeners gracefully. When that fails, he uses the Unix kill command. The situation returns to normal as soon as the second listener is terminated. The DBA promises to research what caused the second listener to be started and why nobody was able to connect to the database as a result:

```
User: can we restart the listener
DBA: let me try
DBA: I cannot stop it the normal way
DBA: because the normal way involves connecting to it
DBA: lsnrctl hangs
User: aaah
DBA: $ lsnrctl status

LSNRCTL for Linux: Version 10.2.0.1.0 - Production on 09-JUN-2007 15:18:28

Copyright (c) 1991, 2005, Oracle. All rights reserved.

Connecting to (DESCRIPTION=(ADDRESS=(PROTOCOL=TCP)(HOST=127.0.0.1)(PORT=1521)))
DBA: hangs at that point
User: ok. makes sense. something is locked up in that process. may be one of the
threads
DBA: ok killing both
User: yeah.
DBA: woo hoo
DBA: i killed the second process
DBA: i can connect now
DBA: SQL*Plus: Release 10.2.0.1.0 - Production on Wed Jun 9 15:21:32 2007

Copyright (c) 1982, 2005, Oracle. All rights reserved.

Connected to:
Oracle Database 10g Release 10.2.0.1.0 - Production

SQL> quit
Disconnected from Oracle Database 10g Release 10.2.0.1.0 - Production
DBA: it was failing before
DBA: check on the report server
```

```
User: yeah. it works fine now
User: great.
DBA: thanks ... two heads are better than one
User: I agree. It's good to know what happened. great. thanks.
DBA: i;ll do some research
DBA: on the phrase "two listeners"
User: ok. cool. gotta go. bye

DBA: l8r
```

One Week Later

When the problem occurred again, very little diagnosis and resolution time were required:

```
User: hi, the oracle server seems to have died last night. can you check. tks
DBA: really?
DBA: that's really bad
User: it was running level 0 backup y'day and I thought because of that queries were
timing out. but looks like it's hosed.
DBA: checking now
User: thank you!
DBA: it may be the same problem that we saw a week ago
DBA: dev
DBA: checking
DBA: yes ... two listeners
DBA: nobody can attach
User: hmmm
DBA: problem cleared
User: tks.
```

Opportunities for Improvement

The DBA in this example has considerable Oracle experience and good problem-solving skills, but there are nevertheless several opportunities for improvement:

- The problem was reported to the DBA by a member of the IT staff, well after the problem started. No monitoring mechanisms were in place to automatically alert the DBA about the loss of service.

- There was no further investigation after the first incident. The problem had been fixed, but the root cause had not been determined. In this case, the listener log file contained many occurrences of the following message: WARNING: Subscription for node down event still pending. This would have been a good place to start the investigation.

Incident Management vs. Problem Management

An *incident* is a single occurrence of a problem. Incident management and problem management are therefore separate aspects of IT management. *Incident management* is concerned with restoring service as rapidly as possible. *Problem management* is concerned with permanently fixing defects so the incidents are not repeated.

In the real-life example in the preceding section, the organization gets high marks for incident management but low marks for problem management. Problem management is facilitated by record keeping—tools such as BMC Remedy Service Desk can be used for this purpose. Knowledge of the event was confined to the DBA and the member of the IT staff who contacted him. Records were not kept, the incident was forgotten, and a second service outage occurred a week later.

Internet Resources

The Internet is a treasure trove of information that can help you in solving a problem. For example, user groups such as the Northern California Oracle Users Group (www.nocoug.org) have made vast collections of electronic presentations and white papers available on their web pages. Often a simple Google search will bring up an answer, but many specialized resources also are available:

- Online Oracle documentation

- Online forums

- Oracle Technology Network

- Ask Tom web site

- Usenet

- Oracle-L mailing list

The highest quality resource is of course the online Oracle documentation, the home page for which is shown in Figure 11-4. This documentation is freely viewable, searchable, and downloadable at https://docs.oracle.com. Documentation for older versions of Oracle software going back to Oracle 7 is also available here. If you need to be able to work offline, you can download as much documentation as you need.

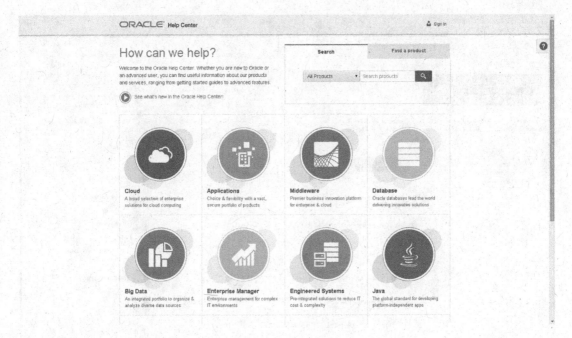

Figure 11-4. *Online Oracle documentation*

■ **Tip** Download the manuals and guides you need to your desktop, laptop, or mobile device so you can read them offline, especially if you prefer the book format instead of the online format.

You also can ask questions on the Oracle forums (https://community.oracle.com), shown in Figure 11-5. Many Oracle experts donate a lot of time answering questions posted here.

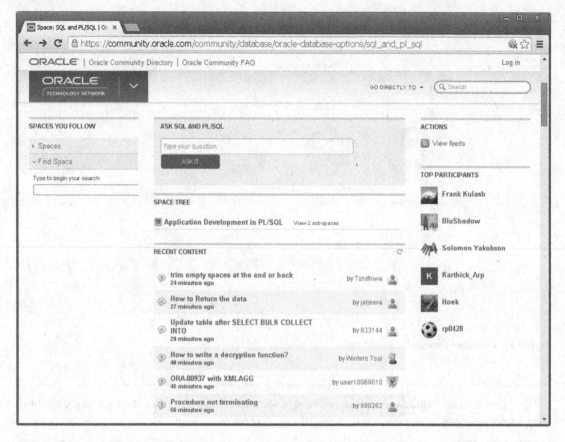

Figure 11-5. *The Oracle forums*

The Oracle Technology Network (`www.oracle.com/technetwork`) is the jumping-off place for all the free resources provided by Oracle Corporation, including articles, sample code, and tutorials. It also contains links to the Oracle documentation and Oracle forums. Figure 11-6 shows the Oracle Technology Network.

Figure 11-6. *The Oracle Technology Network*

Working with Oracle Support

You can search the Oracle knowledge base My Oracle Support (MOS) and obtain technical support from Oracle Support if you are paying annual support fees to Oracle and have a valid Customer Support Identifier (CSI). The support fees are typically 22 percent of the cost of your Oracle licenses. If you choose to forgo Oracle support, you will not be entitled to any patches (fixes for software bugs) or upgrades.

The web page for Oracle Support is `http://support.oracle.com`, shown in Figure 11-7. The tabs on the page indicate the range of things you can do here—for example, read headlines, search the knowledge base, request service, download patches, participate in forums, and so forth.

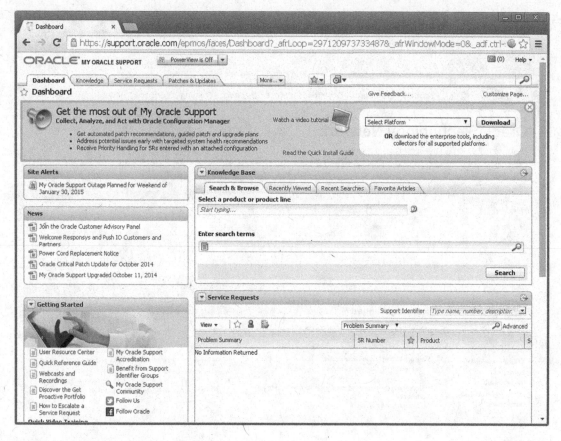

Figure 11-7. *Working with Oracle Support*

If you cannot find an answer in the Oracle knowledge base, you can create a service request. The priority of the service request and the corresponding service-level commitment depend on the impact to your organization. For instance, a production outage is classified as Severity 1 and is given the highest level of attention.

Remote Diagnostic Agent (RDA)

Chapter 9 touched on RDA collections. An RDA collection, shown in Figure 11-8, collects all the information about the database and operating system into one compact package that can be attached to a service request. The RDA collection eliminates the need for Oracle engineers to ask questions about the database environment and shortens the time required for problem resolution.

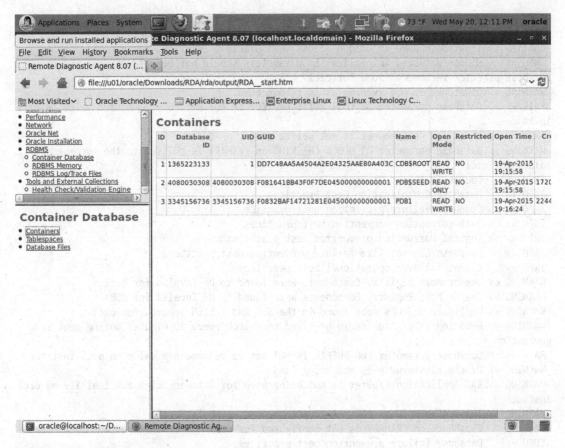

Figure 11-8. An RDA collection

■ **Tip** An RDA collection is a great problem-solving tool and facilitates collaboration among DBAs. A best practice for Oracle database administration is to install the RDA utility in every database environment to avoid losing time when faced with a severe problem that requires vendor support. Periodic RDA collections also serve as a record of changes to the database environment.

ORAchk Oracle Configuration Audit Tool

ORAchk is a tool provided by Oracle Support and can be downloaded from My Oracle Support. As the name implies, it checks whether you are using best practices for your Oracle Database configuration. Here is the summary output produced by the tool in my VM environment:

```
INFO =>    Oracle Data Pump Best practices.
FAIL =>    Bash is vulnerable to code injection (CVE-2014-6271)
WARNING => Linux Swap Configuration does NOT meet Recommendation
WARNING => physical memory is not sufficient
```

```
INFO =>    Important Storage Minimum Requirements for Grid & Database Homes
FAIL =>    DB_UNIQUE_NAME on primary has not been modified from the default,
confirm that database name is unique across your Oracle enterprise. for orcl
INFO =>    Hidden database initialization parameters should not be set
per best practice recommendations for orcl
WARNING => OSWatcher is not running as is recommended.
FAIL =>    Database parameter DB_LOST_WRITE_PROTECT is NOT set to recommended value on orcl
instance
INFO =>    umask for RDBMS owner is not set to 0022
WARNING => Database parameter DB_BLOCK_CHECKING on PRIMARY is NOT set to the recommended
value. for orcl
INFO =>    Operational Best Practices
INFO =>    Database Consolidation Best Practices
INFO =>    Computer failure prevention best practices
INFO =>    Data corruption prevention best practices
INFO =>    Logical corruption prevention best practices
INFO =>    Database/Cluster/Site failure prevention best practices
INFO =>    Client failover operational best practices
WARNING => One or More Registry Components were found to be Invalid for orcl
WARNING => One or More Registry Components were found to be Invalid for PDB1
WARNING => Duplicate objects were found in the SYS and SYSTEM schemas for orcl
WARNING => Redo log file size should be sized to switch every 20 minutes during peak redo
generation for orcl
FAIL =>    Database parameter LOG_BUFFER is NOT set to recommended value on orcl instance
WARNING => Oracle clusterware is not being used
WARNING => RAC Application Cluster is not being used for database high availability on orcl
instance
WARNING => "DISK_ASYNCH_IO is NOT set to recommended value for orcl
FAIL =>    Flashback on PRIMARY is not configured for orcl
INFO =>    Database failure prevention best practices
WARNING => fast_start_mttr_target has NOT been changed from default on orcl instance
WARNING => Database Archivelog Mode should be set to ARCHIVELOG for orcl
FAIL =>    Primary database is NOT protected with Data Guard (standby
database) for real-time data protection and availability for orcl
FAIL =>    Active Data Guard is not configured for orcl
INFO =>    Oracle recovery manager(rman) best practices
INFO =>    Consider increasing the COREDUMPSIZE size
INFO =>    Consider investigating changes to the schema objects such as DDLs or new object
creation for PDB1
INFO =>    Consider increasing the PGA size for PDB1
WARNING => Consider increasing the value of the session_cached_cursors database parameter
for orcl
INFO =>    Consider investigating the frequency of SGA resize operations and take
corrective action for orcl
FAIL =>    There should be no duplicate parameter entries in the database init.ora(spfile)
file for orcl
```

As you can see, there are numerous opportunities for improvement in this VM environment. Detailed output is produced in HTML format. In the exercises, you are asked to run ORAchk in your VM environment and study the findings.

Automatic Diagnostic Repository (ADR)

The history of Oracle errors is stored in a directory structure called the Automatic Diagnostic Repository (ADR). Oracle provides a tool called adrci (ADR Command Interpreter) to query the ADR and to create packages containing diagnostic information. These packages can be attached to service requests that you initiate with Oracle Support. You see an example of using adrci later in this chapter.

Error Codes

With a few exceptions, such as locking problems, the most important symptom of a problem is the error code. These error codes are all listed in *Oracle Database Error Messages*—part of the Oracle documentation set—and there are literally tens of thousands of them. Here is a simple example featuring the very first Oracle error in the book, ORA-00001. The user is trying to insert a record that already exists:

```
SQL*Plus: Release 12.1.0.1.0 Production on Mon Apr 6 01:07:28 2015

Copyright (c) 1982, 2013, Oracle.  All rights reserved.

Last Successful login time: Sun Apr 05 2015 23:28:38 -04:00

Connected to:
Oracle Database 12c Enterprise Edition Release 12.1.0.1.0 - 64bit Production
With the Partitioning, OLAP, Advanced Analytics and Real Application Testing options

PDB1@ORCL> insert into employees select * from employees;
insert into employees select * from employees
*
ERROR at line 1:
ORA-00001: unique constraint (HR.EMP_EMAIL_UK) violated
```

■ **Tip** When investigating a problem, the best question to ask is, "What is the Oracle error code?" Sometimes applications mask the error code, and this hinders the investigation into a problem.

A very limited amount of advice about each Oracle error code is provided in *Oracle Database Error Messages*. Here is what you find in the case of ORA-00001:

```
ORA-00001: unique constraint (string.string) violated
Cause: An UPDATE or INSERT statement attempted to insert a duplicate key. For
Trusted Oracle configured in DBMS MAC mode, you may see this message if a duplicate
entry exists at a different level.
Action: Either remove the unique restriction or do not insert the key.
```

■ **Tip** Oracle supplies the oerr utility for Unix platforms; it displays the text of an error message as well as the cause and action. To display the text associated with ORA-00001, simply type oerr ora 1.

Notice that an Oracle error code has two parts: a facility code and a five-digit number, separated by a hyphen. Leading zeros are often omitted—for example, ORA-00600 and ORA-600 refer to the same error. Here is an example of an error message produced by the Recovery Manager (RMAN) tool:

```
RMAN-06171: not connected to target database
Cause: A command was issued but no connection to the target database has been
established.
Action: Issue a CONNECT TARGET command to connect to the target database.
```

You must learn to identify which Oracle error codes indicate problems with the infrastructure supported by the DBA and which codes indicate errors made by a user or problems with an application. For example, Table 11-1 lists the standard named exceptions that are part of the PL/SQL programming language—they indicate problems with the application in question.

Table 11-1. *Named Exceptions in PL/SQL*

Name	Error Code
ACCESS_INTO_NULL	ORA-06530
COLLECTION_IS_NULL	ORA-06531
CURSOR_ALREADY_OPEN	ORA-06511
DUP_VAL_ON_INDEX	ORA-00001
INVALID_CURSOR	ORA-01001
INVALID_NUMBER	ORA-01722
LOGIN_DENIED	ORA-01017
NO_DATA_FOUND	ORA-01403
NOT_LOGGED_ON	ORA-01012
PROGRAM_ERROR	ORA-06501
ROWTYPE_MISMATCH	ORA-06504
SELF_IS_NULL	ORA-30625
STORAGE_ERROR	ORA-06500
SUBSCRIPT_BEYOND_COUNT	ORA-06533
SUBSCRIPT_OUTSIDE_LIMIT	ORA-06532
SYS_INVALID_ROWID	ORA-01410
TIMEOUT_ON_RESOURCE	ORA-00051
TOO_MANY_ROWS	ORA-01422
VALUE_ERROR	ORA-06502
ZERO_DIVIDE	ORA-01476

■ **Tip** Errors reported in the Oracle alert log usually represent infrastructure errors. A good example is ORA-01653: Unable to extend table HR.EMPLOYEES by 1024 in tablespace EXAMPLE.

Four Errors

I have enough space to discuss only a few errors. I selected the four errors in this section for discussion because they are common and frequently misunderstood.

ORA-01555: Snapshot Too Old

Here is the minimal explanation of the ORA-01555 error found in *Oracle Database 11g Error Messages*:

```
ORA-01555: Snapshot too old; rollback segment number string with name "string" too
small
Cause: rollback records needed by a reader for consistent read are overwritten by
other writers
Action: If in Automatic Undo Management mode, increase undo_retention setting.
Otherwise, use larger rollback segments
```

Consider a query that begins at 9 a.m. and completes at 10 a.m. Suppose that the query is counting the number of records in a very large table, and suppose that the table is very active—that is, records are constantly being inserted into the table. Suppose that Oracle's answer to the query is 10 billion records. Does the answer indicate the number of records at 9 a.m., at 10 a.m., or at some intermediate time between those times?

If you were working with another database technology such as IBM's DB2 or Informix, Microsoft's SQL Server, or Sybase, the answer would be 10 a.m. because the query would not complete until it had locked all the records in the table; it would wait for all insert, update, and delete operations to complete, and it would block others from starting. In other words, readers block writers, and writers block readers. With Oracle, on the other hand, readers do *not* block writers, and writers do *not* block readers. Instead, Oracle determines what the answer to the query would have been at the instant the query *started*—that is, at 9 a.m. This manner of operation is called *read consistency*.[1] Read consistency extends to a single query by default or can extend to an entire transaction. For example, the entire contents of a database can be exported by using read-consistent mode to ensure that there are no conflicts or inconsistencies in the data.

To ensure read consistency, Oracle must construct a snapshot of the database at the time the query or transaction started. If the required data has changed since the query started, Oracle must obtain a prior version of the data from the rollback segments. However, the rollback segments are a shared resource, and the information they contain may be overwritten if other transactions need the space. Therefore, Oracle may not be able to construct the snapshot—that is, the snapshot may be *too old to be reconstructed*.

Prior to Oracle 9*i*, the number and size of rollback segments were left to the DBA. Beginning with Oracle 9*i*, this task should be entrusted to Oracle by changing the value of the UNDO_MANAGEMENT setting to AUTO. If the Snapshot too old error occurs, increase the value of the UNDO_RETENTION setting and ensure, through trial and error, that the tablespace specified by the UNDO_TABLESPACE setting is big enough, adding data files or increasing the size of data files as necessary. The default value of the UNDO_RETENTION setting is 900 seconds (15 minutes); a large value such as 14,400 (4 hours) may be more appropriate, depending on the circumstances, but must be supported by an undo tablespace that is large enough. Note that you can never completely avoid the Snapshot too old error because it is always possible for queries to take so long that the available resources are exhausted. Also, transactions that modify the data typically take precedence over transactions that read the data—that is, the modified transactions overwrite the information in the rollback segments if space is short, regardless of the value of the UNDO_RETENTION setting. You can prevent this by imposing a *retention guarantee* on the undo tablespace by using the ALTER TABLESPACE command. You must take more care than usual to ensure that the undo tablespace is adequately sized if a retention guarantee is in effect.

---

[1]SQL Server offers read consistency beginning with SQL Server 2005. However, it is not the default manner of operation.

ORA-00060: Deadlock Detected

Once again, you see only a minimal explanation in *Oracle Database 11g Error Messages*:

```
ORA-00060: deadlock detected while waiting for resource
Cause: Transactions deadlocked one another while waiting for resources.
Action: Look at the trace file to see the transactions and resources involved. Retry
if necessary.
```

This error is frequently encountered but is one of the least understood Oracle errors. A *deadlock* is a situation in which two transactions interfere with each other; each is waiting for a lock on a resource locked by the other. *The correct thing for the application to do when this error is received is to issue the* ROLLBACK *command and retry the transaction.*

Create two tables, PARENT and CHILD, related to each other by a referential constraint (foreign key), and populate them with data by using the following commands:

```
CREATE TABLE parent (
  parent_ID INTEGER NOT NULL,
  CONSTRAINT parent_PK PRIMARY KEY (parent_id)
);

CREATE TABLE child (
  child_ID INTEGER NOT NULL,
  parent_ID INTEGER NOT NULL,
  CONSTRAINT child_PK PRIMARY KEY (child_id),
  CONSTRAINT child_FK FOREIGN KEY (parent_ID) references parent
);

INSERT INTO parent (parent_ID) values (1);
INSERT INTO parent (parent_ID) values (2);
INSERT INTO child (child_ID, parent_ID) values (1,1);
INSERT INTO child (child_ID, parent_ID) values (2,2);
```

Suppose that two users try to delete the data from the CHILD table, but each deletes records in a different order. At step 3 in the following example, user A is blocked because user B has already locked the requested record. User B is blocked in turn at step 4, and a deadlock results. To resolve the deadlock, Oracle picks either user A or user B as a victim, and any effects of the last command issued by the victim are rolled back. To allow the other user to proceed, the victim must then issue the ROLLBACK command to release any other locks it still holds—it can then retry its transaction:

```
/* Step 1: User A */ DELETE FROM child WHERE child_ID=1;

/* Step 2: User B */ DELETE FROM child WHERE child_ID=2;

/* Step 3: User A */ DELETE FROM child WHERE child_ID=1;

/* Step 4: User B */ DELETE FROM child WHERE child_ID=2;
```

In the preceding example, two users are modifying the *same* data. Deadlock also occurs in the next example, *even though the users are modifying different data*. At step 3, user A is blocked because Oracle needs to verify the absence of child records before deleting a parent record. In the absence of an index on the child_ID column of the Child table, Oracle attempts to lock the entire Child table and is prevented from doing so because user A has a lock on one of the records in the table. User B is blocked in turn at step 4, and a deadlock results:

```
/* Step 1: User A */ DELETE FROM child WHERE child_ID=1;

/* Step 2: User B */ DELETE FROM child WHERE child_ID=2;

/* Step 3: User A */ DELETE FROM parent WHERE parent_ID=1;

/* Step 4: User B */ DELETE FROM parent WHERE parent_ID=2;
```

Defects in database design such as un-indexed foreign keys can increase the frequency of deadlocks, but deadlocks can happen anytime more than one user is using the database. All database programs must anticipate the possibility and take the appropriate action when a deadlock happens—that is, *issue the* ROLLBACK *command and retry the transaction.*

ORA-00600: Internal Error Code

Oracle reports an ORA-00600 error in the alert log whenever it encounters an unexpected condition—the frequent cause is an Oracle bug—and stops processing the SQL statement it was processing at the time. Here is the verbiage from *Oracle Database 11g Error Messages*:

```
ORA-00600: internal error code, arguments: [string], [string], [string], [string],
[string], [string], [string], [string]
Cause: This is the generic internal error number for Oracle program exceptions. This
indicated that a process encountered an exceptional condition.
Action: Report as a bug - the first argument is the internal error number.
```

■ **Caution**   ORA-00600 errors should *always* be investigated, and the DBA should confirm that the error was not triggered by a corrupted data block.

Here is an example of an ORA-00600 incident, from detection to diagnosis. The following code produces an ORA-00600 error in Oracle Database 11.1.0.6. Notice that an ORA-00600 error has a number of arguments, each enclosed in square brackets. The first such argument is the most important and is used to further classify the error:

```
[oracle@localhost ~]$ sqlplus hr/oracle@pdb1

SQL*Plus: Release 12.1.0.1.0 Production on Sun Apr 5 23:28:38 2015

Copyright (c) 1982, 2013, Oracle.  All rights reserved.

Last Successful login time: Sun Apr 05 2015 23:27:29 -04:00
```

```
Connected to:
Oracle Database 12c Enterprise Edition Release 12.1.0.1.0 - 64bit Production
With the Partitioning, OLAP, Advanced Analytics and Real Application Testing options

PDB1@ORCL> @demo
PDB1@ORCL>
PDB1@ORCL> -- create a demo table
PDB1@ORCL> CREATE TABLE scores AS
  2  SELECT o.object_type,
  3    o.object_name,
  4    TRUNC(dbms_random.value(1,101)) AS score
  5  FROM all_objects o;

Table created.

PDB1@ORCL>
PDB1@ORCL> -- create an index
PDB1@ORCL> CREATE INDEX scores_ix ON scores
  2    (object_type, score
  3    );

Index created.

PDB1@ORCL>
PDB1@ORCL> -- list the top 3 scoring objects in each category
PDB1@ORCL> WITH object_types(object_type) AS
  2    ( SELECT MIN(object_type) FROM scores
  3    UNION ALL
  4    SELECT
  5      (SELECT MIN(object_type) FROM scores WHERE object_type > u.object_type
  6      )
  7    FROM object_types u
  8    WHERE object_type IS NOT NULL
  9    )
 10  SELECT l.*
 11  FROM object_types o,
 12    lateral
 13    (SELECT /*+ INDEX(s) */ *
 14    FROM scores s
 15    WHERE s.object_type = o.object_type
 16    ORDER BY s.object_type,
 17      s.score
 18    FETCH FIRST 3 ROWS ONLY
 19    ) l;
  ( SELECT MIN(object_type) FROM scores
                                    *
ERROR at line 2:
ORA-00600: internal error code, arguments: [qctcte1], [0], [], [], [], [], [],
[], [], [], [], []
```

The first thing to do is to check the Oracle alert log. If you have forgotten where it is, you can check the value of the BACKGROUND_DUMP_DEST setting:

```
PDB1@ORCL> SHOW parameter background_dump_dest;

NAME                                     TYPE        VALUE
------------------------------------ ----------- -------------------------------
background_dump_dest                     string      /u01/app/oracle/diag/rdbms/orc
                                                     l/orcl/trace
```

Here is what appears in the Oracle alert log. The alert log indicates that full details are found in a trace file:

```
Sun Apr 05 23:28:48 2015
Errors in file /u01/app/oracle/diag/rdbms/orcl/orcl/trace/orcl_ora_14018.trc
(incident=60308):
ORA-00600: internal error code, arguments: [qctcte1], [0], [], [], [], [], [], [], [], [],
[], []
Incident details in: /u01/app/oracle/diag/rdbms/orcl/orcl/incident/incdir_60308/orcl_
ora_14018_i60308.trc
Use ADRCI or Support Workbench to package the incident.
See Note 411.1 at My Oracle Support for error and packaging details.
Sun Apr 05 23:28:50 2015
Dumping diagnostic data in directory=[cdmp_20150405232850], requested by (instance=1,
osid=14018), summary=[incident=60308].
Sun Apr 05 23:28:50 2015
Sweep [inc][60308]: completed
Sweep [inc2][60308]: completed
```

Next, you use the adrci tool and create a package of information that can be sent to Oracle Support. The specific command is ips (Incident Packaging Service). Notice that ADR differentiates between a problem and an incident:

```
[oracle@localhost trace]$ adrci

ADRCI: Release 12.1.0.1.0 - Production on Sun Apr 5 23:35:21 2015

Copyright (c) 1982, 2013, Oracle and/or its affiliates.  All rights reserved.

ADR base = "/u01/app/oracle"
adrci> set homepath diag/rdbms/orcl/orcl
adrci> show problem

ADR Home = /u01/app/oracle/diag/rdbms/orcl/orcl:
*************************************************************************
PROBLEM_ID PROBLEM_KEY        LAST_INCIDENT LASTINC_TIME
---------- ------------------ ------------- ----------------------------------
1          ORA 4031           7555          2014-01-21 15:06:16.283000 -05:00
2          ORA 600 [qctcte1]  60308         2015-04-05 23:28:48.283000 -04:00
2 rows fetched
```

```
adrci> ips create package incident 60308
Created package 1 based on incident id 60308, correlation level typical
adrci> ips generate package 1 in /u01/oracle
Generated package 1 in file /u01/oracle/ORA600qct_20150405233734_COM_1.zip, mode complete
adrci> exit
```

An alternative to creating a service request is to research the problem yourself by using the MetaLink knowledge base. Specifically, you have to use a search tool called the ORA-600 Troubleshooter, shown in Figure 11-9. You must provide the first argument of the ORA-00600 error you encountered and the version of Oracle Database you are using.

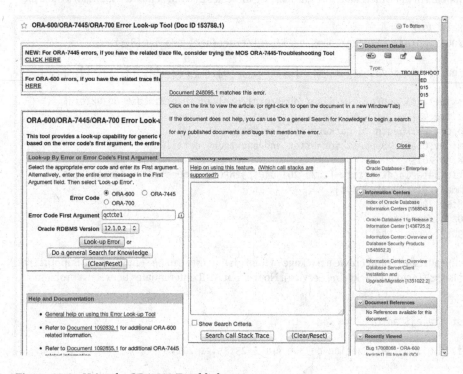

Figure 11-9. Using the ORA-600 Troubleshooter

When you click the Look-Up Error button, Oracle shows you a research note discussing this particular error.

ORA-07445: Exception Encountered

An ORA-07445 error causes the instant termination of the Oracle server process that was handling the query being processed at the time. This sort of error occurs when an Oracle server process attempts to perform an illegal operation such as reading an area of memory that is not allocated to it—the operating system detects the illegal operation and forces the Oracle server process to shut itself down. ORA-00600 and ORA-7445 errors should be handled in the exact same way.

Summary

Here is a short summary of the concepts touched on in this chapter:

- Your activities can be divided among four quadrants depending on their urgency and importance. The ideal place to spend time is the quadrant of activities that are important but not urgent—for example, keeping records, identifying the root causes of incidents and eliminating them, updating documentation, and automating common tasks.

- The first step in solving a problem is to *define* the problem. The second step is to *investigate* the problem. The third step is to *analyze* the data. The fourth step is to *solve* the problem. The last step is to *implement* the solution in a safe and controlled manner.

- Best practices for problem management include fixing problems proactively, finding the root cause of problems, using good tools, using standard operating procedures, using RDA collections, and keeping work records.

- An *incident* is a single occurrence of a problem. *Incident management* is concerned with restoring service as rapidly as possible. *Problem management* is concerned with permanently fixing defects so incidents are not repeated.

- High-quality Internet resources include the Oracle documentation site, Oracle Technology Network, and Oracle-L mailing list.

- If you have purchased an Oracle support contract, you can search the Oracle knowledge base MetaLink and escalate problems to the Oracle Support team.

- You can use the RDA tool to document the Oracle Database configuration. The ORAchk configuration audit tool can be used to determine whether best practices are being followed for Oracle Database configuration.

- The history of Oracle errors is stored in a directory structure called the Automatic Diagnostic Repository (ADR). Oracle provides a tool called adrci (ADR Command Interpreter) to query the ADR and to create packages containing diagnostic information to send to the Oracle Support team.

- An Oracle error code has two parts: a facility code and a five-digit number, separated by a hyphen. The DBA must learn to identify which Oracle error codes indicate problems with the database infrastructure and which codes indicate errors made by a user or a problem with an application. The named exceptions defined by PL/SQL are examples of error codes that indicate problems in the application, not in the database infrastructure.

- An ORA-01555: Snapshot too old error message means the query has taken so long that the undo information required to re-create the required read-consistent snapshot of the database has been overwritten by other transactions—that is, the snapshot is too old to be reconstructed.

- An ORA-00060: Deadlock detected error message means Oracle detected that two transactions are blocking each other and picked one of them as a victim. The appropriate action the victim must take is to issue the ROLLBACK command and retry its transaction.

- An ORA-00600: Internal error code error message indicates that Oracle encountered an unexpected condition and stopped processing the query in question. ORA-00600 errors should always be investigated, and the DBA should confirm that they were not triggered by corrupted data blocks.

- An ORA-07445: Exception encountered error message means the Oracle server process attempted to perform an illegal operation and was forced by the operating system to terminate itself.

Exercises

- Download the RDA tool from My Oracle Support, if you have a valid support contract, and run it in your VM environment. You have to unset the TWO_TASK environment variable (unset TWO_TASK) before running the tool. Use the custom RDA profile DB12c (./rda.sh -p DB12c) to limit the scope of the collection to Oracle Database only. Review all the sections of the RDA report.

- Download the ORAchk tool from My Oracle Support, if you have a valid support contract, and run it in your VM environment. You have to unset the TWO_TASK environment variable (unset TWO_TASK) before running the tool. Examine each finding in the detailed HTML report, and decide whether it should be accepted. Consult the Oracle Database documentation to determine how to implement the findings you have accepted.

- Reproduce one of the deadlock examples in your database. Check whether any messages are recorded in the alert log. Check whether a trace file is produced, and review it. What happens if the victim simply retries its last SQL command instead of issuing the ROLLBACK command and retrying its entire transaction?

- Stop after step 3 of one of the deadlock examples. Session A is now blocked by session B, but Oracle cannot take any action because this is not yet a deadlock scenario. Use a GUI tool such as SQL Developer, Enterprise Manager, Toad, or DBArtisan to identify the blocking process and terminate it.

- In what kind of problem scenarios might users not receive any error messages?

- Users are complaining that their application is behaving sluggishly. How would you check the database environment for signs of trouble?

- Categorize the following errors into user errors and infrastructure errors. What should be done to fix each of them?

```
ORA-01017: invalid username/password; logon denied
ORA-00923: FROM keyword not found where expected
ORA-01653: unable to extend table HR.EMPLOYEES by 128 in tablespace EXAMPLE
ORA-12154: TNS:could not resolve the connect identifier specified
ORA-12541: TNS:no listener
ORA-12514: TNS:listener does not currently know of service requested in
connect descriptor
```

- Review the ORA-00600 example discussed in this chapter. Could the SQL statement be rewritten in a way that avoids the error?

■ ■ ■

Backups

As to our Conduct in the Affair of Extinguishing Fires, tho' we do not want Hands or Good-Will, yet we seem to want Order and Method, and therefore I believe I cannot do better than to offer for our Imitation, the Example of a City in a Neighbouring Province. There is, as I am well inform'd, a Club or Society of active Men belonging to each Fire Engine; whose Business is to attend all Fires with it whenever they happen; and to work it once a Quarter, and see it kept in order.

—Benjamin Franklin, in an anonymous letter to the *Pennsylvania Gazette* (of which he was the editor) following a disastrous fire in Philadelphia in the eighteenth century

American national hero Benjamin Franklin often wrote anonymous letters to the *Pennsylvania Gazette*, a prominent newspaper that he owned and edited. In one such letter, he coined the famous phrase "an ounce of prevention is worth a pound of cure"; and, in addition to making several suggestions for the prevention of fires, he proposed that Philadelphia imitate his native Boston in establishing fire stations and employing firefighters. Not only should all efforts be made to prevent fires, but the city should be adequately prepared to handle the next inevitable fire.

Backups are to a database what fire stations and fire fighters are to a city. You may protect the database against damage the best you can, but you must be prepared if the database is ever damaged, through user or operator error or hardware failure, and needs to be repaired. A backup is a snapshot of a database or a part of a database; if the database is damaged, the damaged parts can be repaired using the backups. Archived logs can be used in conjunction with a backup to replay transactions that changed data after the backup was performed. This chapter describes how to create various kinds of backups; the next chapter describes how to use them to repair databases. If you are impatient, note that you can create a backup with two simple words: BACKUP DATABASE. But as the leading mind of the European renaissance, Leonardo da Vinci, said: "Those who are in love with practice without knowledge are like the sailor who gets into a ship without rudder or compass and who never can be certain whether he is going. Practice must always be founded on sound theory."

Why Do You Need Backups?

Oracle guru Tom Kyte likes to say that "*Why* is probably the right answer." "Why do you need backups?" is a wise question because consideration of the answer will dictate your backup strategy; it might even determine whether you need backups at all. Backups consume resources: disk space, tapes, CPU cycles,

IO bandwidth, network bandwidth, tape-drive bandwidth, operator time, and so on. None of those are free. The necessary hardware and software are not free, either. Consider, for example, the following scenarios:

- A new version of the application is to be deployed, and many objects in the database will be modified. The developers have requested that a backup be created just before the new version is deployed. However, you might be able to recover the database using previous backups and archived redo logs, and a new backup may not be necessary. Also, you can use Oracle flashback technology to recover the database without using backups. If the database is very large but only a small portion will be affected by the new deployment, an alternative might be to duplicate the tables that will be affected, using CREATE TABLE AS commands—the original data can be restored from the duplicate tables if the deployment is unsuccessful.

- Consider a reporting database that contains only materialized views[1] that reflect the data in other databases. If the materialized views become damaged, they can be completely refreshed using the original data. The entire database can be re-created from scripts. In this scenario, you do not need good backups; you just need good scripts.

- I once managed a database named Flatline that was used to store archived data that had been deleted from the transactional databases but needed to be retained for an extended period for legal reasons. New data was loaded into the database only once a month. Obviously, it needed backups only once a month.

- Oracle provides read-only tablespaces for archived data. These don't need as many backups as the rest of the database.

- Development and testing databases may not need backups if they can be cloned from production databases or rebuilt using scripts and seed data.

- *Standby databases* are databases that are continuously synchronizing themselves with the primary database. They have many uses: they can be used for reporting purposes; they provide switchover capability in the event of a planned outage of the primary database; they provide failover capability in the case of an unplanned ouage; and they can be backed up in lieu of backing up the production database so as to offload the CPU and I/O overhead from the production database to the standby database. Standby databases don't need to be backed up unless they are being backed up in lieu of backing up the production database.

An appropriate backup strategy is one that meets the needs of the business while remaining cost-effective. A different strategy might be needed for each database in the enterprise, the goal being to "provide cost-effective stewardship of the IT assets and resources used in providing IT services."[2] Mission-critical databases such as those used in e-commerce have the most demanding requirements. The requirement for a mission-critical e-commerce database might be to "make backups without impacting database performance and quickly recover from failures." Such a requirement typically dictates the use of advanced hardware and software, with all the associated cost. For example, advanced options such as parallel backup, parallel recovery, single-block recovery, and database flashback are available only with the Enterprise Edition of Oracle Database.

---

[1]A *materialized view* is an SQL statement that has been precomputed, or materialized. These views are typically used to *pre-join* tables in the interest of computational efficiency. Their contents typically are not as accurate as the contents of the tables referenced in the SQL expression, but they are useful in situations such as month-end reporting where the most recent data is not required. Another typical use is to store a local copy of data from a remote database.
[2]This is the goal of financial management, as stated in the IT Service Management (ITSM) literature. Chapter 15 discusses ITSM.

Types of Backup

It bears repeating that an appropriate backup strategy is one that meets the needs of the business while remaining cost-effective. You have many choices to make; I describe some of them here.

Tape Backups vs. Disk Backups

The two main storage choices are tape and disk. Each choice has advantages and disadvantages. It is generally accepted that disk backups are not a substitute for tape backups. A common practice is to make backup copies on disk when possible and have them copied to tape in a separate operation.

Advantages and Disadvantages of Tape Backups

On the plus side, tapes are relatively cheap compared to disks, which means multiple backups can be retained without too much expense; multiple backups obviously offer extra protection. Tapes are also more reliable than disks; disks are electromechanical devices and therefore more prone to failure. Also, tapes are serial-access devices and can achieve very high sustained reading and writing speeds.

On the minus side, the process of retrieving a single file from tapes is slower than with disks because the serial nature of tapes requires that the entire preceding portions be read first. Also, tapes usually are not kept online; they are typically ejected from the tape drive and may even be sent offsite for storage in secure fire-proof facilities—for this reason, they may not be readily available in an emergency. A DBA working remotely might not be able to initiate database recovery without the assistance of "remote hands" to perform actions like inserting tapes into a tape drive. Also, tape backup management is itself a specialized IT activity; the DBA may need assistance from IT personnel with the required knowledge.

In general, tapes are faster in serial-access situations, such as copying large numbers of files to a blank tape. They are slower in random-access situations, such as retrieving one file from tape.

Advantages and Disadvantages of Disk Backups

On the plus side, backup and recovery can be initiated by the DBA without "remote hands" assistance and without requiring specialized knowledge of the tape backup technology that is being used.

On the minus side, disks are relatively expensive compared to tape, which means the available capacity is usually much more limited and there may not be enough space available to create a backup copy of the database, let alone multiple backups. Another minus is that disks—unlike tapes—cannot be sent offsite for safekeeping.

Full Backups vs. Partial Backups

Backups require the use of computer resources such as storage disks and storage tapes as well as memory, CPU cycles, and network bandwidth. They must therefore be scheduled so as not to interfere with normal database operations; typically, they are scheduled for nights and weekends. If the database is very large, you may not have the time and resources to create a backup of the entire database in a single operation; instead, you might spread the activity over the course of a week and create a backup of just a portion of the database every night. Also, some portions of the database may be designated as *read-only*, and it is not necessary to create multiple backups of this data.

219

Level 0 Backups vs. Level 1 Backups

A full backup is also called a *level 0* backup. This is a backup containing every data block. A *level 1* backup is one that contains only those data blocks that have changed since the level 0 backup. A level 1 backup is also called an *incremental* backup. A level 0 backup might be created on weekends when there is plenty of time available, and a level 1 backup might be created every night when there is less time available. A feature called *block change tracking* can be used to avoid having to examine every block; the changed blocks are listed in the *block change tracking file*.

Physical Backups vs. Logical Backups

The term *physical backup* refers to exact copies of data blocks and data files produced by a tool such as Recovery Manager (RMAN). The term *logical backup* refers to a structured copy of the data in the tables such as is produced by Data Pump Export or a CREATE TABLE AS SELECT command.

A logical backup can be much smaller than the corresponding physical backup because there is typically much unused space in the data blocks and the data files and because the database contains index data in addition to table data. However, logical backups cannot be used to restore the database; they can only be used to re-create the *data* in an otherwise functional database.

If the database (or part of it) is restored from physical backups, then the redo logs can be used to recover all modifications to the data made since the physical backup was initiated. If a logical backup is used to re-create data, any modifications to the data made after the logical backup was initiated are lost.

Consistent Backups vs. Inconsistent Backups

Many databases are used around the clock. If the data in the database is being modified while the backup is being created, the backup may contain internal consistencies because each data block in the database is visited just once during a backup operation, and any subsequent changes to the block will not be captured. The only way to guarantee a consistent backup is to make the database unavailable and prevent changes during the backup operation. However, inconsistent physical backups are very useful because the information contained in the redo log files can be used to fix any inconsistencies in such backups.

Hot vs. Cold Backups

Hot backups (also called *online backups*) are backups that are created while the database (or relevant portion thereof) is accessible by users and can be modified while the backup is underway. *Cold backups* (also called *offline backups*) are backups that are created while the database (or relevant portion thereof) is in a state in which it cannot be modified while the backup is underway.

Hot backup and *online backup* are generally considered synonymous with *inconsistent backup*, whereas *cold backup* and *offline backup* are considered synonymous with *consistent backup*. However, if the database was not shut down gracefully, a cold backup also may contain inconsistencies. And it is possible to make a consistent *logical* backup of the database while the database is online. Finally note that an online backup of a portion of the database that cannot be modified (for example, a read-only tablespace) is guaranteed to be consistent.

Oracle-Managed Backups vs. User-Managed Backups

Backups created using RMAN are called *Oracle-managed backups*, and backups created by other methods are called *user-managed backups*. For example, Network Appliance provides an advanced technology that can be used to create snapshots of the largest databases in seconds or minutes by recording only the *addresses* of the blocks in the database instead of the *data* contained in the blocks—a copy of a block is made only if the data in one of these blocks is subsequently changed.

Advantages of Oracle-Managed Backups

Backups created using RMAN have many advantages:

- Arguably, the biggest advantage of RMAN is its ease of use. The entire database can be backed up with the simple words BACKUP DATABASE.

- Another great advantage of RMAN is that it stores history data. The history data is needed during recovery operations, but it can be queried by the DBA at any time; a typical use is to verify that the database has been backed up.

- RMAN offers features that are not available anywhere else. Examples are incremental backups, detection of corrupted blocks, and recovery of single blocks.

Advantages of User-Managed Backups

Some types of user-managed backups offer great advantages. For example, snapshot technology has the advantage of lightning speed of both backup and recovery. Making a backup of a file is lightning fast because it only requires that the addresses of blocks be recorded, not the data contained in the blocks—recovery of a file is also lightning fast because it only requires that one list of block addresses be switched with another. The best of both worlds is achieved when snapshots are registered in the RMAN repository—this allows RMAN to use the snapshots for database recovery.

Practical Demonstration: Physical Backups

Here is a practical demonstration of the use of RMAN to create a backup copy of the database. As you will see, this can be accomplished with a few short commands. Please follow along in your VM; you will learn best by doing. For this exercise, restore your VM to the snapshot that you took prior to installing a second ORACLE_HOME in Chapter 5; you won't use it in this and future chapters. However, you can always restore your VM to the snapshot containing the second ORACLE_HOME if you so choose.

Hot backups are desirable because the database remains available during the backup operation. But at this point, RMAN cannot perform a hot backup because the database is in NOARCHIVELOG mode. Remember that in ARCHIVELOG mode, archive copies of the online redo logs are made before they are allowed to be overwritten. If the database ever needs to be restored from a backup, you will need the archive copies of any redo logs that were active during the time of the backup. Let's go ahead and put the database into ARCHIVELOG mode.

First, unset the TWO_TASK variable that tries to connect you to the pdb1 pluggable database. Then connect to the CDB using the SYS account with SYSDBA privilege.

```
[oracle@localhost ~]$ unset TWO_TASK
[oracle@localhost ~]$ sqlplus "/ as sysdba"

SQL*Plus: Release 12.1.0.1.0 Production on Mon Nov 3 20:58:16 2014

Copyright (c) 1982, 2013, Oracle.  All rights reserved.

Connected to:
Oracle Database 12c Enterprise Edition Release 12.1.0.1.0 - 64bit Production
With the Partitioning, OLAP, Advanced Analytics and Real Application Testing options
```

Shut down the CDB, and then reopen it in MOUNT mode.

```
CDB$ROOT@ORCL> shutdown immediate;
Database closed.
Database dismounted.
ORACLE instance shut down.
CDB$ROOT@ORCL> startup mount;
ORACLE instance started.

Total System Global Area  413372416 bytes
Fixed Size                  2289016 bytes
Variable Size             335544968 bytes
Database Buffers           71303168 bytes
Redo Buffers                4235264 bytes
Database mounted.
```

You can now switch the database into ARCHIVELOG mode. As a separate step, you also need to start the archive process; it is the process responsible for automatically making archive copies of the online redo logs as they fill up. Finally, you need to ensure that the archiver is automatically started whenever the database is started. This involves setting the LOG_ARCHIVE_START database-initialization parameter to TRUE:

```
CDB$ROOT@ORCL> alter database archivelog;

Database altered.

CDB$ROOT@ORCL> alter system archive log start;

System altered.

CDB$ROOT@ORCL> alter system set log_archive_start=true scope=spfile;

System altered.
```

Next, open the database and test your work by manually closing an online redo log and checking that an archive copy is automatically made by the archiver process:

```
CDB$ROOT@ORCL> alter database open;

Database altered.

CDB$ROOT@ORCL> alter system switch logfile;

System altered.

CDB$ROOT@ORCL> select name from v$archived_log;

NAME
--------------------------------------------------------------------------------
/u01/app/oracle/fast_recovery_area/ORCL/archivelog/2014_11_03/o1_mf_1_129_b5jgj5
m7_.arc
```

```
CDB$ROOT@ORCL> exit
Disconnected from Oracle Database 12c Enterprise Edition Release 12.1.0.1.0 - 64bit
Production
With the Partitioning, OLAP, Advanced Analytics and Real Application Testing options
```

You are now ready to use RMAN to perform an online backup. Let's change the value of the NLS_DATE_ FORMAT environment variable—it affects the format in which dates are displayed. The default setting does not include minutes and seconds values, which you would like to have during this session. This is an optional step—display settings have no impact on the integrity of backups:

```
[oracle@localhost ~]$ export NLS_DATE_FORMAT='YYYY/MM/DD HH24:MI'
```

When you invoke RMAN, it displays version information and gives you a command prompt:

```
[oracle@localhost ~]$ rman

Recovery Manager: Release 12.1.0.1.0 - Production on Mon Nov 3 09:25:22 2014

Copyright (c) 1982, 2013, Oracle and/or its affiliates.  All rights reserved.

RMAN>
```

Next you establish a command session with the database using the command CONNECT TARGET. RMAN displays the database name (ORCL in this case) and the *DBID*, a unique numeric identifier used to distinguish between databases with the same name:

```
RMAN> connect target

connected to target database: ORCL (DBID=1365223133)
```

All that remains is to instruct RMAN to make a backup copy of the database. The command is as simple as backup database. RMAN first tells you that information about the backup will be stored in the control file of the database instead of a separate *recovery catalog*, which is a separate Oracle database dedicated to storing information about database backups:

```
RMAN> backup database;

Starting backup at 2014/11/03 21:31
using target database control file instead of recovery catalog
allocated channel: ORA_DISK_1
channel ORA_DISK_1: SID=41 device type=DISK
```

RMAN then makes a backup of the files in the CDB:

```
channel ORA_DISK_1: starting full datafile backup set
channel ORA_DISK_1: specifying datafile(s) in backup set
input datafile file number=00003 name=/u01/app/oracle/oradata/ORCL/datafile/o1_mf_
sysaux_9fxmvhl3_.dbf
input datafile file number=00001 name=/u01/app/oracle/oradata/ORCL/datafile/o1_mf_
system_9fxmx6s1_.dbf
input datafile file number=00004 name=/u01/app/oracle/oradata/ORCL/datafile/o1_mf_
undotbs1_9fxn0vgg_.dbf
```

```
input datafile file number=00006 name=/u01/app/oracle/oradata/ORCL/datafile/o1_mf_
users_9fxn0t8s_.dbf
channel ORA_DISK_1: starting piece 1 at 2014/11/03 21:31
channel ORA_DISK_1: finished piece 1 at 2014/11/03 21:37
piece handle=/u01/app/oracle/fast_recovery_area/ORCL/backupset/2014_11_03/o1_mf_nnndf_
TAG20141103T213136_b5jgncy1_.bkp tag=TAG20141103T213136 comment=NONE
channel ORA_DISK_1: backup set complete, elapsed time: 00:06:11
```

RMAN then makes a backup of the files in the pdb1 database:

```
channel ORA_DISK_1: starting full datafile backup set
channel ORA_DISK_1: specifying datafile(s) in backup set
input datafile file number=00012 name=/u01/app/oracle/oradata/ORCL/F0832BAF1472128
1E045000000000001/datafile/o1_mf_sysaux_9fxvnjdl_.dbf
input datafile file number=00011 name=/u01/app/oracle/oradata/ORCL/F0832BAF1472128
1E045000000000001/datafile/o1_mf_system_9fxvnjdq_.dbf
input datafile file number=00014 name=/u01/app/oracle/oradata/ORCL/F0832BAF1472128
1E045000000000001/datafile/o1_mf_apex_226_9gfgd96o_.dbf
input datafile file number=00013 name=/u01/app/oracle/oradata/ORCL/F0832BAF1472128
1E045000000000001/datafile/o1_mf_users_9fxvoh6n_.dbf
channel ORA_DISK_1: starting piece 1 at 2014/11/03 21:37
channel ORA_DISK_1: finished piece 1 at 2014/11/03 21:40
piece handle=/u01/app/oracle/fast_recovery_area/ORCL/F0832BAF14721281E045000000000001/
backupset/2014_11_03/o1_mf_nnndf_TAG20141103T213136_b5jgzymm_.bkp tag=TAG20141103T213136
comment=NONE
channel ORA_DISK_1: backup set complete, elapsed time: 00:02:17
```

There is still another database left to process. This is the *seed* database, which is used only to create a new pluggable database:

```
channel ORA_DISK_1: starting full datafile backup set
channel ORA_DISK_1: specifying datafile(s) in backup set
input datafile file number=00007 name=/u01/app/oracle/oradata/ORCL/datafile/o1_mf_
sysaux_9fxn22p3_.dbf
input datafile file number=00005 name=/u01/app/oracle/oradata/ORCL/datafile/o1_mf_
system_9fxn22po_.dbf
channel ORA_DISK_1: starting piece 1 at 2014/11/03 21:40
channel ORA_DISK_1: finished piece 1 at 2014/11/03 21:41
piece handle=/u01/app/oracle/fast_recovery_area/ORCL/F081641BB43F0F7DE045000000000001/
backupset/2014_11_03/o1_mf_nnndf_TAG20141103T213136_b5jh49xl_.bkp tag=TAG20141103T213136
comment=NONE
channel ORA_DISK_1: backup set complete, elapsed time: 00:00:56
Finished backup at 2014/11/03 21:41
```

Finally, RMAN backs up up the control file and the spfile:

```
Starting Control File and SPFILE Autobackup at 2014/11/03 21:41
piece handle=/u01/app/oracle/fast_recovery_area/ORCL/autobackup/2014_11_03/o1_
mf_s_862695669_b5jh693f_.bkp comment=NONE
Finished Control File and SPFILE Autobackup at 2014/11/03 21:41
```

You can ask RMAN to summarize the results of the backup operation with the LIST BACKUP command. Three backup sets correspond to the three databases that were processed—the CDB, the pluggable database pdb1, and the seed database:

```
RMAN> list backup of database;

List of Backup Sets
===================

BS Key  Type LV Size       Device Type Elapsed Time Completion Time
------- ---- -- ---------- ----------- ------------ ----------------
1       Full    1.47G       DISK        00:06:06     2014/11/03 21:37
        BP Key: 1   Status: AVAILABLE  Compressed: NO  Tag: TAG20141103T213136
        Piece Name: /u01/app/oracle/fast_recovery_area/ORCL/backupset/2014_11_03/o1_mf_
        nnndf_TAG20141103T213136_b5jgncy1_.bkp
  List of Datafiles in backup set 1
  File LV Type Ckp SCN    Ckp Time          Name
  ---- -- ---- ---------- ----------------  ----
  1       Full 3470428    2014/11/03 21:31  /u01/app/oracle/oradata/ORCL/datafile/
                                            o1_mf_system_9fxmx6s1_.dbf
  3       Full 3470428    2014/11/03 21:31  /u01/app/oracle/oradata/ORCL/datafile/
                                            o1_mf_sysaux_9fxmvhl3_.dbf
  4       Full 3470428    2014/11/03 21:31  /u01/app/oracle/oradata/ORCL/datafile/
                                            o1_mf_undotbs1_9fxn0vgg_.dbf
  6       Full 3470428    2014/11/03 21:31  /u01/app/oracle/oradata/ORCL/datafile/
                                            o1_mf_users_9fxn0t8s_.dbf
BS Key  Type LV Size       Device Type Elapsed Time Completion Time
------- ---- -- ---------- ----------- ------------ ----------------
2       Full    813.77M     DISK        00:02:12     2014/11/03 21:40
        BP Key: 2   Status: AVAILABLE  Compressed: NO  Tag: TAG20141103T213136
        Piece Name: /u01/app/oracle/fast_recovery_area/ORCL/F0832BAF1472128
        1E045000000000001/backupset/2014_11_03/o1_mf_nnndf_TAG20141103T213136_b5jgzymm_.bkp
  List of Datafiles in backup set 2
  Container ID: 3, PDB Name: PDB1
  File LV Type Ckp SCN    Ckp Time          Name
  ---- -- ---- ---------- ----------------  ----
  11      Full 3471051    2014/11/03 21:37  /u01/app/oracle/oradata/ORCL/F0832BAF14
                                            721281E045000000000001/datafile/o1_mf_
                                            system_9fxvnjdq_.dbf
  12      Full 3471051    2014/11/03 21:37  /u01/app/oracle/oradata/ORCL/F0832BAF14721281E045
                                            000000000001/datafile/o1_mf_sysaux_9fxvnjdl_.dbf
  13      Full 3471051    2014/11/03 21:37  /u01/app/oracle/oradata/ORCL/F0832BAF14721281E045
                                            000000000001/datafile/o1_mf_users_9fxvoh6n_.dbf
  14      Full 3471051    2014/11/03 21:37  /u01/app/oracle/oradata/ORCL/F0832BAF14
                                            721281E045000000000001/datafile/o1_mf_
                                            apex_226_9gfgd96o_.dbf
BS Key  Type LV Size       Device Type Elapsed Time Completion Time
------- ---- -- ---------- ----------- ------------ ----------------
3       Full    553.52M     DISK        00:00:54     2014/11/03 21:41
        BP Key: 3   Status: AVAILABLE  Compressed: NO  Tag: TAG20141103T213136
        Piece Name: /u01/app/oracle/fast_recovery_area/ORCL/F081641BB43F0F7
        DE045000000000001/backupset/2014_11_03/o1_mf_nnndf_TAG20141103T213136_b5jh49xl_.bkp
```

```
List of Datafiles in backup set 3
Container ID: 2, PDB Name: PDB$SEED
File LV Type Ckp SCN   Ckp Time          Name
---- -- ---- ---------- ---------------- ----
5      Full 2654251   2014/01/27 15:35 /u01/app/oracle/oradata/ORCL/datafile/o1_mf_
                                        system_9fxn22po_.dbf
7      Full 2654251   2014/01/27 15:35 /u01/app/oracle/oradata/ORCL/datafile/o1_mf_
                                        sysaux_9fxn22p3_.dbf
```

```
RMAN> exit;
```

```
Recovery Manager complete.
```

Practical Demonstration: Logical Backups

The Data Pump Export tool is very powerful and flexible. It has features such as parallel unloading and the ability to select precise subsets of data.

First you have to create a *directory object* and map it to a directory on disk. This allows the Data Pump PL/SQL routines to write to disk:

```
[oracle@localhost ~]$ sqlplus sys/oracle@pdb1 as sysdba

SQL*Plus: Release 12.1.0.1.0 Production on Wed Nov 12 19:59:31 2014

Copyright (c) 1982, 2013, Oracle.  All rights reserved.

Connected to:
Oracle Database 12c Enterprise Edition Release 12.1.0.1.0 - 64bit Production
With the Partitioning, OLAP, Advanced Analytics and Real Application Testing options

PDB1@ORCL> create directory PDB1_DATA_PUMP_DIR as '/u01/app/oracle/admin/orcl/dpdump/';

Directory created.

PDB1@ORCL> grant all on directory PDB1_DATA_PUMP_DIR to system;

Grant succeeded.

PDB1@ORCL> quit
Disconnected from Oracle Database 12c Enterprise Edition Release 12.1.0.1.0 - 64bit
Production
With the Partitioning, OLAP, Advanced Analytics and Real Application Testing options
```

Let's export the data from the HR schema, one of the sample schemas included in your VM. Notice the use of the flashback_time qualifier, which ensures that any changes made to the data while the export is in progress are not copied:

```
[oracle@localhost ~]$ expdp userid=system/oracle@pdb1 schemas=hr directory=pdb1_data_pump_
dir flashback_time=sysdate

Export: Release 12.1.0.1.0 - Production on Thu Nov 13 11:11:43 2014
```

```
Copyright (c) 1982, 2013, Oracle and/or its affiliates.  All rights reserved.

UDE-28002: operation generated ORACLE error 28002
ORA-28002: the password will expire within 6 days


Connected to: Oracle Database 12c Enterprise Edition Release 12.1.0.1.0 - 64bit Production
With the Partitioning, OLAP, Advanced Analytics and Real Application Testing options
Starting "SYSTEM"."SYS_EXPORT_SCHEMA_01":  userid=system/********@pdb1 schemas=hr
directory=pdb1_data_pump_dir flashback_time=sysdate
Estimate in progress using BLOCKS method...
Processing object type SCHEMA_EXPORT/TABLE/TABLE_DATA
Total estimation using BLOCKS method: 448 KB
Processing object type SCHEMA_EXPORT/USER
Processing object type SCHEMA_EXPORT/SYSTEM_GRANT
Processing object type SCHEMA_EXPORT/ROLE_GRANT
Processing object type SCHEMA_EXPORT/DEFAULT_ROLE
Processing object type SCHEMA_EXPORT/TABLESPACE_QUOTA
Processing object type SCHEMA_EXPORT/PRE_SCHEMA/PROCACT_SCHEMA
Processing object type SCHEMA_EXPORT/SEQUENCE/SEQUENCE
Processing object type SCHEMA_EXPORT/TABLE/TABLE
Processing object type SCHEMA_EXPORT/TABLE/GRANT/OWNER_GRANT/OBJECT_GRANT
Processing object type SCHEMA_EXPORT/TABLE/COMMENT
Processing object type SCHEMA_EXPORT/PROCEDURE/PROCEDURE
Processing object type SCHEMA_EXPORT/PROCEDURE/ALTER_PROCEDURE
Processing object type SCHEMA_EXPORT/TABLE/INDEX/INDEX
Processing object type SCHEMA_EXPORT/TABLE/CONSTRAINT/CONSTRAINT
Processing object type SCHEMA_EXPORT/TABLE/INDEX/STATISTICS/INDEX_STATISTICS
Processing object type SCHEMA_EXPORT/VIEW/VIEW
Processing object type SCHEMA_EXPORT/TABLE/CONSTRAINT/REF_CONSTRAINT
Processing object type SCHEMA_EXPORT/TABLE/TRIGGER
Processing object type SCHEMA_EXPORT/TABLE/STATISTICS/TABLE_STATISTICS
Processing object type SCHEMA_EXPORT/STATISTICS/MARKER
. . exported "HR"."COUNTRIES"                          6.437 KB       25 rows
. . exported "HR"."DEPARTMENTS"                        7.101 KB       27 rows
. . exported "HR"."EMPLOYEES"                          17.05 KB      107 rows
. . exported "HR"."JOBS"                               7.078 KB       19 rows
. . exported "HR"."JOB_HISTORY"                        7.171 KB       10 rows
. . exported "HR"."LOCATIONS"                          8.414 KB       23 rows
. . exported "HR"."REGIONS"                            5.523 KB        4 rows
Master table "SYSTEM"."SYS_EXPORT_SCHEMA_01" successfully loaded/unloaded
******************************************************************************
Dump file set for SYSTEM.SYS_EXPORT_SCHEMA_01 is:
  /u01/app/oracle/admin/orcl/dpdump/expdat.dmp
Job "SYSTEM"."SYS_EXPORT_SCHEMA_01" successfully completed at Thu Nov 13 11:23:12 2014
elapsed 0 00:10:19
```

On checking the size of the dump file, you find that it is significantly smaller than the physical backup you performed earlier:

```
[oracle@localhost ~]$ ls -l /u01/app/oracle/admin/orcl/dpdump/expdat.dmp
-rw-r-----. 1 oracle oracle 573440 Nov 13 11:23 /u01/app/oracle/admin/orcl/dpdump/expdat.dmp
```

You can obtain a concise list of Data Pump Export options using the command expdp help=y. Some useful options are COMPRESSION, CONTENT, DIRECTORY, DUMPFILE, FILESIZE, FLASHBACK_TIME, FULL, PARALLEL, PARFILE, SCHEMAS, TABLES, and TABLESPACES.

Common RMAN Commands

The RMAN commands that you will most frequently encounter (in addition to BACKUP) are LIST, REPORT, CROSSCHECK, DELETE, SHOW, and CONFIGURE; Table 12-1 provides some examples. For a complete description of these and other commands, please refer to the Oracle Database 12c reference manuals.

Table 12-1. Common RMAN Commands

Command	Purpose
LIST BACKUP OF DATABASE SUMMARY	Produces a summary of all backups recorded in the control file (and recovery catalog if one is being used).
LIST BACKUP OF DATABASE COMPLETED AFTER 'SYSDATE - 1'	Produces a detailed listing of all backups completed over the last 24 hours.
CROSSCHECK BACKUP	Checks whether all the pieces of the backups recorded in the control file are still on disk and have not been inadvertently removed. Backup pieces that can no longer be located are designated as *expired*.
DELETE EXPIRED BACKUP	Removes information about a backup from the control file (or recovery catalog if one is being used) if the backup pieces cannot be found on disk.
REPORT OBSOLETE	Produces a list of backups that are older than the retention policy that is in effect. You can use the SHOW RETENTION POLICY command to determine which retention policy is in effect.
DELETE FORCE NOPROMPT OBSOLETE	Removes information about a backup from the control file (or recovery catalog if one is being used) if the backup is older than the retention policy in effect. The backup pieces are also removed from disk. The FORCE qualifier instructs RMAN not to complain about missing backup pieces. The NOPROMPT qualifier instructs RMAN not to prompt for confirmation before beginning the delete operation.
DELETE ARCHIVELOG ALL COMPLETED BEFORE 'SYSDATE - 7'	Deletes archived redo logs older than seven days.
SHOW ALL	Lists all the RMAN configuration parameters.
CONFIGURE CONTROLFILE AUTOBACKUP ON	Instructs Oracle to make a backup copy of the control file automatically whenever a new data file is added to the database. This is the default mode of behavior; I have included this command only to illustrate how to change backup options.

Listing 12-1 demonstrates the use of these commands. You put all the commands into a *command file* called rman.rcv. You also set the NLS_DATE_FORMAT environment variable to force RMAN to print the time of each operation, not just the date.

Listing 12-1. Common RMAN Commands

```
[oracle@localhost ~]$ cat rman.rcv
SET ECHO ON;
CONNECT TARGET;
LIST BACKUP OF DATABASE COMPLETED AFTER 'SYSDATE - 1';
CROSSCHECK BACKUP;
DELETE EXPIRED BACKUP;
REPORT OBSOLETE;
DELETE FORCE NOPROMPT OBSOLETE;
REPORT UNRECOVERABLE DATABASE;
DELETE ARCHIVELOG ALL COMPLETED BEFORE 'SYSDATE - 7';
SHOW ALL;
CONFIGURE CONTROLFILE AUTOBACKUP ON;
EXIT;

[oracle@localhost ~]$ rman <rman.rcv

Recovery Manager: Release 12.1.0.1.0 - Production on Thu Nov 13 12:40:17 2014

Copyright (c) 1982, 2013, Oracle and/or its affiliates.  All rights reserved.

RMAN>
echo set on

RMAN> CONNECT TARGET;
connected to target database: ORCL (DBID=1365223133)

RMAN> LIST BACKUP OF DATABASE COMPLETED AFTER 'SYSDATE - 1';
using target database control file instead of recovery catalog

List of Backup Sets
===================

BS Key  Type LV Size       Device Type Elapsed Time Completion Time
------- ---- -- ---------- ----------- ------------ ---------------
1       Full    1.42G       DISK        00:02:39     2014/11/13 12:25
        BP Key: 1    Status: AVAILABLE  Compressed: NO  Tag: TAG20141113T122241
        Piece Name: /u01/app/oracle/fast_recovery_area/ORCL/backupset/2014_11_13/o1_mf_
        nnndf_TAG20141113T122241_b69t73mo_.bkp
  List of Datafiles in backup set 1
  File LV Type Ckp SCN    Ckp Time          Name
  ---- -- ---- ---------- ----------------  ----
  1       Full 3503504    2014/11/13 12:22  /u01/app/oracle/oradata/ORCL/datafile/
                                            o1_mf_system_9fxmx6s1_.dbf
  3       Full 3503504    2014/11/13 12:22  /u01/app/oracle/oradata/ORCL/datafile/
                                            o1_mf_sysaux_9fxmvhl3_.dbf
  4       Full 3503504    2014/11/13 12:22  /u01/app/oracle/oradata/ORCL/datafile/
                                            o1_mf_undotbs1_9fxn0vgg_.dbf
  6       Full 3503504    2014/11/13 12:22  /u01/app/oracle/oradata/ORCL/datafile/
                                            o1_mf_users_9fxn0t8s_.dbf
```

```
BS Key  Type LV Size       Device Type Elapsed Time Completion Time
------- ---- -- ---------- ----------- ------------ ---------------
2       Full 818.72M   DISK        00:01:22     2014/11/13 12:26
        BP Key: 2   Status: AVAILABLE  Compressed: NO  Tag: TAG20141113T122241
        Piece Name: /u01/app/oracle/fast_recovery_area/ORCL/F0832BAF1472128
        1E045000000000001/backupset/2014_11_13/o1_mf_nnndf_TAG20141113T122241_b69tdcfl_.bkp
  List of Datafiles in backup set 2
  Container ID: 3, PDB Name: PDB1
  File LV Type Ckp SCN    Ckp Time           Name
  ---- -- ---- ---------- ---------------- ----
  11      Full 3503588    2014/11/13 12:25 /u01/app/oracle/oradata/ORCL/F0832BAF14
                                           721281E045000000000001/datafile/o1_mf_
                                           system_9fxvnjdq_.dbf
  12      Full 3503588    2014/11/13 12:25 /u01/app/oracle/oradata/ORCL/F0832BAF14
                                           721281E045000000000001/datafile/o1_mf_
                                           sysaux_9fxvnjdl_.dbf
  13      Full 3503588    2014/11/13 12:25 /u01/app/oracle/oradata/ORCL/F0832BAF14721281E045
                                           000000000001/datafile/o1_mf_users_9fxvoh6n_.dbf
  14      Full 3503588    2014/11/13 12:25 /u01/app/oracle/oradata/ORCL/F0832BAF14
                                           721281E045000000000001/datafile/o1_mf_
                                           apex_226_9gfgd96o_.dbf


BS Key  Type LV Size       Device Type Elapsed Time Completion Time
------- ---- -- ---------- ----------- ------------ ---------------
3       Full 553.52M   DISK        00:00:45     2014/11/13 12:27
        BP Key: 3   Status: AVAILABLE  Compressed: NO  Tag: TAG20141113T122241
        Piece Name: /u01/app/oracle/fast_recovery_area/ORCL/F081641BB43F0F7
        DE045000000000001/backupset/2014_11_13/o1_mf_nnndf_TAG20141113T122241_b69th2kc_.bkp
  List of Datafiles in backup set 3
  Container ID: 2, PDB Name: PDB$SEED
  File LV Type Ckp SCN    Ckp Time           Name
  ---- -- ---- ---------- ---------------- ----
  5       Full 2654251    2014/01/27 15:35 /u01/app/oracle/oradata/ORCL/datafile/o1_mf_
                                           system_9fxn22po_.dbf
  7       Full 2654251    2014/01/27 15:35 /u01/app/oracle/oradata/ORCL/datafile/o1_mf_
                                           sysaux_9fxn22p3_.dbf
```

RMAN> CROSSCHECK BACKUP;
```
allocated channel: ORA_DISK_1
channel ORA_DISK_1: SID=43 device type=DISK
crosschecked backup piece: found to be 'AVAILABLE'
backup piece handle=/u01/app/oracle/fast_recovery_area/ORCL/backupset/2014_11_13/o1_mf_
nnndf_TAG20141113T122241_b69t73mo_.bkp RECID=1 STAMP=863526163
crosschecked backup piece: found to be 'AVAILABLE'
backup piece handle=/u01/app/oracle/fast_recovery_area/ORCL/F0832BAF1472128
1E045000000000001/backupset/2014_11_13/o1_mf_nnndf_TAG20141113T122241_b69tdcfl_.bkp RECID=2
STAMP=863526331
crosschecked backup piece: found to be 'AVAILABLE'
backup piece handle=/u01/app/oracle/fast_recovery_area/ORCL/F081641BB43F0F7
DE045000000000001/backupset/2014_11_13/o1_mf_nnndf_TAG20141113T122241_b69th2kc_.bkp RECID=3
STAMP=863526418
```

```
crosschecked backup piece: found to be 'AVAILABLE'
backup piece handle=/u01/app/oracle/fast_recovery_area/ORCL/autobackup/2014_11_13/o1_
mf_s_863526476_b69tjz6k_.bkp RECID=4 STAMP=863526479
Crosschecked 4 objects
```

RMAN> DELETE EXPIRED BACKUP;
```
using channel ORA_DISK_1
specification does not match any backup in the repository
```

RMAN> REPORT OBSOLETE;
```
RMAN retention policy will be applied to the command
RMAN retention policy is set to redundancy 1
Report of obsolete backups and copies
Type                 Key   Completion Time     Filename/Handle
-------------------- ----- ------------------- --------------------
Archive Log          1     2014/11/13 12:02    /u01/app/oracle/fast_recovery_area/ORCL/
archivelog/2014_11_13/o1_mf_1_132_b69s1o12_.arc
```

```
RMAN> DELETE FORCE NOPROMPT OBSOLETE;
RMAN retention policy will be applied to the command
RMAN retention policy is set to redundancy 1
using channel ORA_DISK_1
Deleting the following obsolete backups and copies:
Type                 Key   Completion Time     Filename/Handle
-------------------- ----- ------------------- --------------------
Archive Log          1     2014/11/13 12:02    /u01/app/oracle/fast_recovery_area/ORCL/
archivelog/2014_11_13/o1_mf_1_132_b69s1o12_.arc
deleted archived log
archived log file name=/u01/app/oracle/fast_recovery_area/ORCL/archivelog/2014_11_13/o1_
mf_1_132_b69s1o12_.arc RECID=1 STAMP=863524967
Deleted 1 objects
```

RMAN> REPORT UNRECOVERABLE DATABASE;
```
Report of files that need backup due to unrecoverable operations
File Type of Backup Required Name
---- ----------------------- --------------------------------------
```

RMAN> DELETE ARCHIVELOG ALL COMPLETED BEFORE 'SYSDATE - 7';
```
released channel: ORA_DISK_1
allocated channel: ORA_DISK_1
channel ORA_DISK_1: SID=43 device type=DISK
specification does not match any archived log in the repository
```

RMAN> SHOW ALL;
```
RMAN configuration parameters for database with db_unique_name ORCL are:
CONFIGURE RETENTION POLICY TO REDUNDANCY 1; # default
CONFIGURE BACKUP OPTIMIZATION OFF; # default
CONFIGURE DEFAULT DEVICE TYPE TO DISK; # default
CONFIGURE CONTROLFILE AUTOBACKUP ON;
CONFIGURE CONTROLFILE AUTOBACKUP FORMAT FOR DEVICE TYPE DISK TO '%F'; # default
CONFIGURE DEVICE TYPE DISK PARALLELISM 1 BACKUP TYPE TO BACKUPSET; # default
CONFIGURE DATAFILE BACKUP COPIES FOR DEVICE TYPE DISK TO 1; # default
```

```
CONFIGURE ARCHIVELOG BACKUP COPIES FOR DEVICE TYPE DISK TO 1; # default
CONFIGURE MAXSETSIZE TO UNLIMITED; # default
CONFIGURE ENCRYPTION FOR DATABASE OFF; # default
CONFIGURE ENCRYPTION ALGORITHM 'AES128'; # default
CONFIGURE COMPRESSION ALGORITHM 'BASIC' AS OF RELEASE 'DEFAULT' OPTIMIZE FOR LOAD TRUE ; #
default
CONFIGURE RMAN OUTPUT TO KEEP FOR 7 DAYS; # default
CONFIGURE ARCHIVELOG DELETION POLICY TO NONE; # default
CONFIGURE SNAPSHOT CONTROLFILE NAME TO '/u01/app/oracle/product/12.1.0/dbhome_1/dbs/snapcf_
orcl.f'; # default

RMAN> CONFIGURE CONTROLFILE AUTOBACKUP ON;
old RMAN configuration parameters:
CONFIGURE CONTROLFILE AUTOBACKUP ON;
new RMAN configuration parameters:
CONFIGURE CONTROLFILE AUTOBACKUP ON;
new RMAN configuration parameters are successfully stored

RMAN> EXIT;

Recovery Manager complete.
```

Horror Stories

All of the following stories are true and are based on personal experience—mine.

A deployment of a new version of a business application was unsuccessful, and the DBA was asked to undo the changes made to the database by recovering the database from the previous night's backups and the redo logs. He discovered that the backup script that was scheduled to run every night had been failing for three months; its defect was that it did not send an alert to the DBA when it failed in its task. Luckily the redo logs were being copied to a file server and none of the archived redo logs had been deleted. The DBA restored the database from the last good backup and started applying the redo logs to recover the missing transactions. Even the tiniest damage to any of the archived redo logs would have abruptly terminated the recovery operation, but, luckily, none of the redo logs were damaged.

■ **Tip**   Implement a script that checks whether the database has been successfully backed up. This script should be *separate* from the backup script. Also consider daily and weekly reports listing backup successes and failures for all databases in the enterprise—such reports are also useful for tracking how data volumes and backup times are growing.

A new DBA was creating a database and was told by a system administrator that the system administration team handled all aspects of backups. The DBA took him at his word, but, unfortunately, this particular server had been built using a new standard: the database administration team was responsible for backups, not the system administration team. This mission-critical database was used for a whole year before and then decommissioned. It had never been backed up.

■ **Tip** Backups should be tested periodically. A recovery test should be conducted before a database is put to use.

A DBA had disabled an automated backup script one night because it would conflict with a deployment of a new version of a business application. The deployment failed and the database in question was successfully restored to its previous state using the previous night's backup and redo logs. However, the DBA forgot to re-enable the automated backup script. One month later, there was another application deployment, which also failed. This time, the database could not be restored, and the data had to be manually re-created.

It happened to me—it could happen to you!

Summary

Here is a short summary of the concepts touched on in this chapter:

- A backup is a snapshot of a database or a part of a database; if the database is damaged, the damaged parts can be repaired using the backups. Archived logs can be used in conjunction with backups to replay transactions that changed data after the backup was performed.

- An appropriate backup strategy is one that meets the needs of the business while remaining cost-effective.

- A common practice is to make backup copies on disk when possible and have them copied to tape in a separate operation.

- Backups require a lot of computer resources and are therefore typically scheduled at nights and on weekends when other activity is at a minimum. If the database is very large, you may not have the time and resources to create a backup of the entire database in a single operation.

- Incremental backups can be used to conserve computer resources. You copy only those data blocks which have changed since the last backup.

- Backups that are performed while the database is being used may contain inconsistencies. The information in the redo log files can be used to eliminate the inconsistencies.

- Physical backups are copies of whole database blocks. Logical backups are copies of the data records themselves.

- Recovery Manager (RMAN) is usually the tool of choice for creating physical backups. Data Pump Export can be used for creating logical backups.

Exercises

- Automate RMAN backups using the Oracle-suggested backup strategy in Chapter 9 of Oracle Database 2-Day DBA.

CHAPTER 13

■ ■ ■

Recovery

These Officers, with the Men belonging to the Engine, at their Quarterly Meetings, discourse of Fires, of the Faults committed at some, the good Management in some Cases at others, and thus communicating their Thoughts and Experience they grow wise in the Thing, and know how to command and to execute in the best manner upon every Emergency.

—Benjamin Franklin in a letter to the *Pennsylvania Gazette*, following a disastrous fire in Philadelphia in the 18th century

In the previous chapter, you learned how to make backup copies of the database. You now turn your attention to repairing the database if it gets damaged. For the purposes of this chapter, you should assume the availability of backup copies made using Recovery Manager (RMAN) but you will discover that backup copies are not the only repair option available. This chapter also acquaints you with a powerful tool called Data Recovery Advisor (DRA), which greatly simplifies the database administrator's job.

Horror Stories

The following are true stories based on personal experiences.

Sometimes we make a mountain out of a molehill. Early in my career, in the days of Oracle 7, a few blocks of data in the company's most critical database were found to be corrupted. Any transaction that touched the affected blocks could not complete, but the database was otherwise functional. This was a large Enterprise Resource Planning (ERP) database that the business depended on for all aspects of its functioning, so the application administrators went into high gear. There were no disk backups because of the sheer size of the database, so the application administrators recalled the tapes from the offsite storage facility. They shut down the database at the end of the day and began restoring it from tapes, hoping to have the database ready for business the next day. However, three-quarters of the way into the restore operation, a defect was found in the tapes, and the application administrators had to requisition the previous set of tapes from the offsite storage facility. The offsite storage facility was 100 miles away, and this necessitated a substantial delay.

After the database files were successfully restored from tape, the administrators began the task of recovering transactions from the archived redo log files; this took a huge amount of time. From start to finish, the restore and recovery operation took 48 hours instead of the original estimate of 12 hours, and the business lost 2 days of work. The mistake was using a one-size-fits-all repair strategy that did not take into consideration the amount of damage; it is not necessary to shut down and restore the entire database if only one data file is damaged. In Oracle Database 12*c*, it is even possible to repair individual blocks without affecting the availability of the rest of the database.

■ **Tip**   An appropriate repair strategy is one that is tailored to the situation and causes minimum downtime. Individual data files and data blocks can be repaired without impacting the rest of the database.

In my second story, which occured more recently in my career, all the king's horses and all the king's men couldn't put Humpty Dumpty together again. The disks crashed, and a large data-warehouse database became unusable. Unfortunately, the disk backups were being stored on the same disks as the database, and restoration from tapes was the only option. Needless to say, any archived redo logs that were not on tape were lost forever, which meant that a significant number of transactions could never be recovered. In a bad case of déjà vu, the first set of tapes was found to be defective, and restoration had to be started afresh using a second set of tapes. But that was not the end of the story; the database was still unusable even after all available redo logs had been applied. It turned out that data was regularly loaded in NOLOGGING mode, which means redo information was not being recorded in the redo logs. Large parts of the database had to be re-created from other sources, and it was several weeks before it was fully functional again.

It happened to me—it could happen to you.

■ **Tip**   Issue the ALTER DATABASE FORCE LOGGING command to prevent users from using NOLOGGING mode without the knowledge of the DBAs.

Types of Recovery

There are several kinds of repair operations. This section describes each in turn.

Restore vs. Recover

These two terms are often used synonymously in everyday usage—for example, the title of this chapter is simply "Recovery," and the title of this section is "Types of Recovery." However, the words *restore* and *recover* have specialized technical meanings for the DBA. The word *restore* refers to the operation of replacing a damaged or missing file such as a data file, a control file, or an archived redo log file from a backup copy. The word *recover* refers to the process of replaying transactions recorded in the redo logs and making the database usable again. Usually, the recovery process is preceded by the restore process. However, Oracle performs automatic recovery operations (a.k.a. *crash recovery*) if the database is restarted after an ungraceful shutdown such as a system crash.

Coincidentally enough, the two most important RMAN commands for repairing a database are RESTORE and RECOVER—they are powerful commands with a rich set of options. Later in this chapter, you see how DRA simplifies the DBA's job.

Full Recovery vs. Partial Recovery

If one part of a database is damaged, the rest of the database usually continues to function. The most· common examples are loss of a data file (except a data file from the SYSTEM tablespace) or corruption of a few blocks of data. It is usually possible to restore and recover the affected parts of the database without impacting the availability of the rest of the database.

■ **Note**   Single-block recovery is available only in the Enterprise Edition.

Complete Recovery vs. Incomplete Recovery

After the affected parts of the database are *restored* from the backup, the transactions in the redo log files must be *recovered*. Sometimes the recovery phase cannot be completed. For example, an archived redo log may be lost or damaged. Or you might intentionally wish to stop the recovery process at a point in time in the past; perhaps you wish to erase the effects of mistakes made by a user. You will hear the term RESETLOGS used in conjunction with an incomplete recovery, and the *incarnation number* of the database is incremented in such cases. Incomplete recovery is also referred to as *point-in-time recovery*.

Traditional vs. Flashback

Point-in-time recovery after user error can be very time-consuming when the database is large or when a large number of redo logs have to be processed. Partial recovery is not an option in such cases because the integrity of the database might be compromised if different parts of the database reflected different points in time. The Enterprise Edition of Oracle Database 12*c* offers the option to unwind transactions by using a special type of log called the *flashback log*. This can be orders of magnitude faster than traditional recovery but is limited by the amount of space reserved for the storage of flashback logs. Note that the flashback method of recovering a database can only be used to perform *logical recovery*; it cannot be used to recover from physical damage to the database such as corruption of data blocks.

Physical Recovery vs. Logical Recovery

All the methods of recovery that I have covered so far can be classified as *physical recovery* because they are not tailored to the affected data. An alternative to physical recovery following user error is *logical recovery*, which is tailored to the affected data. Here are some examples:

- If an index is corrupted, it can be dropped and re-created without compromising the data in the underlying table.

- If data is inadvertently deleted, it might be possible to reconstruct it from paper records.

- The Data Pump Import utility can be used to restore a table from a logical backup made by using that utility. This is illustrated in Listing 13-1.

Oracle Database 12*c* also offers a variety of methods for logical recovery based on the information contained in the undo segments. These methods are called *flashback methods*; I'll present more information about them later in this chapter.

Listing 13-1. Logical Recovery of a Single Table by Using the Data Pump Import Utility

```
[oracle@localhost ~]$ impdp system/oracle@pdb1 directory=pdb1_data_pump_dir dumpfile=expdat.
dmp tables=hr.employees table_exists_action=replace

Import: Release 12.1.0.1.0 - Production on Wed Dec 3 18:11:50 2014

Copyright (c) 1982, 2013, Oracle and/or its affiliates.  All rights reserved.

Connected to: Oracle Database 12c Enterprise Edition Release 12.1.0.1.0 - 64bit Production
With the Partitioning, OLAP, Advanced Analytics and Real Application Testing options
Master table "SYSTEM"."SYS_IMPORT_TABLE_01" successfully loaded/unloaded
```

```
Starting "SYSTEM"."SYS_IMPORT_TABLE_01":  system/********@pdb1 directory=pdb1_data_pump_dir
dumpfile=expdat.dmp tables=hr.employees table_exists_action=replace
Processing object type SCHEMA_EXPORT/TABLE/TABLE
Processing object type SCHEMA_EXPORT/TABLE/TABLE_DATA
. . imported "HR"."EMPLOYEES"                            17.05 KB      107 rows
Processing object type SCHEMA_EXPORT/TABLE/GRANT/OWNER_GRANT/OBJECT_GRANT
Processing object type SCHEMA_EXPORT/TABLE/COMMENT
Processing object type SCHEMA_EXPORT/TABLE/INDEX/INDEX
Processing object type SCHEMA_EXPORT/TABLE/CONSTRAINT/CONSTRAINT
Processing object type SCHEMA_EXPORT/TABLE/INDEX/STATISTICS/INDEX_STATISTICS
Processing object type SCHEMA_EXPORT/TABLE/CONSTRAINT/REF_CONSTRAINT
Processing object type SCHEMA_EXPORT/TABLE/TRIGGER
Processing object type SCHEMA_EXPORT/TABLE/STATISTICS/TABLE_STATISTICS
Processing object type SCHEMA_EXPORT/STATISTICS/MARKER
Job "SYSTEM"."SYS_IMPORT_TABLE_01" successfully completed at Wed Dec 3 18:12:37 2014 elapsed
0 00:00:43
```

Flashback Technology

The information contained in the undo segments can be used to reconstruct prior versions of the data. The amount of information available in the undo segments is governed by the size of the undo segments and by the UNDO_RETENTION setting. The default value of the UNDO_RETENTION setting is only 900 seconds (15 minutes)—you should increase it to a more appropriate value. Also make sure the undo segments are fairly large.

■ **Note**   The more-advanced flashback features such as Flashback Transaction Query, Flashback Table, and Flashback Database are available only with the Enterprise Edition of Oracle Database 12c.

Flashback Query

If data in a table is inadvertently changed, you can obtain the prior values of the data items by using the undo segments and construct suitable SQL statements to correct the data, as in the following example. First, let's increase the salary of employee 101 by $1,000:

```
SQL> UPDATE employees
  2     SET salary=salary + 1000
  3   WHERE employee_id = 101;

1 row updated.

SQL> SELECT salary
  2     FROM employees
  3   WHERE employee_id = 101;
```

```
     SALARY
----------
     18000

SQL> COMMIT;

Commit complete.
```

Next, determine what the employee's salary used to be, one hour ago. You can do so with the AS OF TIMESTAMP clause:

```
SQL> SELECT salary
  2    FROM employees AS OF TIMESTAMP SYSDATE - 1/24
  3   WHERE employee_id = 101;

     SALARY
----------
     17000
```

You can formulate an UPDATE command to change the employee's salary back to the original value. Notice the use of the AS OF TIMESTAMP clause once again:

```
SQL> UPDATE employees
  2     SET salary = (SELECT salary
  3                     FROM employees AS OF TIMESTAMP SYSDATE - 1/24
  4                    WHERE employee_id = 101)
  5   WHERE employee_id = 101;

1 row updated.

SQL> COMMIT;

Commit complete.

SQL> SELECT salary
  2    FROM employees
  3   WHERE employee_id = 101;

     SALARY
----------
     17000
```

Flashback Versions

If a row of data is changed multiple times, you can use the VERSIONS BETWEEN clause to search for prior versions of the row in the undo segments. VERSIONS_STARTTIME and VERSIONS_XID are *pseudocolumns* that tell you when each version was created and which transaction created it. The absence of these values indicates the time prior to the window specified in the query. In the following example, you can see the original value of the employee's salary ($17,000), the transaction that changed the value to $18,000, and the transaction that reversed the change:

```
SQL> COLUMN versions_starttime FORMAT a32
SQL> SELECT versions_starttime,
  2           versions_xid,
  3           salary
  4      FROM employees VERSIONS BETWEEN TIMESTAMP SYSDATE - 1/24 AND SYSDATE
  5      WHERE employee_id = 101;

VERSIONS_STARTTIME                    VERSIONS_XID        SALARY
--------------------------------   ----------------   ----------
28-NOV-07 02.15.02 PM                 05000F0031030000      17000
28-NOV-07 02.14.31 PM                 09001000D4030000      18000
                                                            17000
```

Flashback Transaction

The SQL statements required to reverse changes can be automatically generated from the undo segments. For example, an INSERT statement can be reversed with a DELETE statement, and vice versa. All you need to do is to select the necessary SQL statements from the flashback_transaction_query view—a DBA-level privilege called SELECT ANY TRANSACTION is required. The transaction identifier (XID) in the following example is the one obtained in the previous section:

```
SQL> SELECT undo_sql
  2      FROM flashback_transaction_query
  3      WHERE XID = '09001000D4030000';

UNDO_SQL
--------------------------------------------------------------------------------
update "HR"."EMPLOYEES" set "SALARY" = '17000' where ROWID = 'AAARAgAAFAAAABYABj';
```

Flashback Table

All changes made to a table can be removed by using the FLASHBACK TABLE command if the information in the undo segments has not yet been overwritten by newer transactions. For example, suppose you inadvertently increase the salary of all employees, as in the following example:

```
SQL> UPDATE employees
  2      SET salary=salary + 1000;

107 rows updated.

SQL> COMMIT;

Commit complete.
```

Before you use the FLASHBACK TABLE command, you must give Oracle permission to restore rows to new locations if necessary. You do this using the ENABLE ROW MOVEMENT clause of the ALTER TABLE command. You can then issue the FLASHBACK TABLE command:

```
SQL> FLASHBACK TABLE employees TO TIMESTAMP SYSDATE - 1/24;
FLASHBACK TABLE employees TO TIMESTAMP SYSDATE - 1/24
                        *
ERROR at line 1:
ORA-08189: cannot flashback the table because row movement is not enabled

SQL> ALTER TABLE employees ENABLE ROW MOVEMENT;

Table altered.

SQL> FLASHBACK TABLE employees TO TIMESTAMP SYSDATE - 1/24;

Flashback complete.
```

Flashback Drop

If an entire table is inadvertently deleted, you can simply recover it from the Recycle Bin by using the FLASHBACK TABLE...TO BEFORE DROP command. Dropped tables remain in the Recycle Bin until they are explicitly purged by using the PURGE command:

```
SQL> CREATE TABLE employees_backup AS SELECT * FROM employees;

Table created.

SQL> SELECT COUNT (*)
  2    FROM employees_backup;

  COUNT(*)
----------
       107

SQL> DROP TABLE employees_backup;

Table dropped.

SQL> DESCRIBE user_recyclebin;
 Name                                      Null?    Type
 ----------------------------------------- -------- ----------------------------
 OBJECT_NAME                               NOT NULL VARCHAR2(30)
 ORIGINAL_NAME                                      VARCHAR2(32)
 OPERATION                                          VARCHAR2(9)
 TYPE                                               VARCHAR2(25)
 TS_NAME                                            VARCHAR2(30)
 CREATETIME                                         VARCHAR2(19)
 DROPTIME                                           VARCHAR2(19)
 DROPSCN                                            NUMBER
```

```
PARTITION_NAME                                  VARCHAR2(32)
CAN_UNDROP                                      VARCHAR2(3)
CAN_PURGE                                       VARCHAR2(3)
RELATED                              NOT NULL   NUMBER
BASE_OBJECT                         NOT NULL   NUMBER
PURGE_OBJECT                        NOT NULL   NUMBER
SPACE                                          NUMBER

SQL> SELECT object_name,
  2          original_name
  3     FROM user_recyclebin;

OBJECT_NAME                      ORIGINAL_NAME
-------------------------------  -------------------------------
BIN$1ethyUzGQEW849KhDJOcJg==$0 EMPLOYEES_BACKUP

SQL> FLASHBACK TABLE employees_backup TO BEFORE DROP;

Flashback complete.

SQL> SELECT COUNT (*)
  2     FROM employees_backup;

  COUNT(*)
----------
       107

SQL> DROP TABLE employees_backup;

Table dropped.

SQL> PURGE user_recyclebin;

Recyclebin purged.

SQL> FLASHBACK TABLE employees_backup TO BEFORE DROP;
FLASHBACK TABLE employees_backup TO BEFORE DROP
*
ERROR at line 1:
ORA-38305: object not in RECYCLE BIN
```

Flashback Data Archive

This feature was introduced in Oracle Database 12c. An archive can be created to store all changes made to data rows during the lifetime of a table. The archive is not dependent on the undo segments, and, consequently, its contents are not lost if the information in the undo segments is overwritten by new transactions. A complete discussion is outside the scope of this chapter.

Flashback Database

The biggest weapon in the armory of flashback features is the FLASHBACK DATABASE command. For example, let's suppose that major changes are being made to the database. You simply need to create a *restore point* by using the CREATE RESTORE POINT command. If the changes need to be tested and test data created before releasing the database to users, you can create a second restore point. If the testing is successful, the test data can be completely erased by reverting to the second restore point, and the database can then be released to users. If the testing is unsuccessful, you can revert to the first restore point to wipe out all traces of your changes.

Using the FLASHBACK DATABASE command requires that the database be shut down and then brought into the MOUNT state. After the command has completed, you must open the database with the RESETLOGS option.

Note that the flashback-database technique depends on a special type of log file called a *flashback log*. The retention of information in flashback logs is governed by the Oracle parameter DB_FLASHBACK_RETENTION_TARGET. Also, the DBA must explicitly enable logging by using the command ALTER DATABASE FLASHBACK ON before opening the database.

LogMiner

You can also recover prior versions of data from the archived redo logs by using a utility called LogMiner, as illustrated in Listing 13-2. LogMiner can construct *undo SQL* that you can use to selectively reverse changes to your data.

Listing 13-2. Logical Recovery Using the LogMiner Utility

```sql
SQL> EXECUTE DBMS_LOGMNR.add_logfile (logfilename => 'C:\APP\IGNATIUS\FLASH_RECOVERY
_AREA\ORCL\ARCHIVELOG\2008_09_20\O1_MF_1_77_4FBYS33F_.ARC', options => DBMS_LOGMNR.N
EW);

PL/SQL procedure successfully completed.

SQL> EXECUTE DBMS_LOGMNR.add_logfile (logfilename => 'C:\APP\IGNATIUS\FLASH_RECOVERY
_AREA\ORCL\ARCHIVELOG\2008_09_20\O1_MF_1_78_4FBYS6J3_.ARC', options => DBMS_LOGMNR.a
ddfile);

PL/SQL procedure successfully completed.

SQL> EXECUTE DBMS_LOGMNR.add_logfile (logfilename => 'C:\APP\IGNATIUS\FLASH_RECOVERY
_AREA\ORCL\ARCHIVELOG\2008_09_20\O1_MF_1_79_4FBYSOOH_.ARC', options => DBMS_LOGMNR.a
ddfile);

PL/SQL procedure successfully completed.

SQL> SELECT sql_undo
  2    FROM v$logmnr_contents
  3    WHERE seg_name = 'EMPLOYEES'
  4      AND ROWNUM < 5;
```

```
SQL_UNDO
------------------------------------------------------
update "HR"."EMPLOYEES"
  set
    "SALARY" = 2600
  where
    "SALARY" = 3250 and
    ROWID = 'AAARcwAAFAAAABUAAA';

update "HR"."EMPLOYEES"
  set
    "SALARY" = 2600
  where
    "SALARY" = 3250 and
    ROWID = 'AAARcwAAFAAAABUAAB';

update "HR"."EMPLOYEES"
  set
    "SALARY" = 4400
  where
    "SALARY" = 5500 and
    ROWID = 'AAARcwAAFAAAABUAAC';

update "HR"."EMPLOYEES"
  set
    "SALARY" = 13000
  where
    "SALARY" = 16250 and
    ROWID = 'AAARcwAAFAAAABUAAD';
```

Note that LogMiner works as advertised only if you have enabled *minimal supplemental logging*. According to the Oracle Database 12c documentation, this "ensures that LogMiner (and any products building on LogMiner technology) has sufficient information to support chained rows and various storage arrangements such as cluster tables and index-organized tables." The command that enables minimal supplemental logging is ALTER DATABASE ADD SUPPLEMENTAL LOG DATA.

A complete discussion of LogMiner can be found in Chapter 18 of *Oracle Database 12c Utilities*.

Data Recovery Advisor

Physical recovery usually requires the use of RMAN . The two most powerful RMAN repair commands are RESTORE DATABASE and RECOVER DATABASE. The first command restores all data files from the last backup. The second command uses the redo logs and recovers all the changes made since the backup. But full database recovery using the RESTORE DATABASE and RECOVER DATABASE commands is not required in all cases. The most appropriate database strategy is one that is tailored to the situation, and RMAN provides a wide range of repair options that may overwhelm the beginner. However, Oracle Database 12c also provides a powerful tool called Data Recovery Advisor (DRA) that greatly simplifies the DBA's job.

Let's demonstrate physical recovery by using DRA to repair corrupt blocks—the same situation described in my first horror story. In those days, Oracle did not offer the capability to repair individual blocks while the rest of the database was still being used, although it did offer the capability to repair individual files. Block recovery is the least invasive of all recovery operations, and DRA makes the process as easy as it is possible to imagine.

I decided to intentionally corrupt one of the data blocks in the Employees table in the sample HR schema, and the DBA_EXTENTS view gave me the information I needed to determine exactly which blocks to corrupt:

```
[oracle@localhost ~]$ sqlplus sys/oracle@pdb1 as sysdba

SQL*Plus: Release 12.1.0.1.0 Production on Wed Dec 3 18:22:19 2014

Copyright (c) 1982, 2013, Oracle.  All rights reserved.

Connected to:
Oracle Database 12c Enterprise Edition Release 12.1.0.1.0 - 64bit Production
With the Partitioning, OLAP, Advanced Analytics and Real Application Testing options

PDB1@ORCL> select block_id from dba_extents where segment_name='EMPLOYEES';

  BLOCK_ID
----------
       200

PDB1@ORCL> select extent_id, file_id, block_id, bytes, blocks
  2  from dba_extents
  3  where segment_name = 'EMPLOYEES';

EXTENT_ID    FILE_ID   BLOCK_ID      BYTES     BLOCKS
---------- ---------- ---------- ---------- ----------
        0         13        200      65536          8

PDB1@ORCL> column file_name format a80
PDB1@ORCL> set linesize 80
PDB1@ORCL> select file_name from dba_data_files where file_id=13;

FILE_NAME
--------------------------------------------------------------------------------
/u01/app/oracle/oradata/ORCL/F0832BAF14721281E045000000000001/datafile/o1_mf_use
rs_9fxvoh6n_.dbf

PDB1@ORCL> exit
Disconnected from Oracle Database 12c Enterprise Edition Release 12.1.0.1.0 - 64bit
Production
With the Partitioning, OLAP, Advanced Analytics and Real Application Testing options
```

I shut down the database and modified the file containing those blocks using a Linux utility called dd (device dump):

```
[oracle@localhost ~]$ dd if=/dev/null of=/u01/app/oracle/oradata/ORCL/F0832BAF1472128
1E045000000000001/datafile/o1_mf_users_9fxvoh6n_.dbf ibs=8192 obs=8192 seek=200 count=1
conv=notrunc
0+0 records in
0+0 records out)
```

Then I started the database. Everything worked normally until I tried to list the contents of the table. SQL*Plus then displayed an error:

```
[oracle@localhost ~]$ sqlplus sys/oracle@pdb1 as sysdba

SQL*Plus: Release 12.1.0.1.0 Production on Wed Dec 3 19:00:58 2014

Copyright (c) 1982, 2013, Oracle.  All rights reserved.

Connected to:
Oracle Database 12c Enterprise Edition Release 12.1.0.1.0 - 64bit Production
With the Partitioning, OLAP, Advanced Analytics and Real Application Testing options

PDB1@ORCL> select * from hr.employees;
select * from hr.employees
*
ERROR at line 1:
ORA-01578: ORACLE data block corrupted (file # 13, block # 202)
ORA-01110: data file 13:
'/u01/app/oracle/oradata/ORCL/F0832BAF14721281E045000000000001/datafile/o1_mf_us
ers_9fxvoh6n_.dbf'

PDB1@ORCL> exit
```

The Oracle-recommended action was, "Try to restore the segment containing the block indicated. This may involve dropping the segment and re-creating it. If there is a trace file, report the error in it to your Oracle representative." But DRA makes short work of the problem, as you shall see:

```
[oracle@localhost ~]$ oerr ora 1578
01578, 00000, "ORACLE data block corrupted (file # %s, block # %s)"
// *Cause:  The data block indicated was corrupted, mostly due to software
//          errors.
// *Action: Try to restore the segment containing the block indicated. This
//          may involve dropping the segment and recreating it. If there
//          is a trace file, report the errors in it to your ORACLE
//          representative.
```

First, let's check whether any *other* blocks are also corrupted. That seems like the smart thing to do—if one block has somehow been corrupted, then other blocks may also have been corrupted, and you can fix all of them at the same time. You use the VALIDATE DATABASE command to check the entire database. (Note that checking the entire database may take a lot of time, and RMAN lets you check individual data files.) The output is shown next (failure messages only):

```
[oracle@localhost ~]$ rman

Recovery Manager: Release 12.1.0.1.0 - Production on Wed Dec 3 19:02:12 2014

Copyright (c) 1982, 2013, Oracle and/or its affiliates.  All rights reserved.

RMAN> connect target;

connected to target database: ORCL (DBID=1365223133)
```

```
RMAN> validate database;

  File Name: /u01/app/oracle/oradata/ORCL/F0832BAF14721281E045000000000001/datafile/
  o1_mf_users_9fxvoh6n_.dbf
  Block Type Blocks Failing Blocks Processed
  ---------- --------------- -----------------
  Data       0                   96
  Index      0                   46
  Other      64                  438

validate found one or more corrupt blocks
See trace file /u01/app/oracle/diag/rdbms/orcl/orcl/trace/orcl_ora_6537.trc for details
```

You then issue the LIST FAILURE, ADVISE FAILURE, and REPAIR FAILURE commands in turn. The LIST FAILURE command tells you what you already know at this point—that the file EXAMPLE01.DBF contains a corrupted block:

```
RMAN> list failure;

Database Role: PRIMARY

List of Database Failures
=========================

Failure ID Priority Status    Time Detected Summary
---------- -------- --------- ------------- -------
202        HIGH     OPEN      03-DEC-14     Datafile 13: '/u01/app/oracle/oradata/ORCL/F0832
BAF14721281E045000000000001/datafile/o1_mf_users_9fxvoh6n_.dbf' contains one or more corrupt
blocks
```

Next you ask DRA to analyze the problem and recommend a course of action. If possible, DRA lists manual methods that can be used to recover from the problem. For example, a data file that has been inadvertently moved to a different directory can be restored to its previous location. In this case, there are no such alternatives, and DRA tells you that the only course is to restore the corrupted block from the backup copies of the database and redo any modifications made to the block since the backup copy was created. DRA automatically creates a RMAN script for the purpose, and the REPAIR FAILURE PREVIEW command lists the contents of the script:

```
RMAN> advise failure;

Database Role: PRIMARY

List of Database Failures
=========================

Failure ID Priority Status    Time Detected Summary
---------- -------- --------- ------------- -------
202        HIGH     OPEN      03-DEC-14     Datafile 13: '/u01/app/oracle/oradata/ORCL/F0832
BAF14721281E045000000000001/datafile/o1_mf_users_9fxvoh6n_.dbf' contains one or more corrupt
blocks
```

```
analyzing automatic repair options; this may take some time
using channel ORA_DISK_1
analyzing automatic repair options complete

Mandatory Manual Actions
========================
no manual actions available

Optional Manual Actions
========================
no manual actions available

Automated Repair Options
========================
Option Repair Description
------ -------------------
1      Recover multiple corrupt blocks in datafile 13
  Strategy: The repair includes complete media recovery with no data loss
  Repair script: /u01/app/oracle/diag/rdbms/orcl/orcl/hm/reco_1931933171.hm

RMAN> repair failure preview;

Strategy: The repair includes complete media recovery with no data loss
Repair script: /u01/app/oracle/diag/rdbms/orcl/orcl/hm/reco_1931933171.hm

contents of repair script:
   # block media recovery for multiple blocks
   recover datafile 13 block 200 to 263;
```

All that is left to do is to execute the script created by DRA. This is done via the simple command REPAIR FAILURE. You can use the NOPROMPT qualifier if you don't want to be prompted for confirmation at various points during the process.

First the corrupted block is restored from the backup copies of the database:

```
RMAN> repair failure;

Strategy: The repair includes complete media recovery with no data loss
Repair script: /u01/app/oracle/diag/rdbms/orcl/orcl/hm/reco_1931933171.hm

contents of repair script:
   # block media recovery for multiple blocks
   recover datafile 13 block 200 to 263;

Do you really want to execute the above repair (enter YES or NO)? y
executing repair script

Starting recover at 03-DEC-14
using channel ORA_DISK_1

channel ORA_DISK_1: restoring block(s)
channel ORA_DISK_1: specifying block(s) to restore from backup set
restoring blocks of datafile 00013
```

```
channel ORA_DISK_1: reading from backup piece /u01/app/oracle/fast_recovery_area/ORCL/F0832B
AF14721281E045000000000001/backupset/2014_12_03/o1_mf_nnndf_TAG20141203T174627_b7z4xync_.bkp
channel ORA_DISK_1: piece handle=/u01/app/oracle/fast_recovery_area/ORCL/F0832BAF14721
281E045000000000001/backupset/2014_12_03/o1_mf_nnndf_TAG20141203T174627_b7z4xync_.bkp
tag=TAG20141203T174627
channel ORA_DISK_1: restored block(s) from backup piece 1
channel ORA_DISK_1: block restore complete, elapsed time: 00:00:03
```

Finally, any modifications made to the block since the backup copy was created are redone with the help of the redo logs:

```
starting media recovery

archived log for thread 1 with sequence 128 is already on disk as file /u01/app/oracle/
fast_recovery_area/ORCL/archivelog/2014_12_03/o1_mf_1_128_b7z6c8oz_.arc
archived log for thread 1 with sequence 129 is already on disk as file /u01/app/oracle/
fast_recovery_area/ORCL/archivelog/2014_12_03/o1_mf_1_129_b7z6dnd4_.arc
archived log for thread 1 with sequence 130 is already on disk as file /u01/app/oracle/
fast_recovery_area/ORCL/archivelog/2014_12_03/o1_mf_1_130_b7z6g2qv_.arc
media recovery complete, elapsed time: 00:00:07
Finished recover at 03-DEC-14
repair failure complete
RMAN> exit

Recovery Manager complete.
```

Documentation and Testing

I'd like to conclude this introduction to the subject of recovery with a brief mention of testing. Not testing recovery procedures is a terrible mistake. A recovery test should always be performed before a new database is put to use. However, it is not feasible to perform periodic testing on a live database. You can use the RMAN command DUPLICATE DATABASE to verify the usability of backups without harming the live database. If the database is too large, you can exclude some tablespaces. A very useful validation technique is the PREVIEW clause, which lets you validate scripts without actually performing the commands in the script.

It is also important to document your recovery procedures. Chapter 15 covers the importance of standard operating procedures (SOPs). Database recovery is the most stressful task a DBA has to perform, and an SOP is exactly what you need to guide you through the situation.

Summary

Here is a short summary of the concepts touched on in this chapter:

- An appropriate repair strategy is one that is tailored to the situation and causes minimum downtime. Individual data files and data blocks can be repaired without impacting the rest of the database. Single-block recovery is available only with the Enterprise Edition.

- The Data Pump Import utility can be used to restore a table from a logical backup made using that utility.

- The word *restore* refers to the operation of replacing a damaged or missing file from a backup copy. The word *recover* refers to the process of relaying transactions recorded in the redo logs.

- A common reason for incomplete recovery is user error. It is the only option if the archived redo logs are damaged.

- Flashback techniques such as flashback query can be used to reverse logical damage caused by user error. These techniques depend on the availability of the required information in the undo segments. The flashback-archive technique can be used to record all changes made to data rows during the lifetime of a table.

- The flashback-database technique can be used to easily recover from major changes or major damage to the database. This technique uses a special kind of log file called a flashback log.

- You can also recover prior versions of data from the archived redo logs by using LogMiner. Enable *supplemental minimal logging* to ensure that LogMiner has sufficient information to support chained rows and various storage arrangements such as cluster tables and index-organized tables.

- Data Recovery Advisor (DRA) simplifies the task of repairing a database. The commands LIST FAILURE, ADVISE FAILURE, and REPAIR FAILURE can be used to easily recovery from any failure. The task can also be performed by using Enterprise Manager.

- Not performing recovery testing is a critical mistake. The DUPLICATE DATABASE command can be used to verify the usability of backups without harming the live database. A standard operating procedure (SOP) for database recovery can be your guide to handling this most stressful of database administration tasks.

Exercises

- Shut down your learning database. Rename the USERS01.DBF file, and then try to open the database. Use DRA to restore the missing file from backups and to recover transactions from the redo logs. Confirm that the database can now be opened for access.

- Flashback features such as flashback query, flashback versions, and flashback transaction depend on the availability of undo information in the undo segments. Information is lost if it is overwritten by newer transactions. Undo retention is governed by the UNDO_RETENTION parameter. Check the value of UNDO_RETENTION in your database. Find out how to increase the value. Add data files to the UNDO tablespace if you think it is not big enough to support this value. How would you determine how much space is enough? Refer to the Oracle documentation and find out how to *guarantee* the retention of undo information.

- The flashback-database feature depends on a special kind of log file called a flashback log, stored in the flash recovery area. The amount of information retained in the flashback logs is covered by the DB_FLASHBACK_RETENTION_TARGET parameter. Check the value of DB_FLASHBACK_RETENTION_TARGET in your database. Find out how to increase the value. Check the value of DB_RECOVERY_FILE_DEST—it tells you the location of the flash recovery area, which is used to store backup copies as well as flashback logs. Check the size of the flash recovery area; is it big enough? Check the V$DATABASE view and determine whether logging of flashback information is enabled; if not, find out how to enable logging.

- Refer to the Oracle Database 12*c* Licensing Information (available at www.oracle. com/technology/documentation) to determine which of the recovery methods discussed in this chapter are available only with the Enterprise Edition of Oracle Database 12*c*.

- Create a restore point by using the CREATE RESTORE POINT command. Modify the data in the Employees table in the HR schema. Shut down the database, and bring it into the mounted state. Use the FLASHBACK DATABASE command to restore the database to the restore point. Open the database by using the RESETLOGS clause. Check the incarnation information in V$DATABASE_INCARNATION. Verify that the modifications you made to the Employees table have been reversed.

- Oracle by Example (OBE) is a collection of tutorials provided by Oracle on various subjects. Perform all the steps in the tutorial on backups and recovery titled "Oracle Database 12*c* 2-Day DBA Series: Performing Backup and Recovery."

CHAPTER 14

■ ■ ■

Database Maintenance

> *"Sometimes," he added, "there is no harm in putting off a piece of work until another day. But when it is a matter of baobabs, that always means a catastrophe. I knew a planet that was inhabited by a lazy man. He neglected three little bushes …"*
>
> —*The Little Prince* by Antoine de Saint-Exupéry

In my first job as a database administrator, working for a Fortune 100 company, I managed only three databases, each no more than 100MB in size, and had ample time for database maintenance. I performed regular database-maintenance procedures to keep the databases in peak operating condition, included data archiving and purging and rebuilding of tables and indexes. I also published graphs of database and application performance every week.

Gartner Research estimated in 2007 that the average amount of data managed by each DBA is 1TB. This allows very little time for database maintenance.

The Maintenance Plan

Here are the components of a simple maintenance plan—they should be automated as much as possible. The following sections of this chapter cover each component in detail.

- Regular backups are absolutely critical to the safety of the database (there may be exceptions, but they only prove the rule). Backup logs should be reviewed frequently, and a recovery exercise should be conducted at least once a year—more often if possible.

- The query optimizer relies on statistical information about the data. By default, statistics are automatically refreshed by Oracle every night, but some sites use a custom approach. Manual intervention may be occasionally needed.

- Data that is no longer needed should be archived and then purged from the database. Tables and indexes that contain a large amount of wasted space should be rebuilt to reclaim space.

- Log files should be reviewed regularly—daily if possible. Old log files should be removed.

- Disk capacity and system capacity should be reviewed regularly. Disk space should be proactively added to the database.

- User activities should be audited.

- Passwords should be changed regularly or when compromised. Unneeded accounts should be locked or removed.

- Patches should be applied to the database when necessary.

■ **Caution**   Index rebuilding and tablespace defragmentation are often conducted without sufficient justification. An old paper by Juan Loaiza, "How to Stop Defragmenting and Start Living: The Definitive Word on Fragmentation," (which you can find on the web) can be considered the last word on the subject.

Backups

Backups are the most important aspect of database maintenance, but the honest truth is that most companies don't pay enough attention to them. Here are some best practices for backups; please refer to Chapter 12 and Chapter 13 for specific information on methods of backups (and recovery).

Generic Best Practices for Database Backups

The following practices apply to all database backups, not just Oracle backups:

- Establish a service-level agreement (SLA) for backups and recovery. Clearly document the maximum amount of data loss that is permitted, backup-retention policies, and how much time is allowed for database recovery.

- Document the backup methodology, and have it formally reviewed. Publish the documentation to an audience that includes the database owner.

- Periodically test the recoverability of backups. Typically this is done in a testing environment. A recovery test establishes how long it will take to recover the database.

- Be prepared to recover from user error—for example, when a user inadvertently updates or deletes the wrong data. I present several options in Chapter 13.

- Have a contingency plan that covers damage to the operating system or hardware— be prepared to move the database to another server.

- Ensure the safety of backups. The traditional method is to send backup tapes offsite. Newer methods involve backups to a *backup appliance* over the network. A combination of *near-line* (disk) and *far-line* (tape or network) backups can be used. Near-line backups reduce the time needed for recovery, whereas far-line backups increase the safety of backups. The tape library should not be a single point of failure—ensure that data can be recovered even if the tape library is damaged.

- Retain multiple backups in case one set of backups is damaged.

- Backup scripts should incorporate error checking and an adequate amount of logging. The logs should be retained for an appropriate time. Notification of backup failures should be sent to the DBAs. Backup failures should be formally investigated.

- Reports of backup successes and failures, the amount of data backed up, and the time it took to perform backups should be generated and sent to an audience that includes the DBAs and the database owner.

- Changes to any aspect of backup procedures, whether temporary or permanent, should be performed under formal change-control procedures.

■ **Tip** Don't forget to perform backups of databases used for development and testing.

Best Practices for Oracle Database Backups

The following practices apply specifically to Oracle database backups:

- Use Recovery Manager (RMAN) for backups. The advantages of RMAN are so numerous and valuable that it would be hard to justify not using it. For example, RMAN checks data blocks for corruption while it is making a backup, single-block recovery is possible with RMAN, and so on.

■ **Tip** Backups performed using third-party software such as Network Appliance Snapshot can be integrated with RMAN.

- Prevent unlogged operations (that is, operations that are not recorded in the redo logs) in databases that use ARCHIVELOG mode; use the ALTER DATABASE FORCE LOGGING command to do this.

- Back up all aspects of the database, including the archived redo logs (for databases that use ARCHIVELOG mode), the control file, and the parameter file (spfile).

- Create logical backups (exports) to supplement physical backups. This creates a certain amount of protection from logical damage, such as data-entry errors. Use a setting such as FLASHBACK_TIME to ensure the consistency of the exported data.

- Make full use of Oracle's flashback features by increasing the value of UNDO_RETENTION from the default value of 15 minutes to a more appropriate value such as 24 hours. This may allow recovery from logical damage without having to resort to physical backups.

- Databases that run in ARCHIVELOG mode should have LAG_ARCHIVE_TARGET set to an appropriate value, such as 15 minutes, to control maximum data loss.

- Incorporate the use of techniques that check for data corruption. These include initialization parameters such as DB_BLOCK_CHECKING, DB_BLOCK_CHECKSUM, and DB_LOST_WRITE_UPDATE, and commands that scan the database, such as VALIDATE DATABASE.

■ **Tip** Oracle Database 11g introduced a single parameter called DB_ULTRA_SAFE that controls the values of DB_BLOCK_CHECKING, DB_BLOCK_CHECKSUM, and DB_LOST_WRITE_UPDATE.

Statistics

The query optimizer requires statistical information about the data, such as the number of rows in each table, in order to generate efficient query plans. This information is collected using the procedures in the DBMS_STATS package. Beginning with Oracle Database 10g, statistical information about the data is refreshed automatically by a scheduled nightly job called GATHER_STATS_JOB; you are free to disable this job in favor of a custom approach. Oracle supplies a wide collection of procedures to collect and manage statistics, including GATHER, DELETE, IMPORT, EXPORT, LOCK, UNLOCK, PUBLISH, and RESTORE procedures. A complete list of them follows, and you can find details in *Oracle Database PL/SQL Packages and Types Reference*.

■ **Caution**   Small changes in statistics can sometimes produce big changes in query plans—not always for the better—and this problem can challenge even the most experienced DBAs. The LOCK and RESTORE procedures can be very useful in improving plan stability.

Archiving and Purging

Database performance commonly degrades as the database grows large. To keep the database performing optimally, you should remove unnecessary data. In some cases, it may be necessary to save a copy of the data in a data archive, such as flat files, XML documents, or the like, before the data is purged from the database. The archiving phase also involves a special backup that is tagged with a high-retention setting, such as seven years.

The freed space is automatically used by new data. Regular purging keeps the size of the database under control and helps keep performance stable. If a large amount of data is purged at a time, the sizes of the tables and indexes are not commensurate with the amount of data they actually contain, and additional maintenance is required to compact and shrink the bloated tables and indexes. This is discussed in the section on rebuilding tables and indexes.

The use of partitioning can completely eliminate the need for archiving, purging, and rebuilding. For example, a table can be divided into partitions in such a way that each month's data is inserted into a separate partition. Queries that require the most recent data perform optimally because the required data is clustered in a relatively small number of data blocks instead of being randomly scattered throughout the table as happens when partitioning is not used. In the case of partitioned tables, purging the data requires only that a partition be dropped; this is a very quick operation. If the old partitions are in a separate tablespace, an alternative to purging is to convert the tablespaces to read-only mode and move them to cheap storage such as WORM drives or unmirrored SATA disks; this is a wonderful way to keep performance optimal without having to remove data. Even the overhead of backups can be kept under control; read-only tablespaces must be backed up only one more time with a high-retention setting and then no longer need to be backed up.

■ **Caution**   Partitioning is an extra-cost option for which Enterprise Edition is a prerequisite. If you are not licensed for Partitioning, you can use partition views or use a do-it-yourself approach.

Rebuilding

The size of a table does not change when records are deleted from it—the indexes associated with the table do not shrink in size either. The wasted space causes three problems:

- The gains that come from caching blocks of data in memory are reduced because fewer records are packed into each block.

- Additional space on disk is required as the database grows.

- Backup and recovery require more time, more space, and more computing resources.

If you are licensed for Diagnostics Pack, you can use the Automatic Segment Advisor to identify tables that would benefit from rebuilding. Alternatively, you can conduct your own investigation of wasted space, using the SPACE_USAGE procedure. Listing 14-1 shows a sample run; you see that 1161 blocks are empty.

Listing 14-1. An Example of the SPACE_USAGE Procedure

```
SQL> SET serveroutput on
SQL>
SQL> DECLARE
  2      l_full_blocks           NUMBER;
  3      l_fs1_blocks            NUMBER;
  4      l_fs2_blocks            NUMBER;
  5      l_fs3_blocks            NUMBER;
  6      l_fs4_blocks            NUMBER;
  7      l_unformatted_blocks    NUMBER;
  8      l_full_bytes            NUMBER;
  9      l_fs1_bytes             NUMBER;
 10      l_fs2_bytes             NUMBER;
 11      l_fs3_bytes             NUMBER;
 12      l_fs4_bytes             NUMBER;
 13      l_unformatted_bytes     NUMBER;
 14  BEGIN
 15      DBMS_SPACE.space:usage (segment_owner         => 'SYSMAN',
 16                              segment_name          => 'MGMT_JOB_EXEC_SUMMARY',
 17                              segment_type          => 'TABLE',
 18                              full_blocks           => l_full_blocks,
 19                              fs1_blocks            => l_fs1_blocks,
 20                              fs2_blocks            => l_fs2_blocks,
 21                              fs3_blocks            => l_fs3_blocks,
 22                              fs4_blocks            => l_fs4_blocks,
 23                              unformatted_blocks    => l_unformatted_blocks,
 24                              full_bytes            => l_full_bytes,
 25                              fs1_bytes             => l_fs1_bytes,
 26                              fs2_bytes             => l_fs2_bytes,
 27                              fs3_bytes             => l_fs3_bytes,
 28                              fs4_bytes             => l_fs4_bytes,
 29                              unformatted_bytes     => l_unformatted_bytes
 30                              );
 31      DBMS_OUTPUT.put_line ('Full blocks:'    || l_full_blocks);
 32      DBMS_OUTPUT.put_line ('Upto 25% free:'  || l_fs1_blocks);
 33      DBMS_OUTPUT.put_line ('Upto 50% free:'  || l_fs2_blocks);
```

```
34      DBMS_OUTPUT.put_line ('Upto 75% free:'       || l_fs3_blocks);
35      DBMS_OUTPUT.put_line ('Upto 100% free:'      || l_fs4_blocks);
36      DBMS_OUTPUT.put_line ('Unformatted blocks:' || l_unformatted_blocks);
37  END;
38  /
Full blocks:294
Upto 25% free:0
Upto 50% free:2
Upto 75% free:1
Upto 100% free:1161
Unformatted blocks:46

PL/SQL procedure successfully completed.
```

Once you have identified tables and indexes that will benefit from compaction, you can reclaim the wasted space using the SHRINK SPACE command, as in Listing 14-2. Note that you have to give Oracle permission explicitly to relocate rows, using the ENABLE ROW MOVEMENT command—Oracle does not do this automatically, so as not to affect any application that has taken advantage of row addresses (ROWIDs).

Listing 14-2. An Example of the SHRINK SPACE Procedure

```
SQL> ALTER TABLE sysman.mgmt_job_exec_summary
  2  ENABLE ROW MOVEMENT;

Table altered.

SQL> ALTER TABLE sysman.mgmt_job_exec_summary
  2  SHRINK SPACE;

Table altered.
```

Log File Maintenance

Log files of all kinds accumulate over time and can fill up the available space. For example, a *trace file* is created whenever certain errors occur, such as ORA-00060 (deadlock) and ORA-00600 (internal error). Listing 14-3 shows the first few lines from such a trace file.

Listing 14-3. An Extract from a Trace File for an ORA-00060 Error

```
Oracle Database 11g Enterprise Edition Release 11.1.0.6.0 - Production
With the Partitioning, OLAP, Data Mining and Real Application Testing options
Windows XP Version V5.1 Service Pack 2
CPU                  : 2 - type 586
Process Affinity     : 0x00000000
Memory (Avail/Total): Ph:451M/2037M, Ph+PgF:2345M/3930M, VA:1243M/2047M
Instance name: orcl
Redo thread mounted by this instance: 1
Oracle process number: 7
Windows thread id: 5196, image: ORACLE.EXE (SHAD)
```

```
*** 2008-06-07 09:32:39.734
*** SESSION ID:(99.609) 2008-06-07 09:32:39.734
*** CLIENT ID:() 2008-06-07 09:32:39.734
*** SERVICE NAME:(SYS$USERS) 2008-06-07 09:32:39.734
*** MODULE NAME:(SQL*Plus) 2008-06-07 09:32:39.734
*** ACTION NAME:() 2008-06-07 09:32:39.734


*** 2008-06-07 09:32:39.734
DEADLOCK DETECTED ( ORA-00060 )

[Transaction Deadlock]

The following deadlock is not an ORACLE error. It is a
deadlock due to user error in the design of an application
or from issuing incorrect ad-hoc SQL. The following
information may aid in determining the deadlock:

Deadlock graph:
                    ---------Blocker(s)-------- ---------Waiter(s)---------
Resource Name       process session holds waits process session holds waits
TM-00011bc5-00000000      7      99   SX   SSX       31     105   SX   SSX
TM-00011bc5-00000000     31     105   SX   SSX        7      99   SX   SSX

session 99: DID 0001-0007-000028EA    session 105: DID 0001-001F-00000041
session 105: DID 0001-001F-00000041   session 99: DID 0001-0007-000028EA

Rows waited on:
  Session 99: no row
  Session 105: no row

----- Information for the OTHER waiting sessions -----
Session 105:
  sid: 105 ser: 881 audsid: 349519 user: 88/IGGY flags: 0x45
  pid: 31 O/S info: user: SYSTEM, term: IGGY, ospid: 5112
    image: ORACLE.EXE (SHAD)
  client details:
    O/S info: user: IGGY\IGNATIUS, term: IGGY, ospid: 4548:6076
    machine: WORKGROUP\IGGY program: sqlplus.exe
    application name: SQL*Plus, hash value=3669949024
  Current SQL Statement:
  DELETE FROM PARENT WHERE ID=2

----- End of information for the OTHER waiting sessions -----

Information for THIS session:

----- Current SQL Statement for this session (sql_id=9vym32vjhdgzc) -----
DELETE FROM PARENT WHERE ID=1
=======================================================
```

The log files are organized into an Automatic Diagnostics Repository (ADR), whose location is controlled by the DIAGNOSTIC_DEST setting. Log files are automatically purged after 30 days—you can change the retention window using the SET CONTROL option of the adrci tool. You can also purge log files manually using the tool's PURGE command, as in Listing 14-4.

Listing 14-4. Using the adrci Tool to Manage Log Files

```
[oracle@localhost ~]$ adrci

ADRCI: Release 12.1.0.1.0 - Production on Mon May 11 01:45:41 2015

Copyright (c) 1982, 2013, Oracle and/or its affiliates.  All rights reserved.

ADR base = "/u01/app/oracle"
adrci> show homepath
ADR Homes:
diag/tnslsnr/localhost/listener
diag/rdbms/orcl/orcl
diag/clients/user_oracle/host_61728193_80
adrci> set homepath diag/rdbms/orcl/orcl
adrci> purge -age 10
adrci> show tracefile
    diag/rdbms/orcl/orcl/trace/orcl_lgwr_24237.trc
    diag/rdbms/orcl/orcl/trace/orcl_dbrm_24231.trc
    diag/rdbms/orcl/orcl/trace/orcl_mmon_24247.trc
    diag/rdbms/orcl/orcl/trace/alert_orcl.log
adrci> exit
```

■ **Tip** Trace files can be very large. The maximum size of a trace file is controlled by the max_dump_file_size initialization setting, whose default value is unlimited. Consider changing the setting to a value that is appropriate for your environment.

Auditing

Oracle provides the ability to audit all aspects of database usage. Audit records can be stored in the AUD$ table owned by SYS or in files outside the database—this is controlled by the AUDIT_TRAIL and AUDIT_FILE_DEST settings. There are a number of useful views on the AUD$ table, the chief ones being DBA_AUDIT_TRAIL and DBA_AUDIT_SESSION. Listing 14-5 shows a sample of the data in the DBA_AUDIT_SESSION table.

Listing 14-5. A Sample Listing of the Contents of the DBA_AUDIT_SESSION View

```
SELECT  TIMESTAMP AS "LOGON",
        logoff_time AS "LOGOFF",
        logoff_lread AS "GETS",
        logoff_pread AS "READS",
        logoff_lwrite AS "WRITES",
        session_cpu AS "CPU"
```

```
    FROM dba_audit_session
  WHERE username = 'IGGY'
    AND logoff_time IS NOT NULL
ORDER BY TIMESTAMP;
```

LOGON	LOGOFF	GETS	READS	WRITES	CPU
11/25 19:07	11/25 19:08	1187	11	364	32
11/25 19:08	11/25 19:16	2105	12	417	32
11/25 19:16	11/25 19:17	1138	3	431	20
11/25 19:18	11/25 19:18	849	0	356	24
11/25 19:18	11/25 19:19	1266	0	516	17
11/25 19:20	11/25 19:29	2655	0	1136	47
11/25 19:33	11/25 19:35	3894	6	1597	49
11/25 19:38	11/25 19:38	154	0	15	3
11/25 19:40	11/25 19:41	71	0	6	11
11/25 19:41	11/25 20:13	2778	10	1059	50
11/25 20:14	11/25 20:28	319540	1123	643	1011
11/28 11:30	11/28 11:30	383	13	6	5
05/26 11:31	05/26 20:10	2427	101	726	100
05/26 14:29	05/26 14:29	58	0	6	0
05/26 14:31	05/26 14:31	58	0	6	0
05/26 14:32	05/26 20:09	258	8	12	21
06/07 09:21	06/07 17:21	3049	114	732	83
06/07 09:32	06/07 17:21	274	15	49	3

18 rows selected.

When creating a database using DBCA, you can choose to enable auditing for logon and logoff events and certain privileged activities such as ALTER DATABASE and ALTER USER. A number of views can be used to determine which activities are being audited, the chief ones being DBA_STMT_AUDIT_OPTS (which SQL commands are being monitored) and DBA_OBJ_AUDIT_OPTS (which tables are being monitored). Listing 14-6 shows a sample of the data in the DBA_STMT_AUDIT_OPTS table.

Listing 14-6. A Sample Listing of the Contents of the DBA_STMT_AUDIT_OPTS View

```
SELECT    audit_option,
          CASE
              WHEN user_name IS NOT NULL
                THEN user_name
              ELSE 'ALL USERS'
          END AS username
    FROM dba_stmt_audit_opts
ORDER BY audit_option, user_name;
```

AUDIT_OPTION	USERNAME
ALTER ANY PROCEDURE	ALL USERS
ALTER ANY TABLE	ALL USERS
ALTER DATABASE	ALL USERS
ALTER PROFILE	ALL USERS
ALTER SYSTEM	ALL USERS

ALTER USER	ALL USERS
CREATE ANY JOB	ALL USERS
CREATE ANY LIBRARY	ALL USERS
CREATE ANY PROCEDURE	ALL USERS
CREATE ANY TABLE	ALL USERS
CREATE EXTERNAL JOB	ALL USERS
CREATE PUBLIC DATABASE LINK	ALL USERS
CREATE SESSION	ALL USERS
CREATE USER	ALL USERS
DROP ANY PROCEDURE	ALL USERS
DROP ANY TABLE	ALL USERS
DROP PROFILE	ALL USERS
DROP USER	ALL USERS
EXEMPT ACCESS POLICY	ALL USERS
GRANT ANY OBJECT PRIVILEGE	ALL USERS
GRANT ANY PRIVILEGE	ALL USERS
GRANT ANY ROLE	ALL USERS
ROLE	ALL USERS
SYSTEM AUDIT	ALL USERS

24 rows selected.

Reviewing audit records regularly is a good practice. Note that Oracle does not delete old audit data automatically—that is the responsibility of the DBA. You should consider archiving the data using the exp or expdp utility before you delete it.

■ **Tip** The AUD$ table is placed in the SYSTEM tablespace when the database is created. The AUD$ table can grow very large, so the SYSTEM tablespace is not a good location for it—it should be housed in a dedicated tablespace instead. Metalink notes 72460.1 *Moving AUD$ to Another Tablespace and Adding Triggers to AUD$* and 1019377.6 *Script to move SYS.AUD$ table out of SYSTEM tablespace* discuss this issue.

User Management

The security of the database is the DBA's responsibility. Here are some simple security rules:

- Passwords should be changed regularly. This is controlled by the PASSWORD_LIFE_TIME, PASSWORD_REUSE_TIME, and PASSWORD_REUSE_MAX settings in the DEFAULT profile. Resist the temptation to relax or disable these settings.

- Shared passwords should be changed when employees are relieved of their responsibilities or leave the company. For example, DBAs typically share the passwords to the SYS and SYSTEM accounts. These passwords should be changed whenever a DBA leaves the organizational group or the company.

- Users should be required to have strong passwords; this is not required by default. Execute the utlpwdmg.sql script from the SYS account to enforce the requirement.

- When a user's job responsibilities change, their database privileges should be changed appropriately. When a user leaves the organization, their account should be removed from the database.

Capacity Management

Regular capacity reviews are part of good database management. Database size and free space should be recorded at regular intervals—the required information can be found in the DBA_DATA_FILES and DBA_FREE_SPACE views, as shown in Listing 14-7. Database size and free space can also be checked using Enterprise Manager. Space should be proactively added to the database as necessary. You should make growth projections and identify opportunities to reclaim disk space. *Capacity management* also refers to use of system resources such as CPU and memory. The information in the Statspack reports and tables can be used to track system utilization, or you can develop a simple system that periodically captures system utilization metrics from the V$SYSSTAT table.

Listing 14-7. Checking Database Size and Free Space

```
SELECT   tablespace:name,
         file_name,
         file_id,
         BYTES / 1024 AS kb,
         autoextensible,
         increment_by * 8192 / 1024 AS next_kb,
         maxbytes / 1024 AS max_kb
    FROM dba_data_files
ORDER BY tablespace:name,
         file_id;
```

TABLESPACE	FILE_NAME	FILE_ID	KB	AUT	NEXT_KB	MAX_KB
SYSAUX	/u01/app/oracle/orad ata/ORCL/datafile/o1 _mf_sysaux_9fxmvhl3_ .dbf	3	1075200	YES	10240	33554416
SYSTEM	/u01/app/oracle/orad ata/ORCL/datafile/o1 _mf_system_9fxmx6s1_ .dbf	1	819200	YES	10240	33554416
UNDOTBS1	/u01/app/oracle/orad ata/ORCL/datafile/o1 _mf_undotbs1_9fxn0vg g_.dbf	4	604160	YES	5120	33554416
USERS	/u01/app/oracle/orad ata/ORCL/datafile/o1 _mf_users_9fxn0t8s_. dbf	6	5120	YES	1280	33554416

Time Series

A *time series* is a sequence of measurements made at periodic intervals. The Statspack tables contain much time series data and can be used for capacity reviews. The Statspack tables STATS$OSSTAT, STATS$SYSSTAT, STATS$SYSTEM_EVENT, and STATS$SYS_TIME_MODEL are of particular interest—they store snapshots of the dynamic performance views V$OSSTAT, V$SYSSTAT, V$SYSTEM_EVENT, and V$SYS_TIME_MODEL, respectively. As illustrated in Listing 14-8, V$OSSTAT offers cumulative values of various OS metrics such as CPU usage, and STATS$OSSTAT contains snapshots of this data; the snapshots are identified by the SNAP_ID column.

Listing 14-8. Comparison of Data in V$OSSTAT and STATS$OSSTAT

```
SQL> SELECT stat_name, value FROM v$osstat;

STAT_NAME                                                          VALUE
----------------------------------------------------------- ----------
NUM_CPUS                                                               2
IDLE_TIME                                                       3769723
BUSY_TIME                                                        668049
USER_TIME                                                        463348
SYS_TIME                                                         204701
AVG_IDLE_TIME                                                   1884476
AVG_BUSY_TIME                                                    333641
AVG_USER_TIME                                                    231300
AVG_SYS_TIME                                                     101963
RSRC_MGR_CPU_WAIT_TIME                                             1278
PHYSICAL_MEMORY_BYTES                                        2136969216
VM_IN_BYTES                                                  1393717248
VM_OUT_BYTES                                                  394657792

13 rows selected.

SQL> SELECT snap_id, osstat_id, value
  2    FROM stats$osstat
  3   WHERE  snap_id IN (3000, 3001);
  SNAP_ID  OSSTAT_ID       VALUE
---------- ---------- ----------
      3000          0           2
      3000          1   654407998
      3000          2    72816975
      3000          3    60092930
      3000          4    12053254
      3000          6      670791
      3000         14           0
      3000         15        1.25
      3000       1008       16396
      3001          0           2
      3001          1   655068971
      3001          2    72864457
      3001          3    60137335
      3001          4    12056331
      3001          6      670791
      3001         14           0
      3001         15  .309570313
      3001       1008      494964

18 rows selected.
```

The time series data in the Statspack tables can be manipulated with SQL queries into a format that is suitable for reports and graphs. First you use the PIVOT operator to create a two-dimensional table of the cumulative values (Listing 14-9). Then you use an analytic function called LAG to compute the difference between the values in successive rows (Listing 14-10). The CPU utilization graph shown in Figure 14-1 was generated using the data produced by the SQL query shown in Listing 14-11.

Listing 14-9. Using the PIVOT Operator to Produce Two-Dimensional Tables

```
SQL> COLUMN busy_time FORMAT 9999999990
SQL> COLUMN idle_time FORMAT 9999999990
SQL>
SQL> SELECT *
  2    FROM (SELECT snap_id, osstat_id, value FROM stats$osstat
  3            WHERE SNAP_ID IN (3000, 3001))
  4        PIVOT
  5        (SUM(value) FOR osstat_id IN (1 AS idle_time, 2 AS busy_time));

   SNAP_ID   IDLE_TIME   BUSY_TIME
---------- ----------- -----------
      3000   654407998    72816975
      3001   655068971    72864457
```

Listing 14-10. Using Analytic Functions to Correlate Data in Different Rows

```
SQL> COLUMN busy_time FORMAT 9999999990
SQL> COLUMN idle_time FORMAT 9999999990
SQL>
SQL> SELECT snap_id,
  2          idle_time - LAG (idle_time) OVER (ORDER BY snap_id) AS idle_time,
  3          busy_time - LAG (busy_time) OVER (ORDER BY snap_id) AS busy_time
  4    FROM (SELECT snap_id, osstat_id, value FROM stats$osstat
  5            WHERE SNAP_ID IN (3000, 3001))
  6        PIVOT
  7        (SUM(value) FOR osstat_id IN (1 AS idle_time, 2 AS busy_time));

   SNAP_ID   IDLE_TIME   BUSY_TIME
---------- ----------- -----------
      3000
      3001      660973       47482
```

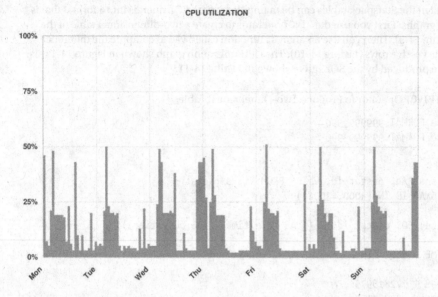

Figure 14-1. *CPU utilization graph produced from the data in the STATS$OSSTAT table*

Listing 14-11. SQL Query to Compute CPU Utilization

```
WITH osstat AS
    (SELECT snap_id,
            LAG (snap_id) OVER (ORDER BY snap_id) AS prev_snap_id,
            idle_time - LAG (idle_time) OVER (ORDER BY snap_id) AS idle_time,
            busy_time - LAG (busy_time) OVER (ORDER BY snap_id) AS busy_time
       FROM (SELECT snap_id, osstat_id, value FROM stats$osstat)
            PIVOT
            (SUM(value) FOR osstat_id IN (1 AS idle_time, 2 AS busy_time)))
SELECT   s1.snap_time,
         o.busy_time / (o.idle_time + o.busy_time) AS cpu_utilization
    FROM osstat o,
         stats$snapshot s1,
         stats$snapshot s2
   WHERE s1.snap_id = o.snap_id
     AND s2.snap_id = o.prev_snap_id
     AND s2.startup_time = s1.startup_time
ORDER BY s1.snap_id;
```

There is a wealth of other useful data in the Statspack tables. For example, STATS$SYSSTAT offers cumulative values for Oracle metrics such as logical reads and physical reads; STATS$SYSTEM_EVENT reports the time spent waiting for I/O, locks, and other resources; and STATS$SYS_TIME_MODEL offers summary information such as the total of the elapsed times of all SQL queries processed by Oracle.

Patching

Oracle periodically releases fixes, known as *patches*, for software bugs. A *one-off patch* is a fix for an individual bug, whereas a *patchset* is a collection of numerous bug fixes. A *critical patch update* (CPU) is a collection of fixes for security-related bugs; Oracle releases one such CPU every quarter. A patchset has an Oracle database version string associated with it; for example, 11.2.0.4 is a patchset associated with Oracle 11*g* Release 2. By contrast, one-off patches and CPUs are identified by a single number; for example, 7210195 was the number of the July 2008 CPU. One-off patches, patches, and patchsets can be downloaded from the Patches & Updates section of the Metalink customer portal.

Some organizations adopt a policy of applying software patches and CPUs whenever they become available. Listing 14-12 is a typical notice regarding the availability of a new CPU that you will receive from Oracle if you have a support contract.

Listing 14-12. Notification about a Critical Patch Update (CPU)

```
July 15th, 2008

Oracle Critical Patch Update July 2008

Dear Oracle customer,

The Critical Patch Update for July 2008 was released on July 15, 2008. Oracle
strongly recommends applying the patches as soon as possible.

The Critical Patch Update Advisory is the starting point for relevant information.
It includes the list of products affected, pointers to obtain the patches, a summary
of the security vulnerabilities for each product suite, and links to other important
documents. Supported products that are not listed in the "Supported Products and
Components Affected" section of the advisory do not require new patches to be
applied.

Also, it is essential to review the Critical Patch Update supporting documentation
referenced in the Advisory before applying patches, as this is where you can find
important pertinent information.

The Critical Patch Update Advisory is available at the following location:

Oracle Technology Network:
http://www.oracle.com/technology/deploy/security/alerts.htm

The next four Critical Patch Update release dates are:

* October 14, 2008
* January 13, 2009
* April 14, 2009
* July 14, 2009

Sincerely, Oracle Security Alerts
```

The notification about a CPU directs you to a web page where you can find more information. Once you have determined the specific patch number applicable to your OS platform, you can download the CPU from My Oracle Support.

CPUs are applied using the opatch utility. Complete instructions are provided with the patch.

Summary

Here is a short summary of the concepts touched on in this chapter:

- Database maintenance is required to keep the database in peak operating condition. Most aspects of database maintenance can be automated. Oracle performs some maintenance automatically: collecting statistics for the query optimizer to use.

- Database backups are the most important responsibility of the DBA. RMAN is the preferred tool for numerous reasons. Recovery testing is vital to validate the backup procedures.

- The query optimizer requires statistical information about the data—for example, the number of rows in each table—in order to generate efficient query plans. This information is collected using the procedures in the DBMS_STATS package. Beginning with Oracle Database 10g, statistical information about the data is collected automatically by a scheduled nightly job; you are free to disable this job in favor of a custom approach.

- Archiving refers to the task of making a copy of old data in preparation for deleting it from the database.

- Purging refers to the task of deleting data that has already been archived.

- Rebuilding refers to the task of compacting tables and indexes from which large amounts of data have been purged.

- Log files and trace files are stored in the Automatic Diagnostics Repository (ADR) and managed using the adrci utility.

- Audit records should be periodically reviewed, archived, and purged.

- Passwords should be changed regularly, shared passwords should be changed when they are compromised, password complexity should be enforced, and accounts should be removed when the owners are relieved of their responsibilities or leave the company.

- The information in DBA_DATA_FILES and DBA_FREE_SPACE can be used to set up a simple system managing disk capacity.

- The Statspack tables STATS$OSSTAT, STATS$SYSSTAT, STATS$SYSTEM_EVENT can be used to produce graphs of system capacity.

Exercises

- Scan your database for corruption using the VALIDATE DATABASE command.

- Determine the start and end times of the maintenance windows in your database. Which maintenance jobs run during these windows?

- Temporarily disable auditing, and move the AUD$ table to a dedicated tablespace.

- Develop a procedure to track the growth of tablespaces and free space. Use the information in the DBA_DATA_FILES and DBA_FREE_SPACE views. Capture the information once a week.

- Explain the autoextensible feature of data files. Is it enabled in your database? What are its advantages? What are its disadvantages?

- Develop a procedure to track the growth of the 20 biggest tables in your database. Use the information in the DBA_SEGMENTS view. Capture the information once a week.

- Using the data in the STATS$SYSSTAT table, create graphs of the following workload metrics: logical reads, physical reads, logical reads per transaction, and physical reads per transaction.

- Download the latest critical patch update, and apply it to your database.

- Locate your database's alert log and listener log. What do they contain? Create an automated process to manage their size.

CHAPTER 15

■ ■ ■

The Big Picture and the Ten Deliverables

And if you don't know Which to Do
Of all the things in front of you,
Then what you'll have when you are through
Is just a mess without a clue ...

Winnie the Pooh in *The Tao of Pooh,* by Benjamin Hoff

What are the deliverables of the database administration role? How likely is it that the deliverables will be completed if you cannot articulate what they are? *Deliverables* are not the same as *current priorities*, because priorities change from day to day; performance improvement may be your priority today, but it may not be your priority when performance returns to acceptable levels. Deliverables are not the same as *assigned tasks*, either, because assigned tasks change from day to day; resetting passwords for forgetful users may be one of your assigned tasks today, but you may not have do it any more if, for example, your organization begins using self-service technology or single sign-on technology, or if the task is assigned to a Service Desk. An example of a deliverable is "databases that meet the needs of the business"—the deliverable does not change from day to day. If there is only one DBA in the organization, then it is the individual's deliverable. If database administration is performed by a team, it is a *shared* deliverable.

This is the most important chapter in this book—I discuss the big IT picture and offer very specific guidance in the form of ten deliverables of the database administration role. Few, if any, other books address this topic.

If you take the lessons in this chapter to heart, you can quickly become a better Oracle DBA than you thought possible. Competency in Oracle technology is only half of the challenge of being a DBA. If you had very little knowledge of Oracle technology but knew exactly "which" needed to be done, you could always find out how to do it—there is Google, and there are online manuals aplenty. Too many Oracle DBAs don't know "which" to do, and what they have when they are through is "just a mess without a clue."

■ **Tip**   This chapter is essentially unchanged from the previous edition, including the use of the now officially deprecated ITIL V2 terminology. After reviewing this chapter, I did not wish to change anything, and I commend it to you as the most important chapter and distinguishing feature of this book. Nothing in this chapter is specific to Oracle Database 12*c*; the entire discussion equally applies to prior and future versions. As regards ITIL V2 terminology, I still believe that you will find it sufficient unless you are a project management professional (PMP).

An Instructive Job Interview

Early in my career, I interviewed for a programmer/analyst job at Hewlett-Packard. The manager who interviewed me gave me the following test. He explained that the problem was to produce a report containing sorted employee information and asked me to draw a flowchart explaining the approach I would use to solve the problem. He gave me some paper and left the room for half an hour. When he left, I wrote a COBOL program that sorted and printed a file of employee records. I prided myself on my programming skills and I was certain the program would work correctly the first time.

When he came back, the manager read my program carefully and complimented me on my programming skills. Then he told me what I had missed. I had written a complete COBOL program but had completely ignored the system development life cycle: initiation, system concept development, planning, requirements analysis, design, development, integration and test, implementation, operations and maintenance, and disposition.

In summary, I was a very good COBOL programmer but did not see the big software development picture.

Well, I did not get the job at Hewlett-Packard, but soon after that I got my first job as a database administrator—at Intel. Database administration became my career, and, in time, I became the manager of a team of DBAs managing a thousand databases for a large service provider. My technical skills were never stronger, but something seemed to be missing. We were burned out from working 60 hours every week, we felt unappreciated, and we were constantly at loggerheads with other groups.

In time, I realized that technical knowledge was not enough. We needed to understand how all the pieces of IT fitted together and how they interacted with each other. In other words, we needed to see the big picture.

WHO IS A SENIOR DBA?

I have attended many interviews for Oracle DBA positions in my career and, with one exception, always found that the interviewers set great store on knowledge of Oracle syntax. A big problem is that the typical interviewer only asks questions about those Oracle features that he or she uses on the job and is most familiar with. Any candidate who has not used those Oracle features is then automatically eliminated.

Jeremiah Wilton was the first Oracle DBA at Amazon.com; he joined the company when it was still a small startup and built the DBA team there. In an interview published in the journal of the Northern California Oracle Users Group (NoCOUG), I asked him the following question.

> *My daughter's piano teacher likes to say that practice makes permanent, not perfect. Just because I've been a database administrator a long time doesn't qualify me as a "senior" database administrator—or does it? Who is a "senior" database administrator? Do I need a college degree? Do I need to be a "syntax junkie"? Do I really need experience with Oracle Streams or ASM to claim the title?*

In his reply, Jeremiah suggested that anybody with a few years of experience under their belt was entitled to call themselves a senior DBA, but he did not value years of experience and knowledge of Oracle syntax very much:

> *To me, senior means that you have used a lot of Oracle's features, solved a lot of problems, and experienced a variety of production situations. Do these qualities necessarily mean that I will want to hire you? No.*

Of far greater importance than seniority is a DBA's ability to solve problems in a deductive and logical manner, to synthesize creative solutions to problems, and to forge positive and constructive business relationships with colleagues and clients. For years at Amazon, we simply tried to hire extraordinarily smart people with a strong interest in working with Oracle and others. Some of Amazon's most senior DBAs started with little or no Oracle experience. I believe that the focus on experience in specific technologies and seniority causes employers to pay more and get less than they could when filling DBA positions.

Jeremiah is proof that experience is overrated; he had no knowledge of Oracle database administration when he started at Amazon.com. He learned his trade on the job and went on to build the database team that Amazon.com relies on today.

How I Became a DBA

I became an Oracle DBA by accident. I was supporting another database technology when Big Bob, the Oracle DBA at my then employer, suddenly resigned. I was asked to take over because I had expressed an interest in becoming an Oracle DBA.

I created a documentation template and asked Bob to spend his remaining time documenting each database using the template. He protested that he did not have the time to provide so much detail and suggested that we meet for an hour or two.

At the meeting, Bob told me not to worry and that I was a smart kid and would soon learn my way around. We ran through the list of databases in about half an hour, spending less than a minute on each while I hastily scribbled notes.

But it wasn't Big Bob's fault, because documentation and record-keeping were not organizational priorities. When the time came for me to take over from him, Big Bob had little more for me than a few passwords, a firm handshake, and lots of good wishes.

THE IMPORTANCE OF COMMUNICATION

Which kind of DBA would you want to maintain your database? One whose speech was sprinkled with incomprehensible Oracle terminology or one who communicated with you in language you understood? I mentioned previously that all the interviews I attended during my job searches, with one single exception, focused on my knowledge of Oracle syntax. A US-based provider of remote DBA services called Database Specialists uses a very unusual approach to interviewing Oracle DBA candidates. Questions about Oracle syntax are not asked. Instead, the interview focuses on the candidate's ability to communicate.

Database Specialists uses a systematic institutional approach to database administration, and the linchpin of the process is communication with its customers. A daily report on every database that is maintained by Database Specialists is sent to the appropriate distribution list. This is not a computer-generated report or graph but an actual memo from a live person. This gives customers visibility into database operations and reassures them that a systematic process of database administration is being followed, even if a memo might sometimes say only "No new issues at this time." All the daily reports are available online in a customer-accessible Internet portal, and they constitute a historical record of all the issues with the database. Here is an example—names and details have been changed to protect customer confidentiality:

```
From: Iggy Fernandez [mailto:ifernandez@dbspecialists.com]
Sent: Friday, February 29, 2008 10:11 AM
To: tsutton@ReallyBigCo.com; gsadler@ReallyBigCo.com;
Cc: archive@dbspecialists.com;
Subject: Daily Database Review for ReallyBigCo PRODDB

Our daily review of this instance has found the following:

    Pollux is now the primary database server and Castor is now the standby
database server. The reversal of roles was performed last night and the
transcript has been sent to Terry. I performed the switchover using the same
method used in the past by Gary, only changing the dates embedded in file names.
    Quoting Terry, the reason for the switchover was: "Having switched to the
standby, we are now using StorageTek instead of NetApp storage. We are working
on replacing the disks in the NetApp array with faster ones."
    The recent performance problems have two symptoms: much higher CPU
utilization than historical norms and continued degradation in I/O performance.
The current hypothesis for increased CPU utilization is that the increase is
correlated with the expansion of the amount of data and the number of users. The
cause of the degradation in I/O performance is under investigation by the system
administrators.
--Iggy
```

When a DBA candidate is interviewed at Database Specialists, the focus is on the candidate's communication skills. The first exercise is to write a daily report of the sort just illustrated. The candidate is shown an extract from the Oracle alert log and asked to write a report discussing the Oracle errors listed in the extract. There is no expectation that the candidate has had previous experience with those errors, and the candidate is welcome to research the answers online; this mimics the approach used by real DBAs in real life. In fact, there may not be any "right" answer.

The second exercise is a role-playing exercise that focuses on *verbal* communication. The exercise mimics a common event in the life of a DBA—a critical problem that has high visibility and requires a number of participants. The candidate is given access to a lab system owned by Database Specialists and is asked to join a telephonic conference. To prepare for the exercise, the candidate is directed to a white paper—available on the Database Specialists web site—that discusses the problem-solving approaches that would be useful during the exercise. Participating on the conference call are members of the Database Specialists team, one of whom represents the customer while the rest represent other IT personnel such as system administrators. The customer describes the problem, and the candidate is expected to ask questions, diagnose the problem, and solve it with the help of the other participants on the call. The problem is actually simulated in a lab database, and the candidate is expected to check the database and communicate the findings. The candidate is welcome to research the problem online, because there is no expectation that he or she has any experience with the specific problem that is being simulated.

Why does this interviewing approach work for Database Specialists? It works because Database Specialists uses a systematic institutional approach to database administration, one in which communication skills are critical.

ITIL

The IT Information Library (ITIL), sponsored by the U.K. government, provides a conceptual overview of and detailed guidance about IT practice. It is a collaborative effort of many IT organizations—not academic theory—and provides guidance that is independent of the hardware and software being used. The first version was issued in the late 1980s, and it is now the international standard for IT practice. The discussion that follows is an adaptation of the framework and terminology presented in the ITIL literature.[1]

The Big Picture

As shown in Figure 15-1, everything starts with the business. The IT department provides IT services to the business. These services are managed using IT service management (ITSM) processes such as Service Level Management, Incident Management, and Change Management. The Infrastructure Management tea006D manages the hardware and software that power the services required by the business—it is divided into a Design and Planning (D&P) team, a Deployment team, and an Operations team. The Application Management team designs and develops the software applications underlying the services used by the business. The ITSM team is the interface between the business and the Infrastructure Management team. In particular, the Service Desk is the single point of contact for all users of the services.

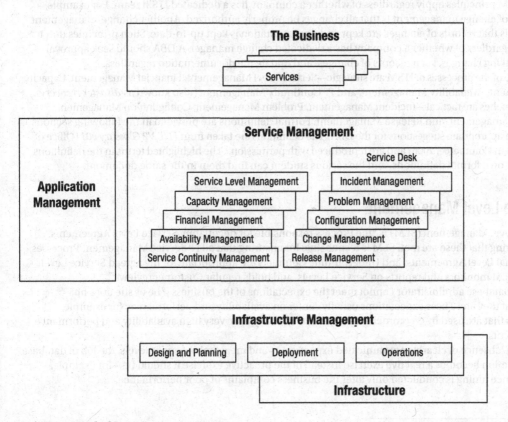

Figure 15-1. The big picture

---

[1]The descriptions and definitions used in this chapter are from ITIL V2.

The preceding is a very formal description of IT practice, and many companies don't have large IT teams. But IT principles don't change whether the IT team consists of a single employee or hundreds of employees. ForH example, service-level expectations always exist, whether they are formally documented in a *service-level agreement* (SLA) or not.

■ **Tip**   The DBA is part of the Operations team. This is an intuitively correct classification because the term *administrator* suggests the day-to-day maintenance of an operational database. However, persons with the title Database Administrator can often be found in the Deployment team and the Applications Management team—a testament to the multidisciplinary job descriptions found in the real world.

IT Service Management Processes

The ITSM team manages the services used by the business. It is the interface between the business and the Infrastructure Management team. The ITSM team uses the ten management processes described in the following sections. Note that the services *managed* by the ITSM team are actually *provided* by the Operations team. ITSM principles apply regardless of whether a company has a dedicated ITSM team. For example, a principle of change management is that all changes be properly authorized. Another change-management principle is that records of changes are kept and documentation is kept up-to-date. Such principles don't change regardless of whether a company has a dedicated change manager. A DBA should seek approval before making changes, keep records of changes, and update the documentation regardless.

Some of the processes of ITSM are strategic—Service Level Management, Financial Management, Capacity Management, Availability Management, and IT Continuity Management (also known as *disaster recovery*). Other branches are tactical—Incident Management, Problem Management, Configuration Management, Change Management, and Release Management. Formal definitions are provided in the following sections along with appropriate suggestions for the DBA. The definitions are taken from *ITIL V2 Glossary v01* (Office of Government Commerce, 2006) and are reproduced with permission.[2] The highlighted terms in the definitions have their own formal definitions, and the serious student can find them in the same document.

Service Level Management

Service Level Management (SLM) is "the Process responsible for negotiating Service Level Agreements, and ensuring that these are met. SLM is responsible for ensuring that all IT Service Management Processes, Operational Level Agreements, and Underpinning Contracts are appropriate for the agreed Service Level Targets. SLM monitors and reports on Service Levels, and holds regular Customer reviews."

The database administrator cannot meet the expectations of the business if he or she does not know what they are. These expectations usually center on availability and performance; for example, databases that are used by e-commerce applications typically have very high availability and performance requirements.

In the absence of clearly communicated expectations and measurable service levels, the job of database administration becomes a reactive exercise instead of the proactive exercise it should be—for example, performance tuning is conducted only after the business complains of poor performance.

---

[2]ITIL ® is a registered trademark and a registered community trademark of the Office of Government Commerce and is registered in the U.S. Patent and Trademark Office. ITIL Glossaries/Acronyms © Crown Copyright Office of Government Commerce. Reproduced with the permission of the Controller of HMSO and the Office of Government Commerce.

Financial Management

Financial Management for IT services is "the Process responsible for managing an IT Service Provider's Budgeting, Accounting and Charging requirements."

Oracle license payments can be a substantial part of the IT department's budget. At the time of writing, a license for Oracle Database Enterprise Edition for a single CPU costs $47,500 or more and depends on the number of cores in the CPU; a license for a four-core Intel CPU costs $95,000. Many features such as partitioning are extra-cost options. Annual support costs are currently 22% of the base price, and development and standby databases must also be separately licensed.

DBAs should understand Oracle's licensing policies and maintain an accurate inventory of installed software. Note that Oracle does not use license keys to unlock software, and it is therefore easy to install inadvertently software that is not properly licensed, such as Enterprise Edition instead of Standard Edition. It should be particularly noted that many features are automatically installed as part of the installation process and cannot be deinstalled. Examples include Partitioning and the various Management Packs. Collector Jobs for Diagnostics Pack are automatically created and scheduled even though very few sites are licensed to use the feature. As described in Chapter 6, the DBA must take explicit steps to deactivate the Management Packs after the database is created.

■ **Tip**   The DBA_FEATURE_USAGE_STATISTICS view shows which Oracle features are being used. This information should be regularly reviewed to ensure that unlicensed features are not being inadvertently used.

IT Service Continuity Management

IT Service Continuity Management (ITSCM) is "the Process responsible for managing Risks that could seriously impact IT Services. ITSCM ensures that the IT Service Provider can always provide minimum agreed Service Levels, by reducing the Risk to an acceptable level and Planning for the Recovery of IT Services. ITSCM should be designed to support Business Continuity Management."

IT continuity management is commonly referred to as *disaster recovery*, and the DBA must be prepared to re-create the database at an alternate location if a disaster should make the primary location unusable. This service is a subset of business continuity management, which is responsible for all aspects of the business, including IT. The DBA is responsible for databases only, and the three approaches that can be used are *hot standby*, *warm standby*, and *cold standby*. In the hot standby approach, an Oracle database is created on a server in the alternate location and is continuously synchronized with the primary database so that failover time can be kept to a minimum. In the warm standby approach, the hardware (including network components) is available at an alternate site but the database has to be re-created from backup tapes—this option is less expensive than the hot standby approach. In the cold standby approach, alternate facilities with power and cabling are identified, but the hardware is only procured in the event of a disaster—this is the cheapest option.

Capacity Management

Capacity Management is "the Process responsible for ensuring that the Capacity of IT Services and the IT Infrastructure is able to deliver agreed Service Level Targets in a Cost Effective and timely manner. Capacity Management considers all Resources required to deliver the IT Service, and plans for short, medium and long term Business Requirements."

In the absence of systematic capacity management, database administration becomes a reactive exercise in which, for example, space is added to databases only when they are close to failure. A systematic approach requires that trends be monitored. This requires periodic checking of database size, free space in tablespaces, CPU utilization, disk utilization, network utilization, and similar parameters, and taking corrective action to prevent the database from failing. DBAs are primarily interested in monitoring database trends; Chapter 10 discusses the use of STATSPACK for that purpose. Automatic Workload Repository (AWR) can also be used for monitoring database trends, but very few sites are licensed to use it.

Availability Management

Availability Management is "the Process responsible for defining, analysing, Planning, measuring and improving all aspects of the Availability of IT services. Availability Management is responsible for ensuring that all IT Infrastructure, Processes, Tools, Roles etc are appropriate for the agreed Service Level Targets for Availability."

Most of the DBA's time can be taken up by tasks relating to availability management. Database tuning (Chapter 16), SQL tuning (Chapter 17), and hardware upgrades are required to keep performance at acceptable levels. Database backups (Chapter 12) are required as insurance against database failures, and recovery testing (Chapter 13) is required to validate the usability of backups and to measure recovery times. An unplanned outage is usually classified as a Sev 1 issue, requiring the immediate attention of the DBA.

Incident Management

Incident Management is "the Process responsible for managing the Lifecycle of all Incidents. The primary Objective of Incident Management is to return the IT Service to Customers as quickly as possible."

The Incident Management process is usually handled by the Service Desk. The Service Desk prioritizes each issue that comes to its attention and engages with the Operations team as necessary until the problem is resolved.

Problem Management

A *problem* is "the root cause of one or more incidents." Problem Management is "the Process responsible for managing the Lifecycle of all Problems. The primary objectives of Problem Management are to prevent Incidents from happening, and to minimize the Impact of Incidents that cannot be prevented. Problem Management includes Problem Control, Error Control and Proactive Problem Management."

Incident Management is a reactive process, whereas Problem Management is a proactive process. An example of an incident is a database outage caused when the archived log area fills up. The incident may be resolved by removing the oldest archived logs, but the root cause of the incident must also be addressed. For example, disk space may be inadequate, and additional disk space may have to be procured. The Problem Management process ensures that chronic problems are identified and fixed.

Change Management

A change is "the addition, modification or removal of anything that could have an effect on IT Services. The Scope should include all Configuration Items, Processes, Documentation etc." Change Management is "the Process responsible for controlling the Lifecycle of all Changes. The primary objective of Change Management is to enable beneficial Changes to be made, with minimum disruption to IT Services."

The Change Management process is tasked with ensuring that changes are appropriately authorized and tested before being applied to the infrastructure that supports the IT services required by the business. The Change Management process is also responsible for ensuring that the risks of the changes are understood and that conflicts are detected. For example, a change to the database may conflict with business tasks.

Configuration Management

Configuration is "a generic term, used to describe a group of Configuration Items that work together to deliver an IT Service, or a recognizable part of an IT Service. Configuration is also used to describe the parameter settings for one or more CIs." Configuration Management is "the Process responsible for maintaining information about Configuration Items required to deliver an IT Service, including their Relationships. This information is managed throughout the Lifecycle of the CI. The primary objective of Configuration Management is to underpin the delivery of IT Services by providing accurate data to all IT Service Management Processes when and where it is needed."

In the terminology of Configuration Management, a database is a configuration item. The Configuration Management process is responsible for creating a repository of information about each configuration item and recording changes made to each configuration item. Systematic configuration management improves the effectiveness of the other branches of IT Service Management. For example, ready access to configuration information can help in resolving incidents (Incident Management) and diagnosing chronic problems (Problem Management).

In Chapter 9, you saw how Remote Diagnostic Assistant (RDA) can be used to assemble information about a database into an HTML framework. In the terminology of Configuration Management, the information collected by RDA is called a *configuration record* and should be stored in a Configuration Management Database (CMDB). You can create a simple CMDB of sorts by linking your RDA collections into an Excel spreadsheet. RDA collections can be run at regular intervals and linked into the spreadsheet. This is an easy way to create and organize a historical record of changes to database configurations.

■ **Note**   An RDA collection is the simplest and quickest way of documenting a database environment.

Release Management

A Releas0065 is "a collection of hardware, software, documentation, Processes or other Components required to implement one or more approved Changes to IT Services. The contents of each Release are managed, tested, and deployed as a single entity." Release Management is "the Process responsible for Planning, scheduling and controlling the movement of Releases to Test and Live Environments. The primary objective of Release Management is to ensure that the integrity of the Live Environment is protected and that the correct Components are released. Release Management works closely with Configuration Management and Change Management."

Release Management is concerned with major changes and additions to the IT infrastructure, such as installation of database software (Chapter 5) and database creation (Chapter 6). You should keep careful notes whenever you install database software and create a database so that the process can be standardized and repeated.

■ **Note**   Oracle provides the Service Level Management Pack for service-level management, the Change Management Pack for change management, the Configuration Management Pack for configuration management, and the Provisioning Pack for release management, but few sites are licensed to use these tools because they are available only with Enterprise Edition and require extra license and support fees on top of those paid for Enterprise Edition.

Start with the End in Mind: The Ten Deliverables

In his best-selling book *The 7 Habits of Highly Effective People* (Free Press, 1989), Stephen Covey distills the secrets of effectiveness into seven principles. In my opinion, the most important habit is "Start with the End in Mind"—how you want your work to be evaluated when you have completed it. When Big Bob turned responsibilities over to me, he had little more for me than the database passwords, a firm handshake, and good wishes—he left me very unhappy.

To be effective as a DBA, you must start with the end in mind—the moment when you hand over responsibilities to your successor. What will you give them other than the database passwords, a firm handshake, and good wishes?

Here are the ten deliverables of the database administration role—they map to the ten deliverables of the Operations team, which are listed in the ITIL literature. In large organizations with many DBAs, these are shared deliverables:

1. *A database that meets the needs of the business*: This is the most important deliverable, if not the only one. The needs of the business include certain levels of *performance, security*, and *availability*. You must understand the needs of the business, you must have a way of evaluating how well the needs are met, and you must have a methodology for meeting those needs. Any chronic performance, security, and availability issues must be discussed with the incoming DBA.

2. *A secure document library*: The absence of a document repository causes a lot of valuable information to be lost. Examples of documents that should be retained include service-level agreements, network diagrams, architecture diagrams, licensing information, E-R diagrams, performance reports, audit reports, software manuals, installation notes, project notes, copies of important correspondence, and so on. Standard operating procedures (SOPs) are another important class of documents; you learn about them later in the chapter. Original software media and files should also be stored in the library for use if the database needs to be rebuilt or if additional databases need to be created. Note that the document library needs to be secure because it contains sensitive and confidential information.

3. *Work logs of service requests, alarms, and changes*: Work logs are important for many reasons. They bring transparency and visibility to the database administration function. From the incident management perspective, it is necessary to review the work logs and identify inefficiencies and root causes. From the problem management perspective, it is necessary to review the work logs and identify chronic problems. From the availability management perspective, it is necessary to review the work logs and identify availability issues. These are just some examples of how work logs help bring about improvements and efficiencies in your ability to provide good service to the business.

4. *Standard operating procedures*: Any database administration task that is done repeatedly should be codified into an SOP. Using a written SOP helps with efficiency and accuracy. We return to this subject later in the chapter.

5. *Procedures and records for backup testing and failover testing*: It is absolutely essential that backup procedures and disaster-recovery procedures be documented. The procedures should be periodically tested, and records should be maintained.

6. *Maintenance and batch schedules, documentation, and records*: Chapter 14 discussed database maintenance. Database maintenance procedures should be documented, and records should be maintained. If the maintenance procedures are automated, log records should also be automatically created. For example, an RMAN catalog can be used to store backup histories. Any repeating tasks or batch jobs that are the responsibility of the DBA should also be adequately documented, and records should be maintained for them.

7. *Database administration tools*: Database administration tools include Oracle-supplied tools such as Database Control, Grid Control, and SQL Developer. The Management Packs, such as Diagnostics Pack, Tuning Pack, Change Management Pack, and Configuration Pack, are very valuable tools, but most organizations don't purchase licenses to use them because of their high cost and because Enterprise Edition is a prerequisite. Other popular tools are Toad from Quest Software and DBArtisan from Embarcadero Technologies002E

8. *Management reports*: Examples of database reports for management are reports on database growth, workload, and performance. STATSPACK and AWR histories should be retained for as long as practicable—the defaults (two weeks in the case of STATSPACK and eight days for AWR) are unsuitable. I suggest retaining data for at least one year if you can afford the space. Baseline snapshots should be retained indefinitely. For example, you can designate the period between 9 a.m. and 10 a.m. every Monday morning as a baseline period so that the snapshots marking the beginning and end of the period are retained indefinitely.

9. *Exception reports*: This deliverable includes reports on SLA violations, security violations, backup failures, and the like. For example, a certain stored procedure or SQL statement may have been identified as critical to the business, and an exception report can be produced by mining STATSPACK data.

10. *Audit reports*: This deliverable typically refers to audit reports conducted by security auditors but can also refer to internal audits of compliance with organizational processes such as Change Management or database reviews by external consultants. The absence of audits indicates a lack of oversight of the database management function.

The Book You Really Need and the Art of the SOP

The book you really need will never be found in bookstores—it is the book containing all the procedures that you need to operate your databases. You're going to have to write that book yourself. Nobody can write the book for you, because you have a unique environment and nobody except you would write a book that caters to a unique environment.

Do you know how to start or stop a database? I thought I did—until I went to work in a large network operations center. We had Solaris, AIX, HP/UX, Linux, and Windows. We had Oracle 8*i*, Oracle 9*i*, and Oracle 10*g*. We had VCS, HP Service Guard, Sun Clusters, Data Guard, and RAC. There were so many variations of the startup and shutdown procedures that I could not remember all of them.

A common task such as adding a data file to a database requires different methods depending on whether you are using cooked files, raw devices, or ASM. Additional complexities are introduced by RAC and Data Guard. Raw files in particular are notoriously difficult to manage—they make it easy to damage the database. And, in my experience, DBAs routinely forget the important step of backing up the data file immediately after it is created.

A TRUE STORY

A DBA stopped a database using the `shutdown` command in preparation for moving some data files to a new location. Unknown to him, the database was managed by Veritas high-availability software, which automatically restarted the database. The database was corrupted when the DBA moved the files.

It happened to me—it could happen to you.

Benefits of SOPs

Here are some of the advantages of SOPs:

- *They improve consistency.* A documented procedure is more likely to be executed consistently than one that is not documented.[3]

- *They improve quality.* It is easier to do a good job if you don't have to rely on memory or invent the procedure.

- *They facilitate continuous improvement.* It is easier to improve the quality of a procedure if it is documented than if it is not documented.

- *They promote transparency.* Would you hire anyone who insisted on charging you a lot of money but refused to tell you what was involved?

- *They improve efficiency.* Things get done faster. They get done correctly the first time. Further, it is easier to improve the efficiency of a procedure if it is documented than if it is not documented. *They facilitate planning.* It is easier to quantify the labor involved in a written procedure than one that is undocumented. This facilitates planning and project management.

- *They can reduce cost.* SOPs established by senior personnel may be delegated to junior personnel who are paid less. Needless to say, there is also a definite cost associated with making mistakes and inefficient execution.

---

[3]I remember a case when a customer vociferously expressed dissatisfaction with the work performed by a certain individual, going so far as to suggest that he be dismissed from service. Management finally agreed that the real problem lay with the "process," not with the performer, and that written procedures would be a better solution than dismissing the performer. I believe that IT management in general is too eager to blame the performer rather than the process. Performers are evaluated every year, but organizational processes are rarely evaluated. I believe that improving organizational processes will inevitably lead to improvements in employee performance. The likelihood that unwritten standards will be violated is much greater than that written standards will be violated. Standards can be violated intentionally or unintentionally. An unintentional violation of unwritten standards usually results when a task is performed by a newcomer to the group or when a veteran performer forgets to use one of the elements of the standard. An unintentional violation of written standard usually results from inadequate training or from sloppy execution. Standards can also be intentionally violated. However, the violator has a convenient excuse if the standard is unwritten, and deliberate violations stem from the belief that the standard is imperfect. It is not difficult for experienced individuals to find something about a procedure that they might choose to do differently if left to their own devices, and therefore organizations that rely on unwritten standards are likely to experience steady erosion of standards.

- *They facilitate knowledge transfer*. Tribal knowledge is lost when the members of the tribe leave to join other tribes or is forgotten with the passage of time. Written documentation is more permanent. Tribal knowledge is also subject to the Telephone game phenomenon.[4]

- *They reduce risk*. SOPs reduce the risk of things going wrong. These risks are exacerbated when regular performers are unavailable because of vacations, illness, resignation, and so on. Mistakes made by IT departments in large organizations often make the front page of the newspaper.

- *They improve employee morale*. Employee morale is high if the organization works well. A dysfunctional organization has low employee morale.

- *They reduce blame games*. It's hard to blame a performer for following a well-established SOP. Responsibility for failure transfers from the performer to the SOP. Of course, the SOP needs to be improved for the next time around.

- *They improve customer satisfaction*. The previous advantages would satisfy almost anybody, but we cannot neglect to mention that SOPs must inevitably improve customer satisfaction. Which customer would not be satisfied with your attention to detail?

A common excuse for not writing SOPs is that most tasks are simple enough. Consider the simple task of shutting down a database. Why does a custom SOP need to be written for this task or customized for each individual database? How customized, you might ask, can this simple task get? Well, the procedures for shutting down a database depend on the Oracle database version; the operating system; any high-availability mechanisms such as VCS, HP Serviceguard, and Sun Cluster; and Oracle components such as RAC and ASM. And here are some of the things a DBA might have to do *before* pressing the buttons that shut down the database:

- Confirm that there are no conflicts with backup schedules.

- Confirm that there are no conflicts with batch schedules.

- Confirm that no incompatible activities have been scheduled at the same time.

- Confirm that there are no conflicts with the SLA for database availability.

- Obtain the permission of the business owners of all applications that are directly or indirectly impacted.

- Send advance notifications to the user community.

- Determine the impact on replication mechanisms and take the appropriate steps to eliminate or mitigate the impact.

- Confirm the availability of other performers to bring down applications gracefully prior to shutting down the database.

- Confirm the access of all performers to databases, servers, and applications.

- Agree on communication mechanisms and performer handoffs.

- Establish escalation procedures for use if things go wrong.

- Establish procedures for use if users or jobs are still connected when the time comes to shut down the database.

---

[4]Telephone is a game in which each participant whispers a sentence to the next. Errors begin to accumulate, and the last participant receives a highly garbled version of the original sentence.

- Blackout alarm mechanisms.

- Send broadcast messages to users just before the shutdown.

Another example of a simple task that can quickly become complicated is resetting a password. Metalink note 270516.1 explains the lengthy sequence of tasks that must be performed to change the SYSMAN password.

Structure of an SOP

The following sections describe an SOP template that can be customized to each site's specific requirements and standards. Each SOP may be divided into the following sections.

Overview

The overview section is provided not so much for the benefit of those executing the SOP but for all those who are peripherally involved, such as customers who need the work done and managers or teams responsible for scheduling, approving, or supervising the work. A minimum of technical jargon should be used, and technical details should be suppressed if appropriate. The following points should be addressed:

- *Purpose*: This is the key section for nontechnical reviewers or managers002E

- *Risks*: A clear description of risks helps in getting approvals to perform the task—it also helps educate the performer. There can even be risks if the task is *not* performed.

- *Labor and billing*: This section specifies the standard fee schedule, which is the standard number of labor hours required to complete the work. In cases where a standard fee schedule cannot easily be constructed because of the variability of the work, guidelines are provided for estimating the work. In some cases, it is appropriate to specify billing details (for example, interdepartmental billing).

- *Scheduling*: This section specifies what advance notice is required, what information needs to be supplied by the requestor, what forms must be completed, and scheduling constraints, if any.

- *Prerequisites*: Clearly documenting the prerequisites improves the chances that they will actually be met. You might want to include a "nice to have" section.

Testing

This section describes what testing should be completed in a laboratory setting before the real work can begin. Here are the reasons for testing:

- *An SOP may not be perfect*. Testing the procedure in a laboratory setting that duplicates the targeted production setting may uncover deficiencies in the procedure.

- *Practice is good preparation*. It may have been a long time since the performer last executed the procedure. Also, the SOP may have omitted some of the details, and practice in a laboratory setting will allow less experienced performers to supply them for themselves.

- *Testing smoothens out the approval process*. In some cases, testing may not be considered necessary because the work is truly routine—for example, adding a user. In other cases, testing may not be practical because of the huge effort required to duplicate the target environment in a laboratory setting. If testing is unnecessary or impractical, then the author of the SOP should indicate as much and explain why.

Approvals

This section describes whose approval is required and the protocols to be observed—for example, verbal approval, written approval, formal meetings, advance notice, and so on. I have observed that most IT organizations fall into one of two categories:

- *Very little attention is paid to change management.* The performers are given free rein to take suitable action. Performer morale is high, but the situation is certainly not desirable from a management viewpoint.

- *A huge amount of attention is paid to change management.* Performers are not permitted to do the slightest work without the approval of "change czars." Performers chafe under this scrutiny and complain of delays and the effort expended in submitting paperwork before artificial deadlines, attending change-management meetings, and answering questions from change czars who do not have expertise in the subject matter.

The approach I recommend is that the SOP explicitly state whose approval is required. The following is a short list:

- The performers who will be actually performing the tasks

- Managers of the performers required to perform the task or tasks

- Representatives of users who will be affected by the task

If all the necessary approvals have been obtained, the approval of the change czars becomes a mere formality.

Notification

This section describes who should be notified before the work begins and the mechanisms and procedures that should be used.

Backup

This section provides step-by-step instructions for creating backups in case the work needs to be undone.

Staging Activities

This section addresses all other preparation steps that are not covered by the approval, notification, and backup sections.

Execution

This section provides step-by-step instructions on how the work should be done.

Verification

This sections states what "successful" execution means. For example, it may require confirmation from a user that they are able to use the application.

Backout

This section provides step-by-step instructions on using the backups if it becomes necessary to reverse the change.

Signoff

This section describes who decides that the performer has executed the work correctly.

Record-Keeping

This section makes the record-keeping requirements explicit. :

Quality Assurance

This section describes any quality assurance procedures that should be used to assess the quality and accuracy of the work.

KILL FIRST, ASK QUESTIONS LATER?

An article titled "A Day in the Life of an Enterprise DBA" was published in the March 1998 issue of *Oracle* magazine, published by Oracle. The protagonist used the Enterprise Manager tool to perform a variety of tasks. Here is how he diagnosed and fixed a slow system.

> To find out who is hitting the system so hard, I start up TopSessions and look at the user-resource usage on the system. I sort based on redo activity to find the culprit. A developer is inserting data into the database and causing significant redo-log activity. A double-click on the user shows me the actual SQL that has been executed. Apparently, the developer is loading data onto the production system during production time. Should I call him before I kill his session? No—**kill first, call later**. He should know better. Soon after, the supervisors report that the system is running well again.

This brings to mind the 2002 James Bond movie *Die Another Day*, starring Pierce Brosnan as James Bond and Rosamund Pike as double agent Miranda Frost. In the movie, Frost describes Bond as follows:

> He's a double 0, and a wild one as I discovered today. He'll light the fuse on any explosive situation and be a danger to himself and others. **Kill first, ask questions later**. I think he's a blunt instrument whose primary method is to provoke and confront ...

Your motto should not be "Kill first, ask questions later" but "Follow the SOP." That way, you won't light the fuse on explosive situations and be a danger to yourself and to others!

Suggested SOPs

Here is a list of common database tasks. As you have seen, even everyday tasks such as stopping a database and changing passwords can be nontrivial. If you don't have the time to write detailed SOPs, you should consider writing at least a few sentences on each topic:

1. *Connecting to a database*: This describes how the DBA connects to the database to perform database administration activities. This SOP is invaluable in an emergency when speed is critical or when the primary DBA is unavailable.

2. *Starting a database*: This describes how to start the database engine and associated components such as ASM, Data Guard, and database applications.

3. *Stopping a database*: This describes how to stop the database engine and associated components.

4. *Backups and recovery*: This describes how to perform an ad hoc backup and how to recover the database from backups.

5. *Removing archived redo logs*: This describes what to do when the archived log destination fills up.

6. *Standby database maintenance*: This describes how to fail over and fail back.

7. *Adding space*: This describes the process for adding data files or increasing the size of data files.

8. *Health checks*: This describes how to check the health of the database and of applications that use the database.

9. *Adding a user*: This describes special procedures and security rules to be followed when adding a user to a database—for example, specific privileges that might be needed by users of particular applications.

10. *Resetting a password*: This describes special procedures to be followed when performing password resets—for example, steps to prevent applications from malfunctioning.

11. *Clearing a lock*: This describes internal procedures to be followed when terminating a process that is blocking other users.

12. *Maintenance activities*: This describes daily maintenance activities, such as investigating backup failures, reviewing the error log, and checking the contents of trace files. It also covers weekly maintenance activities such as regenerating statistics, monthly maintenance activities such as preparing for month-end batch processing, and quarterly maintenance activities such as preparing for quarter-end processing.

Summary

Here is a short summary of the concepts this chapter touched on:

- IT services are managed using the principles of IT service management (ITSM). The Infrastructure Management team manages the hardware and software that power the services required by the business—it is divided into a Design and Planning (D&P) team, a Deployment team, and an Operations team. The Application Management team designs and develops the software applications underlying the services used by the business. The ITSM team is the interface between the business and the Infrastructure Management team. In particular, the Service Desk is the single point of contact for all users of the services.

- The DBA is part of the Operations team. This is an intuitive classification, because the term *administration* suggests the day-to-day maintenance of an operational database. However, people with that title can often be found in the Deployment team and the Applications Management team.

- Some of the processes of ITSM are strategic: Service Level Management, Financial Management, Capacity Management, Availability Management, and IT Continuity Management (a.k.a disaster recovery). Other branches are tactical: Incident Management, Problem Management, Configuration Management, Change Management, and Release Management.

- Oracle provides Management Packs for a number of ITSM processes, but most sites are not licensed to use them, because they are available only with Enterprise Edition and require extra license and support fees.

- Oracle makes it very easy to download, install, and activate software, but this causes organizations to be vulnerable to using unlicensed software. Particular care has to be taken in the case of the Management Packs, which few sites are licensed to use but which are automatically installed and activated during the installation process.

- Every database requires a disaster recovery plan. The three approaches that can be used are *hot standby*, *warm standby*, and *cold standby*. A cold standby is the cheapest option and is simply a plan for the procurement and provisioning of hardware at a previously identified location, complete reinstallation of software, and database recovery from backup tapes.

- STATSPACK and AWR histories can be used to monitor trends in workloads and performance. They should be maintained for as long as practicable. Baselines should be retained indefinitely.

- Incident management is a reactive process, with the goal being to restore service as soon as possible. Problem management is a proactive process, with the goal being to identify and eliminate chronic problems.

- Configuration management is the linchpin of the other ITSM processes. Oracle provides the Configuration Management Pack, but few sites are licensed to use it—RDA is a cheap and simple substitute.

- These are the ten deliverables for the database administration role: databases that meet the needs of the business; a secure document library; work logs of service requests, alarms, and changes; standard operating procedures (SOPs); backup testing and failover testing procedures and records; maintenance and batch schedules, documentation, and records; database administration tools; management reports; exception reports; and audit reports.

- Any database administration task that is done repeatedly should be codified into an SOP. Using a written SOP has many benefits, including efficiency, quality, and consistency.

Exercises

- Download *Oracle Database Licensing Information, 12c Release 1 (12.1)* from the Oracle website. Also download *Oracle Technology Global Price List*. Review the contents of the DBA_FEATURES_USAGE_INFO view in your database. Which extra-cost options and Management Packs have been automatically installed in your practice database? Which extra-cost options and Management Packs are already in use? For example, have AWR collections been automatically scheduled by the Oracle installer? Compute what the total licensing and annual support costs might be if your database was not solely for self-educational purposes.

- Download *ITIL V2 Glossary* from www.best-management-practice.com/gempdf/ITIL_Glossary_May_v2_2007.pdf. Find the definitions of the terms in the various ITIL definitions provided in this chapter.

- Write an SOP to add a data file to your database. Include enough detail that somebody who was unfamiliar with Oracle (for example, a Windows system administrator) would be able to perform this simple task. Remember to include the step of backing up the data file immediately after it was created.

Further Reading

- *ICT Infrastructure Management.* Office of Government Commerce, 2002. This book describes information and communications technology (ICT) management and its relationship to IT Service Management. This refers to the ITIL V2 publication.

- *ITIL V2 Glossary v01.* Office of Government Commerce, 2006. This is a glossary of terms, definitions, and acronyms used by ITIL V2. You can download it from www.best-management-practice.com/gempdf/ITIL_Glossary_May_v2_2007.pdf.

- Mullins, Craig S. *Database Administration: The Complete Guide to DBA Practices and Procedures (2nd Edition).* Addison-Wesley Professional, 2012.

- *Service Delivery.* Office of Government Commerce, 2000. This book describes the strategic aspects of IT Service Management, specifically the Service Level Management, Financial Management, Capacity Management, IT Continuity Management, and Release Management processes. This refers to the ITIL V2 publication.

- *Service Support.* Office of Government Commerce, 2001. This book describes the tactical aspects of IT Service Management, specifically the Service Desk, Incident Management, Problem Management, Configuration Management, Change Management, and Release Management processes. This refers to the ITIL V2 publication.

- Van Bon, Jan. *Foundations of IT Service Management: Based on ITIL.* Van Haren Publishing, 2005. This book is much more affordable than the publications of the Office of Government Commerce and is suitable for beginners.

Database Tuning

CHAPTER 16

■ ■ ■

Database Tuning

Citius, Altius, Fortius—Swifter, Higher, Stronger

—Motto of the Olympic Games

Database tuning can be a complex exercise, but it can be facilitated by a systematic approach. This chapter describes a systematic five-step approach to performance tuning. It also presents the most important tools provided by Oracle to help with performance tuning; Statspack is given equal time because tools such as Automatic Workload Repository (AWR) and Automatic Database Diagnostic Monitor (ADDM) require licenses and are not available at most sites.[1] In particular, you learn a powerful method of mining the Statspack and AWR repositories for data on performance trends. This data can be graphed by using tools such as Microsoft Excel.

Of course, I can only give you a brief introduction to the vast topic of database tuning. If you want to continue your study of this topic, the best book you will every find is *Database Performance Tuning Guide* in the Oracle documentation set. I recommend that you do the exercises listed at the end of the chapter—they will familiarize you with the most common tools for database tuning. The best way to learn is by doing.

■ **Tip** The SQL scripts in this chapter use blank lines for extra readability. When executing them in SQL*Plus, use the command `set sqlblanklines on` to prevent them from erroring out.

Using a Systematic Five-Step Tuning Method

Once upon a time, a database-tuning expert saw a drunken man on his hands and knees searching for something under a bright streetlight. "Have you lost something?" he asked the drunk.

"My keys," said the drunk.

The performance expert offered to help, and he too got on his hands and knees to search for the lost keys. After concluding that no keys were to be found under the streetlight, he began questioning the drunk. "When was the last time you remember seeing your keys?" he asked.

"At the bar," said the drunk.

"Then why are you searching here?"

"Because it is so much brighter here!"

The story is fictional, and the moral is that you must concentrate your efforts in the appropriate place. You shouldn't focus your exertion wherever it is most convenient to do so—the problem might not be in the Oracle database at all.

---

[1] In 2007, the president of a well-known consulting company reported that only 2 of its 70 clients had licenses for Diagnostics Pack.

Here is an example of a case where poor performance was reported but the database was *not* the problem. The output shown in Listing 16-1 was produced by using the dbms_monitor.session_trace:enable procedure to trace a poorly performing batch process and then using the tkprof utility to summarize the trace data. The session was traced for about 40 minutes, and the data shows that the Oracle database spent only 140.08 seconds executing SQL queries. The bulk of the time—2,138.67 seconds—was spent waiting for further instructions from the program. This clearly showed that the database was *not* the problem.

Listing 16-1. Sample Output of the tkprof Utility

OVERALL TOTALS FOR ALL NON-RECURSIVE STATEMENTS

call	count	cpu	**elapsed**	disk	query	current	rows
Parse	14114	0.37	0.40	0	0	0	0
Execute	78466	107.84	109.89	195	1105246	26768	13139
Fetch	72200	19.88	29.78	2100	432976	0	84080
total	164780	128.09	**140.08**	2295	1538222	26768	97219

Misses in library cache during parse: 4
Misses in library cache during execute: 4

Elapsed times include waiting on following events:

Event waited on	Times Waited	Max. Wait	Total Waited
SQL*Net message to client	87649	0.00	0.09
SQL*Net message from client	**87649**	**0.57**	**2138.67**
db file sequential read	2295	0.26	10.80
SQL*Net break/reset to client	1084	0.00	0.07
log file sync	1813	0.15	18.02
latch: session allocation	8	0.29	2.14
latch: cache buffers chains	1	0.00	0.00
latch: library cache	3	0.00	0.01
log file switch completion	1	0.97	0.97
latch: redo writing	1	0.04	0.04

In his book *The Art and Science of Oracle Performance Tuning*, Christopher Lawson outlines a systematic five-step method for solving any performance-tuning problem:[2]

1. *Define* the problem. This requires patient listening, skillful questioning, and even careful observation. "The database is slow" is an example of a poorly defined problem. "The database is slow between 10 a.m. and 11 a.m. every day" is more precise. "This report now takes twice as long as it used to take only a week ago" is another example of a precisely defined problem. Ask the user for the history of the problem. Ask what previous efforts have been made to solve the problem. Ask what changed recently in the environment—for example, software or hardware upgrades. Ask whether all users are affected or only some. Ask whether the problem occurs at specific times of the day or week. Ask whether all parts of the application are equally affected or just certain parts.

---

[2]This was presented in Chapter 11 as a general method of solving any performance problems; refer to the flowchart shown in Figure 11-2.

2. *Investigate* the problem, and collect as much pertinent evidence as possible. Examples include Statspack reports, graphs of database workload and DB time, and session traces. Study the environment, and find out what may be affecting the database—for example, other databases and applications may be competing for resources with your database.

3. *Analyze* the data collected in the second step, and isolate the cause of the performance problem. This is often the most challenging part of the performance-tuning exercise. If the cause of the problem is not found, go back to step 1 or step 2.

4. *Solve* the problem by creating a solution that addresses the root cause. Solutions are not always obvious, and, therefore, this step may require a great deal of ingenuity and creativity.

5. *Implement* the solution in a safe and controlled manner. Conduct an appropriate level of testing. Obtain "before" and "after" measurements, if possible, in order to quantify the performance improvement. If the expected improvement is not obtained, go back to step 2.

Oracle Database versions may change, and software tools may change, but the five performance-tuning steps never change. A problem may be simple and require only a few minutes of your time, or it may be tremendously complex and require weeks of your time, but the five steps always remain the same. A simple example follows; you will be asked to duplicate it in the "Exercises" section at the end of the chapter:

1. The users told the DBA that the problem was restricted to certain parts of the application and that there had not been a problem the previous day. On questioning the application developers, the DBA learned that there had been an application upgrade the previous night.

2. The DBA used the `spreport.sql` script to generate Statspack reports for a one-hour period for the previous day and the current day. The DBA also traced a number of database sessions by using the `DBMS_MONITOR.SET_SQL_TRACE` procedure.

3. Examination of the Statspack report for the current day showed large numbers of `enq: TM - contention` events; sessions were waiting, trying to lock an entire table. These events were not observed in the Statspack report for the previous day. The table in question was identified by searching through the trace files.

4. The `enq: TM - contention` event indicates an unindexed foreign key. If a foreign key is not indexed, Oracle must lock the entire child table when a record is deleted from the parent table in the foreign-key relationship. The DBA queried the `DBA_CONSTRAINTS`, `DBA_CONS_COLUMNS`, and `DBA_IND_COLUMNS` views to identify the missing index and brought this to the attention of the developers.

5. All that was left to do was to implement the solution in a safe and controlled manner. The developers followed the necessary change-control procedures before creating the necessary index.

■ **Tip** A good question to ask during the investigation phase is, "What changed?"

Analyzing DB Time

The best way to analyze database performance is to find out where the database is spending time. This is powerfully summarized by the Statspack and AWR reports. To demonstrate this, I used the Swingbench tool[3] to perform large numbers of transactions in my test database on my laptop. I then used the `spreport.sql` and `awrrpt.sql` scripts to generate the Statspack and AWR reports for a one-hour period; both scripts can be found in `ORACLE_HOME\rdbms\admin`. Listing 16-2 shows the first page of the Statspack report, and Listing 16-3 shows the first page of the corresponding AWR report.

Listing 16-2. First Page from a Sample Statspack Report

```
STATSPACK report for

Database      DB Id Instance  Inst Num  Startup  Time    Release   RAC
~~~~~~~~      --------- --------- --------  --------- -----  ---------- ---
          1365223133 orcl         1 05-Jul-14 22:59 12.1.0.1.0  NO

Host Name          Platform              CPUs Cores Sockets  Memory (G)
~~~~          ---------------- ----------------------  ----- ----- -------  -------------
          localhost.locald Linux x86 64-bit        1     0      0        1.5

Snapshot      Snap Id   Snap Time            Sessions    Curs/Sess Comment
~~~~~~~~      --------- ------------------   --------    --------- --------
Begin Snap:      111 18-Apr-15 14:00:15           2        4.5
  End Snap:      171 18-Apr-15 15:00:10           3        4.3
  Elapsed:          59.92 (mins)   Av Act Sess:         0.9
  DB time:          56.77 (mins)       DB CPU:  1.30 (mins)

Cache Sizes      Begin         End
~~~~~~~~~~~      ------      ----------
Buffer Cache:      52M    Std Block Size:        8K
Shared Pool:      172M      Log Buffer:    3,912K

Load Profile          Per Second   Per Transaction   Per Exec   Per Call
~~~~~~~~~~~~          -----------   ---------------   --------   --------
     DB time(s):           1.0             0.1        0.01       0.02
      DB CPU(s):           0.0             0.0        0.00       0.00
      Redo size:      30,328.6         2,658.6
  Logical reads:       1,520.9           133.3
  Block changes:         288.9            25.3
 Physical reads:         195.8            17.2
Physical writes:           0.1             0.0
     User calls:          43.9             3.9
         Parses:          30.6             2.7
    Hard parses:           5.3             0.5
W/A MB processed:          0.3             0.0
         Logons:           1.4             0.1
       Executes:         153.6            13.5
      Rollbacks:           0.0             0.0
   Transactions:          11.4
```

---

[3]The Swingbench tool can be downloaded from www.dominicgiles.com.

```
Instance Efficiency Indicators
~~~~~~~~~~~~~~~~~~~~~~~~~~~~~~~~~~~~

              Buffer Nowait %:   100.00       Redo NoWait %:   99.99
              Buffer  Hit  %:     87.13   Optimal W/A Exec %:  100.00
             Library Hit  %:      93.56      Soft Parse %:     82.80
         Execute to Parse %:      80.05       Latch Hit %:    100.00
   Parse CPU to Parse Elapsd %:    6.93    % Non-Parse CPU:    82.42


    Shared Pool Statistics       Begin       End
                                 ------      ------
                Memory Usage %:   90.17      94.15
        % SQL with executions>1:  79.38      80.00
      % Memory for SQL w/exec>1:  74.63      79.55


Top 5 Timed Events                                           Avg   %Total
~~~~~~~~~~~~~~~~~~~~                                          wait   Call
Event                             Waits      Time (s)  (ms)   Time
------------------------------- ----------- ---------- ------ ------
PL/SQL lock timer                 143,791     1,398      10   37.3
db file sequential read           311,592     1,254       4   33.5
log file sync                      20,819       684      33   18.2
write complete waits                  212       208     979    5.5
CPU time                                       155             4.1
```

The most important part of the Statspack report is the Top 5 Timed Events section. It is preceded by details concerning the workload processed by the database. In Listing 16-2, you can see that the DB time was 56.77 minutes during an elapsed interval of 59.92 minutes. *DB time* is the sum of the response times of all database calls made by the connected sessions; it can be much larger than the clock time if multiple sessions are simultaneously active. Note that actual CPU usage was only 55 seconds during the entire period—just 4.1% of the total DB time. The rest of the time was spent waiting for overhead activities such as reading data from disk (db file sequential read operations) and writing redo information to the online redo logs (log file sync operations). Each db file sequential read operation retrieves one database block from disk. The average time for each operation was 4 milliseconds. The average time for each log file sync operation was 33 milliseconds—too large for comfort—but such operations accounted for only 18.2% of DB time.

Listing 16-3 shows the first page of the AWR report for the same period. The format is very similar to that of the Statspack report, but there is some variance in the numbers because the methods used by AWR are different than those of Statspack.

Listing 16-3. First Page from a Sample AWR Report

```
WORKLOAD REPOSITORY report for

DB Name         DB Id       Instance     Inst Num Startup Time     Release     RAC
------------ ------------ ------------ --------- --------------- ----------- ---
ORCL         1365223133 orcl           1 05-Jul-14 23:00 12.1.0.1.0   NO

Host Name        Platform                         CPUs Cores Sockets Memory(GB)
--------------- --------------------------- ---- ----- ------- ----------
localhost.locald Linux x86 64-bit                  1                    1.46
```

	Snap Id	Snap Time	Sessions	Curs/Sess	PDBs
Begin Snap:	164	18-Apr-15 14:00:41	42	1.8	1
End Snap:	170	18-Apr-15 15:00:33	42	1.3	1
Elapsed:		59.87 (mins)			
DB Time:		56.41 (mins)			

Load Profile	Per Second	Per Transaction	Per Exec	Per Call
DB Time(s):	0.9	0.2	0.01	0.04
DB CPU(s):	0.0	0.0	0.00	0.00
Redo size (bytes):	30,844.9	5,302.4		
Logical read (blocks):	1,014.9	174.5		
Block changes:	158.9	27.3		
Physical read (blocks):	115.6	19.9		
Physical write (blocks):	28.4	4.9		
Read IO requests:	103.7	17.8		
Write IO requests:	22.6	3.9		
Read IO (MB):	0.9	0.2		
Write IO (MB):	0.2	0.0		
User calls:	25.7	4.4		
Parses (SQL):	32.5	5.6		
Hard parses (SQL):	6.1	1.1		
SQL Work Area (MB):	-0.3	-0.1		
Logons:	1.4	0.2		
Executes (SQL):	165.0	28.4		
Rollbacks:	0.0	0.0		
Transactions:	5.8			

Instance Efficiency Percentages (Target 100%)

Buffer Nowait %:	99.97	Redo NoWait %:	99.99
Buffer Hit %:	88.61	In-memory Sort %:	100.00
Library Hit %:	93.58	Soft Parse %:	81.20
Execute to Parse %:	80.32	Latch Hit %:	100.00
Parse CPU to Parse Elapsd %:	7.29	% Non-Parse CPU:	60.09

Top 10 Foreground Events by Total Wait Time

Event	Waits	Total Wait Time (sec)	Wait Avg(ms)	% DB time	Wait Class
db file sequential read	329,858	1671	5	49.4	User I/O
log file sync	20,833	691.7	33	20.4	Commit
write complete waits	216	224.4	1039	6.6	Configuration
cursor: pin S wait on X	264	85.7	324	2.5	Concurrency
DB CPU		77.5		2.3	
resmgr: cpu quantum	3,286	76.9	23	2.3	Scheduler
read by other session	627	31.4	50	.9	User I/O
db file parallel read	943	22.1	23	.7	User I/O
library cache load lock	186	19.6	106	.6	Concurrency
db file scattered read	827	15.1	18	.4	User I/O

The best way to tune this database would seem to be to get faster disks; another alternative would be to increase the size of the buffer cache so that less data has to be read from disk. The ADDM report automatically analyzes the components of DB time and makes appropriate suggestions, some of which are shown in Listing 16-4. The ADDM script is addmrpt.sql, and it too can be found in ORACLE_HOME\ rdbms\admin.

Listing 16-4. Recommendations from a Sample ADDM Report

```
Findings and Recommendations
----------------------------


Finding 1: "User I/O" wait Class
Impact is .48 active sessions, 51.59% of total activity.
-------------------------------------------------------
Wait class "User I/O" was consuming significant database time.


   No recommendations are available.


Finding 2: Top SQL Statements
Impact is .3 active sessions, 32.39% of total activity.
-------------------------------------------------------
SQL statements consuming significant database time were found. These
statements offer a good opportunity for performance improvement.


   Recommendation 1: SQL Tuning
   Estimated benefit is .16 active sessions, 17.46% of total activity.
   ------------------------------------------------------------------
   Action
      Run SQL Tuning Advisor on the SELECT statement with SQL_ID
      "c13sma6rkr27c".
      Related Object
         SQL statement with SQL_ID c13sma6rkr27c.
         SELECT PRODUCTS.PRODUCT_ID, PRODUCT_NAME, PRODUCT_DESCRIPTION,
         CATEGORY_ID, WEIGHT_CLASS, WARRANTY_PERIOD, SUPPLIER_ID,
         PRODUCT_STATUS, LIST_PRICE, MIN_PRICE, CATALOG_URL, QUANTITY_ON_HAND
         FROM PRODUCTS, INVENTORIES WHERE PRODUCTS.CATEGORY_ID = :B3 AND
         INVENTORIES.PRODUCT_ID = PRODUCTS.PRODUCT_ID AND
         INVENTORIES.WAREHOUSE_ID = :B2 AND ROWNUM < :B1
   Rationale
      The SQL statement executed in container PDB1 with database ID
      3345156736.
   Rationale
      The SQL spent 96% of its database time on CPU, I/O and Cluster waits.
      This part of database time may be improved by the SQL Tuning Advisor.
   Rationale
      Database time for this SQL was divided as follows: 100% for SQL
      execution, 0% for parsing, 0% for PL/SQL execution and 0% for Java
      execution.
   Rationale
      SQL statement with SQL_ID "c13sma6rkr27c" was executed 13518 times and
      had an average elapsed time of 0.03 seconds.
```

```
Rationale
    I/O and Cluster wait for TABLE "SOE.INVENTORIES" with object ID 96079
    consumed 89% of the database time spent on this SQL statement.
Rationale
    Top level calls to execute the PL/SQL statement with SQL_ID
    "0w2qpuc6u2zsp" are responsible for 100% of the database time spent on
    the SELECT statement with SQL_ID "c13sma6rkr27c".
    Related Object
        SQL statement with SQL_ID 0w2qpuc6u2zsp.
        BEGIN :1 := orderentry.neworder(:2 ,:3 ,:4 ); END;
```

Understanding the Oracle Wait Interface

Statspack gets its data from the Oracle *wait interface*—the collection of *dynamic performance views* that track all aspects of database activity. Performance-monitoring tools can query these tables by using SQL. Some of the most important views in the wait interface are described in the following sections.

V$SYSSTAT and V$SESSTAT

V$SESSTAT and V$SYSSTAT contain almost 400 counters describing every aspect of the workload handled by the database. V$SESSTAT contains session-level counters—almost 400 of them for each session—and V$SYSSTAT contains system-level counters, each one being the total of all the session-level counters of the same type. In other words, each row in V$SESSTAT gives you the value of a counter for one session, and each row in V$SYSSTAT gives you the total value for all sessions. Four of these counters (logons current, opened cursors current, session cursor cache current, and workarea memory allocated) represent current levels; the rest are cumulative counters that keep incrementing from the time the database was started.

Because the majority of these counters are cumulative, the way to monitor the rate of activity is to observe the values of the counters at fixed intervals and calculate the difference. This is the approach used by the Statspack report. Some of the most important counters are described here:

- CPU used by this session is the amount of CPU used by one session in the case of V$SESSTAT. It is the amount of CPU used by all sessions put together in the case of V$SYSSTAT.

- consistent gets and db block gets are the number of blocks read in *consistent* and *current* mode, respectively; current mode is used to find the most up-to-date version of a block, and consistent mode is used to find the state of a block at a prior point in time. The sum of consistent gets and db block gets is the number of *logical reads* performed by the database.

- physical reads is the number of blocks that are not found in the memory cache and have to be physically retrieved from the disk.

- physical writes is the number of modified blocks that are written to disk.

- user commits and user rollbacks track transaction rates.

A complete list of the workload metrics tracked in the V$SYSSTAT and V$SESSTAT views is available in *Oracle Database 12c Reference*.

V$SESSION_EVENT and V$SYSTEM_EVENT

Whereas V$SESSTAT and V$SYSSTAT track the workload handled by the database, V$SESSION_EVENT and V$SYSTEM_EVENT track the amount of time spent waiting in over 100 different categories—for example, waiting for I/O or waiting for a lock. All the counters are cumulative; V$SESSION_EVENT has session-level counters, and V$SYSTEM_EVENT has system-level counters. You saw some examples of these counters in the Top 5 Timed Events example (Listing 16-2) earlier in this chapter; a complete list and explanation of each wait event is provided in *Oracle Database 11g Reference*. Here are some more examples:

- db file sequential read tracks the amount of time spent reading single blocks from tables.

- db file scattered read tracks the amount of time spent performing full table scans.

- enq: TX - contention is the amount of time spent waiting for row locks.

- enq: TM - contention is the amount of time spent waiting for table-level locks.

Mining the Statspack Repository

Statspack gets its data by performing *snapshots* of the dynamic performance tables such as V$SYSSTAT and V$SYSTEM_EVENT. This data is stored in tables that mimic the structure of the dynamic performance tables; for example, the STATS$SYSSTAT table corresponds to the V$SYSSTAT view, and the STATS$SYSTEM_EVENT table corresponds to the V$SYSTEM_EVENT view.

The Statspack repository can be mined for historical data that can be graphed using tools such as Microsoft Excel. The graphs show any historical trends and repeating patterns.

■ **Tip** A stable database exhibits distinct repeating patterns; for example, the workload may peak during the day and subside at night. These patterns are the signature of the database. Deviations from established patterns can be a sign that something is wrong with the database. The Statspackreports for the affected periods can be analyzed and compared with the reports for baseline periods.

In Chapter 10, you saw examples of SQL queries to mine the Statspack repository. Listing 10-8 showed an SQL query to track logical reads per second and physical reads per second over a period of time. That query is a good way to monitor trends and changes in the database workload; you can modify it to include other workload metrics. The corresponding graph is shown in Figure 10-2. Listing 10-9 showed an SQL query to extract performance information on specific SQL queries of your choice.

In Listing 16-5, you see another valuable SQL query; it provides the distribution of DB time for each available time period. It is a fairly long query, but you can download the text from the Source Code section of the Apress web site (www.apress.com). You have to specify a range of snapshots; the appropriate range can be obtained from the STATS$SNAPSHOT table. As explained earlier in this chapter, the distribution of DB time is precisely the information you need to tune the database. CPU time is obtained from the STATS$SYSSTAT table, and the wait time for each type of event is obtained from the STATS$SYSTEM_EVENT table. The classifications in the V$EVENT_NAME view are used to group events into categories such as Application, Concurrency, Commit, User IO, and System IO. The PIVOT operator is used to convert rows into columns; this makes it easy to perform further analysis on the data. The LAG function is used to compute the amount of increase in each row of data. Finally, you divide CPU time and wait time by the length of the observed interval to compute *average active sessions* for each category of time. The AWR analog of this query is available in the Google group for this book (https://groups.google.com/forum/#!forum/beginning-oracle-database-12c-administration).

Sample output of this query is shown in Figures 16-1 and 16-2. Each graph shows data for the same database, one week at a time. Even if you knew very little about performance tuning, you could instinctively tell which week was a good week for the database and which week was a bad week. The graph in Figure 16-1 exhibits very regular patterns, indicating database stability. The graph in Figure 16-2 is for another week in the same database, but the regular patterns are missing. I hope these examples convince you of the importance of becoming familiar with the workload and performance patterns in your database.

Listing 16-5. SQL Query to Show Patterns and Trends in the Distribution of DB Time

```
set linesize 132
set pagesize 10000
set tab off
set trimout on
set trimspool on
set sqlblanklines on

alter session set nls_date_format = 'yyyy/mm/dd hh24:mi';

column aas_cpu format 999.99
column aas_other format 999.99
column aas_application format 999.99
column aas_concurrency format 999.99
column aas_commit format 999.99
column aas_user_io format 999.99
column aas_system_io format 999.99

WITH
  timed_events AS

  -- Get wait time from the STATS$SYSTEM_EVENT table.
  -- Select snapshots between start_snap_id and end_snap_id.
  -- Convert wait microseconds into seconds.
  -- Merge some wait classes into the "Other" class (wait_class# = 0).
  -- Ignore the "Idle" class (wait_class = 6).
  -- Wait classifications are those found in the V$EVENT_NAME view.

  -- Get CPU usage from the STATS$SYSSTAT table.
  -- Select snapshots between start_snap_id and end_snap_id.
  -- Convert CPU centiseconds into seconds.

  (SELECT   snap_id,
            CASE
                WHEN wait_class# IN (0, 2, 3, 7, 10, 11, 12)
                THEN 0
                ELSE wait_class#
            END AS wait_class#,
            time_waited_micro / 1000000 AS time_spent
```

```
   FROM    stats$system_event NATURAL JOIN v$event_name
   WHERE   snap_id between &&start_snap_id and &&end_snap_id
   AND     wait_class# != 6

           UNION ALL

   SELECT  snap_id,
           100 as wait_class#,
           VALUE / 100 as time_spent
   FROM    stats$sysstat
   WHERE   snap_id between &&start_snap_id and &&end_snap_id
   AND     name = 'CPU used by this session'),
```

----

pivoted_data AS

-- Create separate columns for each wait class and for CPU time.

```
(SELECT   *
   FROM    (SELECT * from timed_events)
           PIVOT (SUM(time_spent)
             FOR wait_class# IN ( 0 AS other,
                                  1 AS application,
                                  4 AS concurrency,
                                  5 AS commit,
                                  8 AS user_io,
                                  9 AS system_io,
                                100 AS cpu))),
```

----

deltas AS

-- Use the LAG analytic function to determine the amount of increase.
-- Partition the rows by database startup time.
-- The STATS$SNAPSHOT view tells us when the database was started.

```
(SELECT   snap_id,

          snap_time,

          (snap_time - LAG(snap_time)
            OVER (PARTITION BY startup_time ORDER BY snap_id)) * 86400
            AS snap_time_d,

          cpu - LAG (cpu)
            OVER (PARTITION BY startup_time ORDER BY snap_id)
            AS cpu_d,
```

```
            other - LAG (other)
              OVER (PARTITION BY startup_time ORDER BY snap_id)
              AS other_d,

            application - LAG (application)
              OVER (PARTITION BY startup_time ORDER BY snap_id)
              AS application_d,

            concurrency - LAG (concurrency)
              OVER (PARTITION BY startup_time ORDER BY snap_id)
              AS concurrency_d,

            commit - LAG (commit)
              OVER (PARTITION BY startup_time ORDER BY snap_id)
              AS commit_d,

            user_io - LAG (user_io)
              OVER (PARTITION BY startup_time ORDER BY snap_id)
              AS user_io_d,

            system_io - LAG (system_io)
              OVER (PARTITION BY startup_time ORDER BY snap_id)
              AS system_io_d

    FROM    pivoted_data NATURAL JOIN stats$snapshot)

-------------------------------------------------------------------------------

-- Compute and print Average Active Sessions for each category of time.

    SELECT  snap_id,
            snap_time,
            cpu_d / snap_time_d AS aas_cpu,
            other_d / snap_time_d AS aas_other,
            application_d / snap_time_d AS aas_application,
            concurrency_d / snap_time_d AS aas_concurrency,
            commit_d / snap_time_d AS aas_commit,
            user_io_d / snap_time_d AS aas_user_io,
            system_io_d / snap_time_d AS aas_system_io

    FROM    deltas

ORDER BY    snap_id;
```

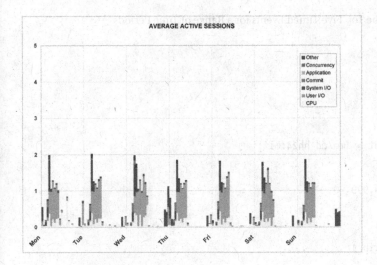

Figure 16-1. *A good week for the database*

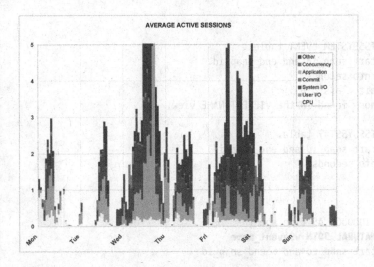

Figure 16-2. *A bad week for the database*

It is also useful to see at a glance the top five timed events for a range of time periods. The query shown in Listing 16-6 lets you do exactly that. You can download the text of this query and the AWR analog from the Google group for this book (https://groups.google.com/forum/#!forum/beginning-oracle-database-12c-administration). Listing 16-7 shows some sample output; it is for the first six periods in the graph shown in Figure 16-1.

Listing 16-6. SQL Query to Display the Top Five Timed Events for a Range of Time Periods

```
set linesize 132
set pagesize 10000
set tab off
set trimout on
set trimspool on
set sqlblanklines on

alter session set nls_date_format = 'mm/dd hh24:mi';

column event format a30
column time_spent_d format 9,999,999.90
column aas format 9999.90
column percentage format 999.90

break on snap_id on snap_time skip 1

WITH

  timed_events AS

  -- Get wait time from the STATS$SYSTEM_EVENT table.
  -- Select snapshots between start_snap_id and end_snap_id.
  -- Convert wait microseconds into seconds.
  -- Ignore the "Idle" class (wait_class = 6).
  -- Wait classifications are those found in the V$EVENT_NAME view.

  -- Get CPU usage from the STATS$SYSSTAT table.
  -- Select snapshots between start_snap_id and end_snap_id.
  -- Convert CPU centiseconds into seconds.

  (SELECT    snap_id,
            event,
            time_waited_micro / 1000000 AS time_spent
     FROM    stats$system_event NATURAL JOIN v$event_name
    WHERE    snap_id between &&start_snap_id and &&end_snap_id
      AND    wait_class# != 6

            UNION ALL

   SELECT    snap_id,
            'CPU used by this session' AS event,
            VALUE / 100 as time_spent
     FROM    stats$sysstat
    WHERE    snap_id between &&start_snap_id and &&end_snap_id
      AND    name = 'CPU used by this session'),
```

----

deltas AS

```
-- Use the LAG analytic function to determine the amount of increase.
-- Partition the rows by database startup time.
-- The STATS$SNAPSHOT view tells us when the database was started.

(SELECT    snap_id,
           snap_time,
           event,
           (snap_time - LAG (snap_time)
             OVER (PARTITION BY startup_time, event ORDER BY snap_id)) * 86400
             AS snap_time_d,
           time_spent - LAG (time_spent)
             OVER (PARTITION BY startup_time, event ORDER BY snap_id)
             AS time_spent_d
   FROM    timed_events NATURAL JOIN stats$snapshot),
```

----

ranks AS

```
-- Use the RANK analytic function to rank the events.
-- Also compute the percentage contribution of each event.

(SELECT    snap_id,
           snap_time,
           event,
           snap_time_d,
           time_spent_d,
           RANK()
             OVER (PARTITION BY snap_id ORDER BY time_spent_d DESC)
             AS rank,
           decode(time_spent_d, 0, 0, time_spent_d / SUM(time_spent_d)
             OVER (PARTITION BY snap_id) * 100)
             AS percentage
   FROM    deltas
  WHERE    time_spent_d IS NOT NULL)
```

```
-- Compute Average Active Sessions for each category of time.
-- List the top 5 events.

  SELECT   snap_id,
           snap_time,
           rank,
           substr(event, 1, 30) as event,
           time_spent_d,
```

```
          time_spent_d / snap_time_d as aas,
          percentage
   FROM   ranks
  WHERE   rank <= 5
ORDER BY  snap_id,
          rank;
```

Listing 16-7. Sample Report Showing the Top Five Timed Events for a Range of Time Periods

SNAP	SNAP_TIME	RANK	EVENT	TIME_SPENT_D	AAS	PERCENT
2201	01/07 01:00	1	CPU used by this session	127.05	.04	47.32
		2	RMAN backup & recovery I/O	74.75	.02	27.84
		3	control file parallel write	17.59	.00	6.55
		4	db file sequential read	16.89	.00	6.29
		5	control file sequential read	10.56	.00	3.93
2211	01/07 02:00	1	log file sync	269.49	.07	36.58
		2	log file parallel write	266.31	.07	36.15
		3	CPU used by this session	151.23	.04	20.53
		4	db file sequential read	31.48	.01	4.27
		5	control file parallel write	15.52	.00	2.11
2221	01/07 03:00	1	log file parallel write	867.97	.24	31.45
		2	CPU used by this session	653.38	.18	23.67
		3	log file sync	608.85	.17	22.06
		4	db file scattered read	273.92	.08	9.93
		5	log buffer space	121.16	.03	4.39
2231	01/07 04:00	1	log file parallel write	2,169.10	.60	30.36
		2	CPU used by this session	1,362.13	.38	19.06
		3	db file scattered read	1,308.39	.36	18.31
		4	db file sequential read	871.71	.24	12.20
		5	log file sequential read	606.94	.17	8.49
2241	01/07 05:00	1	db file scattered read	3,154.11	.88	82.63
		2	db file sequential read	264.16	.07	6.92
		3	CPU used by this session	102.78	.03	2.69
		4	log file parallel write	101.61	.03	2.66
		5	control file parallel write	84.06	.02	2.20
2251	01/07 06:00	1	db file scattered read	3,327.81	.92	71.27
		2	CPU used by this session	827.02	.23	17.71
		3	db file sequential read	261.75	.07	5.61
		4	read by other session	122.51	.03	2.62
		5	control file parallel write	58.31	.02	1.25

Using the Statspack Report

A Statspack report is generated from two *snapshots* of the database. These snapshots are a copy of the contents of the various dynamic performance tables that are continuously accumulating information about activity in the database. AWR and ADDM were offered as replacements for Statspack beginning with Oracle Database 10g and are no longer documented in the Oracle manuals. However, you can use AWR and ADDM only with Enterprise Edition and only if you have a license for Diagnostics Pack—an extra-cost option available only with Enterprise Edition. In my experience, very few organizations have the requisite licenses. I therefore emphasize the use of Statspack and use it a lot in my own work. Note that Oracle did make several incremental enhancements to Statspack in Oracle Database 10g and 11g, thus further increasing its usefulness and relevance. However, you will have to refer to Chapter 21 of *Oracle Database 9i Performance Tuning Guide and Reference* for documentation on Statspack because it is not documented in the Oracle Database 10g and 11g manuals. A useful introduction to Statspack as well as installation instructions can be found in spdoc.txt in the ORACLE_HOME\rdbms\admin folder.

The Statspack report contains a wealth of other information that can help you diagnose and solve your performance problem. In Listing 16-2, you saw the first page of a sample Statspack report, of which the most interesting section was the Top 5 Timed Events section. Here is a list of other interesting sections of the Statspack report:

- SQL Ordered by CPU lists the SQL queries that consume the most CPU.

- SQL Ordered by Elapsed Time lists the SQL queries that take the longest.

- SQL Ordered by Gets lists the SQL queries that perform the most logical reads.

- SQL Ordered by Reads lists the SQL queries that perform the most physical reads.

- Instance Activity Stats lists workload data from the V$SYSSTAT dynamic performance view.

- File Read Histogram Stats lists workload and performance metrics for each file in the database.

- Segments by Logical Reads and Segments by Physical Reads show which tables and indexes have the most logical reads and physical reads. They are only available in level-7 snapshots. Refer to Chapter 21 of *Oracle Database 9i Performance Tuning Guide and Reference* for information on the different snapshot levels and how to change them.

Summary

Here is a short summary of the concepts touched on in this chapter:

- When a performance problem is reported, the database might not be the cause. A systematic method should be used to identify the root cause.

- The five steps for addressing any performance problem are define, investigate, analyze, solve, and implement.

- The best way to analyze database performance is to find out where the database is spending its time. This is summarized by the Top 5 Timed Events section of the Statspack report.

- Statspack gets its data from the Oracle wait interface—the collection of dynamic performance views that track all aspects of database activity. Important views include V$SYSSTAT, V$SESSTAT, V$SESSION_EVENT, and V$SYSTEM_EVENT.

- The Statspack repository can be mined for historical data that can be graphed using tools such as Microsoft Excel. This is a good way to monitor trends and changes in the database workload and database performance. You can also track performance of individual queries over time. It is also useful to see at a glance the top five timed events for a range of time periods.

- A stable database exhibits distinct repeating patterns; for example, the workload may peak during the day and subside at night. These patterns are the signature of the database. Deviations from established patterns can be a sign that something is wrong with the database; the Statspack reports for the affected periods can be analyzed and compared with the reports for baseline periods.

- The Statspack report contains a wealth of information that can help you diagnose and solve a performance problem. Examples include SQL Ordered by CPU, SQL Ordered by Elapsed Time, SQL Ordered by Gets, SQL Ordered by Reads, Instance Activity Stats, File Read Histogram Stats, Segments by Logical Reads, and Segments by Physical Reads.

Exercises

1. In this exercise, you will duplicate the locking problem described in this chapter. You will need to use the HR sample schema as well as Statspack. If you have not already installed Statspack in your test database, run the scripts spcreate.sql and spauto.sql in the $ORACLE_HOME/rdbms/admin folder. The instructions are in spdoc.txt in the same folder.

    a. Query the DBA_CONSTRAINTS and DBA_CONS_COLUMNS views, and confirm that the manager_id column of the employees table in the HR schema is a *foreign key* that links to the employee_id column of the same table. Use the following commands:

    ```
    SELECT constraint_name
      FROM dba_constraints
     WHERE owner = 'HR'
       AND table_name = 'EMPLOYEES'
       AND constraint_type = 'P';

    SELECT constraint_name,
           owner,
           table_name
      FROM dba_constraints
     WHERE constraint_type = 'R'
       AND r_owner = 'HR'
       AND r_constraint_name = 'EMP_EMP_ID_PK';
    ```

```
SELECT column_name,
       position
  FROM dba_cons_columns
 WHERE owner = 'HR'
   AND constraint_name = 'EMP_EMP_ID_PK';

SELECT column_name,
       position
  FROM dba_cons_columns
 WHERE owner = 'HR'
   AND constraint_name = 'EMP_MANAGER_FK';
```

b. Drop the emp_manager_ix index on the manager_id column of the employees table. Use the command drop index hr.emp_manager_ix.

c. Find the name of each employee's manager. Use the following command:

```
SELECT e2.first_name AS manager_first_name,
       e2.last_name AS manager_last_name,
       e1.first_name AS employee_first_name,
       e1.last_name AS employee_last_name
  FROM hr.employees e1,
       hr.employees e2
 WHERE e2.employee_id = e1.manager_id
ORDER BY 1, 2, 3, 4;
```

d. Connect to the database as the HR user, and update one of the records in the employees table. For example, issue the command update employees set phone_number=phone_number where first_name='Alexander' and last_name='Hunold'. Do not commit this transaction.

e. Connect to the database again and attempt to delete the manager of the employee whose record you just updated. For example, issue the command delete from employees where first_name='Lex' and last_name='De Haan'. Oracle will block this command.

f. Connect to the database as the system user. Query the v$session_wait table, and find the session ID of the blocked session. Because you know it is waiting for an enq: TM - contention event to complete, you can use the command select sid as session_id, wait_time_micro from v$session_wait where event = 'enq: TM - contention'.

g. Query the V$SESSION view, and obtain the *serial number* of the blocked process. Use the command select serial# as serial_num from v$session where sid=&session_id.

h. Begin tracing the blocked session by using the DBMS_MONITOR.SESSION_ TRACE_ENABLE session. Issue the command execute dbms_monitor. session_trace:enable(&session_id, &serial_num, TRUE). Refer to *Oracle Database 11g PL/SQL Packages and Types Reference* for a description of the session_trace:enable procedure.

i. Generate a Statspack snapshot by using the statspack.snap procedure. Using a special version of the procedure, capture performance information for the blocked session in addition to system-wide information; issue the command execute statspack.snap(i_session_id => &session_id).

j.   Resume the first session, and issue the `rollback` command. This will release the blocked session, and Oracle will display the error `ORA-02292: integrity constraint (HR.EMP_MANAGER_FK) violated - child record found`.

k.   Identify the trace file for the second session by using the command `select tracefile from v$process where addr = (select paddr from v$session where sid = &session_id)`. Review the trace file, and locate the lines similar to the following line:

```
WAIT #4: nam='enq: TM - contention' ela= 855599225
name|mode=1414332421 object #=71472
table/partition=0 obj#=-1 tim=198871373294
```

l.   Confirm that the object number listed in the trace file corresponds to the employees table. Use the command `select owner, object_type, object_name from dba_objects where object_id=&object_id`.

m.   Perform the experiment once more, and confirm that additional wait messages appear in the trace file.

n.   Navigate to the folder where the trace file is located, and invoke the `tkprof` utility from the command line. You have to specify the name of the trace file and choose a name for the output file. Review the output file created by `tkprof`.

o.   Generate another Statspack snapshot by using the `statspack.snap` procedure with the same parameter used in step 9. Use the command `execute statspack.snap(i_session_id => &session_id)`.

p.   Connect to the database as the `system` or `perfstat` user, and generate a Statspack report from the snapshots obtained in step i and step o. Run the `spreport.sql` script by using the command `@?/rdbms/admin/spreport.sql`.

q.   Review the Statspack report. In particular, review the Top 5 Timed Events section. Also pay attention to the sections of the report that provide information on the blocked session you were tracking.

r.   Connect to the database as the `HR` user, and re-create the index you dropped at the start at the exercise. Use the command `create index hr.emp_manager_ix on hr.employees (manager_id)`.

2.   Download the Swingbench tool, and run the Order Entry benchmark for an hour. Review the AWR, ADDM, and Statspack reports for the run. Tune the database, and attempt to improve performance.

Further Reading

- The free *Oracle Database 12c Performance Tuning Guide* offers a detailed and comprehensive treatment of performance-tuning methods, and the price is right.

- Chapter 21 of *Oracle Database 9i Performance Tuning Guide and Reference* explains how to install and use Statspack. Note that Statspack is not documented in the reference guides for Oracle Database 10g, 11g, and 12c, even though it has been upgraded for all these versions. Refer to the upgrade notes in `$ORACLE_HOME/rdbms/admin/spdoc.txt` in your virtual machine.

CHAPTER 17

■■■

SQL Tuning

Every limbo boy and girl

All around the limbo world

Gonna do the limbo rock

All around the limbo clock

"Limbo Rock," recorded by Chubby Checker in 1962

Perhaps the most complex problem in database administration is SQL tuning, and it may not be a coincidence that I left it for the very end. The paucity of books devoted to SQL tuning is perhaps further evidence of the difficulty of the topic.

The only way to interact with Oracle, to retrieve data, to change data, and to administer the database is SQL. Oracle itself uses SQL to perform all the work that it does behind the scenes. SQL performance is therefore the key to database performance; all database performance problems are really SQL performance problems, even if they express themselves as contention for resources.

This chapter presents some of the causes of inefficient SQL and some common techniques of making SQL more efficient, but you spend most of your time working through a case study. I present a fairly typical SQL statement and show you how to improve it in stages until it hits the theoretical maximum level of performance that is possible to achieve.

Defining Efficiency

The *efficiency* of an SQL statement is measured by the amount of computing resources such as CPU cycles used in producing the output. Reducing the consumption of resources is the goal of SQL tuning. Elapsed time is not a good measure of the efficiency of an SQL statement because it is not always proportional to the amount of resources consumed. For example, contention for CPU cycles and disk I/O causes execution delays. The number of logical read operations is a better way to measure the consumption of computing resources because it is directly proportional to the amount of resources consumed—the fewer the logical read operations, the less CPU consumption.

Identifying Inefficient SQL Statements

When an application is performing poorly or a batch job takes a long time, you have to identify SQL statements that are consuming a lot of resources and are candidates for tuning. The simplest way to do this is to watch the operation of the database by using a GUI tool such as Enterprise Manager or SQL Developer. In Figure 17-1, you can see a query being run by SYSTEM.

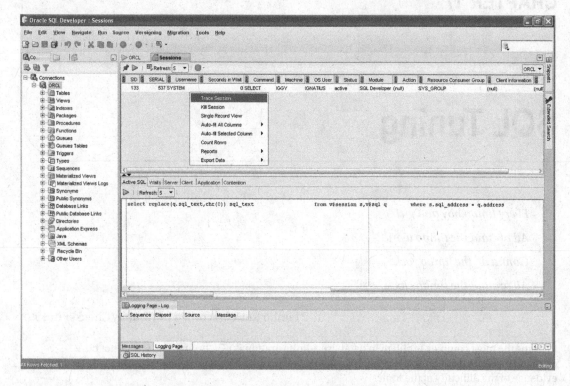

Figure 17-1. *Using SQL Developer to monitor sessions*

A systematic way of identifying tuning candidates in a batch job is to *trace* the job. If you ask Oracle to trace a job, it records SQL statements and execution details in a *trace file*. The simplest way to start tracing a session is to use Enterprise Manager or SQL Developer as in Figure 17-1. You can also use the SET_SQL_TRACE_IN_SESSION command as in the following example:

```
EXECUTE dbms_system.set_sql_trace:in_session(133, 537, true);
```

You can then use the tkprof tool to summarize the information in a more readable form, as in Listing 17-1. You can see that a particular statement was executed 163 times—execution statistics are also displayed. In this case, the number of logical reads—the number of buffers gotten for consistent read—is zero because the information is coming from dynamic performance tables, not from actual database tables.

Listing 17-1. Using tkprof to Summarize a Trace File

```
C:\app\IGNATIUS\diag\rdbms\orcl\orcl\trace>tkprof orcl_ora_6744.trc
output = orcl_ora_6744.tkprof

TKPROF: Release 11.1.0.6.0 - Production on Sun Sep 28 21:59:38 2008

Copyright (c) 1982, 2007, Oracle.  All rights reserved.

C:\app\IGNATIUS\diag\rdbms\orcl\orcl\trace>type orcl_ora_6744.tkprof
```

```
Trace file: orcl_ora_6744.trc
Sort options: default

********************************************************************************
count    = number of times OCI procedure was executed
cpu      = cpu time in seconds executing
elapsed  = elapsed time in seconds executing
disk     = number of physical reads of buffers from disk
query    = number of buffers gotten for consistent read
current  = number of buffers gotten in current mode (usually for update)
rows     = number of rows processed by the fetch or execute call
********************************************************************************

select replace(q.sql_text,chr(0)) sql_text
from v$session s,v$sql q
where s.sql_address = q.address
and s.sql_hash_value = q.hash_value
and s.sid = :SID

call     count       cpu    elapsed       disk      query    current       rows
-------  ------  --------  ---------  ---------  ---------  ---------  ---------
Parse        61      0.00       0.00          0          0          0          0
Execute      61      0.00       0.03          0          0          0          0
Fetch        61      0.00       0.02          0          0          0        305
-------  ------  --------  ---------  ---------  ---------  ---------  ---------
total       183      0.00       0.06          0          0          0        305

Misses in library cache during parse: 1
Misses in library cache during execute: 1
Optimizer mode: ALL_ROWS
Parsing user id: 5

Rows     Row Source Operation
-------  ---------------------------------------------------
      5  NESTED LOOPS  (cr=0 pr=0 pw=0 time=11 us cost=0 size=640 card=1)
      1   MERGE JOIN CARTESIAN (cr=0 pr=0 pw=0 time=0 us cost=0 size=108 card=1)
      1    NESTED LOOPS  (cr=0 pr=0 pw=0 time=0 us cost=0 size=39 card=1)
      1     FIXED TABLE FIXED INDEX X$KSLWT (ind:1) (cr=0 pr=0 pw=0 time=0 us cost=0
           size=26 card=1)
      1     FIXED TABLE FIXED INDEX X$KSLED (ind:2) (cr=0 pr=0 pw=0 time=0 us cost=0
           size=13 card=1)
      1    BUFFER SORT (cr=0 pr=0 pw=0 time=0 us cost=0 size=69 card=1)
      1     FIXED TABLE FIXED INDEX X$KSUSE (ind:1) (cr=0 pr=0 pw=0 time=0 us cost=0
           size=69 card=1)
      5   FIXED TABLE FIXED INDEX X$KGLCURSOR_CHILD (ind:1) (cr=0 pr=0 pw=0 time=6
          us cost=0 size=532 card=1)
********************************************************************************
```

Another way to identify tuning candidates is to examine a Statspack or Automatic Workload Repository (AWR) report. They were discussed in Chapter 16.

Understanding the Causes of Inefficient SQL

You may not even realize that you are dealing with inefficient SQL because powerful hardware can compensate for much inefficiency. In fact, one simple method of "improving" performance is simply to throw powerful hardware at the problem.[1] In other cases, a statement may take so little time to execute that you may not realize it is inefficient. There are many different causes for poor performance of SQL statements, and there are many solutions; a short discussion cannot do them justice.

Also keep in mind that, given enough time, effort, and money, it is always possible to extract more performance from an SQL statement. The example used in this chapter perfectly illustrates the point; you keep improving its performance until you hit the theoretical maximum level of performance. However, it is not usually possible to give so much time and attention to individual statements. The amount of effort you are willing to expend is usually governed by business requirements and the return on your investment.

The most frequently cited cause of inefficient SQL is the failure of the query optimizer to generate an efficient query-execution plan, but there are many others. Here are some examples:

- There are usually many ways to write the same query, and not all of them are equally efficient. Failure to use advanced features of the language is a common cause of inefficient SQL.

- Poor application-development practices may increase the amount of inefficient SQL. For example, giving users the ability to generate new types of queries (a.k.a. *ad hoc queries*) is usually a perfect recipe for poor performance. Another example of poor application-development practices is insufficient testing.

- Logical and physical database design can play a big role in SQL performance. Examples are inadequate indexing and partitioning of data, and insufficient attention to disk layouts.

- Inadequate database maintenance can cause SQL performance to degrade as time passes. A perfect example is the absence of an archiving strategy to keep the amount of data under control.

It bears repeating that hardware limitations—including CPU speed, memory size, and disk speed—play a big role in performance. If the system does not have enough memory, data may have to be frequently retrieved from disk. The workload handled by the database server also plays a major role in performance; your SQL statement will run slowly if it has to compete for resources with SQL statements submitted by other users. Often this is the result of poor coordination of workloads. For example, it is poor practice to perform batch processing during the day when most OLTP work is performed. Sometimes this is the result of poor capacity planning. For example, an online store may not have properly planned for the increase in transaction volumes during popular holidays.

---

[1] In *Oracle on VMware*, Dr. Bert Scalzo makes a persuasive case for "solving" problems with hardware upgrades: "*Person hours cost so much more now than computer hardware even with inexpensive offshore outsourcing. It is now considered a sound business decision these days to throw cheap hardware at problems*".

Ways to Improve SQL

Given enough time, effort, and money, it is usually possible to extract more performance from any SQL statement. However, it is not usually possible to give so much time and attention to individual statements. The amount of effort you are willing to expend is usually governed by business requirements and the return on your investment. The goal is usually to bring performance of poorly performing SQL statements to a level that is acceptable to the users of the database. The following sections describe some techniques that can be used to improve performance.

Indexes

A common reason for inefficient processing of SQL statements is the lack of appropriate indexes and other paths to reach the required data. Imagine how difficult it would be to find an item of information in a book if those items were not organized into appropriate chapters and there was no index of key words at the back of the book. Chapter 7 discussed indexes.

Most tables have a primary key and therefore have at least one index—that is, the index on the items composing the primary key. This index is used to ensure that no two records contain the same values of these data items. The absence of such an index would make it harder to ensure this. Indexes should also be created for any *foreign keys* in a table—that is, data items that link the table to another table—unless the table in question is small enough that the lack of such indexes will not have an impact on performance. Indexes should also be created for data items that are restricted in SQL queries.

The dba_indexes and dba_ind_columns views show what indexes have been created, as in the following example from the tuning exercise in this chapter:

```
SQL> SELECT table_name,
  2            index_name
  3      FROM user_indexes
  4      WHERE table_name in ('MY_TABLES', 'MY_INDEXES');
```

TABLE_NAME	INDEX_NAME
MY_INDEXES	MY_INDEXES_FK1
MY_INDEXES	MY_INDEXES_I1
MY_INDEXES	MY_INDEXES_PK
MY_TABLES	MY_TABLES_PK

```
SQL> SELECT table_name,
  2            index_name,
  3            column_name,
  4            column_position
  5      FROM user_ind_columns
  6      WHERE table_name in ('MY_TABLES', 'MY_INDEXES');
```

TABLE_NAME	INDEX_NAME	COLUMN_NAME	COLUMN_POSITION
MY_INDEXES	MY_INDEXES_PK	OWNER	1
MY_INDEXES	MY_INDEXES_PK	INDEX_NAME	2
MY_INDEXES	MY_INDEXES_I1	INDEX_TYPE	1
MY_INDEXES	MY_INDEXES_FK1	TABLE_OWNER	1

MY_INDEXES	MY_INDEXES_FK1	TABLE_NAME	2
MY_TABLES	MY_TABLES_PK	OWNER	1
MY_TABLES	MY_TABLES_PK	TABLE_NAME	2

Database designers have several kinds of indexes at their disposal. The most common are listed here:

- Most indexes are of the *b*tree* (balanced tree) type and are best suited for online transaction-processing environments. Index entries are stored in a structure that has a root node, branches, and leaves; hence the name.

- *Reverse key indexes* are a specialized type of b*tree index in which the key values are reversed (for example, *IGGY* becomes *YGGI*) to prevent concentrations of similar entries in index blocks and consequent contention for blocks.

- *Function-based indexes* and indexes on *virtual columns* (columns defined in terms of other columns) are indexes not on the data values contained in columns but on combinations of these values. For example, an index on UPPER(name) is an example of a function-based index.

- *Bitmap indexes* are a specialized kind of index used in data warehouses for columns that contain only a few values—for example, model, year, and color. Each value is represented by a *bitmap* (an array of 0s and 1s), and each element of the bitmap represents one record in the table.

In addition to indexes, database designers have other data structures at their disposal. Examples include clusters, index-organized tables, and partitioned tables.

■ **Tip**   Oracle does not use an index unless the query optimizer perceives a benefit in doing so. You can verify that an index is being used by issuing the MONITORING USAGE clause of the ALTER INDEX command and reviewing the contents of the v$object_usage view after a suitable time has passed. If Oracle is not using an index, you can use the techniques in the following sections to increase the chances that it will do so. If an index is never used, you should consider whether it can be removed safely, because indexes slow down insert, update, and delete operations and occupy valuable space within the database.

Hints

Hints for the optimizer can be embedded inside an SQL statement if the optimizer does not find an acceptable query plan for the statement. Each hint partially constrains the optimizer, and a full set of hints completely constrains the optimizer. In fact, a desirable query plan can be preserved by capturing the complete set of hints that describes it in a *stored outline*. For details, refer to *Oracle Database 12c Performance Tuning Guide*.

The most commonly used hints are in the following list. You can find detailed information on these and other hints in *Oracle Database 12c SQL Language Reference*:

- The LEADING hint instructs Oracle to process the specified tables first, in the order listed.

- The ORDERED hint instructs Oracle to process the tables in the order listed in the body of the SQL statement.

- The INDEX hint instructs Oracle to use the specified index when processing the specified table.

- The FULL hint instructs Oracle not to use indexes when processing the specified table.

- The NO_MERGE hint instructs Oracle to optimize and process an inline view separately from the rest of the query.

- The USE_NL, USE_HASH, and USE_MERGE hints are used in conjunction with the LEADING hint or the ORDERED hint to constrain the choice of join method (nested loops, hash, or sort-merge) for the specified table.

Here is an example of an SQL query that incorporates hints to guide and constrain the optimizer. Oracle is instructed to visit the my_indexes table before the my_tables table. Oracle is also instructed to use an index on the index_type data item in my_indexes and an index on the owner and table_name data items in my_tables, if such indexes are available. Note that hints must come directly after the SELECT keyword and must be enclosed between special markers—for example, /*+ INDEX(MY_INDEXES (INDEX_TYPE)) */:

```
SELECT          /*+ INDEX(MY_INDEXES (INDEX_TYPE))
                    INDEX(MY_TABLES (OWNER TABLE_NAME))
                    LEADING(MY_INDEXES MY_TABLES)
                    USE_NL(MY_TABLES)
                */
    DISTINCT my_tables.owner,
             my_tables.table_name,
             my_tables.tablespace:name
        FROM my_tables, my_indexes
       WHERE my_tables.owner = my_indexes.table_owner
         AND my_tables.table_name = my_indexes.table_name
         AND my_indexes.index_type = :index_type;
```

Statistics

Statistical information on tables and indexes and the data they contain is what the query optimizer needs to do its job properly. The simplest way to collect statistics is to use the procedures in the DBMS_STATS package. For example, DBMS_STATS.GATHER_TABLE_STATS can be used to collect statistics for a single table, and DBMS_STATS.GATHER_SCHEMA_STATS can be used to collect statistics for all the tables in a schema. You see some examples in the tuning exercise in this chapter.

However, the question of how and when to collect statistics does not have an easy answer, because changes in statistics can lead to changes in query-execution plans that are *not* always for the better. A perfect example of how fresh statistics can degrade performance occurs when statistics are collected on a table that contains very volatile data. The statistics describe the data that existed when the statistics were collected, but the data could change soon thereafter; the table could be empty when the statistics were collected but could be filled with data soon thereafter.

Here is what various Oracle experts have said on the subject. The quote that ties all the other quotes together is the last. You have to *understand* your data in order to create a strategy that works best for your situation:

> *It astonishes me how many shops prohibit any unapproved production changes and yet reanalyze schema stats weekly. Evidently, they do not understand that the purpose of schema reanalysis is to change their production SQL execution plans, and they act surprised when performance changes!*[2]

> *I have advised many customers to stop analyzing, thereby creating a more stable environment overnight.*[3]

> *Oh, and by the way, could you please stop gathering statistics constantly? I don't know much about databases, but I do think I know the following: small tables tend to stay small, large tables tend to stay large, unique indexes have a tendency to stay unique, and nonunique indexes often stay nonunique.*[4]

> *Monitor the changes in execution plans and/or performance for the individual SQL statements...and perhaps as a consequence regather stats. That way, you'd leave stuff alone that works very well, thank you, and you'd put your efforts into exactly the things that have become worse.*[5]

> *It is my firm belief that most scheduled statistics-gathering jobs do not cause much harm only because (most) changes in the statistics were insignificant as far as the optimizer is concerned—meaning that it was an exercise in futility.*[6]

> *There are some statistics about your data that can be left unchanged for a long time, possibly forever; there are some statistics that need to be changed periodically; and there are some statistics that need to be changed constantly.... The biggest problem is that you need to understand the data.*[7]

Beginning with Oracle 10g, statistics are automatically collected by a job that runs during a nightly maintenance window. This default strategy may work for many databases. You can use the procedures in the DBMS_STATS package to create a custom strategy. Complete details of the DBMS_STATS package can be found in *Oracle Database PL/SQL Packages and Types Reference*. Here is a representative list of the available procedures:

- The GATHER_*_STATS procedures can be used to manually gather statistics. For example, GATHER_TABLE_STATS gathers statistics for a single table, and GATHER_SCHEMA_STATS gathers statistics for all the indexes and tables in a schema.

- The DELETE_*_STATS procedures can be used to delete statistics.

---

[2]Don Burleson, "Optimizing Oracle Optimizer Statistics," Oracle FAQ's, March 1, 2004, www.orafaq.com/node/9.
[3]Mogens Norgaard in the *Journal of the Northern California Oracle Users Group*.
[4]Dave Ensor as remembered by Mogens Norgaard and quoted in the *Journal of the Northern California Oracle Users Group*.
[5]Mogens Norgaard in the *Journal of the Northern California Oracle Users Group*.
[6]Wolfgang Breitling in the *Journal of the Northern California Oracle Users Group*.
[7]Jonathan Lewis in the *Journal of Northern California Oracle Users Group*.

- The EXPORT_*_STATS procedures can be used to copy the statistics to a special table. IMPORT_*_STATS can be used to import desired statistics. For example, statistics can be exported from a production database and imported into a development database; this ensures that both databases use the same query-execution plans.

- The GATHER_STATS_JOB job retains previous statistics. The RESTORE_*_STATS procedures can be used to restore statistics from a previous point in time. The default retention period used by the GATHER_STATS_JOB is 31 days; you can change this by using the ALTER_STATS_HISTORY_RETENTION procedure.

- The LOCK_*_STATS procedures can be used to lock statistics and prevent them from being overwritten. Oddly enough, locking statistics can be a useful practice not only when data is static, but also when it is volatile.

- Possibly the most important procedures are the SET_*_PREFS procedures. They can be used to customize how the GATHER_STATS_JOB collects statistics. The available options are similar to those of the GATHER_*_STATS procedures.

■ **Caution**   One class of statistics that is not collected automatically is the system statistics. An example is sreadtim, the time taken to read one random block from disk. You can must collect system statistics manually by using the GATHER_SYSTEM_STATS procedure. For details, refer to *Oracle Database 12c PL/SQL Packages and Types Reference*.

Tuning by Example

Let's experience the process of tuning an SQL statement by creating two tables, my_tables and my_indexes, modeled after dba_tables and dba_indexes, two dictionary views. Every record in my_tables describes one table, and every record in my_indexes describes one index. The exercise is to print the details (owner, table_name, and tablespace:name) of tables that have at least one bitmap index.

Note that the SELECT ANY DICTIONARY, ALTER SYSTEM, ADVISOR, and CREATE CLUSTER privileges are needed for this exercise. Connect as SYSTEM, and grant them to the HR account. Also take a minute to extend the password expiry date of the HR account; if you neglect to do so, you will receive the message "ORA-28002: the password will expire within 7 days" when you connect to the HR account and will not be able to use the autotrace feature required for this exercise:

```
[oracle@localhost ~]$ sqlplus system/oracle@pdb1

SQL*Plus: Release 12.1.0.1.0 Production on Sun Feb 1 12:20:00 2015

Copyright (c) 1982, 2013, Oracle.  All rights reserved.

Last Successful login time: Sun Feb 01 2015 12:19:50 -05:00

Connected to:
Oracle Database 12c Enterprise Edition Release 12.1.0.1.0 - 64bit Production
With the Partitioning, OLAP, Advanced Analytics and Real Application Testing options
```

```
PDB1@ORCL> grant select any dictionary to hr;

Grant succeeded.

PDB1@ORCL> grant alter system to hr;

Grant succeeded.

PDB1@ORCL> alter user hr identified by oracle;

User altered.

PDB1@ORCL> grant advisor to hr;

Grant succeeded.

PDB1@ORCL> grant create cluster to hr;

Grant succeeded.

PDB1@ORCL> exit
Disconnected from Oracle Database 12c Enterprise Edition Release 12.1.0.1.0 - 64bit
Production
With the Partitioning, OLAP, Advanced Analytics and Real Application Testing options
```

You also need to create a role called plustrace in order to trace SQL statements in SQL*Plus. Log in to the SYS account, and execute the plustrace.sql script in the sqlplus/admin folder in ORACLE_HOME. Then grant the newly created plustrace role to public:

```
[oracle@localhost ~]$ sqlplus sys/oracle@pdb1 as sysdba

SQL*Plus: Release 12.1.0.1.0 Production on Sun Feb 1 13:43:46 2015

Copyright (c) 1982, 2013, Oracle.  All rights reserved.

Connected to:
Oracle Database 12c Enterprise Edition Release 12.1.0.1.0 - 64bit Production
With the Partitioning, OLAP, Advanced Analytics and Real Application Testing options

PDB1@ORCL> @?/sqlplus/admin/plustrce
PDB1@ORCL>
PDB1@ORCL> drop role plustrace;
drop role plustrace
        *
ERROR at line 1:
ORA-01919: role 'PLUSTRACE' does not exist

PDB1@ORCL> create role plustrace;

Role created.
```

```
PDB1@ORCL>
PDB1@ORCL> grant select on v_$sesstat to plustrace;

Grant succeeded.

PDB1@ORCL> grant select on v_$statname to plustrace;

Grant succeeded.

PDB1@ORCL> grant select on v_$mystat to plustrace;

Grant succeeded.

PDB1@ORCL> grant plustrace to dba with admin option;

Grant succeeded.

PDB1@ORCL>
PDB1@ORCL> set echo off
PDB1@ORCL> grant plustrace to public;

Grant succeeded.

PDB1@ORCL> exit
Disconnected from Oracle Database 12c Enterprise Edition Release 12.1.0.1.0 - 64bit
Production
With the Partitioning, OLAP, Advanced Analytics and Real Application Testing options
```

Creating and Populating the Tables

Create and populate the two tables as follows. When I performed the experiment, 2,371 records were
inserted into my_tables, and 3,938 records were inserted into my_indexes:

```
PDB1@ORCL> CREATE TABLE my_tables AS
  2  SELECT dba_tables.* FROM dba_tables;

Table created.

PDB1@ORCL> CREATE TABLE my_indexes AS
  2  SELECT dba_indexes.*
  3  FROM dba_tables,
  4    dba_indexes
  5  WHERE dba_tables.owner      = dba_indexes.table_owner
  6  AND dba_tables.table_name = dba_indexes.table_name;

Table created.

PDB1@ORCL> /* Count the records in the my_tables table */
PDB1@ORCL> SELECT COUNT(*) FROM my_tables;
```

```
  COUNT(*)
----------
      2371

PDB1@ORCL> /* Count the records in the my_indexes table */
PDB1@ORCL> SELECT COUNT(*) FROM my_indexes;

  COUNT(*)
----------
      3938
```

Establishing a Baseline

Here is a simple SQL statement that prints the required information (owner, table_name, and tablespace:name) about tables that have an index of a specified type. You join my_tables and my_indexes, extract the required pieces of information from my_tables, and eliminate duplicates by using the DISTINCT operator:

```
SELECT DISTINCT my_tables.owner,
  my_tables.table_name,
  my_tables.tablespace:name
FROM my_tables,
  my_indexes
WHERE my_tables.owner      = my_indexes.table_owner
AND my_tables.table_name   = my_indexes.table_name
AND my_indexes.index_type = :index_type
```

Observe that you have not yet created appropriate indexes for my_tables and my_indexes, nor have you collected statistical information for use in constructing query-execution plans. However, you will soon see that Oracle can execute queries and join tables even in the absence of indexes and can even generate statistical information dynamically by sampling the data.

Some preliminaries are required before you execute the query. You must activate the autotrace feature and must ensure that detailed timing information is captured during the course of the query (statistics_level=ALL). The autotrace feature is used to print the most important items of information relating to efficiency of SQL queries. More-detailed information is captured by Oracle if statistics_level is appropriately configured:

```
PDB1@ORCL> ALTER SESSION SET statistics_level=ALL;

Session altered.

PDB1@ORCL> SET AUTOTRACE ON statistics
PDB1@ORCL> VARIABLE index_type VARCHAR2(32);
PDB1@ORCL> EXEC :index_type := 'FUNCTION-BASED NORMAL';

PL/SQL procedure successfully completed.

PDB1@ORCL> column owner format a30
PDB1@ORCL> column table_name format a30
PDB1@ORCL> column tablespace:name format a30
PDB1@ORCL> set linesize 100
```

```
PDB1@ORCL> set pagesize 100
PDB1@ORCL> SELECT DISTINCT my_tables.owner,
  2    my_tables.table_name,
  3    my_tables.tablespace:name
  4  FROM my_tables,
  5    my_indexes
  6  WHERE my_tables.owner       = my_indexes.table_owner
  7  AND my_tables.table_name = my_indexes.table_name
  8  AND my_indexes.index_type = :index_type;
s
```

OWNER	TABLE_NAME	TABLESPACE_NAME
SYS	WRI$_OPTSTAT_TAB_HISTORY	SYSAUX
SYS	XS$NSTMPL_ATTR	SYSTEM
XDB	X$PT6UFI5W7S9D1VDEOGP5LBKOKHIF	SYSAUX
WMSYS	WM$CONSTRAINTS_TABLE$	SYSAUX
SYS	SCHEDULER$_JOB	SYSTEM
WMSYS	WM$HINT_TABLE$	SYSAUX
APEX_040200	WWV_FLOW_LIST_OF_VALUES_DATA	SYSAUX
SYS	WRI$_OPTSTAT_HISTGRM_HISTORY	
SYS	WRI$_OPTSTAT_OPR	SYSAUX
SYS	WRI$_OPTSTAT_OPR_TASKS	SYSAUX
SYS	SCHEDULER$_WINDOW	SYSTEM
WMSYS	WM$VERSIONED_TABLES$	SYSAUX
APEX_040200	WWV_FLOW_WORKSHEET_RPTS	SYSAUX
APEX_040200	WWV_FLOW_COMPANY_SCHEMAS	SYSAUX
OBE	OEHR_CUSTOMERS	APEX_2264528630961551
APEX_040200	WWV_FLOW_MAIL_LOG	SYSAUX
SYS	XS$ACL_PARAM	SYSTEM
SYS	WRI$_OPTSTAT_HISTHEAD_HISTORY	
SYS	WRI$_OPTSTAT_IND_HISTORY	SYSAUX
SYS	WRI$_OPTSTAT_AUX_HISTORY	SYSAUX
SYS	DBFS$_MOUNTS	SYSTEM
APEX_040200	WWV_FLOW_REPORT_LAYOUTS	SYSAUX
APEX_040200	WWV_FLOW_WORKSHEETS	SYSAUX
APEX_040200	WWV_FLOW_WORKSHEET_CONDITIONS	SYSAUX

```
24 rows selected.

Statistics
----------------------------------------------------------
          4  recursive calls
        238  consistent gets
          0  physical reads
          0  db block gets
        124  redo size
       1768  bytes sent via SQL*Net to client
        554  bytes received via SQL*Net from client
          3  SQL*Net roundtrips to/from client
          0  sorts (memory)
          0  sorts (disk)
         24  rows processed
```

Twenty-four rows of data are printed. The name of the tablespace is not printed in the case of two tables; the explanation is left as an exercise for you. But the more interesting information is that relating to the efficiency of the query. This is printed because you activated the autotrace feature. Here is an explanation of the various items of information:

- *Recursive calls* are all the internal queries that are executed behind the scenes in addition to your query. When a query is submitted for execution, Oracle first checks its syntax. It then checks the semantics—that is, it de-references synonyms and views and identifies the underlying tables. It then computes the *signature* (a.k.a. *hash value*) of the query and checks its cache of query-execution plans for a reusable query plan that corresponds to that signature. If a query plan is not found, Oracle has to construct one; this results in *recursive calls*. The number of recursive calls required can be large if the information Oracle needs to construct the query plan is not available in the *dictionary cache* and has to be retrieved from the database or if there are no statistics about tables mentioned in the query and data blocks have to be sampled to generate statistics dynamically.

- *DB block gets* is the number of times Oracle needs the latest version of a data block. Oracle does not need the latest version of a data block when the data is simply being read by the user. Instead, Oracle needs the version of the data block that was current when the query started. The latest version of a data block is typically required when the intention is to modify the data. Note that db block gets is 0 in all the examples in this chapter.

- *Consistent gets*, a.k.a. *logical reads*, is the number of operations to retrieve a consistent version of a data block that were performed by Oracle while constructing query plans and while executing queries. Remember that all data blocks read during the execution of any query are the versions that were current when the query started; this is called *read consistency*. One of the principal objectives of query tuning is to reduce the number of consistent get operations that are required.

- *Physical reads* is the number of operations to read data blocks from the disks that were performed by Oracle because the blocks were not found in Oracle's cache when they were required. The limit on the number of physical reads is therefore the number of consistent gets.

- *Redo size* is the amount of information Oracle writes to the journals that track changes to the database. This metric applies only when the data is changed in some way.

- *Bytes sent via SQL*Net to client, bytes received via SQL*Net from client,* and *SQL*Net roundtrips to/from client* are fairly self-explanatory; they track the number and size of messages sent to and from Oracle and the user.

- *Sorts (memory)* and *sorts (disk)* track the number of sorting operations performed by Oracle during the course of your query. Sorting operations are performed in memory if possible; they spill onto the disks if the data does not fit into Oracle's memory buffers. It is desirable for sorting to be performed in memory because reading and writing data to and from the disks are expensive operations. The amount of memory available to database sessions for sorting operations is controlled by the value of PGA_AGGREGATE_TARGET.

- *Rows processed* is the number of rows of information required by the user.

The preceding explanations should make it clear that a lot of overhead is involved in executing a query—for example, physical reads are required if data blocks are not found in Oracle's cache. The amount of overhead during any execution varies depending on the contents of the *shared pool* (cache of query-execution plans) and *buffer cache* (cache of data blocks) at the time of execution. You can gauge the complete extent of overhead by flushing both the shared pool and buffer cache and then re-executing the query:

```
PDB1@ORCL> ALTER SYSTEM FLUSH SHARED_POOL;

System altered.

PDB1@ORCL> ALTER SYSTEM FLUSH BUFFER_CACHE;

System altered.
```

After the flush, 201 recursive calls, 344 consistent gets (including 237 physical reads), and 10 sort operations are required:

```
Statistics
----------------------------------------------------------
        190  recursive calls
          0  db block gets
        344  consistent gets
        237  physical reads
          0  redo size
       1768  bytes sent via SQL*Net to client
        554  bytes received via SQL*Net from client
          3  SQL*Net roundtrips to/from client
         10  sorts (memory)
          0  sorts (disk)
         24  rows processed
```

Let's now flush only the buffer cache and execute the query again to quantify the precise amount of overhead work involved in constructing a query-execution plan. Recursive calls and sorts fall from 1,653 to 0, and consistent gets fall from 498 to 108. The amount of overhead work dwarfs the actual work done by the query. The number of consistent gets is 108; it will not decrease if you repeat the query again. The baseline number that you will attempt to reduce in this tuning exercise is therefore 108. Notice that the number of physical reads is less than the number of consistent gets even though you flushed the buffer cache before executing the query. The reason is that the consistent gets metric counts a block as many times as it is accessed during the course of a query, whereas the physical reads metric counts a block only when it is brought into the buffer cache from the disks. A block might be accessed several times during the course of the query but might have to be brought into the buffer cache only once:

```
Statistics
----------------------------------------------------------
          1  recursive calls
          0  db block gets
        228  consistent gets
        222  physical reads
          0  redo size
       1768  bytes sent via SQL*Net to client
```

```
 554  bytes received via SQL*Net from client
   3  SQL*Net roundtrips to/from client
   0  sorts (memory)
   0  sorts (disk)
  24  rows processed
```

Executing the query yet one more time, we see that physical reads has fallen to zero because all data blocks are found in Oracle's cache:

```
Statistics
----------------------------------------------------------
   0  recursive calls
   0  db block gets
 228  consistent gets
   0  physical reads
   0  redo size
1768  bytes sent via SQL*Net to client
 554  bytes received via SQL*Net from client
   3  SQL*Net roundtrips to/from client
   0  sorts (memory)
   0  sorts (disk)
  24  rows processed
```

Table 17-1 summarizes the findings. The first time you executed the query, Oracle had to construct a query-execution plan but found most of the required dictionary information in its cache. The second time you executed the query, Oracle had to reread all the dictionary execution into cache—this explains the recursive calls and the physical reads—as well as all the data blocks required during the actual execution of the query. The third time you executed the query, Oracle did not have to construct an execution plan, but all the data bocks required during the execution of the query had to be obtained from disk. The fourth time you executed the query, all the required data blocks were found in Oracle's cache.

Table 17-1. Overhead Work Required to Construct a Query-Execution Plan

Metric	First Execution	Second Execution	Third Execution	Query Plan Overhead	Fourth Execution
Recursive calls	4	190	1	189	0
Consistent gets	238	344	228	116	228
Physical reads	0	237	222	15	0

The number of consistent gets will not go down if you repeat the query a fifth time; 228 is therefore the baseline number you will try to reduce in this tuning exercise.

Examining the Query Plan

It is now time to examine the query plan that Oracle has been using. A simple way to do so is to use the dbms_xplan.display_cursor procedure. The following query plan was displayed after I flushed the shared pool and the buffer cache earlier in the exercise.

```
PDB1@ORCL> SELECT * FROM TABLE(dbms_xplan.display_cursor(format=>'TYPICAL IOSTATS LAST'));

PLAN_TABLE_OUTPUT
--------------------------------------------------------------------------------------------------------
SQL_ID  2794xwzhab8yb, child number 0
--------------------------------------------------------------------------------------------------------
SELECT DISTINCT my_tables.owner,   my_tables.table_name,
my_tables.tablespace_name FROM my_tables,   my_indexes WHERE
my_tables.owner     = my_indexes.table_owner AND my_tables.table_name
= my_indexes.table_name AND my_indexes.index_type = :index_type

Plan hash value: 457052432

-----------------------------------------------------------------------------------------------------------------------
| Id | Operation          | Name       | Starts | E-Rows |E-Bytes| Cost (%CPU)| E-Time    | A-Rows |   A-Time    | Buffers | Reads |
-----------------------------------------------------------------------------------------------------------------------
|  0 | SELECT STATEMENT   |            |      1 |        |       |  69 (100)|           |     24 |00:00:00.01 |     228 |   222 |
|  1 |  HASH UNIQUE       |            |      1 |    985 | 66980 |  69   (0)| 00:00:01 |     24 |00:00:00.01 |     228 |   222 |
|* 2 |   HASH JOIN        |            |      1 |    985 | 66980 |  69   (0)| 00:00:01 |     29 |00:00:00.01 |     228 |   222 |
|* 3 |    TABLE ACCESS FULL| MY_INDEXES |      1 |    985 | 34475 |  42   (0)| 00:00:01 |     29 |00:00:00.01 |     139 |   136 |
|  4 |    TABLE ACCESS FULL| MY_TABLES  |      1 |   2371 | 78243 |  27   (0)| 00:00:01 |   2371 |00:00:00.01 |      89 |    86 |
-----------------------------------------------------------------------------------------------------------------------

Predicate Information (identified by operation id):
---------------------------------------------------

   2 - access("MY_TABLES"."OWNER"="MY_INDEXES"."TABLE_OWNER" AND "MY_TABLES"."TABLE_NAME"="MY_INDEXES"."TABLE_NAME")
   3 - filter("MY_INDEXES"."INDEX_TYPE"=:INDEX_TYPE)
```

The hash signature (SQL_ID) of the SQL statement is 2794xwzhab8yb, and that of the query execution plan is 457052432. You obtain different values when you try the exercise in your database. Oracle caches as many plans as possible for future reuse and knows how to translate a hash value into the precise place in memory where the SQL statement or plan is stored. Whenever an SQL statement is submitted for execution, Oracle computes its signature and searches for a statement with identical text and semantics in the cache. If a statement with identical text and semantics is found, its plan can be reused. If Oracle finds a statement with identical text but does not find one that also has identical semantics, it must create a new execution plan; this execution plan is called a *child cursor*. Multiple plans can exist for the same statement—this is indicated by the *child number*. For example, two users may each own a private copy of a table mentioned in an SQL statement, and therefore different query plans are needed for each user.

The execution plan itself is shown in tabular format and is followed by the list of filters (a.k.a. *predicates*) that apply to the rows of the table. Each row in the table represents one step of the query-execution plan. Here is the description of the columns:

- *Id* is the row number.

- *Operation* describes the step—for example, TABLE ACCESS FULL means all rows in the table are retrieved.

- *Name* is an optional piece of information; it is the name of the object to which the step applies.

- *Starts* is the number of times the step is executed.

- *E-Rows* is the number of rows that Oracle *expected* to obtain in the step.

- *E-Bytes* is the total number of bytes that Oracle *expected* to obtain in the step.

- *Cost* is the *cumulative* cost that Oracle *expected* to incur at the end of the step. The unit is best understood as the estimated time to read a single block from disk (sreadtim) recorded in the "system statistics." In other words, the cost is the number of data blocks that could be retrieved in the time that Oracle expects . The percentage of time for which Oracle expects to use the CPU is displayed along with the cost.

- *E-Time* is an estimate of the *cumulative* amount of time to complete this step and all prior steps. Hours, minutes, and seconds are displayed.

- *A-Rows* is the number of rows that Oracle *actually* obtained in the step.

- *A-Bytes* is the total number of bytes that Oracle *actually* obtained in the step.

- *Buffers* is the cumulative number of consistent get operations that were *actually* performed in the step and all prior steps.

- *Reads* is the *cumulative* number of physical read operations that were actually performed in the step and all prior steps.

A little skill is needed to interpret the execution plan. Notice the indentation of the operations listed in the second column. The correct sequence of operations is obtained by applying the following rule: *perform operations in the order in which they are listed, except that if the operations listed after a certain operation are more deeply indented in the listing, then perform those operations first (in the order in which those operations are listed).* On applying this rule, you see that the operations are performed in the following order:

Id	Operation	Name	Starts	E-Rows	E-Bytes	Cost (%CPU)	E-Time	A-Rows	A-Time	Buffers	Reads
* 3	TABLE ACCESS FULL	MY_INDEXES	1	985	34475	42 (0)	00:00:01	29	00:00:00.01	139	136
4	TABLE ACCESS FULL	MY_TABLES	1	2371	78243	27 (0)	00:00:01	2371	00:00:00.01	89	86
* 2	HASH JOIN		1	985	66980	69 (0)	00:00:01	29	00:00:00.01	228	222
1	HASH UNIQUE		1	985	66980	69 (0)	00:00:01	24	00:00:00.01	228	222
0	SELECT STATEMENT		1			69 (100)		24	00:00:00.01	228	222

First, all the rows of data in the my_indexes table are retrieved (TABLE ACCESS FULL), and a lookup table (a.k.a. *hash table*) is constructed from rows that satisfy the filter (a.k.a. *predicate*) my_indexes.index_type = :index_type. This means a signature (a.k.a. *hash value*) is calculated for each row of data satisfying the predicate. This signature is then translated into a position in the hash table where the row will be stored. This makes it tremendously easy to locate the row when it is required later. Because my_indexes and my_tables are related by the values of owner and table_name, a hash signature is constructed from these values.

Next, all the rows of data in the my_tables table are retrieved (TABLE ACCESS FULL). After retrieving each row of data from the my_tables table, rows of data from the my_indexes table satisfying the join predicate my_tables.owner = my_indexes.owner AND my_tables.table_name = my_indexes.table_name are retrieved from the lookup table constructed in the previous step (HASH JOIN); and if any such rows are found, the required data items (owner, table_name, and tablespace:name) are included in the query results. Duplicates are avoided (HASH UNIQUE) by storing the resulting rows of data in another hash table; new rows are added to the hash table only if a matching row is not found.

Of particular interest are the columns in the execution plan labeled E-Rows, E-Bytes, Cost, and E-Time. These are estimates generated by Oracle. Time and cost are straightforward computations based on rows and bytes, but how does Oracle estimate rows and bytes in the first place? The answer is that Oracle uses a combination of rules of thumb and any available statistical information available in the data dictionary; this statistical information is automatically refreshed every night by default. In the absence of statistical information, Oracle samples a certain number of data blocks from the table and estimates the number of qualifying rows in each block of the table and the average length of these rows; this is referred to as *dynamic sampling*.

Observe the values in the E-Rows and A-Rows columns in the execution plan. Oracle's estimate of the number of qualifying rows in my_tables is surprisingly accurate. The reason is that Oracle Database 12*c* automatically generates statistics during a CREATE TABLE AS SELECT (CTAS) operation. However, there are wide discrepancies between the E-Rows and A-Rows values in other lines of the execution plan.

Indexes and Statistics

Let's create an appropriate set of indexes on your tables. First you define primary key constraints on my_tables and my_indexes. Oracle automatically creates unique indexes because it needs an efficient method of enforcing the constraints. You also create a foreign-key constraint linking the two tables and create an index on the foreign key. Finally, you create an index on the values of index_type because your query restricts the value of index_type. You then refresh statistics on both tables:

```
ALTER TABLE my_tables
ADD (CONSTRAINT my_tables_pk PRIMARY KEY (owner, table_name));

ALTER TABLE my_indexes
ADD (CONSTRAINT my_indexes_pk PRIMARY KEY (owner, index_name));

ALTER TABLE my_indexes
ADD (CONSTRAINT my_indexes_fk1 FOREIGN KEY (table_owner, table_name)
REFERENCES my_tables);

CREATE INDEX my_indexes_i1 ON my_indexes (index_type);

CREATE INDEX my_indexes_fk1 ON my_indexes (table_owner, table_name);

EXEC DBMS_STATS.gather_table_stats(user,tabname=>'MY_TABLES');
EXEC DBMS_STATS.gather_table_stats(user,tabname=>'MY_INDEXES');
```

```
Plan hash value: 931433591
```

Id	Operation	Name	Starts	E-Rows	E-Bytes	Cost (%CPU)	E-Time	A-Rows	A-Time	Buffers
0	SELECT STATEMENT		1			31 (100)		24	00:00:00.04	109
1	HASH UNIQUE		1	29	1972	31 (0)	00:00:01	24	00:00:00.04	109
* 2	HASH JOIN		1	29	1972	31 (0)	00:00:01	29	00:00:00.04	109
3	TABLE ACCESS BY INDEX ROWID BATCHED	MY_INDEXES	1	29	1015	4 (0)	00:00:01	29	00:00:00.01	20
* 4	INDEX RANGE SCAN	MY_INDEXES_I1	1	29		1 (0)	00:00:01	29	00:00:00.01	2
5	TABLE ACCESS FULL	MY_TABLES	1	2371	78243	27 (0)	00:00:01	2371	00:00:00.01	89

```
Predicate Information (identified by operation id):
---------------------------------------------------

   2 - access("MY_TABLES"."OWNER"="MY_INDEXES"."TABLE_OWNER" AND "MY_TABLES"."TABLE_NAME"="MY_INDEXES"."TABLE_NAME")
   4 - access("MY_INDEXES"."INDEX_TYPE"=:INDEX_TYPE)
```

You find tremendous improvement in the accuracy of the estimates and a substantial improvement in the efficiency of the query plan after indexes are created and statistics are gathered. Oracle now correctly estimates that 29 rows will be retrieved from the my_indexes table. Oracle uses the index on the values of index_type to efficiently retrieve the 15 qualifying rows. This execution plan requires only 109 consistent gets.

Using SQL Access Advisor

If you are using Enterprise Edition and have a license for the Tuning Pack, you can use a feature called SQL Tuning Advisor to help you with SQL tuning. You've already created indexes and generated statistics; you can now look to SQL Tuning Advisor for fresh ideas. SQL Advisor finds a better plan that reduces the number of consistent gets to 80 and creates a *profile* that, if accepted, will increase the likelihood that the better plan is chosen. This profile consists of OPT_ESTIMATE hints, which are scaling factors that are used to adjust the calculations of the optimizer. The next section shows how explicit hints can be used to obtain this plan:

```
PDB1@ORCL> VARIABLE tuning_task VARCHAR2(32);
PDB1@ORCL> EXEC :tuning_task := dbms_sqltune.create_tuning_task (sql_id => '2794xwzhab8yb');

PL/SQL procedure successfully completed.

PDB1@ORCL> EXEC dbms_sqltune.execute_tuning_task(task_name => :tuning_task);

PL/SQL procedure successfully completed.

PDB1@ORCL> SET LONG 100000;
PDB1@ORCL> SET PAGESIZE 1000
PDB1@ORCL> SET LINESIZE 200
PDB1@ORCL> COLUMN recommendations FORMAT a200
PDB1@ORCL> SELECT DBMS_SQLTUNE.report_tuning_task (:tuning_task) AS recommendations FROM
DUAL;

RECOMMENDATIONS
--------------------------------------------------------------------------------
GENERAL INFORMATION SECTION
--------------------------------------------------------------------------------
Tuning Task Name    : TASK_11
Tuning Task Owner   : HR
Workload Type       : Single SQL Statement
Scope               : COMPREHENSIVE
Time Limit(seconds): 1800
Completion Status   : COMPLETED
Started at          : 04/12/2015 21:33:14
Completed at        : 04/12/2015 21:33:21


--------------------------------------------------------------------------------
Schema Name   : HR
Container Name: PDB1
SQL ID        : 2794xwzhab8yb
SQL Text      : SELECT DISTINCT my_tables.owner,
                  my_tables.table_name,
                  my_tables.tablespace:name
                FROM my_tables,
                  my_indexes
                WHERE my_tables.owner      = my_indexes.table_owner
                AND my_tables.table_name = my_indexes.table_name
                AND my_indexes.index_type = :index_type
Bind Variables: :
 1 -  (VARCHAR2(128)):FUNCTION-BASED NORMAL
```

```
-------------------------------------------------------------------------------
FINDINGS SECTION (1 finding)
-------------------------------------------------------------------------------

1- SQL Profile Finding (see explain plans section below)
-------------------------------------------------------
  A potentially better execution plan was found for this statement.

  Recommendation (estimated benefit: 28.5%)
  -----------------------------------------
  - Consider accepting the recommended SQL profile.
    execute dbms_sqltune.accept_sql_profile(task_name => 'TASK_11',
            task_owner => 'HR', replace => TRUE);

  Validation results
  ------------------
  The SQL profile was tested by executing both its plan and the original plan
  and measuring their respective execution statistics. A plan may have been
  only partially executed if the other could be run to completion in less time.

                          Original Plan  With SQL Profile  % Improved
                          -------------  ----------------  ----------
  Completion Status:         COMPLETE        COMPLETE
  Elapsed Time (s):          .033816         .002418        92.84 %
  CPU Time (s):              .0319           .0021          93.41 %
  User I/O Time (s):         0               0
  Buffer Gets:               109             80             26.6 %
  Physical Read Requests:    0               0
  Physical Write Requests:   0               0
  Physical Read Bytes:       0               0
  Physical Write Bytes:      0               0
  Rows Processed:            24              24
  Fetches:                   24              24
  Executions:                1               1

  Notes
  -----
  1. Statistics for the original plan were averaged over 10 executions.
  2. Statistics for the SQL profile plan were averaged over 10 executions.

-------------------------------------------------------------------------------
EXPLAIN PLANS SECTION
-------------------------------------------------------------------------------

2- Using SQL Profile
--------------------
Plan hash value: 3284819692
```

```
---------------------------------------------------------------------------
| Id  | Operation                       | Name          | Rows | Bytes | Cost |
---------------------------------------------------------------------------
|   0 | SELECT STATEMENT                |               |   29 |  1972 |   37 |
|   1 |  SORT UNIQUE                    |               |   29 |  1972 |   37 |
|   2 |   NESTED LOOPS                  |               |   29 |  1972 |   33 |
|   3 |    TABLE ACCESS BY INDEX ROWID| MY_INDEXES    |   29 |  1015 |    4 |
|*  4 |     INDEX RANGE SCAN            | MY_INDEXES_I1 |   29 |       |    1 |
|   5 |    TABLE ACCESS BY INDEX ROWID| MY_TABLES     |    1 |    33 |    1 |
|*  6 |     INDEX UNIQUE SCAN           | MY_TABLES_PK  |    1 |       |      |
---------------------------------------------------------------------------

Predicate Information (identified by operation id):
---------------------------------------------------

   4 - access("MY_INDEXES"."INDEX_TYPE"=:INDEX_TYPE)
   6 - access("MY_TABLES"."OWNER"="MY_INDEXES"."TABLE_OWNER" AND
            "MY_TABLES"."TABLE_NAME"="MY_INDEXES"."TABLE_NAME")

---------------------------------------------------------------------------
```

Optimizer Hints

Hints for the optimizer can be embedded in an SQL statement if the optimizer does not find an acceptable query plan for the statement. Each hint partially constrains the optimizer, and a full set of hints completely constrains the optimizer.[8] Let's instruct Oracle to use the my_indexes_fk1 index to efficiently associate qualifying records in the my_indexes table with matching records from the my_tables table:

```
SELECT /*+ INDEX(MY_INDEXES (INDEX_TYPE))
  INDEX(MY_TABLES (OWNER TABLE_NAME))
  LEADING(MY_INDEXES MY_TABLES)
  USE_NL(MY_TABLES)
  */
  DISTINCT my_tables.owner,
  my_tables.table_name,
  my_tables.tablespace:name
FROM my_tables,
  my_indexes
WHERE my_tables.owner      = my_indexes.table_owner
AND my_tables.table_name   = my_indexes.table_name
AND my_indexes.index_type = :index_type;
```

---

[8]The use of hints is a defense against *bind variable peeking*. To understand the problem, remember that a query-execution plan is constructed once and used many times. If the values of the bind variables in the first invocation of the query are not particularly representative of the data, the query plan that is generated will not be a good candidate for reuse. *Stored outlines* are another defense against bind variable peeking. It is also possible to turn off bind variable peeking for your session or for the entire database; this forces Oracle to generate a query plan that is not tailored to one set of bind variables. However, note that bind variable peeking does work well when the data has a uniform distribution.

The LEADING hint specifies the order in which tables are processed, the INDEX hint specifies that an index be used, and the USE_NL hint specifies that tables be joined using the simple *nested loop* method (instead of the *hash* method used in previous executions). The use of the my_indexes_fk1 index reduces the number of consistent gets to 37.

```
Plan hash value: 3667498330

----------------------------------------------------------------------------------------------------------------------------
| Id | Operation                           | Name           | Starts | E-Rows |E-Bytes| Cost (%CPU)| E-Time   | A-Rows |  A-Time     | Buffers |
----------------------------------------------------------------------------------------------------------------------------
|  0 | SELECT STATEMENT                    |                |      1 |        |       | 33 (100)|          |     24 |00:00:00.01 |      80 |
|  1 |  HASH UNIQUE                        |                |      1 |     29 |  1972 | 33   (0)| 00:00:01 |     24 |00:00:00.01 |      80 |
|  2 |   NESTED LOOPS                      |                |      1 |        |       |         |          |     29 |00:00:00.01 |      80 |
|  3 |    NESTED LOOPS                     |                |      1 |     29 |  1972 | 33   (0)| 00:00:01 |     29 |00:00:00.01 |      51 |
|  4 |     TABLE ACCESS BY INDEX ROWID BATCHED| MY_INDEXES  |      1 |     29 |  1015 |  4   (0)| 00:00:01 |     29 |00:00:00.01 |      20 |
|* 5 |      INDEX RANGE SCAN               | MY_INDEXES_I1  |      1 |     29 |       |  1   (0)| 00:00:01 |     29 |00:00:00.01 |       2 |
|* 6 |     INDEX UNIQUE SCAN               | MY_TABLES_PK   |     29 |      1 |       |  0   (0)|          |     29 |00:00:00.01 |      31 |
|  7 |    TABLE ACCESS BY INDEX ROWID      | MY_TABLES      |     29 |      1 |    33 |  1   (0)| 00:00:01 |     29 |00:00:00.01 |      29 |
----------------------------------------------------------------------------------------------------------------------------

Predicate Information (identified by operation id):
--------------------------------------------------------

   5 - access("MY_INDEXES"."INDEX_TYPE"=:INDEX_TYPE)
   6 - access("MY_TABLES"."OWNER"="MY_INDEXES"."TABLE_OWNER" AND "MY_TABLES"."TABLE_NAME"="MY_INDEXES"."TABLE_NAME")
```

Extreme Tuning

It does not appear possible to reduce consistent get operations any further because you are already using indexes to maximum advantage. Here is a summary of the previous execution strategy:

- Using the my_indexes_i1 index, collect the addresses of rows of the my_indexes table that qualify for inclusion.

- Using the addresses obtained in the previous step, retrieve the qualifying rows from the my_indexes table. There are 29 rows that qualify, and, therefore, you have to perform this step 29 times.

- For every qualifying row retrieved from the my_indexes table, use the my_tables_pk index and obtain the address of the matching row in the my_tables table. Obviously, 29 rows qualify.

- Using the addresses obtained in the previous step, retrieve the 29 matching rows from the my_tables table.

- Eliminate duplicates from the result.

It may appear that you have tuned the SQL statement as much as you can. However, there *is* a way to retrieve records quickly without the use of indexes, and there *is* a way to retrieve data from two tables without actually visiting two tables. *Hash clusters* allow data to be retrieved without the use of indexes; Oracle computes the hash signature of the record you need and translates the hash signature into the address of the record. Clustering effects can also significantly reduce the number of blocks that need to be visited to retrieve the required data. Further, *materialized views* combine the data from multiple tables and enable you to retrieve data from multiple tables *without* visiting the tables themselves. You can combine hash clusters and materialized views to achieve a dramatic reduction in the number of consistent get operations; in fact, you need only one consistent get operation.

First you create a hash cluster, and then you combine the data from my_tables and my_indexes into another table called my_tables_and_indexes. In the interests of brevity, you select only those items of information required by the query—items of information that would help other queries would normally be considered for inclusion:

```
PDB1@ORCL> CREATE CLUSTER my_cluster (index_type VARCHAR2(27)) SIZE 8192 HASHKEYS 5;

Cluster created.

PDB1@ORCL> CREATE MATERIALIZED VIEW LOG ON my_tables WITH ROWID;

Materialized view log created.
```

Next, you create a materialized view of the data. You use *materialized view logs* to ensure that any future changes to the data in my_tables or my_indexes are immediately made to the copy of the data in the materialized view. You enable *query rewrite* to ensure that your query is automatically modified and that the required data is retrieved from the materialized view instead of from my_tables and my_indexes. Appropriate indexes that would improve the usability and maintainability of the materialized view should also be created; I leave this as an exercise for you:

```
PDB1@ORCL> CREATE MATERIALIZED VIEW LOG ON my_indexes WITH ROWID;

Materialized view log created.

PDB1@ORCL> CREATE MATERIALIZED VIEW my_mv
  2   CLUSTER my_cluster (index_type)
  3   REFRESH FAST ON COMMIT
  4   ENABLE QUERY REWRITE
  5   AS
  6   SELECT t.ROWID AS table_rowid,
  7     t.owner AS table_owner,
  8     t.table_name,
  9     t.tablespace:name,
 10     i.ROWID AS index_rowid,
 11     i.index_type
 12   FROM my_tables t,
 13     my_indexes i
 14   WHERE t.owner = i.table_owner
 15   AND t.table_name = i.table_name;

Materialized view created.

PDB1@ORCL> EXEC DBMS_STATS.gather_table_stats(user, tabname=>'MY_MV');

PL/SQL procedure successfully completed.

PDB1@ORCL> SELECT DISTINCT my_tables.owner,
  2     my_tables.table_name,
  3     my_tables.tablespace:name
  4   FROM my_tables,
  5     my_indexes
```

```
6  WHERE my_tables.owner      = my_indexes.table_owner
7  AND my_tables.table_name   = my_indexes.table_name
8  AND my_indexes.index_type  = :index_type;
```

It's now time to test the query again. You find that the number of consistent gets has been reduced to 6.

```
Plan hash value: 1006555447
```

Id	Operation	Name	Starts	E-Rows	E-Bytes	Cost (%CPU)	E-Time	A-Rows	A-Time	Buffers
0	SELECT STATEMENT		1			1 (100)		24	00:00:00.01	6
1	HASH UNIQUE		1	985	41370	1 (0)	00:00:01	24	00:00:00.01	6
* 2	TABLE ACCESS HASH	MY_MV	1	985	41370	1 (0)	00:00:01	29	00:00:00.01	6

```
Predicate Information (identified by operation id):
---------------------------------------------------

   2 - access("MY_MV"."INDEX_TYPE"=:INDEX_TYPE)
```

But Wait, There's More!

Executing a query obviously requires at least one consistent get operation. However, there is no need to execute the query if the query results have been previously cached and the data has not changed. Oracle 11*g* introduced the RESULT_CACHE hint to indicate that the data should be obtained from cache if possible. Note that this feature is available only with the Enterprise Edition. In the following example, you can see that the number of consistent gets has been reduced to zero!

```
PDB1@ORCL> SELECT /*+ RESULT_CACHE
 2   */
 3    DISTINCT my_tables.owner,
 4    my_tables.table_name,
 5    my_tables.tablespace:name
 6  FROM my_tables,
 7    my_indexes
 8  WHERE my_tables.owner      = my_indexes.table_owner
 9  AND my_tables.table_name   = my_indexes.table_name
10  AND my_indexes.index_type  = :index_type;

Statistics
----------------------------------------------------------
          0  recursive calls
          0  db block gets
          0  consistent gets
          0  physical reads
          0  redo size
       1751  bytes sent via SQL*Net to client
        554  bytes received via SQL*Net from client
          3  SQL*Net roundtrips to/from client
          0  sorts (memory)
          0  sorts (disk)
         24  rows processed
```

Id	Operation	Name	Starts	E-Rows	E-Bytes	Cost (%CPU)	E-Time	A-Rows	A-Time
0	SELECT STATEMENT		1			1 (100)		24	00:00:00.01
1	RESULT CACHE	as25n73upsfxq720679pkz3t68	1					24	00:00:00.01
2	HASH UNIQUE		0	985	41370	1 (0)	00:00:01	0	00:00:00.01
* 3	TABLE ACCESS HASH	MY_MV	0	985	41370	1 (0)	00:00:01	0	00:00:00.01

Predicate Information (identified by operation id):
----

   3 - access("MY_MV"."INDEX_TYPE"=:INDEX_TYPE)

You saw four query plans in this exercise:

- The first query plan did not use any indexes because none had been created at the time.

- Qualifying records in my_indexes were efficiently identified by using the index on the values of index_type and were placed in a lookup table. All the records in my_tables were then retrieved and compared with the records in the lookup table.

- Qualifying records in my_indexes were efficiently identified using the index on the values of index_type. An index on the values of table_owner and table_name was then used to efficiently find the corresponding records in my_tables.

- A materialized view was used to combine the data from my_tables and my_indexes, and a *hash cluster* was used to create clusters of related records.

Summary

Here is a short summary of the concepts touched on in this chapter:

- The efficiency of an SQL statement is measured by the amount of computing resources used in producing the output. The number of logical read operations is a good way to measure the consumption of computing resources because it is directly proportional to the amount of resources consumed.

- Inefficient SQL can be identified by using tools such as Enterprise Manager and Toad, by tracing a batch job or user session, and by examining Statspack reports.

- Common causes for inefficient SQL are as follows: failure to use advanced features such as analytic functions, poor application development practices, poor logical and physical database design, and inadequate database maintenance.

- Hardware limitations and contention for limited resources play a major role in performance.

- The primary key of a table is always indexed. Indexes should be created on foreign keys unless the tables in question are small enough that the lack of an index will not have an impact on performance. Indexes should also be created on data items that are restricted in SQL queries. The dba_indexes and dba_ind_columns views show what indexes have been created. Most indexes are of the b*tree type. Other types of indexes are reverse key indexes, function-based indexes, and bitmap indexes. Clusters, index-organized tables, and table partitions are other options available to the database designer.

- Hints for the optimizer can be embedded in an SQL statement. Each hint partially constrains the optimizer, and a full set of hints completely constrains the optimizer. A desirable query plan can be preserved by capturing the set of hints that describes it in a stored outline.

- Statistical information on tables and indexes and the data they contain is what the query optimizer needs to do its job properly. Table and index statistics are automatically collected by a job called GATHER_STATS_JOB that runs during a nightly maintenance window. The DBMS_STATS package contains a variety of procedures for customizing the statistics collection strategy. System statistics are not collected automatically; they should be manually collected using the GATHER_SYSTEM_STATS procedure.

- One of the principal objectives of query tuning is to reduce the number of consistent get operations (logical reads) required. The theoretical lower bound on the number of consistent get operations is 1.

- The cost of creating a query plan can far exceed the cost of executing a query. Plan reuse is therefore critical for database performance. Dynamic sampling, necessitated by the absence of statistics, can dramatically increase the cost of creating a query plan.

- If you are using the Enterprise Edition and have a license for the Tuning Pack, you can use SQL Tuning Advisor to help you with SQL tuning.

Exercises

1. Enable tracing of your SQL query by using the dbms_monitor.session_trace:enable and dbms_monitor.session_trace:disable procedures. Locate the trace file, and review the recursive calls. Also review the PARSE, EXECUTE, and FETCH calls for your query.

2. Re-create the my_tables_and_indexes materialized view with all the columns in my_indexes and my_tables instead of just those columns required in the exercise. Does the materialized view need any indexes?

3. Insert new data into my_tables and my_indexes, and verify that the data is automatically inserted into the materialized view.

Index

■ A

Active workload repository (AWR), 67
ad hoc queries, 316
ADR. *See* Automatic diagnostic repository (ADR)
ADVISOR privilege, 321
ALTER_STATS_HISTORY_RETENTION
      procedure, 321
ALTER SYSTEM privilege, 321
Architectural choices, Oracle
    dedicated server, 64
    MAA, 66
    RAC, 65
    shared server, 65
    standby database, 65
Archived redo logs, 67
Archiver (ARCHn), 50, 53
ARCHn. *See* Archiver (ARCHn)
ASM. *See* Automatic storage management (ASM)
Automatic Database Diagnostic Monitor
      (ADDM), 309
Automatic diagnostic repository (ADR), 207
Automatic memory management, 106
Automatic storage management (ASM), 80, 105
Automatic Workload Repository (AWR), 175, 182,
      185, 187, 278, 293, 309
Average active sessions, 302
AWR. *See* Automatic Workload
      Repository (AWR)
awrrpt.sql script, 296

■ B

Background processes
    ARCHn, 53
    CKPT, 53
    DBWn, 52
    LGWR, 52
    PMON, 53
    SMON, 53

Backup database
    consistent backups *vs.* inconsistent
      backups, 220
    e-commerce, 218
    full backups *vs.* partial backups, 219
    hot *vs.* cold backups
      offline backup, 220
      online backups, 220
    level 0 backups *vs.* level 1 backups
      block change tracking file, 220
      incremental backup, 220
    logical backups, 226–227
    oracle-managed backups *vs.* user-managed
      backups
      advantages, 221
      RMAN, 220
    physical backups, 221–226
    resources, 217
    RMAN commands, 228, 230–232
    tape backups *vs.* disk backups
      advantages and disadvantages, 219
      remote hands assistance, 219
      serial-access devices, 219
Backups, 67
Bitmap indexes, 318
b*tree (balanced tree) indexes, 318
Buffer cache, 52, 327
Bytes received via SQL*Net from client item, 326
Bytes sent via SQL*Net to client item, 326

■ C

Capacity management
    DBA_DATA_FILES, 263
    DBA_FREE_SPACE, 263
    time series
      analytic functions, 265
      PIVOT operator, 264–265
      SQL Query, 266
      V$OSSTAT and STATS$OSSTAT, 264

CDB. *See* Container database (CDB)
Checkpoint process (CKPT), 53
Child cursor, 329
CKPT. *See* Checkpoint process (CKPT)
Client installations
  instant client
    basic and SQL*Plus package, 75
    OUI, 75
    su–and sed command, 76
    TNS_ADMIN, 77
    tnsnames.ora, 76
Client software, 49
Cloud computing, 70, 72
CMDB. *See* Configuration Management
    Database (CMDB)
Configuration files
  listener.ora, 49
  pfile, 49
  spfile, 49
  tnsnames.ora, 49
Configuration Management Database (CMDB), 279
Consistent gets, 326
Container database (CDB), 53
Control files, 51, 67
Counters
  consistent gets and db block gets, 300
  CPU, 300
  in Oracle Database 11g Reference, 301
  physical reads, 300
  physical writes, 300
  user commits and rollbacks track transaction
    rates, 300
CPU. *See* Critical patch update (CPU)
CPU cycles, 313
CPU sizing, 69
CREATE CLUSTER privilege, 321
CREATE TABLE AS SELECT (CTAS) operation, 331
Critical patch update (CPU)
  one-off patch, 267
  security-related bugs, 267
CSI. *See* Customer support identifier (CSI)
Customer support identifier (CSI), 203

■ D

Database
  banks and e-commerce web sites, 9
  create database and GUI tools, 9
  ITIL, 9
Database administrators (DBAs)
  communication skills, 274
  confidentiality, protection, 274
  database specialists, 273
  deliverables

audit reports, 281
backup, failover testing, 280
business needs, 280
database administration tools, 281
exception reports, 281
maintenance procedures, 281
management reports, 281
secure document library, 280
standard operating procedures, 280
work logs, 280
individual deliverable, 271
job interview, 272–273
report writing exercise, 274
role-playing exercise, 274
shared deliverable, 271
SOP (*see* Standard operating procedure (SOP))
systematic institutional approach, 273–274
Database backups, 51
Database configuration assistant (DBCA)
  administrative password accounts, 103
  AL32UTF8, 106
  archived redo logs, 105
  automatic memory management, 106
  character sets tab, 106
  confirmation screen, 109
  connection mode tab, 106
  database creation, 98–99
  database-creation scripts, 107
  database name and instance name (SID), 101
  database templates, 97
  data files, 105
  EM cloud control, 102
  EM express, 102
  fast recovery area, 105–106
  file storage/ASM, 105
  listener, 104
  memory tab, 106
  opening screen, 97
  sizing tab, 106
  success message, 109–110
  templates
    custom database, 100
    data warehouse, 100
    general purpose/transaction processing, 100
  validity checks, 108
  variables, 105
Database creation. *See* also DBCA
  basic database administration tasks
    enterprise manager database
      express, 114–116
    starting the database, 114
    starting the listener, 113
    stopping the database, 112
    stopping the listener, 113

components, 110
control files, 112
data files, 111
graphical user interfaces, 92
initialization parameters, 111
listener, creation and configuration (*see* NetCA)
next-next-next installation type, 92
Nosejob video, 91
redo log groups, 112
service provider, 91
unconventional Oracle installation, 91
X window system, 92
Database Definition Language (DDL)
creation commands, employee Table, 30
indexes, 30
tables, 30
variable character (VARCHAR2)/numeric, 30
Database design. *See also* Physical database design
logical, 117
physical, 117
Database maintenance
archiving, 256
auditing
DBA_AUDIT_SESSION View, 260–261
DBA_STMT_AUDIT_OPTS View, 261–262
backups
ALTER DATABASE FORCE LOGGING
command, 255
ARCHIVELOG mode, 255
change-control procedures, 255
data corruption, 255
far-line (tape or network), 254
flashback features, 255
logical backups, 255
near-line (disk), 254
RMAN, 255
SLA, 254
capacity (*see* Capacity management)
Log file, 258–260
patches, 267–268
plan, 253–254
purging, 256
rebuilding
SHRINK SPACE procedure, 258
SPACE_USAGE procedure, 257–258
SPACE_USAGE procedure, 258
statistics
DBMS_STATS package, 256
GATHER_STATS_JOB, 256
user management, 262
Database Management Systems (DBMS)
data integrity, 21–22
data security, 22
transaction management, 20–21

Database Manipulation Language (DML)
DELETE, 32
INSERT, 31
MERGE, 32–33
UPDATE, 32
Database templates, 97
Database tuning
ADDM report, 299–300
AWR report, 297–298
five-step tuning method, 293
overview, 293
Statspack report, 296–297, 301, 308–309
wait interface, 300–301
Database writer (DBWn), 52
Data definition language (DDL), 51
Data dictionary
querying, 171
table and view, 169–171
views, 168
Data files
AWR, 67
block size, 50
extent, 50
pages, 50
Statspack, 67
SYSTEM and SYSAUX tablespaces, 67
tablespaces, 49
undo and temporary space, 67
Data guard, 65
Data loading
data marts and data warehouses, 149
data pump utility
data_pump_dir, 153
expdp and impdp utility, 153, 155–156
oracle database 10g, 153
export and import utility
data pump, 149
exp utility, features, 150–151
imp utility, features, 152
PL/SQL routines, 149
triggers, 152
INSERT command, 149
SQL*Loader
control file, 156
data files, 156
DB2 load utility, 156
session, 157–158
SQL server bcp utility, 156
Data modeling. *See* Database design
Data pump export, 150
Data Recovery Advisor (DRA)
ADVISE FAILURE command, 247
Block recovery, 244
DBA_EXTENTS view, 245

Data Recovery Advisor (DRA) (*cont.*)
    dd (device dump), 245
    LIST FAILURE command, 247
    RECOVER DATABASE, 244
    REPAIR FAILURE command, 248–249
    RESTORE DATABASE, 244
    segment and re-creation, 246
    VALIDATE DATABASE command, 246
A Day in the Life of an Enterprise DBA, 286
DBA_CONSTRAINTS and
        DBA_CONS_COLUMNS views, 310
DBA_CONSTRAINTS and
        DBA_CONS_COLUMNS views, 311
dba_ind_columns view, 317–318
dba_indexes and dba_ind_columns views, 338
dba_indexes view, 317–318
DBA privileges, account creation, 161–162
DB block gets, 326
DBCA. *See* Database configuration
        assistant (DBCA)
DBMS_STATS.GATHER_SCHEMA_STATS
    procedure, 319
DBMS_STATS.GATHER_TABLE_STATS
    procedure, 319
dbms_xplan.display_cursor procedure, 329
DBWn. *See* Database writer (DBWn)
DDL. *See* Database Definition Language (DDL)
DDL. *See* Data definition language (DDL)
Deadlock, 210
Dedicated server architecture, 64
Dedicated server process, 52
DELETE_*_STATS procedures, 320
Dictionary cache, 52, 326
Disaster recovery. *See* IT Service Continuity
        Management (ITSCM)
Disk sizing, 66, 71
Disk speed
    CPU sizing, 69
    memory sizing, 68
    network sizing, 69
Dispatcher process, 65
DISTINCT operator, 324
DML. *See* Database Manipulation Language (DML)
DRA. *See* Data Recovery Advisor (DRA)
Dynamic performance views, 300

■ E

Efficiency
    causes of inefficiency, 316
    definition, 313
    identifying inefficiency, 313–315
Elasticity, 70

Embedded SQL
    Java Program, 34–35
    phrase #sql, 34
Engineered systems, 69
Enterprise Manager
    Database Express, 162
    e-mail messages, 175
    Grid Control, 162
    monitoring backups, 180
    password resets, 162
    server technologies, 189
Enterprise manager cloud control
        (EM cloud control), 102
Enterprise manager database
        express, 102, 114–116
Enterprise Resource Planning (ERP), 235
Event logs, 51
Exadata
    cloud computing, 70
    configurations, 70
Exports, 67
EXPORT_*_STATS procedures, 321
Export utility, 150

■ F

Fast recovery area, 105
File placement, 68
Flashback recovery area, 51
Flashback technology
    BEFORE DROP command, 241–242
    Data Archive, 242
    FLASHBACK DATABASE command, 243
    FLASHBACK TABLE command, 241
    flashback_transaction_query, 240
    Query
        SQL statements, 238
        TIMESTAMP clause, 239
    UNDO_RETENTION setting, 238
    undo segments, 238
    VERSIONS_STARTTIME and
        VERSIONS_XID, 239–240
Function-based indexes, 318

■ G

GATHER_SCHEMA_STATS procedure, 320
GATHER_STATS_JOB procedure, 321, 339
GATHER_TABLE_STATS procedure, 320

■ H

Hash clusters, 335

■ I, J, K

IaaS. *See* Infrastructure as a service (IaaS)
IMPORT_*_STATS procedures, 321
Import utility, 150
Index-organized table (IOT), 121
Infrastructure as a service (IaaS), 70
Inter-process communication (IPC), 51
IPC. *See* Inter-process communication (IPC)
ITIL. *See* IT Infrastructure Library (ITIL)
IT Information Library (ITIL)
    IT practice guidance, 275
    ITSM, 275
IT Infrastructure Library (ITIL), 9, 23
ITSCM. *See* IT Service Continuity Management
       (ITSCM)
IT Service Continuity Management (ITSCM), 277
    availability management, 278
    change management, 278
    CMDB
        RDA, 279
        repository, creation, 279
    DBA approaches
        cold standby, 277
        hot standby, 277
        warm standby, 277
    incident management, 278
    problem management, 278
    release management, 279
IT service management (ITSM), 275
    application management team, 275
    big picture, 275
    branches, 276
    capacity management, 277
        AWR, 278
        monitoring database trends, 278
    change management, 275–276
    financial management, 277
    incident management, 275
    infrastructure management team, 275
    ITSCM, 277
    Oracle license, 277
    principle, 276
    processes, 276
    service level management, 275
    SLM, 276

■ L

LAG function, 301
Latches, 51
LEADING hint, 335
LGWR. *See* Log-writer (LGWR)
Licensing

database
    enterprise edition, 64
    Oracle express edition, 63
    standard edition, 63
    evaluation, 63
    freely download, 63
    high-end configuration, 61
    low-end configuration, 62–63
    media packs, 64
    Oracle's data guard technology, 61
    Oracle software, 61
    prototype, 63
    RAC, 61
Life cycle of database session, 55–56
LOCK_*_STATS procedures, 321
Log buffer, 52
Log file maintenance
    adrci Tool, 260
    errors
        ORA-00060 (deadlock), 258
        ORA-00600 (internal error), 258
    trace file, 258–259
Logical backups
    Data Pump Export tool, 226
    expdp help=y, 228
    flashback_time qualifier, 226, 227
    vs. physical backups, 220
Log-writer (LGWR), 50, 52

■ M

MAA. *See* Maximum availability
       architecture (MAA)
Many-to-one architecture
    cache fusion, 54
    ODA, 54
    scale up/out, 54
Materialized view logs, 336–337
Maximum availability architecture (MAA), 66, 71
Memory sizing
    buffer cache, 68
    shared pool, 68
    stack space, 68
Monitoring
    backups, 180
    capacity
        CPU utilization percentage, 188–189
        tables and views, 188
    changes, 178
    database availability
        12c 2 day DBA manual, 178
        alert log, 176–178
        diag trace, 178
        oracle enterprise manager, 178

Monitoring (*cont.*)
  growth
    capturing and storing, 182
    DBA_DATA_FILES view, 180
    enterprise manager, report, 181
    ten biggest tables, 181
  performance
    average elapsed times, t
      wo SQL queries, 185–187
    execution statistics, 185
  security
    AUDIT CREATE SESSION, 179
    connection/disconnections, history, 179
    password policy, 180
  third-party tools, 189
  workload
    database stability, distinct pattern, 183–184
    excel graph, 184
    tables and views, 182–183
MOS. *See* My Oracle support (MOS)
MTS. *See* Multithreaded server (MTS)
Multithreaded server (MTS), 52
My Oracle support (MOS), 192, 203, 205

■ **N**

Nested loop methods, 335
NetCA. *See* Net configuration assistant (NetCA)
Net configuration assistant (NetCA)
  listener configuration, 93
  listener name field, 94
  opening screen, 92–93
  port number, 96
  protocol selection, 95
  single listener, 96
  success message, 97
Network interface, 80
Network sizing, 69
NoCOUG. *See* Northern California Oracle
      Users Group (NoCOUG)
Northern California Oracle Users Group
    (NoCOUG), 8, 272

■ **O**

ODA. *See* Oracle database appliance (ODA)
OEL. *See* Oracle enterprise linux (OEL)
OFA. *See* Optimal flexible architecture (OFA)
OLTP. *See* Online transaction processing (OLTP)
One-to-many configuration
  CDB, 53
  Oracle multitenant option, 53
  PDB/non-CDB compatibility
    guarantee, 53–54
Online and offline backups, 220
Online redo log files, 67

Online transaction processing (OLTP), 65
Optimal flexible architecture (OFA), 68
ORA-00060 error (deadlock detected), 210–211
ORA-00600 error (internal error code)
  adrci tool, 213
  BACKGROUND_DUMP_DEST setting, 213
  bug—and stops processing, 211
  incident packaging service (IPS), 213
  MetaLink knowledge, 214
  ORA-600 troubleshooter, 214
  Oracle alert log, 211, 213
  Oracle database 12c enterprise edition, 212
ORA-01555 error (snapshot too old)
  Oracle database 11g error messages, 209
  read consistency, 209
  rollback segments, 209
  UNDO_MANAGEMENT setting, 209
  UNDO_RETENTION setting, 209
ORA-07445 error (exception encountered), 214
Oracle7 Tuning guide, 126
Oracle architecture
  archived redo log files, 50
  components, 48
  concepts, 56–57
  configuration files, 49
  control file, 51
  database backups, 51
  database *vs.* instance, 49
  data files, 49–50
  event logs, 51
  instance, 51–53
  life cycle of database session, 55–56
  many-to-one architecture, 54
  one-to-many configuration, 53–54
  redo log files, 50
  software, 49
  Spotlight software tool, 47–48
  temporary files, 50
Oracle database 10g, 150
Oracle database 11g utilities, 150
Oracle database 11g error messages, 210–211
Oracle Database 12c
  CDD, 8
  full-screen editor, 8
  new connection, creating, 5–6
  GUI tool, 8
  SQL Developer, 5
  VAX/VMS, 8
  VirtualBox virtualization software, 4
  VM, 4
Oracle database 12c SQL language
    reference, 143
Oracle database appliance (ODA), 54
  configuration, 70
  pay-as-you-grow model, 69
  RAC deployment, 69

Oracle enterprise linux (OEL), 74
Oracle home, 49
ORACLE_HOME_BACKSLASH\rdbms\BACKSLASH\
    admin page, 296–297, 299, 309
Oracle index
    balanced tree/b-tree, 119
    bitmap index, 121
    concatenated index, 119
    foreign keys, 120
    function-based indexes, 119–120
    IOT, 121
    local and global, 126
    primary key, 120
    query optimizer, 120
    QUICK_TUNE procedure, 120
    structure, 119
    table, 118
    unique vs. non-unique, 118
Oracle multitenant option, 49, 53–54
Oracle partition
    advantages, 122
    methods, 121
        composite, 125–126
        hash, 124
        interval, 123
        list, 122–123
        range, 123
        reference, 124–125
    partition pruning, 121
Oracle's cache, 328
Oracle's data guard architecture, 64
Oracle technology network (OTN), 74
Oracle universal installer (OUI), 75, 81
OTN. See Oracle technology network (OTN)
OUI. See Oracle universal installer (OUI)

■ P

PaaS. See Platform as a service (PaaS)
Partition views
    bitmap index, 127, 129
    denormalization, 130
    index, 128
    materialized, 130
    Oracle7 Tuning guide, 126
    schemas, 127
    table-creation statements, 128
    UNION-ALL, 126
PDB. See Pluggable database (PDB)
Performance-tuning problem,
        systematic step method, 294
pfile, 49
Physical backups
    ARCHIVELOG mode, 221
    CONNECT TARGET command, 223
    LIST BACKUP command, 225

NLS_DATE_FORMAT, 223
NOARCHIVELOG mode, 221
online redo logs, 222
recovery catalog, 223
seed database, 224
vs. logical backups, 220
Physical database design
    cluster, 131–132
    index (see Oracle index)
Physical reads, 326–327
PIVOT operator, 301
Platform as a service (PaaS), 70
Pluggable database (PDB), 53
PMON. See Process monitor (PMON)
Problems fixing, DBA
    error codes
        facility, 208
        five-digit number, 208
        named exceptions, PL/SQL, 208
        Oracle database error messages, 207
        Recovery Manager (RMAN) tool, 208
    four quadrants, 192
    incident management vs. problem
        management, 200
    internet resources
        online Oracle documentation, 200–201
        Oracle forums, 201–202
        Oracle technology network, 202–203
    Oracle, 204
        ADR, 207
        MOS, 203
        ORAchk, configuration audit tool, 205–206
        RDA collection, 204–205
    problem management, 194–195
    systematic method
        analysis, 193
        define, 193
        implementation, 193
        investigation, 193
        solve, 193
        work flow diagram, 193–194
    unresponsive listener
        define, 196
        implementation, 198–199
        improvement, 199
        investigation and analysis, 197–198
    work records, 195–196
Procedural language/SQL (PL/SQL)
    condition checking, 40
    employee_updates procedure, 41–44
    loops, 40
    subroutines, 40
    triggers, 41, 44
Process monitor (PMON), 53
Program global area, 50
Partitioned views. See Partition views

■ Q

Query-execution plan, 328
    A-bytes column, 330
    A-rows column, 330
    buffers column, 330
    cost column, 330
    E-bytes column, 329
    E·rows column, 329
    E-time column, 330
    Id column, 329
    name column, 329
    operation column, 329
    reads, 330
    starts column, 329
Query optimizer, 316, 334

■ R

RAC. *See* Real application clusters (RAC)
RAID. *See* Redundant array of inexpensive
    disks (RAID)
Railroad diagrams
    FROM_clause, 27–29
    GROUP_BY_clause, 27–29
    hypothetical ROW command, 27
    inline view, 30
    ORDER_BY_clause, 28
    scalar subquery, 30
    SELECT_list, 27–29
    SELECT statement, 27
    subquery diagram, 30
    WHERE_clause, 28–29
RDA. *See* Remote diagnostic agent (RDA)
RDA. *See* Remote diagnostic assistant (RDA)
Read consistency, 326
Real application clusters (RAC), 49, 54, 61, 65, 71, 74
Recovery Manager (RMAN), 180
    complete recovery *vs.* incomplete recovery
        point-in-time recovery, 237
        RESETLOGS, 237
    documentation and testing, 249
    DRA, 244–249
    flashback features. *See* Flashback technology
    full recovery *vs.* partial recovery, 236
    LogMiner, 243–244
    physical recovery *vs.* logical recovery
        Data Pump Import utility, 237
        flashback methods, 237
    redo log files, 235
    restore *vs.* recover, 236
    traditional vs. flashback, 237
Recursive calls, 326
Recycle pool, 52
Redo log files
    archiver, 50

LGWR process, 50
    round-robin, 50
Redo log group, 50
Redo size, 326
Redundant array of inexpensive disks (RAID), 68
Relational Database Management
    Systems (RDBMS)
    chains of records, 10
    hashing, 9
    relational operators, 12–13
    RP-1 Physical Data Independence, 23
    SEQUEL, 11
Relational operators, RDBMS
    difference, 12
    efficiency, 19
    join, 12
    projection, 12
    relational algebra expressions, 19–20
    selection, 12
    table expressions, 18–19
    union, 12
Remedy service desk, 200
Remote Diagnostic Agent (RDA), 204–205
    database information, 167
    HTML framework, 166
    system information, 166–167
Remote diagnostic assistant (RDA), 279
Request for proposal (RFP) process, 66
RESTORE_*_STATS procedures, 321
RESULT_CACHE hint, 337
Reverse key indexes, 318
RMAN. *See* Recovery Manager (RMAN)
RMAN commands
    description, 228
    rman.rcv, 228
ROLLBACK command, 210
Rows processed item, 326

■ S

Schemas
    blocks of storage, 138
    data dictionary views, 138
    DBA_OBJECTS, 136
    DBA_TABLES view, 138, 140
    DBA_, USER_, and ALL_ dictionary
        views, 140–141
    definition, 135
    objects, 135–136
    relational model, 136
    segment, 138
    SYS schema, 136–137
    tables and indexes, 138
    triggers, 136
    virtual tables, 136

SCN. *See* System change number (SCN)
SELECT ANY DICTIONARY privilege, 321
SEQUEL. *See* Structured English Query
      Language (SEQUEL)
Server installations
    downloading and installation steps, Oracle
       software
      firefox preferences panel, 80
      install database software, 83
      languages list, 84
      license agreement, 81
      my Oracle support, 81
      OS groups, 86
      OUI, 81
      prerequisite checks, 86
      root.sh, 87–88
      runInstaller script, 81
      single instance database, 83
      skip software updates, 82
      software location path, 85
      standard edition, 84
      success message, 89
      /tmp directory and unzip, 81
      www.oracle.com, 80
    network interface, 80
    RAC/ASM, 80
Server software, 49
Service level management (SLM), 276
SET_*_PREFS procedures, 321
SET_SQL_TRACE_IN_SESSION command, 314
SGA. *See* System global area (SGA)
Shared disk approach, 54
Shared nothing/federated approach, 54
Shared pool, 52, 327
Shared server, 65
Shared SQL area, 52
SLM. *See* Service level management (SLM)
SMON. *See* System monitor (SMON)
Snapshots, 301, 309
Software executables, 67
Software installation
    client installations, 75–78
    database administrator, 73
    HTML and PDF formats, 74
    Oracle database examples, 89
    OTN, 74
    prerequisites and preinstallation requirements
      OEL, 74
      RAC, 74
      yum installer, 74
    reference manuals, 74
    server installations, 80–89
    SQL developer, 78–80
Sorts (disk) item, 326
Sorts (memory) item, 326

spdoc.txt file, 309
spfile, 49
spreport.sql script, 296
SQL access advisor, 332–334
SQL developer
    blocking session
      identification, 165
      termination, 166
    browsing database and SQL commands, 79
    command-line tool, 80
    database connection, 78–79
    examining table structure, 164
    execution plan, checking, 163–164
    GUI tool, 78, 80
    OTN account, 78
SQL Developer, 35–36
SQL*Net roundtrips to/from client, 326
SQL*Plus
    neatly formatted report, 35–36
    report-writing tool, 35
SQL query
    patterns and trends in distribution of
      DB time, 302–305
    range of time periods, 306–308
SQL tuning
    autotrace, 321
    baselines, establishing, 324, 328
    description, 313, 317, 321
    efficiency, 313
    extreme tuning, 335
    FULL hint, 319
    INDEX hint, 319
    indexes, 317–318, 331
    inefficient
      causes of, 316
      identifying, 313–315
    LEADING hint, 318
    my_indexes table, 319
    NO_MERGE hint, 319
    ORDERED hint, 318
    plustrace, 322–323
    query plans, examining, 329
    SQL access advisor, 332–334
    statistics, 319–321, 331
    statistics_level, 324–325
    tables, creating and populating, 323
    USE_HASH hint, 319
    USE_MERGE hint, 319
SQL tuning advisor, 332
Standard operating procedure (SOP)
    advantages, 282–283
    approval and protocol, 285–286
    database, shut down, 284
    database tasks, 287
    labor and billing, 284

Standard operating procedure (SOP) (*cont.*)
    prerequisites, 284
    purpose, 284
    risks, 284
    scheduling, 284
    shut down, database, 282–283
    structure, 284
    testing, 284
Standby database, 65
Statspack, 67, 175, 182, 185
Statspack report
    analyzing time, 296
    mining data from, 301, 308
    using, 309
STATS$SNAPSHOT table, 301
STATS$SYSSTAT table, 301
STATS$SYSTEM_EVENT table, 301
Structured English Query Language (SEQUEL), 11–12
Structured query language (SQL)
    DDL, 30–31
    DML, 30–33
    duplicate data records, 37
    embedded, 34–35
    inefficient SQL Query, 26
    nullable data items, 40
    performance improvement, 25–26
    railroad diagrams, 27–30
    redundancy, 37–39
    SQL Developer, 35–36
    SQL*Plus, 35–36
Swingbench tool, 312
System change number (SCN), 53
System global area (SGA), 51
System monitor (SMON), 53

■ T

Tables, creating and populating, 323
Temporary files, 50
Third-Party tools
    table structure, 172
    Toad and DBArtisan, 171
tkprof tool, 314–315
tkprof utility, 294
Transaction management
    atomicity, 21
    consistency, 21
    durability, 21
    isolation, 21

■ U

Unconventional Oracle installation, 91
Usable space, 68
User management
    ALTER PROFILE command, 143
    ALTER USER command, 145, 148
    attributes, modification, 148
    CREATE USER command, 141
        DBA_USERS, schema
            attributes, 142
        DEFAULT profile, definition, 143
    CREATE USER command, 141
        DBA_USERS, schema
            attributes, 143
        DEFAULT profile, definition, 144
    dba_role_privs, 147
    dba_sys_privs, 147
    dba_tab_privs, 147
    DROP USER command, 148–149
    GRANT command, 144
    REVOKE command, 148
    SYSTEM account, 141
    user ifernand, 146
    USERS tablespace, 145

■ V

V$SESSION_EVENT view, 301
V$SESSTAT view, 300
Virtual machine (VM)
    Oracle VirtualBox, 4
VM. *See* Virtual machine (VM)
VM environment, 205–206
V$EVENT_NAME view, 301
V$SYSSTAT view, 300–301
V$SYSTEM_EVENT view, 301

■ W

Wait interface
    overview, 300
    V$SESSION_EVENT view, 301
    V$SESSTAT view, 300

■ X, Y, Z
X window system, 92

 *For the Complete Technology & Database Professional*

IOUG represents the **voice of Oracle technology and database professionals -** empowering you to be **more productive in your business** and career by **delivering education,** sharing **best practices** and providing technology direction and **networking opportunities.**

Context, Not Just Content

IOUG is dedicated to helping our members become an #IOUGenius by staying on the cutting-edge of Oracle technologies and industry issues through practical content, user-focused education, and invaluable networking and leadership opportunities:

- *SELECT Journal* is our quarterly publication that provides in-depth, peer-reviewed articles on industry news and best practices in Oracle technology

- Our #IOUGenius blog highlights a featured weekly topic and provides content driven by Oracle professionals and the IOUG community

- Special Interest Groups provide you the chance to collaborate with peers on the specific issues that matter to you and even take on leadership roles outside of your organization

- COLLABORATE is our once-a-year opportunity to connect with the members of not one, but three, Oracle users groups (IOUG, OAUG and Quest) as well as with the top names and faces in the Oracle community.

Who we are...

... **more than 20,000** database professionals, developers, application and infrastructure architects, business intelligence specialists and IT managers

... **a community of users** that share experiences and knowledge on issues and technologies that matter to you and your organization

Interested? Join IOUG's community of Oracle technology and database professionals at www.ioug.org/Join.

Independent Oracle Users Group | phone: (312) 245-1579 | email: membership@ioug.org
330 N. Wabash Ave., Suite 2000, Chicago, IL 60611